PENGUIN BOOKS

KHARTOUM

Michael Asher is a graduate of the University of Leeds, and has served in both the Parachute Regiment and the SAS. He is the author of sixteen books, including works of travel, biography, military history, four novels and the best-selling *The Real 'Bravo Two Zero'*. A Fellow of the Royal Society of Literature, he has won awards for desert exploration from the Royal Geographical and Royal Scottish Geographical Society. He has also presented three documentaries for Channel 4.

Michael Asher lived in the Sudan for ten years. A fluent speaker of both Arabic and Swahili, he now lives near Nairobi, Kenya, with his wife, Arabist and photographer Mariantonietta Peru, and his two children. Michael Asher currently runs small-group, self-contained treks by camel in the deserts of the Sudan. Access his website at www.lost-oasis.org

Khartoum

The Ultimate Imperial Adventure

MICHAEL ASHER

PENGUIN BOOKS

PENGUIN BOOKS

Published by the Penguin Group
Penguin Books Ltd, 80 Strand, London WC2R 0RL, England
Penguin Group (USA) Inc., 375 Hudson Street, New York, New York 10014, USA
Penguin Group (Canada), 90 Eglinton Avenue East, Suite 700, Toronto, Ontario, Canada M4P 2Y3
(a division of Pearson Penguin Canada Inc.)
Penguin Ireland, 25 St Stephen's Green, Dublin 2, Ireland
(a division of Penguin Books Ltd)
Penguin Group (Australia), 250 Camberwell Road, Camberwell, Victoria 3124, Australia
(a division of Pearson Australia Group Pty Ltd)
Penguin Books India Pvt Ltd, 11 Community Centre, Panchsheel Park, New Delhi – 110 017, India
Penguin Group (NZ), 67 Apollo Drive, Mairangi Bay, Auckland 1310, New Zealand
(a division of Pearson New Zealand Ltd)
Penguin Books (South Africa) (Pty) Ltd, 24 Sturdee Avenue, Rosebank, Johannesburg 2196, South Africa

Penguin Books Ltd, Registered Offices: 80 Strand, London WC2R 0RL, England

www.penguin.com

First published by Viking 2005
Published in Penguin Books 2006

4

Copyright © Michael Asher, 2005
All rights reserved

The moral right of the author has been asserted

Set in Monotype Bembo
Typeset by Rowland Phototypesetting Ltd, Bury St Edmunds, Suffolk
Printed in Great Britain by Clays Ltd, St Ives plc

ISBN-13: 978-0-140-25855-4

www.greenpenguin.co.uk

To the memory of the brave soldiers,
British, Sudanese, Egyptian and others, who fought and died in
the Nile Campaigns, 1883–9

Contents

List of Illustrations

Section One

Section Two

Section Three

List of Maps

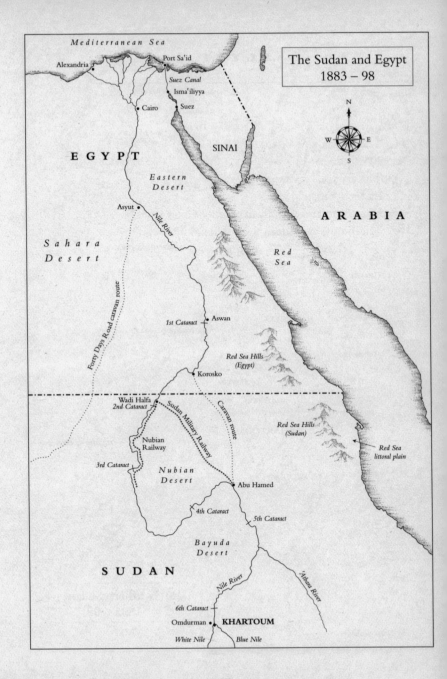

Mediterranean Sea

Alexandria

Port Sa'id

Suez Canal

Isma'iliyya

Cairo

Suez

SINAI

ARABIA

The Sudan and Egypt
1883 – 98

N
W   E
S

EGYPT

Eastern
Desert

Sahara
Desert

Asyut

Nile River

Red
Sea

1st Cataract

Aswan

Forty Days Road caravan route

Red Sea Hills
(Egypt)

Korosko

Caravan route

Wadi Halfa
2nd Cataract

Sudan Military Railway

Nubian
Railway

Red Sea Hills
(Sudan)

Red Sea
littoral plain

3rd Cataract

Nubian
Desert

Abu Hamed

4th Cataract

5th Cataract

Bayuda
Desert

SUDAN

Nile River

'Atbara River

6th Cataract

Omdurman

KHARTOUM

White Nile

Blue Nile

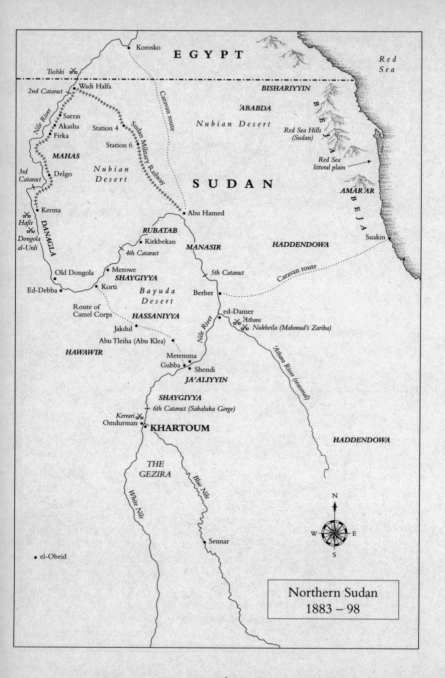

EGYPT

SUDAN

Red Sea

Korosko

Tushki

2nd Cataract
Wadi Halfa
Sarras
Akasha
Firka

Station 4

Station 6

MAHAS

Nile River

Sudan Military Railway

Caravan route

BISHARIYYIN

'ABABDA

Nubian Desert

Red Sea Hills (Sudan)

Red Sea littoral plain

B E J A

3rd Cataract
Delgo

Nubian Desert

Kerma

Hafir

Dongola al-Urdi

DANAGLA

Abu Hamed

RUBATAB
Kirkbekan
4th Cataract

MANASIR

HADDENDOWA

AMARAR

B E J A

Suakin

Merowe

SHAYGIYYA

Old Dongola

Ed-Debba
Korti

Bayuda Desert

5th Cataract

Berber

Caravan route

Route of Camel Corps

HASSANIYYA

Jakdul

Abu Tleiha (Abu Klea)

HAWAWIR

Metemma
Gubba
Shendi

JA'ALIYYIN

Nile River

ed-Damer
'Atbara
Nukheila (Mahmud's Zariba)

'Atbara River (seasonal)

SHAYGIYYA
6th Cataract (Sabaluka Gorge)

Kerrari
Omdurman

KHARTOUM

THE GEZIRA

White Nile

Blue Nile

HADDENDOWA

Sennar

el-Obeid

N
W E
S

Northern Sudan
1883 – 98

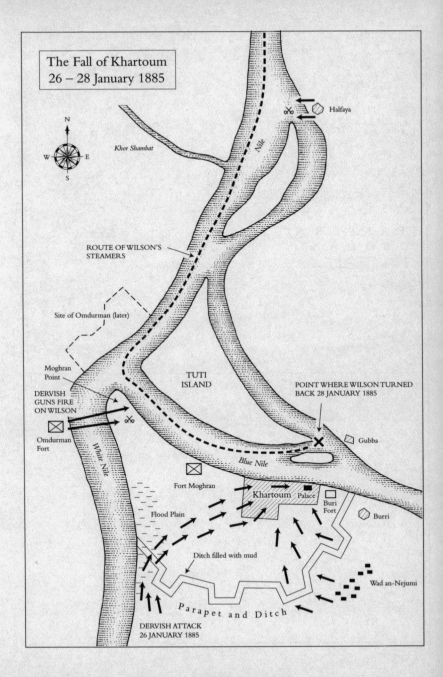

The Fall of Khartoum
26 – 28 January 1885

Khor Shambat

Nile

Halfaya

ROUTE OF WILSON'S
STEAMERS

Site of Omdurman (later)

Moghran
Point

TUTI
ISLAND

POINT WHERE WILSON TURNED
BACK 28 JANUARY 1885

DERVISH
GUNS FIRE
ON WILSON

Omdurman
Fort

Gubba

White Nile

Blue Nile

Fort Moghran

Khartoum   Palace   Buri
Fort

Burri

Flood Plain

Ditch filled with mud

Parapet and Ditch

Wad an-Nejumi

DERVISH ATTACK
26 JANUARY 1885

Handub ⚔
Sinkat ⚔
                    • Suakin
Tamaai ⚔   ⚔ Trinkitat
              ⚔ et-Teb
         ⚔
      Tokar

R e d
S e a

ARABIA

E A S T E R N
S U D A N

• Kassala
(To Italy)

Massawa •
(Later to Italy)

N
W   E
S

xvi

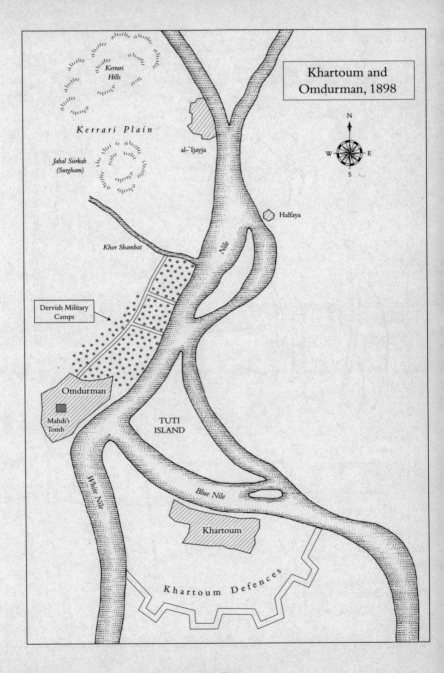

Khartoum and
Omdurman, 1898

Kerrari
Hills

Kerrari Plain

Jabal Surkab
(Surgham)

al-ʿIjayja

Halfaya

Nile

Khor Shambat

Dervish Military
Camps

Omdurman

TUTI
ISLAND

Mahdi's
Tomb

White Nile

Blue Nile

Khartoum

Khartoum Defences

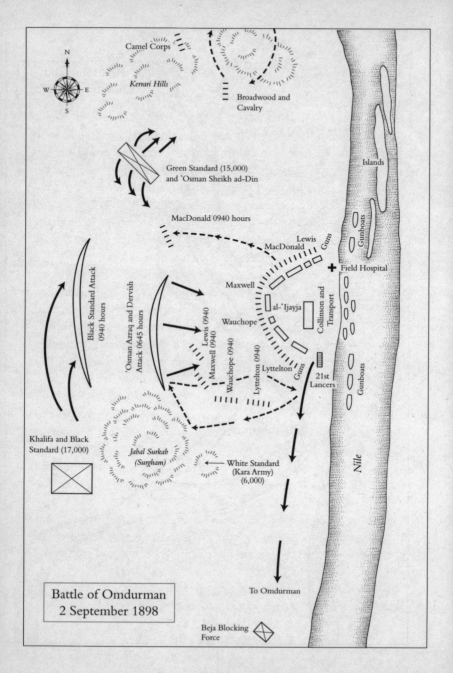

Battle of Omdurman
2 September 1898

Camel Corps

Kerrari Hills

Broadwood and Cavalry

Green Standard (15,000) and 'Osman Sheikh ad-Din

MacDonald 0940 hours

Lewis

MacDonald

Guns

Maxwell

al-'Ijayja

Field Hospital

Black Standard Attack 0940 hours

'Osman Azraq and Dervish Attack 0645 hours

Lewis 0940

Wauchope

Collinson and Transport

Maxwell 0940

Wauchope 0940

Lyttelton 0940

Lyttelton

Guns

21st Lancers

Khalifa and Black Standard (17,000)

Jabal Surkab (Surgham)

White Standard (Kara Army) (6,000)

Gunboats

Islands

Gunboats

Nile

To Omdurman

Beja Blocking Force

Acknowledgements

I should like to thank my editor at Penguin, Eleo Gordon, for her patience in waiting, for fighting my corner, and especially for allowing me to change tack and embark on what turned out to be a great adventure for me. I would like to thank all Viking-Penguin staff for their dedication and professionalism.

My thanks also go to my agent, Anthony Goff, of David Higham Associates, and his assistant, Georgia Glover, for their tireless loyalty.

I could not have completed the book without the help of my good friends and partners in Khartoum, George and Eleonora Pagoulatos, and George's brothers Tanash and Gerossimos and their wives, proprietors of the Acropole Hotel and the Acropole Tourist Corporation. I would like to add a very special thanks for the patience and companionship of my drivers Ramadan – already famous as the companion of Paul Theroux and others – and Ahmad.

I could not have completed my library research without the help of the staff of the British Institute of East Africa Studies in Nairobi, the London Library, the British Library, and the Palestine Exploration Fund. I owe them all a great debt. I am also grateful for the help of my neighbours, Esmond and Chryssee Bradley Martin, in Nairobi.

I suppose authors don't always make the best husbands and fathers, so I much appreciate the encouragement and patience of my wife, Mariantonietta, and my children, Burton and Jade.

Michael Asher
Langata, Nairobi, Kenya, 2005

Prologue

The deserter Gustav Klootz had seen death before, but never carnage like this. The bodies were scattered over a distance of two miles through the thorn-scrub: eleven thousand Egyptian soldiers and camp-followers in piles, hacked, stabbed and shot to ribbons. Swarms of dervishes were moving among them, dipping their ten-foot-long spears ritually in the wounds. They were stripping the corpses of everything – weapons, ammunition, boots, watches, even the blood-soaked uniforms themselves. The sky was already black with circling vultures. Some of the dead were smouldering from bullets fired at point-blank range. The dervishes claimed they were infidels being consumed by hellfire. Klootz saw one dead soldier hanging suspended from a huge baobab tree, where he had probably climbed in a futile attempt to escape the slaughter.

Among the corpses was that of Klootz's former commander, Lieut. General William Hicks. Nearby were the bodies of the two men for whom Klootz had served as orderly – the giant Prussian Major Baron Gotz von Seckendorff, and the drunken Irish war-correspondent Edmund O'Donovan, of the *Daily News*. O'Donovan in particular had been furious at Klootz's betrayal. 'What must be the condition of an army,' he had written in his journal after Klootz had absconded, 'when even a European servant deserts to the enemy?'[1]

Klootz, a tall, blond Berliner with socialist notions, had joined the dervishes at er-Rahad a week previously and had converted to Islam. He had contributed to the massacre by alerting the enemy to the column's weakness. He had once won the Iron Cross for bravery with the Uhlans, but still he was nauseated by what he saw on the battlefield. 'I had the greatest difficulty in keeping myself from breaking down,' he said, 'when I saw the mutilated corpses of those with whom but a short while before I had laughed and spoken.'

The savage attack by forty thousand screaming dervishes had smashed into the Egyptian column in the forest of Shaykan, Kordofan Province, in the western Sudan, that morning, 5 November 1883. Hicks's force had been moving tactically in three ragged squares, one up and two back. The leading square had buckled instantly under the onslaught. The riflemen in the flanking squares were so exhausted and racked with thirst that they could hardly focus. They had wheeled and fired blindly into the mêlée, killing their own comrades as well as the enemy. 'Almost at the same instant,' said Mohammad Nur al-Barudi, Hicks's cook, who had survived after being shot and slashed with a sword, 'the dervishes simultaneously attacked from the woods on both sides and from front and rear. The wildest confusion followed. Squares fired on each other, on friends and enemies . . . the surging mass of dervishes now completely circled the force and gradually closed in on them.'[2] Any remnants of discipline among Hicks's force evaporated. The squares fractured into thrashing knots of men, who were cut to pieces. 'No proper formation could be preserved among the soldiers,' an unnamed survivor said. 'They fought in detached groups, each body of men surrounded by [dervishes], who picked them off in turn.'[3]

The only organized resistance came from the eleven European officers and their bodyguard of Bashi-Bazuks, or irregular cavalry – mostly Turks, Albanians and Shaygiyya tribesmen from the northern Sudan. On point of the column when the attack came, they drew up with their backs to a baobab tree, and fought to the last man. Hicks himself was one of the last to die. He emptied his revolver three times, loading and reloading automatically. When his rounds were spent, he charged a body of dervish horsemen brandishing his sword so maniacally that they actually ran away. His stallion wounded, he slipped out of the saddle and fought the enemy off with his blade, until he was speared to death. '[Hicks] was full of courage like an elephant,' said Sheikh 'Ali Gulla, a dervish wounded earlier in the fighting. 'He feared nothing . . . the bravest of all the brave men I have known.'[4] Afterwards, the heads of both Hicks and Seckendorff were cut off and carried as trophies to the dervish camp, where Klootz was required to identify them. Later they were stuck on spikes over the gate of el-Obeid.

The Egyptian colonial government had walked into this massacre through over-confidence and a desire for decisive action. For two years a rebel force based in Kordofan had inflicted on them defeat after defeat. Columns had been ambushed and wiped out, garrisons had been slaughtered. Then, in January 1883, Kordofan's capital, el-Obeid, had fallen. The Khedive Tewfiq had at first dismissed the rebellion as a local disturbance by religious fanatics. By early 1883, though, it had become clear that if el-Obeid was not retaken the whole of the Sudan might be lost.

The rebellion was led by a Muslim holy man named Mohammad Ahmad, who claimed to be the Mahdi – the direct successor of the Prophet Mohammad. His followers were known as *daraweesh*, after the Sudanese colloquial word for 'holy men' – anglicized as 'dervishes'. Preaching death to anyone who refused his own brand of Islam, the Mahdi had subverted tens of thousands of tribesmen from the Nile Valley and the western Sudan, united in their shared religion and their hatred of Turco-Egyptian rule.

In September, the Khedive Tewfiq had sent the Hicks expedition to recapture el-Obeid and put an end to the Mahdi once and for all. It was the largest modern army ever dispatched into the interior of the Sudan: 8,300 infantry, nearly two thousand cavalry, an artillery battery of sixteen Krupp mountain-guns and Nordenfeldt machine-guns, and a baggage-train of two thousand men and some six thousand camels, mules and donkeys. It should have been formidable weighed against the motley rabble the Mahdi could muster, many of whom were armed with swords, sticks or spears. But the Egyptian force had one major weakness: its morale.

Many of the troops had been captured by the British fighting for the Egyptian nationalist leader, Colonel 'Arabi Pasha, at Tel el-Kebir in the Nile Delta the previous year. Most had been sent to the Sudan in shackles. A British officer who had inspected them in Cairo before departure had been shocked to discover that some had cut off their own trigger-fingers to avoid being re-enlisted. Others had even rubbed lime into their eyes to ruin their eyesight.

Almost all had obtained forged certificates proving that they could not be called on for further service.

As for Hicks himself, his name had been literally picked out of a hat in Cairo's Shepheard's Hotel. Though he had never held a major executive command before, he was a courageous, competent officer, concerned simply with getting the job done. Fifty-three years old, married with two children, his ambition was to obtain a secure full-time post in the Egyptian service. He had arrived in the Sudan with dreams of a knighthood, and later of taking over from the current Sirdar or Commander-in-Chief of the Egyptian army, Sir Evelyn Wood, VC. Tall, rugged and physically tough, Hicks was a retired honorary colonel of the Indian army. He had survived more than twenty actions in India and Abyssinia, and had been mentioned in dispatches twice. Despite the calumnies poured on him afterwards, he was no fool.

In June, he had suggested that the army should be used simply to defend the Sudan's capital, Khartoum, and the Jazira – the area to the south between the Blue and White Niles. Here, in April, his field force had held steady and had scored one of a handful of victories against the rebels in the past two years. Dervish horsemen had charged to within a few yards of the square, but had been flattened by volleys from the Egyptian troops. Six hundred dervishes had been left dead on the battlefield, including a brother of the Mahdi. 'The Egyptian soldiers were much steadier than I expected,' Hicks had written after the first engagement, 'but I don't know that they will be so steady when we cross to the Kordofan side, where we shall meet many more rifles and guns.'[5]

Hicks was correct in his assessment. Fighting in sight of the Nile, with the support of armed steamers, was one thing: marching out into the arid steppes of Kordofan was quite another. What Hicks did not know was that the Egyptian *fellahin* had a traditional terror of the desert.

As an Englishman in the service of the Egyptian Khedive, though, Hicks was in a difficult position. The Khedive was not master in his own country. Ousted in 1879 and replaced by the nationalist Colonel 'Arabi Pasha, he had been reinstated by the

British after the battle of Tel el-Kebir in 1882. Since then, Khedive Tewfiq had ruled only in name. The real authority in Egypt was Her Britannic Majesty's agent in Cairo, Sir Edward Malet.

Malet agreed with Hicks that the army should be used only to defend Khartoum, but his hands were tied by his own government. Prime Minister William Ewart Gladstone, a Liberal, was reluctant to get drawn into affairs in the Sudan. His Foreign Secretary, George Leveson-Gower, Lord Granville, had obliged Malet to carry on the pretence that, in its relations with the Sudan, the Egyptian government was in fact independent.

Sir Evelyn Baring, who took over Malet's job three days after Hicks had left, had been opposed to the expedition from the start. He later blamed the massacre on British hypocrisy. Gladstone's government, he said, could not claim to have been unaware of the dangers. In March 1883 a British officer, Lieut. Colonel John Donald Hammill Stewart of the 11th Hussars, had been sent to Khartoum. He had produced a report outlining the risks of an expedition into hostile territory, which had been scathing about the cowardliness of the Egyptian troops and their officers. Stewart had been clear in his opinion that, should Hicks be defeated, the whole of the Sudan would probably be lost.

Instead of showing a firm hand, though, Gladstone's government had allowed Hicks's men to go like lambs to the slaughter. If, against all odds, Hicks succeeded, they would enjoy the kudos. If he failed, they believed – quite wrongly – that they could wash their hands of the whole matter. The Khedive Tewfiq, unfettered by advice from Malet, also chose to ignore Stewart's warning. His government was determined to show the British they were still capable of handling trouble in their own back yard.

Hicks, who had *de facto* authority in the Sudan, could have disputed the Khedive's instructions by arguing that his superiors in Cairo were unaware of conditions on the ground. It had been impressed on him, though, that his appointment was a fine opportunity to distinguish himself. 'It is most important that this campaign is a successful one,' he had written in January, 'as the retention or loss of the Sudan depends on it.'[6] Originally sent to

Khartoum as second-in-command, he had fought hard to get himself appointed commander-in-chief. Having attained his wish, it would have seemed churlish of him to refuse to march. It would also have been anathema to a professional soldier who had just been given his first big command, and might even have opened him to a charge of cowardice. In any case, he had his Krupps and Nordenfeldts, and hoped these modern weapons would make up for his worthless soldiers.

Hicks set out with his army from Khartoum on 5 September 1883, on a campaign that, as *Times* correspondent Frank Power commented, 'even the most sanguine look forward to with the greatest gloom'. Power was supposed to accompany Hicks but was providentially evacuated back to Khartoum with dysentery on the third day out. Long before, though, he had confidently predicted that all Hicks's Krupps and machine-guns would not deter the Mahdi's fanatics. If fifty dervishes managed to get inside the Egyptian square, he declared, the whole column would be lost.[7]

Had Hicks followed his instincts he might still have prevailed. His original plan had been to approach el-Obeid from the north, which entailed using a short-cut passing through the fringes of the Sahara desert. Hicks was dissuaded from this plan by 'Ala ad-Din Pasha, a former Ottoman cavalry officer whom Hicks himself had proclaimed civil governor-general of the Sudan, and who was to die with him at Shaykan. 'Ala ad-Din preferred the more southerly route, along the Khor al-Habl, a seasonal watercourse likely to yield more abundant water. Reluctantly agreeing to take this route, Hicks planned to leave small garrisons at intervals along it to safeguard a withdrawal. These posts would also serve as way stations for supply caravans due to move up later from the Nile. Again, the governor-general deterred him, persuading him that to divide their force would be dangerous. The small garrisons, 'Ala ad-Din said, would in any case be picked off piecemeal by the rebels.

Hicks was a good officer but felt unable to delegate, because none of his men had had staff experience. He neglected strategy and intelligence. His biggest mistake, though, was in allowing his instincts and experience to be overruled by 'Ala ad-Din. On the southern course, the expedition was in hostile territory. Here, the dervishes operated a scorched-earth policy, moving tribes from their villages, polluting or filling in wells, and manipulating the movement of the column. From the day Hicks left the White Nile at ed-Duem on 22 September, three thousand rebel scouts shadowed him all the way.

Frank Power's observations had proved tragically prescient. After harassing the column for weeks, on 1 or 2 November – the actual date is disputed – the dervishes had occupied the water-pool at Birka, forty miles south of el-Obeid. This gave Hicks no choice but to turn north to another pool with the unenticing name of Fula al-Masarin, the 'Pool of the Entrails'. His path took him through the forest of Shaykan, where there was dense cover from *kitr* trees and thorn-scrub. The scrub here was so dense, in fact, that the force was unable to keep formation. It was an ideal spot for an ambush.

On the night of 3 November the Egyptians dug in behind earthworks, the remains of which were still to be found fifty years afterwards. By dawn the next day – 4 November – the Mahdi's riflemen had crept through the scrub to within yards of the enemy. That morning the Mahdi himself arrived. 'We dervishes were anxious to attack at once,' said Bela Ahmad Siraj, one of the Mahdi's men, interviewed years later, 'but the Mahdi restrained us. So we contented ourselves with skirmishing and firing rifles at the [enemy]. So fierce was the fire that the bark was stripped from the trees as if they had been washed by soap.'[8]

Almost every bullet found a target, and the Egyptians fired back ineffectually at their invisible assailants. 'The bullets are flying in all directions,' wrote Major Arthur Herlth, an Austrian cavalry officer on Hicks's staff, 'and camels, mules and men keep dropping down; we are all cramped up together, so the bullets cannot fail to strike. We are faint and weary and have no idea what to do . . .'[9] The firefight continued all day. It was unseasonally hot, and by evening the Egyptian soldiers were too thirsty and demoralized to build a thorn enclosure – a zariba. The following morning, 5 November, they assembled in three squares at about 1000 hours.

When they moved off, they left scores of dead behind them, and even artillery pieces whose crews had been wiped out. The Egyptians, by now almost blind with thirst, advanced slowly through the forest, which was less dense here than it had been the previous day. They had been pressing forward for no more than an hour when the dervishes launched their final devastating charge.

As Power had predicted, the Mahdi's men were not perturbed by Hicks's Krupps or Nordenfeldts. Their best weapon was the country, and they had used it brilliantly. They had no problems with morale. They outnumbered the Egyptians at least four to one, and believed they were fighting for God. That most of the enemy were fellow Muslims mattered not a jot. If they were not Mahdists, they were unbelievers. To the dervishes, all fair-skinned foreigners, British, Austrian, German, Egyptian, Albanian, Anatolian, Circassian or Greek, Christian or Muslim, were 'Turks', and fuel for the fire.

Besides, the Mahdi had assured his men that they were invulnerable. He had declared that the enemy's bullets would turn to water. Many of the dervishes wore *hejabs* – magic amulets made of verses from the Quran rolled inside a leather pouch. These gave them protection against blades and bullets. Claiming a direct revelation from the Prophet Mohammad, the Mahdi also announced that on the day of battle forty thousand angels would join them, swooping down on the unbelievers like giant raptors. Later, some of the tribesmen swore they had actually *seen* these dark angels on the battlefield.

After the massacre, the dervish army remained near Shaykan for a week, collecting the spoils of war – sacks of biscuits, rice and barley, suits of mail, camels, horses, mules, donkeys, rifles, pistols, ammunition, swords, bayonets, shovels, clothing, watches, gold, silver and cash, as well as the Krupps and Nordenfeldts, and their shells. Klootz, now known among the dervishes as Mustafa, was given charge of Hicks's injured white stallion. He was told to use the medical supplies he had collected on the battlefield to salve its wound.

Between two and three hundred Egyptian soldiers who had survived by hiding under the piles of dead were herded together. They were stripped naked and sent to el-Obeid with ropes round their necks. Those who were not executed later were left to beg in the market place, and eventually died of starvation. A few hundred dervishes had been killed. These included the Sheikh of the Kinana tribe from the White Nile, and fourteen of his men, who had been blown to shreds by a single artillery shell – proving, at least, that Hicks's men did get their guns into action. These and the other dervish dead were buried with simple ceremony, while the enemy dead were left for the vultures.

The Mahdi had revived the primitive communism of traditional Islam. All loot was supposed to be handed in to the communal hoard, the *bayt al-mal*. Some booty was auctioned, some distributed as presents, but he gave short shrift to any private acquisitiveness. Tribesmen who had cached weapons or treasure on the battlefield for later collection were flogged with hippo-hide whips until they died or revealed where it was. Seven slaves in the service of the Mahdi's own uncle, Sayid Mohammad Taha, had their right hands and left feet slashed off publicly for concealing plunder.

When the stench of the dead grew too oppressive, the dervishes decamped for el-Obeid. On the day after the victory, there had been a hundred-gun salute in the town. Now, there were scenes of savage ecstasy as the victorious warriors marched in trailing shrouds of dust. First came the banners, scarlet, black and green, followed by ranks of footmen tens of thousands strong. The tips of their leaf-bladed spears danced and scintillated, still stained with the enemy's blood. The men were drunk with victory, moving to a mesmerizing chant of *la ilaha illa-llah* (there is no god but Allah). According to Father Joseph Ohrwalder, an Austrian Catholic missionary who was a prisoner in el-Obeid at the time, their voices were like the sound of a rushing stream. Some warriors, intoxicated by the mantra, wheeled and circled out of the columns, brandishing their spears and letting out blood-curdling roars.

After them came the cavalry, trotting, reining in, and launching suddenly into ferocious mock charges, with their spears thrust out.

They were followed by the prisoners – a handful of naked *fellahin*, who were dragged forward by ropes, kicked, thumped, jeered at and spat upon. Finally, after the captured guns, came the Mahdi himself, mounted on a white camel.

The crowd went wild with excitement. Men rushed to kiss his feet, and to touch his robes, while others hurled themselves flat and kissed the ground on which his camel had walked. The women ululated in shrill voices, chanting, 'The Mahdi! God's Expected One!' Mohammad Ahmad had performed a miracle. He had gathered an army of tribesmen and peasants from scratch. He had taken on the largest government force ever sent into the region and annihilated it. His warriors had charged modern rifles, cannons and machine-guns, armed only with swords, spears and sticks.

From this day on, the Mahdi became an object of veneration. The very water with which he made his ablutions was collected and handed out as a cure-all for ailments. The Mahdi was believed to be replete with *baraka*, the mystical life force possessed by all holy men, which could be passed on by touch. Those who had believed from the beginning that he was the Messiah foretold in legend could point to Shaykan as proof. Those who had not believed could either profess themselves convinced, or go along for the ride. Nobody who had witnessed the treatment of looters at Shaykan was now likely to dispute Mohammad Ahmad's claim – at least not in public.

Even the Mahdi himself had not expected such a complete victory. He knew that he was no longer leading a rebellion. The balance of power had tipped, and he now had the Sudan in the palm of his hand. The government still possessed garrisons in the other provinces, some of them commanded by Europeans – Frank Lupton in Bahr al-Ghazal, Emin Pasha in Fashoda, Rudolf von Slatin in Darfur. Most were held by small numbers of ill-equipped troops isolated in remote outposts in the trackless wilderness. They did not perturb the Mahdi. The only obstacle that remained to the *sirat al-mustaqim* – the straight path of true Islam – lay three hundred miles to the east, where a thin grey line of soldiers manned the ramparts of Khartoum.

Part One

1

Three days of blood, noise and smoke in the forest of Shaykan in November 1883 were the dawn of the Mahdist state in the Sudan, the first radical Islamic realm, and the only African nation ever to win independence from a colonial power by force of arms. Its success was to send shock-waves through the western world. Rising to its crescendo at the time of Queen Victoria's Diamond Jubilee, its defeat was to become the climactic adventure of the British colonial era.

Before Mohammad 'Ali Pasha's army crossed the southern frontiers of Egypt in 1820, there was no such country as the Sudan. A million square miles of arid hills, mountains, river valleys, swamps, lakes, lush savannahs, sterile desert, desolate coast and marginal steppe, it was a chequerboard of cultivating and nomadic tribes. These peoples, speaking four hundred different languages, were of almost every conceivable kind and combination of Arab and African culture. It was an amorphous territory without borders. The Arabs, who had begun to settle there in the twelfth century, had named it *bilad as-Sudan* or the Land of the Blacks.

For centuries the region had been riddled with feuds, small wars and squabbles between rival tribes, chiefs and petty sultans. Throughout the eighteenth century the most powerful princedom in the Sudan was the Funj sultanate, with its capital at Sennar on the Blue Nile. Founded two hundred years earlier as a partnership between Arab nomads and settled farmers, by the 1820s it was almost moribund, its power dwindling year by year. When Mohammad 'Ali's force arrived at Sennar in 1821, they met with little opposition.

Mohammad 'Ali Pasha was Viceroy of Egypt, an Albanian soldier-of-fortune in the service of the Ottoman Empire. His nominal master was the Ottoman Sultan in Constantinople, who held the dual role of temporal monarch and Khalifa (Caliph) of Islam: the successor of the Prophet Mohammad, the Shadow of God on Earth. After Mohammad 'Ali's conquest, therefore, the Sudan became in essence a colony *of a colony* of the Ottoman Empire.

Mohammad 'Ali's invasion force had come mainly in search of black slaves, to be organized into a new army of riflemen known as Jihadiyya – Sudanese battalions with Turco-Egyptian officers, trained on European lines.[1] Yet the Turco-Egyptian occupation was more than a crude attempt at exploitation. Mohammad 'Ali Pasha dreamed of turning both Egypt and its new southern extension into modern and prosperous countries. Though some of his successors were venal, corrupt and incompetent, others were men of energy and vision who tried to continue Mohammad 'Ali's dream. They introduced new crops and agricultural schemes, settled nomads, built schools and hospitals, constructed railways, erected telegraph lines, established a postal system and improved steamer-transport on the Nile.

To pay for these improvements the Sudanese were subjected to taxation so severe it amounted almost to confiscation. Revenues were collected by Bashi-Bazuks – Turkish irregulars, Christian and Muslim, whose principal trade, as Hicks Pasha noted, was 'robbery and murder'.[2] 'They are like ferrets in a rabbit warren,' he wrote. 'A Bashi-Bazuk paid £50 by the Government spends £500 and amasses large sums besides.'[3]

Suffocating taxation was one of the main sources of discontent behind the Mahdist revolt. The second was the prohibition of the slave trade. In 1877, Mohammad 'Ali's grandson, Isma'il Pasha, now styled 'Khedive' instead of 'Viceroy', was obliged by Britain to sign a convention for the suppression of slavery. The agreement prohibited all public commerce in slaves throughout Egyptian territory, and provided for the ending of private slavery in the Sudan within twelve years. To help enforce the embargo, the

Khedive appointed his first European governor-general of the Sudan, an Englishman named Charles George Gordon.

Gordon had already served Isma'il Pasha for three years, having succeeded British explorer Sir Samuel Baker as governor of Gondokoro Province, a month's trip by steamer up the White Nile from Khartoum. As governor-general, he declared war on the slave trade. He closed slave markets, halted caravans, and had slave-merchants publicly hanged. When the slave-traders in the Bahr al-Ghazal region revolted, he unleashed the cattle-nomads of the steppes against them.

To the Sudanese, the slave trade was a traditional part of life. It was not forbidden in Islam, and they did not consider it wrong. They could not understand why outsiders wanted to abolish it, when it was self-evidently profitable to everyone. No one in the Sudan or Egypt – except Gordon, and the slaves – had any real interest in stopping the trade. Its suppression was a devastating blow to the Sudanese economy. Coupled with the exorbitant taxes, it caused deep discontent among Sudanese of all tribes and classes.

Privately, Khedive Isma'il Pasha opposed both the ban on slavery and the appointment of Gordon. His hands were tied, though, by his vast debts to Britain and other European creditors. Within thirteen years he had plunged his country £91 million into the red – a sum he could never hope to pay back. When, in 1876, he suspended repayments, Britain, France, Germany and Russia set up a commission to ensure settlement. Inevitably Isma'il objected, and he was brusquely deposed and replaced by his more malleable son, Tewfiq. The prime conspirator in this palace coup was the British member of the commission, Sir Evelyn Baring, a former artillery officer turned diplomat and a scion of the banking firm Baring Brothers.

The deposition of Isma'il, though, had unforeseen consequences. Incensed by the knowledge that Egypt had been sold out to foreign creditors, revolutionary forces seized their chance. A flood of anti-foreign sentiment raised in its current a popular nationalist leader, Colonel Ahmad 'Arabi Pasha – an officer of *fellahin* origin. Supported by the Egyptian army, 'Arabi Pasha occupied Alexandria. His followers slaughtered foreigners, looted the city and threatened passage through the Suez Canal. The 'puppet' Khedive, Tewfiq, fled from Cairo.

The British could not, of course, let this threat to their financial interests go unopposed. Eighty per cent of shipping passing through the Suez Canal flew the British flag. A month after Tewfiq escaped, the Royal Navy's Mediterranean fleet bombarded 'Arabi's shore batteries in Alexandria harbour. In September, the fleet landed an Anglo-Indian expeditionary force, thirty thousand strong. Led by imperial trouble-shooter Lieut. General Sir Garnet Wolseley, it smashed 'Arabi Pasha at Tel el-Kebir in the Nile Delta.

Tewfiq was reinstated as Khedive. The defeated Egyptian army was placed under British command and reconstructed from scratch. Egypt was now controlled by the British, but it remained a province of the Ottoman Empire. Meanwhile, the disturbances under 'Arabi Pasha and the British invasion had left Egypt's control of the Sudan gravely debilitated. Sudanese were everywhere infuriated by the loss of the slave trade, impoverished by the brutal taxes, and alienated by the innovations the Turco-Egyptians had introduced. If they were to throw off the Ottoman yoke it was now or never. When, in 1881, a Sufi adept named Mohammad Ahmad declared himself the Mahdi, or Expected Guide, and called on the Faithful to expel the Turks, his message fell on fertile ground.

2

The narrow serpent of land the local Arabs called *al-khartum* or the Elephant's Trunk lies where the Blue and White Niles meet. In September, when the rivers are in spate, the confluence is a vast sheet of fast-flowing water over a mile wide and fifteen feet above the low water mark. During the flood season, the Blue Nile, surging down six thousand feet from Lake Tana in Abyssinia, slowing up through the clay plains of Rosseires, attains a soup-like thickness from its baggage of silt. Its surface is littered with tree-trunks, dead animals and vegetation. At the Moghran point, where the rivers meet, its dark colour is clearly distinguishable from the delicate jade of the White Nile, whose journey, a thousand miles from the Victoria Nyanza through the equatorial swamps of the Sudd, is of a gentler, more meandering kind.

Until the 1830s, Khartoum was no more than a Shilluk fishing village, consisting of a few *tukuls*, or grass-roofed huts. The town was established as a military and civil headquarters by Khurshid Pasha, the Sudan's first Turco-Egyptian governor-general or *hikimdar*, who built a mosque, a hospital, a military barracks and the original *hikimdar*'s palace – on the site where the Republican Palace stands today.

The town came into its own in the 1840s with the opening up of the White Nile basin, the tropical region far to the south. The area had traditionally been considered impenetrable due to the fearful swamp of the Sudd, the tse-tse fly and the truculent Nilotic tribes. The Turco-Egyptians wanted to create an 'equatorial empire', and they began to send armed steamers to blaze trails south. Two new Provinces were established, with their capitals at Fashoda and Gondokoro.

These pioneering expeditions were soon followed by the boats of ivory-hunters. At first the ivory trade was restricted to the Egyptian government. When its monopoly was abolished in 1840, adventurers flocked to the Sudan to make their fortunes in elephants' teeth. The profits were enormous, mainly because the tribes of the White Nile, such as the Bongo and the Bari, had no idea of its value. In the 1840s, two shillings' worth of Venetian glass beads would buy an entire tusk. As the price on the world market was twenty shillings per kilo, and the average tusk weighed eight and a half kilos, this represented a rather satisfactory gross return to the ivory-hunter of 168 shillings per tusk. Khartoum was ideally situated as a base for their ventures up the White Nile.

Slavery had been known in the Sudan since the earliest times. It developed in the nineteenth century as a by-product of the ivory trade. Ivory merchants would march inland from the river at the head of small armies of hired guns. They would recruit and arm local tribesmen as their proxies. They would surround villages, capture their inhabitants, and torture them till they revealed where their ivory was hidden. They would take the tusks, then burn the village, and murder everyone but the young men, young women and children. The cattle would be given to the neighbouring tribesmen who had aided them. The survivors of the raid would be forced to carry the ivory to the Nile, where the traders' boats were waiting. They became the 'currency' of the ivory merchants, used to offset their expenses and to pay their mercenaries from the north.

Khartoum stood at the point where all roads met. It was both the entrepôt of river commerce and the main junction of the overland camel-trails. Caravans brought slaves, ivory, ostrich feathers and gum arabic from Darfur in the west and Abyssinia in the east. They carried textiles and manufactured goods from Egypt in the north. By the late 1870s the city had a population of about fifty thousand, more than half of whom were slaves.

In 1850, Liverpool merchant George Melly commented that Khartoum 'looked like the end of the world'.[4] Thirty-four years later it still had the air of a frontier town. The banks of the Blue Nile were shaded in palm-groves that stretched as far as Moghran point, and the city itself was full of trees. The Nile banks were more verdant than they are today. Lion, rhino and hippopotamus were never far off. Crocodiles were a constant menace to water-carriers and women washing their clothes in the river. One huge crocodile, known as the Sheikh, was venerated. Despite the number of victims he had swallowed, chasing him was considered a crime.

The Blue Nile waterfront was a scene of relentless activity. *Sagiyyas* – wooden water-wheels – creaked as they drew water, sloshing it into feeder channels to be carried through the many gardens that stretched to the river bank. There was a *sagiyya* at work every hundred yards. In a couple of instances they had been replaced by steam pumps, whose cough and clatter could be heard clear across the Nile. In the lanes between the gardens there was a continual procession of slaves and porters balancing water-pots on their heads with elegant grace.

Access to the landing jetties was by steps in the stone embankment. Vessels of all descriptions were endlessly weighing anchor and putting in. Apart from the governor-general's *dhahabiyya* or houseboat, there were fishing smacks, consular vessels, native sailing boats or *nuggars*, government 'penny-steamers' and armed trading vessels flying a dozen different flags. From time to time the governor of Berber Province would put in an appearance in his galley-like vessel rowed by twelve muscular black slaves.

The *hikimdar*'s palace or *saraya* was the most impressive building on the waterfront. It was a U-shaped construction of red brick with a two-storey frontage and two single-storey wings. The lower floor was occupied by government clerks, while the upper floor, reached by staircases on both sides, housed the officials. The palace's main gate was an arched doorway on the western side, facing the Muderiyya, the civil headquarters of the city of Khartoum – standing on the site of the present-day Ministry of the Interior.

Beyond the Muderiyya was the Austrian Consulate, a large house bearing the double-eagle arms of the Austro-Hungarian Empire on its door. The consul, sixty-year-old Martin Ludwig Hansall, was the leading personality in the town. One of Khartoum's earliest European residents, he had arrived here as a member of the Catholic Mission in 1853. He was a teacher at the Mission School and secretary to the Bishop of Khartoum. Appointed Austrian consul and protector of the Catholic Mission in 1862, he was a fervent churchgoer, though his devotion did not prevent him retaining a harem of no less than seven native girls.

Next door to Hansall's consulate stood the telegraph and post offices. Beyond that was the Roman Catholic Mission, established by Austro-Hungarian Jesuits in 1848. Covering an extensive area, it was walled and gated, and famous for its neatly manicured gardens, planted with banana, fig, jasmine and mimosa trees. It was graced with libraries, cloisters, the Mission school, in which Hansall taught, and, above all, the church. Frank Power of *The Times* found the sound of its bell comforting. 'It is queer to hear [the bell] ringing the Angelus each day,' he wrote, 'among the palm trees, and above the clatter of Arabs, slaves, naked men and women and the cries of tropical birds.'[5]

The 'native' town lay behind the riverside area. It was separated from the Nile bank by a vast open space dotted with pits from which sand and soil had been removed for brick-making. The town was a labyrinth of thatched huts and mud-brick dwellings, centred round two covered *souqs* and a mosque with a cone-shaped minaret. The poorer quarters of the town, including its brothels, lay in the area today occupied by Jamhuriyya Street – the modern city's principal thoroughfare.

The city had a tolerable climate for part of the year, but was unpleasant in the flood season. During the rains, the pits in the space behind the waterfront would fill up with water. The entire area would devolve into a malarial swamp, buzzing with mosquitoes and rumbling with the croak of a million frogs. The connection between the mosquito and malaria was still unknown. In 1878 alone, malaria accounted for the lives of no less than seventeen priests and nuns of the Catholic Mission at Khartoum.

With its largely makeshift houses, the city was also at the mercy of the *haboob*, the violent line squalls that came in May to June. These were whirling columns of yellow dust and clay particles thousands of feet high that slammed into the place at gale-force. They could rip off roofs and knock houses and *tukuls* flat. In 1839, a *haboob* destroyed thousands of houses and sank eleven boats on the White Nile.

As for terrestrial enemies, the rivers protected the town on the northern side, and a rough crescent of ramparts ran from Burri Fort on the Blue Nile west towards the White Nile. Because of the fifteen-foot variation in river levels from wet to dry season, the ramparts had a critical gap on the western side. The wall, stretching a distance of four miles, had been built on the assumption that a large force would be available to man it. In mid-November 1883, the garrison could muster only two thousand troops.

3

By then, the atmosphere in Khartoum had grown tense. Every Sunday, Lieut. Colonel Henry de Coetlogon ran the fast steamer *Bordain* to ed-Duem on the White Nile, desperate for any word from Hicks. Every Saturday, though, he arrived back in Khartoum empty-handed. Sir Evelyn Baring's telegraph rattled out day and night from Cairo, asking for news in vain.

Forty-four-year-old de Coetlogon, acting commander of the Khartoum garrison, had escaped the fate of Hicks and his fellow officers largely by incompetence. Hicks had thought him rude and insubordinate, and had been obliged to 'pitch into him' on more than one occasion. In the end he had left him behind. An undistinguished officer, born in Munich, de Coetlogon had joined the East Yorkshire Regiment at the age of nineteen. He had been passed over for promotion many times, and it had taken him fifteen years to obtain a captaincy. Retiring as honorary major in 1881, he had served for two years in India before entering the Egyptian army.

He had moved into the *hikimdar*'s palace on the south bank of the Blue Nile, where a telegraph office had been set up. Apart from himself, the place was occupied only by Frank Power of *The Times*, the twenty-five-year-old monocled Irishman who doubled as sketcher for the *Pictorial News*, and who had been providentially invalided out of Hicks's column. The building's vast empty rooms and long corridor gave the place a bleak feeling that fuelled Power's sombre mood. Still weak from his long attack of dysentery, the eccentric Dubliner was haunted by paranoia. 'It is now thirty-two days since Hicks Pasha and his immense army marched from Duem where I left,' he had written on 27 October, 'and since then *not one word, good or bad*, has been heard of him and his eleven thousand men . . . If it is bad, we Christians, Turks and Cairo Arabs here, will not have ten minutes to live, as the Arabs here are to a man secretly for the Mahdi.'[6]

Power had been *Times* correspondent with the Turkish forces at Plevna during the Turco-Russian war. He had seen fighting and bloodshed but had never known strain like this. Unable to sleep, he was up every morning at four o'clock. He walked to a local café in Muderiyya Square, passing through the arched gate of the palace. The guard of twenty-five Sudanese soldiers with their sergeant would turn out and present arms. Power sat in the square under a palm-tree, among rowdy backgammon and pensive chess-players, until the heat got up at about ten o'clock. He wrote dispatches, drew sketches, and watched the vendors and passers-by in the local bazaar.

The market was a constant swirl of noise and movement – a sideshow that never grew dull. Tarboosh-clad government em-ployees swept past on huge white Nubian donkeys, almost the size of mules. Coptic clerks and accountants, Turks, Circassians, Albanians and Armenians scurried to the Muderiyya. Arabs of the Shanabla or Shukriyya appeared, looming over the crowds disdainfully on their camels, bringing with them the odours of sand and uncured hide. Files of black slaves, naked but for loin-cloths, tramped past carrying water-skins like bloated maggots from the Nile. There were women of all shapes and sizes – long-legged Dinka and Shilluk maidens, dusky Nubian women, Nubas from Kordofan with their hair plaited into fantastic styles, decked with cowries and gold. There were Danagla and Ja'aliyyin tribesmen from the Nile Valley, in sweeping white *jallabiyyas* and layered white turbans – hired guns of the slave-traders, Nile sailors, ser-vants, hawkers and pedlars. As they passed, many would look askance at the monocled Irishman. 'Have you heard from your general yet?' was the question everyone asked.

Days became weeks, but still Power had no answer to that question. Then, on 21 November, *Bordain* put in quietly at the jetty below the governor-general's palace by night. On board were Lieut. Colonel Henry de Coetlogon, and a tribesman with a spear wound in his back. The tribesman claimed to be the only survivor of Hicks's army.

Later that night the Greek consul, Nikolaos Leontides, a native of the Isle of Leros, answered a knock at his door and was surprised to find standing outside the French consul, Alphonse Marquet, the richest merchant in Khartoum. 'Come to my house, by the garden,' Marquet said. Intrigued, Leontides walked along the waterfront and entered Marquet's garden. He found a gloomy huddle there in the lamplight: Marquet, Henry de Coetlogon, Frank Power, Martin Hansall, and acting governor-general Hussain Yusri, a Syrian. De Coetlogon told Leontides what everyone else there already knew: he had picked up a survivor of the Hicks mission, and his message had been unequivocal: the expedition had been wiped out.

'Hicks, his staff, O'Donovan, and the twelve thousand men have been massacred,' Frank Power wrote grimly later. 'Colonel de Coetlogon and I are in Khartoum, where the volcano has not yet "erupted", but the Mahdi has three hundred thousand men [sic] with rifles and artillery, and we have only two thousand soldiers, no retreat, and the town and country to the Red Sea red hot for the rebels.'[7]

4

The next morning, Sir Evelyn Baring was sitting in the office of his spacious Qasr ad-Dubbara residence in Cairo when a clerk brought in a telegram from de Coetlogon in Khartoum. Baring read the message carefully, then glanced out for a moment over his lawn, a carpet of green baize running as far as a low wall by the waters of the Nile. Beyond the wrought-iron gates with their royal cipher, he could see upriver as far as the Abbassiyya barracks, where the British army of occupation was garrisoned, and beyond that, the tower of All Saints Anglican Cathedral at Bulaq. He betrayed no surprise at the news of Hicks's massacre. In fact, rumours that the column was in difficulties had been emanating from the French consul-general for several days. Baring had himself calculated that if Hicks and his men were alive, they must by now be out of provisions.

After considering his priorities for a moment, he penned an immediate dispatch to Rear-Admiral Sir William Hewett RN,

VC, Commander-in-Chief of the Royal Navy's East India Station. Hewett was to order a squadron of warships at once to the Red Sea, to secure the Sudan's ports – Suakin and Massawa. Only after this was done did Baring wire the Foreign Secretary, Lord Granville, in London. Granville's main concern was the imminent threat to Egypt herself. He advised Baring to talk to his military experts, Lieut. General Sir Evelyn Wood, Sirdar of the Egyptian army, Lieut. General Sir Frederick Stephenson, commanding the British army in Egypt, and Lieut. General Valentine Baker, commanding the Egyptian gendarmerie. Together they could decide on the best course.

In Khartoum, there was panic. The Mahdi's vast army was now equipped with the most modern weapons. Numerous tribes who had remained on the fence until the victory at Shaykan were said to be flocking to his banners. Provincial governors who had hitherto been prepared to resist were said to be ready to hand over their provinces to the new Messiah. The Mahdi and his hordes were expected outside Khartoum at any moment. By 1 December Alphonse Marquet, the city's richest merchant, had packed up and left on his boat downriver to Berber. It was the signal for a general exodus. 'Greeks, Copts, Turks, Maltese, Bengalese, Madrasees, Algerians, Italians – consuls and merchants . . .' Power wrote, 'all trooping down before the river to Berber is closed.'[8] By the end of the month almost all the consuls and even the priests, nuns and staff from the Catholic Mission had gone.

Four days after the news of Hicks's defeat, Generals Wood, Stephenson and Baker hurried under the wide verandas of Baring's house and made their way up the short flight of stairs to his drawing-room. None of them was a stranger to the Agency – all had at one time or another been invited to Sir Evelyn and Lady Baring's Tuesday 'at homes', where as many as forty guests would be entertained in their elegant but somewhat sterile ballroom and music-room. Now, the generals settled uncomfortably into chairs of white wood, in a hospital-like ambience of spotless walls and ceiling, and were served tea by turbaned Indian servants in white and gold livery whom Baring had brought with him from Delhi.

It was a grim and realistic meeting. The three officers agreed that the massacre of Hicks was the death-knell of Turco-Egyptian rule in the Sudan. Even Khartoum could not now be saved. They recommended holding the capital only until the other garrisons could be pulled out. Then the whole of the Sudan would have to be evacuated, with the exception of the Red Sea ports.

After they had departed, Baring retired to his office and wrote out a wire, relaying this advice to Lord Granville in London. Baring did not find the policy of abandoning the Sudan a hard pill to swallow. Committed to Egypt's re-establishment, he felt that the key to success was financial solvency. Jettisoning the vast deserts and swamps to the south would be an immense blow to Egypt's pride, but a great asset to her exchequer. That the idea might horrify the Khedive and the Egyptian government did not disturb him – he was a man accustomed to making unpopular decisions. Forty-two years old, he had left the army twelve years earlier and taken a post as private secretary to his cousin, Lord Northbrook, who had been appointed Viceroy of India. During his term as 'Vice-Viceroy', Baring had not been liked. People feared and respected him, or feared and disliked him, but he had few real friends.

With his bear-like features and hooded, inscrutable eyes, Sir Evelyn was not a man easily dislodged from his posture of diplomatic calm. He had a quintessentially English distrust of bravado, immodesty and self-advertisement, but beneath the frost there was a keen sense of the absurd. He had shared this with the nonsense poet Edward Lear, a friend from his youth. Baring was also loyal by nature: he had become engaged at the age of twenty-one, and remained faithful to his fiancée until they were able to marry fourteen years later. Inevitably nicknamed 'Over-Baring', he sometimes appeared pompous and peremptory. At heart, though, he was a straightforward man – friendly, plain and outspoken – who genuinely believed in the intrinsic benevolence of the British Empire. The task he had been given on taking over as British agent had been an impossible one. He was expected both to oversee the withdrawal of British forces from Egypt, and to implement administrative reforms that would replace the autocratic government of the Khedives. Baring knew that these two objectives were mutually exclusive. If British troops were withdrawn from Egypt, the reforms could not be carried out. The only solution was to continue British occupation.

Now he turned his considerable acumen to the evacuation of Egyptian garrisons from the Sudan. The most logical way would be to make use of the Red Sea port of Suakin, opening up the caravan route from there to Berber, on the Nile. The distance was only 240 miles, although the way was desert with few water-sources. Suakin port and its satellite outposts, Sinkat and Tokar, were still in Khedival hands, but the Suakin–Berber route was blocked by the Beja tribes, who had joined the dervishes. Mustered by an outstanding pro-Mahdist leader named 'Osman Digna, the Beja had been active since the previous summer, when they had raided the post at Sinkat.

That winter they wiped out a force of 160 men, on its way to Sinkat. A month later Captain Lyndoch Moncrieff, RN, British consul at Jeddah, was killed at et-Teb advancing with a battalion of Egyptian infantry to relieve Tokar. Of an entire Sudanese Jihadiyya battalion thrown at 'Osman Digna in mid-November, only two officers and thirty-three men came back alive. On 19 November Baring wired to Lord Granville that Egyptian authority in the eastern Sudan had virtually ceased to exist.

Opening the road from Suakin to Berber was going to require a substantial force. The question was, where would that force come from? The Khedive Tewfiq's solution was to send the re-invented Egyptian army under Sir Evelyn Wood. Lord Granville would not hear of it. Wood's army had not yet completed its training, and in any case had been raised to serve only within the confines of Egypt itself. Deploying Stephenson's British troops was out of the question as far as Gladstone was concerned, and the use of Ottoman forces was likely to have political complications. The only available corps was Valentine Baker's gendarmerie.

It was well equipped, but it was a police force. Like the army, it was never chartered for service outside its own country. Apart from about two hundred Turks who were in good fighting fettle, its officers and men were of the same dubious substance out of which Hicks's column had been cobbled. Baring also had grave doubts about its commander, fifty-seven-year-old Valentine Baker. He did not trust his judgement, and was afraid he would do something rash.[9]

Baker, who was living in a suite at Shepheard's Hotel in Ezbekiyya Square with his wife and two daughters, was the younger brother of the Nile explorer Sir Samuel Baker. He shared his peer's relentless courage and lack of tact. Like Sam, a thickset, powerful, uncouth-looking man, Val had originally been one of the British army's brightest stars – a personal friend of the Prince of Wales, and colonel of one of the smartest-of-the-smart cavalry regiments, the 10th Hussars. Nine years before, however, Baker had been convicted of indecent assault on a young girl called Rebecca Dickinson in the carriage of a train bound for Waterloo. Whether or not he was guilty is still disputed. The most astonishing aspect of the case was not the assault, but the fact that someone in his privileged position failed to get away with it.

Unfortunately for him, he picked the wrong woman. Even more unfortunately, her cause was taken up by Queen Victoria, who wanted to make an example of the kind of roués she thought were ruining the Prince of Wales. On conviction, Baker was given a year in prison, a £500 fine, and was cashiered from the army for good.

Two years later he resurfaced in Constantinople, where Sultan 'Abdal Hamid II threw him a lifeline as a mercenary. He fought with distinction as a cavalry officer during the Turco-Russian war. In 1882, after Tel el-Kebir, he was transferred to Egypt with the rank of lieutenant-general. Hicks, who encountered him during his first days in Cairo, thought him 'one of the nicest men I have ever met – so evidently with a head on his shoulders, and he *looks* as if his life had had some heavy cloud over it'.[10]

It was Baker himself who had drawn up the original blueprint for the new Egyptian army. He had envisaged it as a force of six thousand Egyptian soldiers with eighty British officers. Baker had hoped to become its first Sirdar, and tried to pull strings with his old friend the Prince of Wales to get himself appointed. But Prime Minister Gladstone, who had never let Queen Victoria intimidate him, gave short shrift to her son. Baker was an ex-convict who had not been invited to Cairo by HM Government. His appointment as Sirdar was out of the question. As consolation prize, Tewfiq gave him the gendarmerie. Baring's reservations about Baker's competence were well founded. The last thing needed on any sensitive military operation was a commander who felt obliged to prove himself. Such a man was likely to endanger the entire force. Understandably, Baker's major aim in life was to redeem his name and regain his rank in the British army. If it meant placing himself in harm's way, then so much the better.

Baring was astute enough to realize this. Sending the gendarmerie was the Khedive's decision, not his, yet Baring would not have allowed Baker to go if there had been any choice. The facts were that two Egyptian garrisons in the port's hinterland – Sinkat and Tokar – were under siege by the dervishes. The British government had refused to give military aid, and had refused to let Egypt use her own army. Baring knew that if no action was taken, the garrisons would fall and Suakin would almost certainly be lost.

Before Baker left, Baring called him to his office and gave him a face-to-face grilling, to impress on him that he must not attempt any 'heroics'. Baker promised faithfully that he would toe the line. Baring put his instructions in writing, and had the letter signed by the Khedive. The orders reiterated that Baker's mission was to open the Suakin–Berber road, and to pacify the region along the coast. He was enjoined not to engage the dervishes unless the conditions were highly favourable, and advised to refrain from any action at all until he had received reinforcements. These were to be six hundred pro-Egyptian tribesmen from the Sudan, raised and led by Zubayr Rahma Pasha, a Sudanese former slave-trader who had been in exile in Cairo for the past six years.

Two days before Christmas 1883, General Valentine Baker landed in the Sudan.

5

In the empty palace in Khartoum, Power had left Hicks's room untouched. 'I have disturbed nothing,' he wrote on 1 December, '. . . his photos, guns and papers &c are lying about as if he only went out for a few moments.'[11] Since the Mahdi had failed to materialize outside the ramparts, Power had become more sanguine. He felt that the city could hold out for months as long as the townspeople remained loyal, and Baker's gendarmes got through. As *Times* correspondent, he was not pleased at the prospect of being liberated by a social leper like Valentine Baker. Rescue by his celebrated elder brother Sir Samuel Baker would have made a better story. He reckoned there were at least fifteen thousand Mahdi supporters among the population, led by thirty prominent men. Various schemes were mooted for dealing with the ringleaders, ranging from poisoning to strangling in their beds. None was ever put into practice.

Much earlier, Henry de Coetlogon had begun to lose his nerve. Three days after receiving the news of the Hicks massacre he had telegraphed Sir Evelyn Wood, claiming that Khartoum and Sennar only had enough provisions to last two months. 'All supplies are cut off,' he wrote. 'To save what remains of the army in the Sudan, a retreat on Berber should be made at once . . . Reinforcements arriving could not reach Khartoum except by land and for that a very large force is necessary . . . Again I say, the only way of saving what remains is to attempt a general retreat on Berber. This is the real state of affairs here, and I beg of you to impress on His Highness the Khedive.'[12]

By New Year's Day 1884, even Power had started to wonder if Baker's force really had been deployed. 'They have done nothing for us yet from Cairo,' he wrote his mother. 'They are leaving it all to fate, and the rebels around us are growing stronger.'[13] His morale had been raised a little when a month earlier Baring had appointed him British consul in Khartoum. Power was flattered. The honour was not at all diminished in his eyes by the fact that he and de Coetlogon were the only British subjects in the town. Still, he had calculated that it would take Baker's men twenty-two days to reach Khartoum by the Nile route, and they were long overdue. At the beginning of January, unable to stand it any longer, de Coetlogon contradicted his earlier pronouncement by demanding twelve thousand men to defend Khartoum. Only six days later he was again asking for an order to withdraw.

6

Over a thousand miles away to the north-east, in Palestine, a British officer of a very different calibre was camping at Tel Abu Hareira on the Dead Sea shore. Herbert Horatio Kitchener, thirty-three years old, was a captain in the Royal Engineers, attached to the Egyptian army as *bimbashi* (major). He had volunteered to spend his leave mapping the Wadi Arabah for the Palestine Exploration Fund.

Kitchener could, if he had chosen, have been commissioned in a smart cavalry unit like Baker's 10th Hussars. His father, a former lieutenant-colonel of the 13th Light Dragoons, had tried to persuade him to apply for one. Kitchener had obstinately refused – his heart had been set on the Royal Engineers. Though the Engineers could not claim the social élan of the cavalry, it was a professional elite. A corps composed only of officers (other ranks served in the Corps of Sappers & Miners), it had never been subject to the purchase system. The practice of buying commissions and promotions had been abolished in the Cardwell reforms in 1871, but many officers currently serving – including Baker and de Coetlogon – had been beneficiaries or victims of the old system.

Kitchener, who had been commissioned in 1870, had spent much of his career in Palestine, Turkey and Cyprus. He spoke both Turkish and Arabic fluently. Already an expert cartographer, he had been suggested for the current job in Palestine by his friend and fellow Sapper Lieut. Colonel Sir Charles Wilson, FRS, Director of the Palestine Exploration Fund, who was currently Sir Evelyn Baring's Military Attaché in Cairo. Kitchener was accompanied by Professor Edward Hull, FRS, Chair of Geology at the Royal College of Science, whom he had come to thoroughly detest.

His sojourn with Hull was quickly to be cut short. On New Year's Eve four Bedouin on fast camels arrived at the camp. They had ridden almost non-stop from Isma'iliyya on the Suez canal with an urgent dispatch for Kitchener. It had come from the Sirdar, Sir Evelyn Wood, and informed him that an Egyptian army column under Hicks Pasha had just been slaughtered in the Sudan. There was an immediate threat to Khartoum – perhaps even to Egypt herself – and Kitchener was ordered to return to Cairo at once.

Tall, slender, luxuriantly moustachioed, Kitchener already possessed the granite features, the face of planes and angles, that would later stare domineeringly out of the First World War recruiting poster, 'Your Country Needs You'. He had been born with a cast in his left eye, which made it difficult for others to tell whom he was looking at. Some felt that he was staring right through them. One of those Irish-bred Englishmen who furnished the British Empire with so many soldiers and adventurers, he was born in County Kerry on 24 June 1850, the second son of Henry Kitchener, a landowner who had long ago sold his commission in the Dragoons. His mother, Frances, was the daughter of a Suffolk vicar.

Kitchener's father had left the army but not the military manner. He was a martinet who ran the household with such rigid order that servants were required to stand outside the room with a watch, waiting for the precise moment to serve breakfast. This obsessive precision, coupled with the strong language Henry used to enforce it, produced a son whose habit was to retire into his own shell as a defence. 'Herbert is very reserved about his feelings,' his mother once commented. 'I am afraid he will suffer a great deal from repression.'[14] The death of his mother when he was fourteen added to his shyness, and he grew up a brusque, aloof young man. At the Royal Military Academy at Woolwich he was something of a mysterious figure, who maintained a distance to prevent anyone imposing their will on him or questioning his decisions. He was noted for his exceptional memory, but his eye-defect ruled him out for team games and marksmanship.

As a young subaltern he was able to get on with foreigners better than with his own peers. This ability, together with his linguistic talent and superb memory, was to make him one of the most brilliant intelligence officers of his generation. During the war against 'Arabi Pasha in 1882, Kitchener took unofficial leave from his job surveying Cyprus and begged a berth on a British steamer bound for Alexandria. There, he reported to Lieut. Colonel A. B. Tulloch, Military Liaison Officer to the fleet commander, forty-two-year-old Admiral Sir Edward Beauchamp Seymour. Explaining that he spoke Arabic, he offered himself for intelligence work. Tulloch accepted, and the two of them went ashore at night disguised as Lebanese officials.

They examined 'Arabi's immense shore batteries in Alexandria harbour, and took a train to Zagazig in the Nile Delta. Jumping off the train after a short distance, they made notes and sketches of the dispositions of 'Arabi's forces. Later they returned to a secret rendezvous on the coast. They were picked up and rowed back to Seymour's flagship, *Invincible*, where they made their report. It was from the decks of *Invincible* that Kitchener witnessed the fleet's bombardment of Alexandria. A few days later, a fair-skinned Syrian was dragged from the Zagazig train and murdered in the belief that he was a British spy.

The thrill of spying behind enemy lines left Kitchener reluctant to go back to his uninspiring survey in Cyprus. On his return, though, he found himself in disgrace. His chief, Major General Sir Robert Biddulph, was furious – he had been absent without leave, which was a court-martial offence. Since he had risked his life on active service, the general was persuaded to turn a blind eye. But he refused Kitchener's request to be permanently attached to British forces in Egypt.

After Wolseley had defeated 'Arabi Pasha in June 1882, though, Kitchener found himself in demand. Few British officers spoke Arabic, and fewer still both Arabic and Turkish. He managed to wangle a place on the list of the first twenty-six regular officers to be transferred to the Egyptian army under Sirdar Evelyn Wood. In January 1883 he joined the Egyptian army as second-in-command of a cavalry unit.

Kitchener's ability to blend in with the local population came in useful now. A few days after Wood's dispatch arrived at his camp on the Dead Sea, he donned Arab dress and assumed the name of 'Abdallah Bey, an Egyptian official. Settling into this new identity, he set off on his horse to ride across the Sinai desert to Isma'iliyya on the Suez canal. It was a distance of two hundred miles, through the territory of Bedouin tribes whose loyalty was doubtful. Professor Hull advised him strongly against it. He reminded him of the murder of the explorer Major E. H. Palmer and his two colleagues by the Sinai Bedouin the previous year. Kitchener laughed at him.

Kitchener and his Bedouin escort rode ten hours a day across the great stony wilderness of the Sinai. He marvelled at the navigational skills of his Arabs, who used the sun and stars, and only lost the way once. For the last two days they rode in the teeth of a savage sandstorm that whipped sand into their faces like a lash. Kitchener was unable to wear his sunglasses for fear of being known as an Englishman. He later claimed that this storm permanently affected his eyes.

A fortnight after getting back to Cairo, Kitchener was dining at Shepheard's Hotel with Major General Sir Gerald Graham, the Sapper officer who had led the assault against 'Arabi Pasha at Tel el-Kebir. Graham, a six-foot-six giant who had also won the VC at Redan in the Crimea, was suddenly handed a message. An old acquaintance of his was about to arrive at Cairo railway station. This man, whom Graham had first known as a subaltern in the trenches of Redan, and had met again in China, was now a major-general.

He was Charles George Gordon, former provincial governor of Gondokoro, and former governor-general of the Sudan. As the

British government's sole response to the Hicks massacre, he was going back to Khartoum. He was under orders to pull out the Egyptian garrisons, and abandon the Sudan once and for all.

<h1 style="text-align:center">7</h1>

Valentine Baker's advance party landed at Suakin in the nick of time. That very day, an Egyptian officer named Qasim Effendi had led a sortie of seven hundred Jihadiyya against the rebels on the mainland. The government troops were ambushed in the rocky chasms of Tamanib by three thousand dervishes. The Albanian Bashi-Bazuks who formed the cavalry detachment high-tailed it at the gallop. The Jihadiyya made a brave stand, but were slaughtered. Only fifty managed to get home. The dervishes chased them back to Suakin, but were repulsed by Baker's gendarmes, who were in the process of disembarking from their transports.

Set on an oval-shaped island amid a labyrinth of coral reefs, Suakin was the only port on the three-hundred-mile stretch of coast between Halayb and Aqiq. It lay at the end of a long bay, but could only be approached by threading carefully through a narrow corridor between coral reefs. 'A glittering white town,' wrote John Colborne, one of Hicks's staff, in 1883, '. . . the houses look at a distance like the pierced walls of a fortress, giving it a medieval and castellated appearance.'[15] The houses were built of coral and limestone, with baroque façades punctuated by *mashrub-iyya* screens, bay windows, verandas, balconies and Quranic texts carved in niches on the walls. Warehouses lined the wharves, and the pasha's palace lay in the centre of the maze, its gate decorated by a lion's head prow taken from a shipwreck.

Beyond the shady awnings on the wharves, the Red Sea stretched, onyx-hued, opaque and languid, vanishing into the sea-mist towards the coast of Arabia. The sea around the island was five or six fathoms deep. The mainland coast was rimmed with a shelf of coral, breached only where freshwater streams cut through to the surf. At ebb-tide the reef became a pattern of lagoons, trapping water in small pools filled with seaweed and the arrowhead shapes of tiny fish. The true shore was a flat brown expanse of sun-baked mud, interrupted by thickets of mangroves. The leopard-hued littoral plain – the Gwineb – stretched to a skyline dominated by the ochre massifs of the Red Sea hills. These were the perimeter walls of the Aulib – a vast wilderness of mountain-desert, over a hundred thousand square miles in area, giving way on the western side to the Nubian desert.

The island was connected to the mainland by a causeway, built by Charles Gordon during his time as governor-general. Captain Harrington, commanding Baker's advance party, thought the causeway wide open. His first act was to build an earth rampart on the mainland side. It was a thousand yards in radius, with a four-foot ditch decked out with sharp stakes and iron spikes. In the port's warehouses, Harrington found a quarter of a million pounds' worth of rotting Manchester goods, but no food. The Egyptian troops who were supposed to be holding the port looked like a ragamuffin army. Discipline had evaporated, and they were weak with hunger. Most were armed with smoothbore weapons that should have been considered antiques.

Harrington was relieved when the first men-of-war of Rear Admiral Billy Hewett's Red Sea squadron steamed up the channel. The ironclad *Ranger* appeared in mid-December and took up a position where its guns could rake the causeway with fire. Hewett arrived in person on his flag-ship *Euryalus* on 16 December, trailed two weeks later by *Woodlark* and the gunboat *Coquette*. Harrington's spearhead party was quickly followed by the main party under Baker's Chief of Staff, Colonel George Sartorius, a forty-three-year-old British artillery officer who had fought in India, and as a mercenary alongside Baker in the Turco-Russian war. He had brought his wife along. The first thing he dealt with on arrival was the food problem. He sent out sorties to the mainland to rustle cattle. If the owners could be found they were paid. If not, the beasts were simply confiscated.

Sartorius also ordered the entire Suakin garrison out for review, and promptly resolved a mutiny among the Albanian Bashi-Bazuks by having them publicly flogged. When the provincial governor, seventy-year-old Sulayman Pasha, objected, Sartorius reported his obstructions to the government in Cairo, and got him sacked. Baker arrived on 23 December to find himself invested with complete civil and military authority.

The morale of Baker's three-thousand-strong gendarmerie battalions was nothing to boast about. They had objected stridently to being transported out of their own country. The two hundred Turks whom Baker had relied on to form the backbone of his force had mutinied in Cairo. They had not embarked for the Sudan at all. Many of the Egyptians had vanished before they took ship at Suez. The bad apples among the rest had been clapped in leg-irons.

Those who did arrive were poorly trained. On mustering in Suakin, it was observed that they could not understand drill commands, did not know left from right, and were unable to form a square. In musketry practice they constantly made the novice's mistake of firing high. Altogether they presented an uninspiring picture. 'It is to be hoped,' commented George Sartorius's wife, somewhat optimistically, 'the enemy will not fight, and will be kept off by the look of the men when in a large body together.'[16]

Zubayr Pasha's irregulars were as bad as the Egyptians. They were hardly capable even of marching and did not know how to fix bayonets. Their junior officers were mostly off the retired list and had forgotten how to give orders. Worst of all, they would only follow Zubayr himself, and the former slave-merchant had not turned up. This was not for lack of commitment on his part, but a home-goal by the British government. They had been influenced by the Anti-Slavery lobby in Britain. Baring had been ordered by Lord Granville not to let Zubayr leave Cairo. 'This was another grand blunder,' wrote Mrs Sartorius, 'that rendered the Suakin expedition almost helpless from the first. With Zubayr Pasha at their head [the irregulars] would have been formidable antagonists to the Sudanese, and have fought in precisely the same fashion. Without him, they were wasted.'[17]

Baker took ship to inspect Suakin's sister port of Massawa further south, and returned in early January with a battalion of Jihadiyya.

A few days later he contacted Baring, boasting that with the troops brought up from Massawa and more irregulars from Zubayr, he could take control of the eastern Sudan without British or Turkish help. The same day, Baker's orders to clear the Suakin–Berber road by military means were revoked.

In Cairo, Baring had organized a coup against the Egyptian government of Prime Minister Sharif Pasha. Sharif had wanted to hold Khartoum at all costs, but on 6 January, Baring had given both the Prime Minister and the Khedive an ultimatum. Egyptian garrisons in the Sudan must be evacuated, and the country must be abandoned. If Sharif and his ministers objected, they could be replaced. Sharif Pasha and the entire Council of Ministers promptly tendered their resignations. Sharif pointed out that there were twenty-one thousand Turco-Egyptian troops still in the Sudan, with all their dependants, all of them loyal to the Ottoman Sultan. They could not be simply left to the miseries of the Mahdi's rule.

Sharif's replacement, Nubar Pasha, an Armenian Christian regarded as an outsider in Cairo, was reconciled to withdrawal. The other ministers in his new cabinet had been carefully chosen, and were unlikely to rock the boat.

Baring suggested that Baker might attempt to open the Berber road by friendly overtures to the local tribes. Baker understood the futility of this idea. No tribal sheikh was likely to sign an alliance with a force that was about to withdraw. In any case, 'peaceful means' was no way of retrieving his personal honour.

Baker had with him about three dozen European officers. An unexpected addition to their number turned up in January. This was Colonel Frederick Gustavus Burnaby of the Royal Horse Guards, who walked into Baker's office one day dressed in a Norfolk jacket and carrying an umbrella. Burnaby had come under his own steam. An old friend of Baker's from the Balkans, he had been invited unofficially by Baker's wife, Fanny, who had told him that there was a scrap on and that Baker needed someone he could trust. Burnaby had taken leave to join the fight, and had borrowed a double-barrelled shotgun – as if potting dervishes was the equivalent of a good pheasant shoot.

Baker himself was delighted to find a kindred spirit, but not everyone admired Burnaby's facetious approach to war. Forty-two years old, the son of a Bedford clergyman, he was a giant of a man, of enormous physical strength and some linguistic talent. He had won fame through his sensational but probably apocryphal account of his travels in Central Asia, *The Road to Khiva*. He had also ballooned across the Channel. Reckless in speech as well as on the battlefield, he had publicly insulted the Prince of Wales. This had earned him the undying enmity of Britain's Commander-in-Chief, Field Marshal George, Duke of Cambridge, who was the Queen's cousin.

Burnaby had impeccable social credentials, but there was a distinct whiff of the exhibitionist about him. He was Kitchener's opposite. He possessed the sort of qualities Sir Evelyn Baring disliked. Indeed, the famous portrait of Burnaby as a young officer by J. G. Tissot, painted in 1870, displays an expression that seems to epitomize the arrogance of the 'imperial race'. A photograph taken not long before his death, with the bloom of youth vanished, reveals an unmistakable psychopathic quality. 'He has the most evil countenance one can imagine,' commented the Arabist Wilfred Scawen Blunt in his journal, '. . . a dull, heavy, fellow . . . with a dash of cunning, and more than a dash of brutality.'[18] Blunt later dismissed Burnaby as nothing more than 'a butcher'.

Towards the end of January, Rear Admiral Hewett, Baker, Burnaby and the other senior officers met to decide a course of action. The garrison at Sinkat, only nine miles from Suakin, was in deep trouble. Its commander, Tewfiq Bey, a Cretan of Jewish origin, was considered the best Turco-Egyptian officer on the coast. He had been holding off the rebels since August 1883. By now, however, he and his men were starving. Donkeys, dogs, cats, rats, boots, belts, shoes, bones, tree-leaves, and even insects had been eaten. Tewfiq was already preparing his men for a suicidal break-out. At Tokar, further south, the garrison was better off. It had food for three months, but it was under constant fire from the dervishes and would very soon be out of ammunition.

Baker knew that the plight of Sinkat was the more urgent, but its relief was impossible. The chances were that his gendarmerie would be annihilated before they even reached the post. Tokar lay on the flat coastal plain. It was true that Consul Moncrieff's force had already been cut to pieces there, but Baker liked to believe his chances were better. A move on Tokar might ease the pressure on Sinkat and give Tewfiq an even chance of breaking out. After the meeting, Baker wired Baring that he had decided to do what he could 'in the Tokar direction'.[19]

Baker was not obliged to relieve either of the garrisons. Baring had drummed into him over and over that he must not attempt any action against the dervishes unless he was absolutely certain of success. Absolute certainty was, of course, subjective, and Baker was a man obsessed. The lust to regain his honour would not allow him to hold back. The genie had been let out of the bottle and could not be reinserted. The only way Baring could have stopped Baker at this point was by giving him a direct order not to advance. No such order was given. On 22 January Baker led his Bashi-Bazuks on a reconnaissance force to Handub, fifteen miles from Suakin, as a feint to distract the dervishes from Sinkat and Tokar. Once again, the Bashi-Bazuks fled on contact with the enemy. It was not an encouraging omen.

Two days later, Valentine Baker embarked his men on steamers for Trinkitat, en route to relieve the garrison at Tokar.

8

Baker and his officers thought they were fighting 'savages'. Burnaby, a man of no profound political convictions and a penchant for self-advertisement, had brought a pheasant gun along to 'administer a reproof' – as if they were naughty schoolchildren. It was part of the prevailing ideology of the era. Even the standard military textbooks contained a section entitled *Wars Against Savages*. 'In all wars against savage races,' the text ran, 'it is noticed that the enemy makes decided efforts to approach against the rear and flanks of the regular troops, which necessitates the formation of more or less flexible squares both in marching and in the engagement.'[20]

To the Beja tribesmen Baker's force was about to confront, though, he and his men were the barbarians. They had a history that spanned no less than forty centuries. They were the Bugiha of Leo Africanus, the Blemmyes of the Romans, the Bugas of the Axumites, and the Medja or Bukas of the pharaohs. They had inhabited the chasms, gorges, plateaux and valleys of the Red Sea hills even before the ancient Egyptian kings had sent their armies here looking for gold.

The 'Amarar, the most ethnically pure of the Beja tribes, claimed to be descended directly from Ham the son of Noah, and to have lived in these hills literally since the grounding of the Ark. They may well have belonged to the same pre-dynastic stock from which the ancestors of the pharaohs had sprung. They had seen many civilizations come and go – the ancient Egyptians, the Greeks, the Romans, the Byzantines, the Arabs, the Ottomans, the Portuguese, the French, the Turco-Egyptians and now the British. None of these powers had controlled them. Except for the arrival of the camel, iron weapons, and a few other innovations, their culture had remained almost untouched in four thousand years.

The Beja were perhaps the most formidable warriors in the Sudan. Their fighting prowess had been honed by generations of blood-feuds and tribal wars. It had been recognized by the pharaohs, who had recruited them as a police force as early as 2000 BC – ironically, the ancient equivalent of Baker's gendarmerie. They were not Arabs. They did not speak Arabic, but Tu-Bedawi, a Cushitic tongue related to Somali. The Arabs were extrovert and open, and loved nothing more than endless conversations round the hearth. They made a cult of generosity and hospitality. The Beja, though, were truculent, taciturn, moody and xenophobic.

Few early travellers had anything good to say about them. The Roman Pomponius Mela, whose civilization the Beja had harassed for half a millennium, considered them 'scarcely human'. Don Stefano de Gama, a sixteenth-century Portuguese sailor, wrote in 1540 that they were 'wild men, amongst whom is no civil society, nor truth nor civility'. The German naturalist George Schwein-furth described them in 1864 as 'inhospitable without exception, false and secretive . . . as repellent as the thorns and as clinging as the prickles of their native plants'.[21]

They were accustomed to wandering their hills in tiny groups. They were reticent with everyone, even other branches of the same family. The landscape they inhabited was austere and merciless, a place without shade or comfort, buffeted by winds that were icy and furnace-like in turn. Their society had evolved as a response to an environment of extremes. These desert hills had produced men and women of an extraordinary mental and physical resilience, with an uncommon determination to survive. Ferocious, inimical and individualist, they had over the centuries achieved a remarkable harmony with this cruellest of possible worlds.

What most outsiders remembered about the Beja was their distinctive hairstyle. Beja warriors considered it a disgrace to cut the hair. They let it grow in great plumes and rats' tails, greased with mutton fat. This style, recognizable on ancient Egyptian tombs as early as Old Kingdom times, was their trademark. British soldiers would later dub them 'fuzzy-wuzzies'.

The Beja had joined the ranks of the dervishes, but were not fervid Muslims. They rarely performed their prayers or fasted in Ramadan. Though the holy cities of Arabia lay just across their horizons, few ever performed the hajj. Over the ages a dozen religions – including Isis-worship and Christianity – had sat lightly on their shoulders, but none had left a mark on them. Their belief in magic was strong. Some Beja clans were supposed to have attained mastery over Jinns or evil spirits. They had no Mahdist traditions, and no empathy with the tribes from the White Nile or the western Sudan. The land west of the Nile was for them beyond the edge of the earth.

They were made up of three major tribes and some smaller ones. The most southerly tribe was the Haddendowa, whose territory extended to the Gash Delta, and who herded cattle as well as camels. The least numerous of the three principal tribes were the 'Amarar, occupying the central area. To the north – spilling over

29

into southern Egypt – were the Bishariyyin, who had a fair admixture of Arab blood, without yielding anything of their culture or language. These tribes were not true nomads at heart. Unlike the Arab Bedouin, they owned and inherited land. Still, the harshness of their landscape forced them to wander. If the rains were abundant, between April and September, they would sow sorghum in the wadis or khors where the rainwater was dammed up for a few days. Then they would move on with their camels and goats, carrying their huts of palmetto fibre on camels' backs. They would return to harvest the grain when it was ripe. But the rains here were capricious. In drought years their flocks and herds would be decimated. In flood years, mountain torrents would wash away their crops as soon as they had been planted.

The Beja lived by the cult of bravery. They hunted lion on foot with swords and shields. It was no uncommon thing to find Beja herdsmen who had killed a leopard – the fastest and most determined of predators – with only a dagger. They also bred the best camel in the world – the Bishari – a trim, greyish-white beast with a large head and pricked-up ears that could outrun any other breed in Africa or the Middle East. So steady was the Bishari's gait that the rider could trot with a glass of tea in his hand and never spill a drop.

The southern tribes had some horses, but the Beja fought mostly on foot. Long-limbed and slimly built, they were nimble, fast and sure-footed. They carried spears, but their preferred weapon was a broad-sword with a straight, double-edged blade and a cross-hilt. Some of these swords were very old, and had been handed down over generations. Some were forged of fine steel, with delicate workmanship. The Beja always preferred cold steel to bullets. Left to themselves they never carried firearms, and had no interest in them. In battle, their tactics never varied. They would approach the enemy under cover, and charge at tremendous velocity.[22] Beja women and even small children thought nothing of fighting beside the men.

Religious fervour alone would probably not have been enough to incite the Beja to revolt. The uprising in the eastern Sudan had come about as a direct result of corruption by two greedy Egyptian officials, who had cheated them of their dues in the carrying trade.

The Haddendowa were the principal carriers on the camel-route from Suakin to Berber. In early 1883 they had been given the contract to carry Hicks's men, equipment and provisions. The price agreed was $7 per camel. The contract had been ratified, and Baring, then Controller of the Public Debt, had disbursed the funds. After delivering men and matériel safely to Berber, the Haddendowa had been paid only $1 per camel. The two men in charge, Rashid Pasha and Ibrahim Bey, had simply pocketed the rest. The resentment this caused was incalculable. The Beja had long memories and were not likely to let such treatment go unpunished. It was precisely at this moment that the means of their revenge appeared. It came in the unlikely person of the Mahdi's appointed agent in the eastern Sudan, 'Osman Digna.

'Osman Digna, then forty-four, was a small, reserved man whom no one would have singled out as destined for heroism. Neither brave nor generous, neither charming nor even honourable by Beja standards, he was not truly one of them. His mother belonged to the Haddendowa, but his father was descended from a Kurdish soldier of Selim the Grim, the Ottoman Sultan whose troops had occupied Suakin in 1516. Morose and unromantic by nature, tight-fisted and churlish, he was not and never had been popular. His influence on the Haddendowa was and remains a mystery. A decade after 'Osman's death, T. R. H. Owen wrote that 'No tribesman remembers him with affection and few with admiration.'[23] But 'Osman did have three qualities that were essential to a great leader. He was astute, he had uncommon determination, and he had tremendous powers of persuasion. He also had luck. At a less favourable instant, his mission to raise the Beja might have failed.

'Osman was a merchant, born in Suakin. He had dabbled in the slave trade but had got his fingers burned when *Wild Swan*, a British anti-slave patrol ship, stopped one of his sambuks. The boat was carrying eighty-four slaves bound for Jeddah. The British asked the Ottoman authorities in Jeddah to search the Digna brothers' premises, and confiscate their property. 'Osman and his two brothers were flung into jail. Later he started a business as a water-supplier, delivering water to a gin factory owned by a Greek merchant. His resentment against the British and the Turks festered. When he got wind of the 'Arabi Pasha revolt in Egypt, he tried to stir up the population of Suakin against the government. The Suakin merchants, quivering at the thought of a British man-of-war steaming into harbour with its guns blazing, asked him to leave. He had removed himself to Berber, but was still to be found in Suakin from time to time.

In April 1883 'Osman Digna had been in Berber when he heard the news that el-Obeid had fallen to the Mahdi. His brother had been among the Mahdi's men, but died of fever before the dervishes took the city. 'Osman had decided to visit the Mahdi in el-Obeid, and his appearance there had been opportune. The Mahdi was quite aware of the key importance of Suakin, and that reinforcements were already being moved to Khartoum along the Suakin–Berber road. The Beja were unpromising recruits for the revolt, but if 'Osman could stir up enough trouble on the Red Sea to close the government's lines of communication, it would be a major boon. On 8 May 1883 the Mahdi gave 'Osman Digna a letter appointing him the official Mahdist *emir* in the eastern Sudan.

As soon as he arrived back on the coast, 'Osman began preaching the Mahdi's cause. He was not well known, and was not liked, respected or trusted. Few were ready to take him seriously. As a young man 'Osman had joined the Majazib, a local order of Sufis, or Islamic mystics, which had gained enormous prestige among the southern Beja tribes. Though only a half-hearted Sufi, 'Osman now appealed to the order's chief, at-Tahir Majzub, who welcomed him. When the Sheikh read the Mahdi's letter, he immediately placed it on his head as a sign of respect. Moments later, he changed his *jallabiyya* for the patched *jibba* tunic and *sirwal* of the dervishes. With at-Tahir's religious authority behind him, 'Osman Digna was in business.

The Sheikh had reasons of his own for going along with the Mahdi's ambitions. His great religious rivals were the powerful

Khatmiyya Brotherhood, run by the al-Mirghani family. The Khatmiyya, whose headquarters were at Kassala, had been specially favoured by the government ever since the Mohammad 'Ali invasion. This had caused at-Tahir deep resentment. He leapt at the chance to join the opposition.

Sinkat, as a key station on the Berber caravan route, was the first place to draw 'Osman's attention. He arrived there with a force of fifteen hundred Haddendowa and 'Amarar on 5 August 1883 and demanded in the name of the Mahdi that both Sinkat and Suakin should be handed over to him. The commander of the Sinkat garrison, Tewfiq Bey, sent out a delegation of Khatmiyya holy men to negotiate. At the same time he had his men fortify their barracks as quickly as possible. Scenting duplicity, 'Osman ordered his Beja to attack. A charge swept them into the barracks, but Tewfiq's men fought back gallantly. 'Osman was wounded three times, and sixty-five of his men were killed, including his brother and cousin. The dervishes lost heart and fell back, making for the hills. 'Osman, carried home by his retinue, lost his taste for fighting at the sharp end. From now on he led every fight from his prayer-mat, half a mile to the rear.

'Osman's popularity dwindled after the attack on Sinkat. But for government inactivity, he might never have taken further part in the Mahdiyya. For a time, his only supporters were the Bishariab and Jemilab clans of the Haddendowa, notorious bandits who would do anything for plunder. The lack of positive action by the Suakin garrison, and some half-hearted efforts on the government's part at conciliation, played into 'Osman's hands. The tribes inter-preted it as weakness. They began to believe that the government was afraid of 'Osman. Before the year was up, his fortunes had changed dramatically. The whole of the northern Haddendowa had joined his flag.

They had already routed Consul Moncrieff at et-Teb, on the plains of Tokar. Now, they waited patiently to do the same to Baker Pasha's gendarmerie.

9

Baker's beach-head was at Trinkitat, a flat peninsula about twelve miles north-east of Tokar. It took him two days to land his force there – about four thousand men, four Krupps, two rocket-batteries and two Gatling guns. In addition to just over a thousand gendarmerie, he had nearly the same number of Jihadiyya, seven hundred of Zubayr's irregulars, and a mixed force of 450 Egyptian and Turkish cavalry.

Tokar lay on the edge of the Khor Baraka, a seasonal delta subject to dangerous flash floods in the rainy season. Here the Red Sea littoral was at its widest. It was a flat plain densely covered with acacia scrub, stretching like a powder-grey billiard table, thirty-five miles towards the natural ramparts of the hills. Tokar itself was no more than a village laid on the starkness, where the Turks had built a fort to defend some brackish wells sunk to the water-table.

The day after Baker landed, telegraph communication was established between Suakin and Cairo by submarine cable. Baker's dispatches had to be sent first to Suakin for transmission, but from there a telegram took only two hours. On 31 January he inaugurated the cable by informing Cairo that he planned to move on Tokar the following day.

Opposite Trinkitat, though, the mainland was a saline crust overlying liquid mud, which made advancing a penance. While Baker supervised the construction of earthworks to shield the assembly-point, Fred Burnaby went ashore with a pathfinder force to mark out routes through the mire. The morass extended for about three miles. On the crest of a ridge marking the edge of the marsh, Baker ordered another redoubt to be thrown up. It was a circular earthwork with a parapet and a ditch all round it, and was immediately christened 'Fort Baker'. According to *Daily News* correspondent John McDonald, embedded with Baker's force, the redoubt was actually no more than a mile and three-quarters from the beach-head. 'But much of the route was vile,' he wrote, 'leading through sea-ooze and mud . . . one can easily comprehend why anybody who crossed from Trinkitat to Fort Baker might estimate the distance from two to ten miles.'[24]

Mules, camels and horses had to battle with the slough. The gendarmes and Jihadiyya removed their packs, pulling and pushing at the beasts to extricate them. Camels had to be patiently unloaded by their handlers, hauled to firmer ground, and reloaded again. Men, animals, guns and equipment were lathered in viscous, stinking, salt-saturated mud. Attempts to improve the worst places with cut brushwood soon failed. Advancing in fits and starts, it took much longer to reach the fort than anticipated. Baker was obliged to postpone his advance for two days.

On 2 February, however, he telegraphed to Cairo that he would move the next morning, with 3,200 men, towards the wells at et-Teb. These wells, an essential stage in the advance, lay about three miles away and were occupied by the dervishes. This was where Moncrieff and his Egyptians had been slaughtered. Baker, thinking that his return to grace was imminent, had begun to feel upbeat. Remembering that Baring had instructed him to hold back unless he was certain of victory, he added, 'there is every chance of success.'[25]

They marched at first light, three battalions in echelon, moving in columns of companies. The Krupp batteries moved at the head and flanks, protected by the main body of cavalry. Cavalry scouts or 'vedettes' formed a mile-wide box around the advancing force. The day was dull and overcast, with the peaty scent of rain in the air. As time wore on, the rain hit them in sudden squalls. Progress was slow, and Baker had to halt the columns frequently to keep the stragglers together. Visibility was poor and the going ponderous. At about 0900 hours, Baker heard shots from the direction of the vedettes on the left front. Cameos of dark figures with shocks of wild hair, naked but for dust-coloured loincloths, appeared suddenly on the skyline. It was as if they had sprung fully armed out of the bowels of the earth.

To the Beja warriors, the Egyptian force was a curious sight. The gendarmes were dressed in brilliant white uniforms with red tarbooshes. They approached in formations that to the tribesmen seemed stiff and wooden, like dolls on parade. They moved forward without making use of the ground at all, presenting excellent targets. 'Osman Digna's men knew from previous experience that as soon as the enemy were fired on they would form a square. This would cut down their ability to return fire. The rear rank would not be able to fire at all. 'Osman was perfectly well aware that the square's weakness lay in its angles. His men would work on these weaknesses, attacking to the left of the front. The enemy artillery did not worry 'Osman. His intention was to get inside its range and attack before it could do much damage. By the time the gun-crews had got their first rounds off, the dervishes would be on them.

Baker ordered the guns to open fire. Three whoffs of smoke and belches of flame licked out from the ranks. Flat claps of percussion broke the silence. The dervishes disappeared as the surface around them erupted in cascades of rock and dust. Almost at once, more crazy-haired tribesmen materialized on ridges to the front and right. A troop of camel-men, hanging together like a swarm of giant flies, trotted out of the middle distance. Baker recognized the build-up to a rush from all sides – the dervishes' only real tactic. He sent Captain Harvey with the Egyptian cavalry to disperse the dervish cameleers.

It was a job for a squadron, but an entire regiment launched into an attack. Instead of beating a hasty retreat, the handful of Beja camel-riders spurred their animals towards the advancing enemy. Burnaby, riding with the Egyptians, was astounded. This was perhaps his first inkling that the encounter was not going to turn into the grouse-shoot he had so confidently imagined. He saw one dervish head his Bishari smack into an Egyptian squadron. The tribesman made a beeline for the squadron commander, and cut him out of the saddle with a dry swish of his broad-sword. The officer, whose sabre was drawn, was too astonished even to parry the blow. As two troopers closed on him, the dervish brought them both down with great sweeps of his blade. Burnaby, still dressed in his Norfolk jacket, and still carrying his umbrella, put a pistol shot through the Beja's head. He and Captain Harvey tried to restore order. A moment later there was the ominous crackle of musketry from behind them, as the infantry in the rear opened erratic fire, bringing down their own comrades. Troopers dropped from their saddles like stones. Many turned their horses and rode away shrieking in terror.

Burnaby's servant, Storey, found himself riding a horse that had gone berserk with fear, and a moment later he was deposited abruptly in a bush in front of a horde of howling Beja. Storey managed to keep hold of his mount's chain collar. He dashed alongside the wildly capering animal, pursued by yelling warriors, and just succeeded in staying on his feet until he caught up with Burnaby, who inquired laconically why on earth he had not mounted.

Meanwhile, Major Giles with the Turkish cavalry had pursued a group of Beja horse half a mile when they suddenly found themselves in a trap. Dervish spearmen leapt out of the brushwood on all sides. Giles ordered his men to withdraw back to the main force. 'By the time the cavalry returned the battle was raging,' wrote *Daily News* man McDonald. 'We had been taken by surprise, but warnings of the coming catastrophe might have been detected previously. The vedettes on our left had for some time been drawing closer to the main body. They were getting out of order, and it seemed as if the responsible officers had forgotten their very existence.'[26]

Dervish fire was incoming from all sides except the rear. At Baker's instructions, Colonel Ahmad Kamal of the gendarmerie ordered the troops to form a square. At first it went with deceptive smoothness. The gendarme battalions formed up with unexpected rapidity on the left, in front and part of the right. The Jihadiyya battalion took its place on the left. At the rear of the square, though, there was utter confusion. At that moment, the main body of 'Osman Digna's dervishes leapt out of the brushwood and hurtled towards the square. They were a chilling sight — some barefoot, half naked, their greased corkscrews of hair flying, carrying elephant-hide shields and throwing sticks, their swords and spears glittering. They crossed the flat ground, not running, but bounding like predators. They had the look not of warriors, but of lycanthropic beasts.

In abject panic the gendarmerie battalions discharged their ammunition into the air. They fired so fast that within fifteen seconds the unfinished square was thick with smoke. Bawled-out orders could not be heard over the din. The confusion spread to the Jihadiyya, who also began belting off wasted rounds. 'The frantic efforts of the Egyptians to get in formation,' wrote McDonald, 'the confused din of orders, and the chaos in the rear, where three hundred camels, with the whole of the transport and commissariat, were struggling to force their way inside the square, defies description . . . What should have been the rear side was an irregular out-bulging mass of horses, mules, camels and men tightly wedged together and extending towards the centre of the square.'[27]

The idea of the square formation was to allow the troops to stand shoulder to shoulder to resist a charge. The dervishes still had not reached them, and there might have been time to reform had the gendarmerie not begun to break ranks out of sheer terror. They surged inwards, away from the charging enemy, pushing back the Bashi-Bazuks and the Jihadiyya. The Sudanese troops held their own for a time, but could not stand alone. Some of the artillerymen inside the square could not even assemble their guns, because the mules carrying them had gone berserk.

At this point the retreating Egyptian cavalry hit them like a whirlwind, pursued by the dervishes. Many of the horses were riderless. 'They were wild with terror,' McDonald recalled. 'In their panic the infantry in their so-called square fired anywhere and anyhow.' An Egyptian cavalry officer smashed against McDonald's horse and was thrown instantly. He was 'doubtless butchered, as most were once dismounted', the *Daily News* man said. Hardly having recovered from the shock, McDonald saw an Egyptian soldier three yards away shot by his own men. Seconds later, an Italian officer, Captain Cavalieri, was also killed by his own side. Outside the square, a round fired by a gendarme missed Baker by a fraction of an inch. The Krupp batteries near Baker were overrun.

His native Chief of Staff was run through next to him. Spouts of arterial blood pumped around him as the artillerymen were slashed and speared to bloody rags.

Before the leaping dervishes had even reached the square, one of the gendarme battalions had crumbled completely. The others, infected by the panic, also broke. The gendarmerie, now feverish with terror, were totally out of control. They threw away their rifles and ran. Burnaby, riding back slowly to the square through swarms of bullets, could not believe what he was seeing. 'The sight was never to be forgotten,' he wrote. 'Some four thousand men running for their lives with a few hundred [dervishes] behind them spearing everyone within reach.'[28] Burnaby saw a mounted Bashi-Bazuk officer galloping away, blasting off his carbine indiscriminately, bringing down friend and foe.

Many of the gendarmes tried to rip off their uniforms as they fled. Some rushed back to the beach-head stark naked. Others grabbed the tails of horses and tried vainly to vault on to their backs. A few of the deserters were shot in the back by their European officers as they ran. Many did not even attempt to escape, but knelt down, clasping their hands and begging for mercy. Baker tried to rally the cavalry but found that the last vestige of military discipline had gone. He had never witnessed anything like this: his soldiers had sunk to the level of terrified beasts, unable even to defend themselves.

Within only eight minutes of the first rush, McDonald reckoned, almost the entire army had been put to flight. Some huddled together with the transport animals and were butchered. The dervishes seized them by the necks, speared them through the back, and then cut their throats. One dervish picked up a gendarme's discarded rifle and, not knowing how to fire it, used it to smash in its owner's skull. 'This frightful carnage,' McDonald wrote, 'lasted most part of the pursuit, upwards of five miles, to [Fort Baker] which we [had] left early in the morning. The yells of the [dervishes] and the cries of their Egyptian victims were appalling.'[29]

The Gatling gun-crews, who had opened fire when the enemy

were already on top of them, were gutted almost instantly by dervish spears. The Krupp teams who had been inside the square kept firing till the end. They were defended mostly by Europeans. These included the force's medical officer, thirty-eight-year-old Dr Armand Leslie, its paymaster, James Morice Bey – a former inspector-general of the Egyptian coastguard service – and two other British officers, Major Watkins and Lieutenant Carrol. As McDonald rode away he saw them fighting off the dervishes with revolvers and swords. 'Their quiet demeanour was as a ray of light and of Divine hope,' he wrote, 'in that hell of fierce triumph and clinging hell.'[30]

Valentine Baker and his British chief of staff, Colonel Hay, had rushed to the remnants of the square in a last ditch attempt to rally the men. As they did so, a troop of dervish warriors stood in their path. Baker and Hay charged recklessly through them. Withdrawing back to the fort, Baker tried to muster his troops to make a last stand. It was impossible. Many of the Egyptians had already reached the beach-head and were clambering back on to the steamers. The ships would have been sunk had the naval officers on board not fired their pistols over the heads of the rabble. When Baker arrived at Trinkitat, the last man back, he was astonished to see his gendarmes being fired at by their own side. It was a fitting climax to the debacle.

So ended General Valentine Baker's vainglorious attempt to restore his good name. Of the 3,200 troops he had led into battle that morning, 2,250 were dead. A total of 112 officers were missing, believed killed in action. This included six Englishmen, and, apart from Burnaby and Baker, almost the entire contingent of Europeans. Of the Turkish battalion only thirty were left; of the Jihadiyya only seventy. Four Krupps, two Gatlings and half a million cartridges had been lost. The Egyptians had thrown away three thousand Remington rifles. The square had broken before the dervishes had even engaged it, and the enemy had numbered less than twelve hundred men.

Baker was stunned. He had known all along that his troops were mediocre, but he had never expected them to run away from an enemy they outnumbered three to one. His chances of retrieving his name were all but lost. There was no time to wallow in it, though. The dervishes were coming, and his job was to get his men back to Suakin as soon as possible. Though he still had three thousand troops garrisoned there, he was afraid that the port would now be vulnerable to attack. To lose Suakin on top of everything else would be disastrous.

Fortunately, 'Osman's men only pursued the Egyptians as far as Fort Baker and the edge of the saltmarsh. Though they prowled around all night, Baker was able to use the ramparts he had built on Trinkitat island to cover the evacuation. As McDonald noted, not a single Egyptian officer assisted him. 'They were in bed or skulking elsewhere,' he wrote. 'The whole work had to be done by Baker Pasha, Colonel Hay, and Mr Bewley, who is chief of the transport. No more rascally set of cowards ever existed than these native officers. There is more excuse for their men . . . but their employment in battle is sheer crime and idiocy.'[31]

The following day, Baker wired the bad news to Baring. The Egyptian troops, he said, had thrown down their weapons and run away, carrying the black troops with them, before the dervish attack had even connected with the square. Baring was shattered. He realized immediately that Baker had done precisely what he had urged him not to. He had taken on a task that was beyond the power of the untrained and undisciplined troops under his command. It was as if Baker had thought he could force them to victory by will alone. Inevitably, it had been a fiasco, and this, following so hard on the Hicks massacre, was exactly what Baring could have done without.

Mulling over the news in his sunny room at Qasr ad–Dubbara, overlooking the Nile, Baring realized that the ramifications of the defeat were serious. Suakin had already been in a vulnerable position before the battle: now it might fall to the dervishes. The garrisons at Sinkat and Tokar were beyond retrieval, the Suakin–Berber road was firmly shut, and the eastern Sudan was virtually cut off from Egypt. The bottom line was that the British government might be forced to send British troops to secure the eastern Sudan. That would be the thin end of the wedge, leading to escalation, and to total military involvement in a country both Baring and HM Government had gone to some trouble to ditch. In fact, Lord Wolseley, Adjutant General of the British army, and his chief, the Duke of Cambridge, were advising Gladstone to do just that.

Yet, in answer to Baker's report, Baring demonstrated a degree of self-control that belied his nickname. His first thought, indeed, was that Baker would blame himself for the massacre. Anything might happen in the next few days, and to have his senior man in the Sudan lose his cool would be a fresh disaster. Remonstration would serve no purpose. Instead, he wired Suakin that he was certain General Baker had done his best, and that Baker retained Baring's full confidence. It was an act of both generosity and nobility on Baring's part. He knew that he should never have agreed to Baker's deployment. 'I was principally responsible for this mistake,' he wrote, '. . . I could have prevented General Baker from going to Suakin, and although I knew the risk . . . I decided not to do so.'[32] It was clear, though, that he felt Baker had let him down, partly because of his need to prove himself, or as Baring put it, his 'special personal inducement . . . to distinguish himself by leading a daring and successful military exploit'.[33]

At Suakin, there was a mood of near hysteria. Granville ordered Admiral Bill Hewett to assume military and civil command. This meant that Baker had been replaced, and also indicated that the British had now taken over control from the Khedive, observing their pledge to protect the Red Sea ports. To secure his authority in the town, Hewett landed 150 British Marines and bluejackets – the first British servicemen officially deployed in the Sudan.

Other adverse consequences of the debacle at et-Teb were quick in coming. On 8 February, unable to hold out any longer, Tewfiq

Bey made his attempt to break out of Sinkat. Tewfiq knew that he had one chance in a hundred of getting his troops, with their wives and children, through the nine miles of rocky ravines to Suakin. But Sinkat had literally been eaten out, even of cockroaches and grasshoppers, and it was either move or suffer a lingering death by starvation. Tewfiq ordered his Krupps to be spiked, and had everything that might have been of use to the dervishes smashed or thrown into the wells. Then he marched out of the town at the head of his men, who were formed into a square, with the women and children in the centre.

They had been marching for an hour when the dervishes fell on them from all sides. The troops fought back bravely, but they were cut down. Only thirty women and six men survived. Tewfiq Bey fell with his men, fighting doggedly. Even 'Osman Digna, not famous for his generosity, praised Tewfiq as the most courageous of all the Ottoman officers in the Sudan. Augustus Wylde, acting British consul in Jeddah, wrote, 'In the annals of the Sudan there has never been a more perfect hero than Tewfiq Bey, and his memory will last and be told in the hillside and the campfire among Sudan warriors long after the present generation has passed away.'[34]

Part Two

1

It was the best part of a thousand miles from Suakin to the borders of Darfur – the western province of the Turco-Egyptian Sudan. Beyond the White Nile, the caravan route crossed through the vast rolling steppe known as the *goz*. On a clear day, the steppe rolls out to infinity under the great blue dome of the African sky, an undulating sea of red sand, yellow grass and thorn forest, stretching all the way across the continent between the 10th and 13th parallels. The *goz* marks the southern boundary of the Sahara desert – the place where Africa and the Arab world meet.

The character of the *goz* changes dramatically from season to season. In the dry it is scarcely fit for man, and one can journey for days without coming across another person. The steppes are hot, dust-choked, monotonous, the thorn-trees grey and brittle. The wadis are empty, the water-pools are expanses of cracked and blistered earth. Even the villages feel like ghost-towns. After the summer rains, though, the grass is no longer yellow but a dozen shades of green, as the thorn-scrub blooms with new leaf. Wadis flow, the great pools fill up with brown water. Men appear out of nowhere, congregating around vast baobab or *tebeldi* trees whose hollowed-out trunks are used as water-tanks. In the nineteenth century – and until quite recently – herds of elephant, giraffe, buffalo, oryx, roan antelope, and hartebeest would cross the Bahr al-Ghazal river and make their way north into the grasslands after the rains. In the 1830s a British traveller named Major Denham reported that elephant herds two thousand strong were to be seen in Darfur.

Elephant and giraffe especially were hunted by the Baggara cattle-nomads of the *goz*, in the summer wet. The Baggara were not a tribe but a loose-knit group of tribes, the descendants of Arab Bedouin who had drifted across the Sahara in the late Middle Ages and taken African women as wives. African in appearance, but Arab in language and culture, they had given up their black tents for grass huts, and their camels for cattle and horses. They had adapted themselves perfectly to life on the marginal steppe.

Hunting elephant and giraffe was not a necessity for the Baggara, but a quest for honour. Though by the 1870s some of the nomads had muskets, they still hunted on horseback with a ten-foot leaf-bladed spear called a *shalagai*. Their courage was the toast of early western travellers. 'They bring down elephants with lance and sword,' wrote the German naturalist George Schweinfurth in 1874, 'a feat scarcely less free from risk than playing with lions and leopards as though they were kittens'.[1]

An elephant hunt was a serious affair that took several weeks and required courage and superb riding skills. One horseman would single out a tusker and ride boldly up, prodding him with his *shalagai* until the animal gave chase. The horseman had to keep about ten yards ahead. He drew the furious beast into bush where the seven-man killing group was concealed. The team would leap out of cover as the tusker passed, and stab him close to the anus with their razor-sharp spears.

The Baggara hunted elephant mainly for ivory, but giraffe were hunted for their meat. Riding down giraffe required horsemanship of an even higher order than an elephant hunt. The giraffe would start running at 500 yards, and with their gangly legs could cover even the most difficult ground at an incredible pace. The Baggara had to gallop flat out just to catch them, and needed absolute concentration. A second's hesitation and the rider was lost. Every season men would be killed running into the low branches of a *talh* tree, or into a pothole unseen in the scrub. Once within spearing distance, the rider had to transfer his *shalagai* to his right hand. He would stab the running animal in the back leg, taking care to avoid the beast's bone-crushing kick. One accurate thrust was all it took to bring down the giraffe.

Though the horsemanship required for chasing giraffe might be exceptional, all Baggara boys grew up in the saddle. Their lives were cycles of movement with their herds of humped zebu cattle, in search of grazing and water. Horses were esteemed, but it was the cattle that occupied pride of place in their culture. They referred to the herds as *faddha umm suf*, or 'silver with hair'. During the dry cool season they remained on the banks of seasonal rivers such as the Bahr al-'Arab or Bahr al-Ghazal, on the southern borders of their territory. In the summer rains, though, when the ground grew swampy, and their herds were plagued by flies, they would follow the rainheads north. Their extreme limit was the sandy belt just south of the desert proper, where the fly could not follow.

In the wet, they pitched their camps on the banks of water-pools or seasonal wadis. The camp would consist of perhaps half a dozen bowl-shaped huts. There would always be a shady tree under which the bachelors sat, and, if lion were about, a zariba of cut thorn-bush in the centre, to protect the cattle after dark. Some sections would plant dhura or dukhn as they passed and return to reap the crop when it was ripe. Apart from beef, they lived on *'asida* – a porridge made from hand-milled grain – cows' milk, and liquid butter.

There was nothing of luxury in a Baggara cattle-camp – not even rugs or woven hangings. The huts themselves were made of local materials – grass, split-cane, bark, palmetto fibre – materials that could be renewed or abandoned as necessary. Everything a family owned could be loaded on the backs of two or three bulls within the space of an hour. In summer they would move perhaps twenty miles in a day. The women and small children rode bulls fitted with ornate litters. The men rode donkeys or horses. When they halted in the afternoon, their huts would be up, the zariba built, and the cows milked, all inside two hours. The huts belonged to the womenfolk. A Baggara man rarely had any personal property other than a wooden bed sprung with giraffe-gut, called an *angareb*, his clothes, his saddle, his dagger and his spears.

The exploits of giraffe and elephant hunters were celebrated in ballads sung by the women at marriages and circumcisions. Any

46

man who had committed a cowardly act would be remembered in such a ballad too. Like the Beja in the east, the Baggara lived by the cult of bravery, and would rather die than be called cowards. 'Their wealth consists of cattle,' Schweinfurth wrote. 'They are not, however, shepherds, as they are represented in the idylls of home, but martial and warlike from their youth; they are bolder robbers than any other of the [Sudanese] nomad races ... I can confidently maintain that they form the finest race of the nomad people dwelling on the Nile [sic] ...'[2]

It was these ferocious horsemen, born of the arid steppes of Kordofan and Darfur, who were to form the backbone of the dervish army. From among them was to rise the man who would 'create' the Mahdi, and who would himself become absolute ruler of the Sudan.

2

'Abdallahi wad Torshayn was born in 1846, somewhere in the *goz* of southern Darfur. His father, Torshayn or 'Ugly Bull', was a *feki* or holy man of the Ta'isha, a Baggara tribe. His chief occupation was writing charms to ward off bullets and blades, concocting potions, curing ailments both physical and spiritual, exorcizing Jinns or evil-spirits, and declaring the conditions propitious for raids and hunts.

Torshayn was at least the third generation of his family to follow the occupation of *feki*. He was the grandson of a famous healer called 'Ali Karrar, who had walked to Darfur from West Africa on the pilgrim route to Mecca. Scores of such pilgrims, known as Takarna, had settled in the Sudan – in places whole villages had been populated by them. 'Ali Karrar, though, had married a Ta'isha girl, and found a niche as a *feki* among the Baggara nomads. Although not known for sure, it is probable that he came from Sokoto in western Nigeria, a 'Caliphate' or Islamic sultanate founded in 1810.

A Sultan of Sokoto named Mohammad Bello had predicted the

imminent appearance of a Mahdi or Expected Guide – a Messiah figure, occurring periodically in Islam, whose role was to purify the religion, and restore justice and harmony. Bello had sent an envoy east to hunt for news of such a Messiah in Wadai (now eastern Chad) and Darfur. Over the following years there were periodic migrations from Sokoto by devotees seeking a Mahdi in the east. 'Ali Karrar may well have been a member of just such an exodus. If so, it seems likely that the idea of an imminent Messiah had a place in 'Abdallahi's earliest mental map.

'Abdallahi was the youngest of Torshayn's three sons. Little is known for certain about his childhood, though it seems that he was a poor scholar, and never learned to read the Quran. His father despaired of him even remembering the verses needed for daily prayers. 'Abdallahi did, however, learn to write charms by imitating Torshayn, though without fully understanding the letters. There was nothing dishonest about this, since to the tribesmen it was not the meaning, but the form of the symbols that carried magical power.

As a young man, he almost certainly took part in elephant and giraffe hunts, as a *feki*. One way the holy man ensured success in such a hunt was by inscribing a Quranic verse on a *loh* or writing-board, washing off the ink into a bowl of water, and passing the water round to be drunk by the hunters. The remainder of the liquid would be rubbed into the horses' flanks. 'Abdallahi must have played his part well, for though he had two full brothers and a half-brother, two of them more accomplished in reading and writing than himself, it was he who took over as tribal *feki* when Torshayn grew old.

3

For the first twenty years of 'Abdallahi's life, Darfur was not a province of the Sudan, but an independent sultanate. Authority lay in the hands of a chief of the sedentary Fur tribe, Sultan Ibrahim Mohammad. From the mid-1860s, though, a slave-trader named

Zubayr Rahma had been the real power in the area. This was the same man who was now exiled in Cairo, and whose irregulars had been sent to help Valentine Baker. Zubayr was a gifted leader and administrator from the Ja'aliyyin tribe, of the northern Sudan. He controlled the trade in ivory and slaves from Darfur's traditional slaving grounds in Dar Fertit, south of the Bahr al-Ghazal.

To reach the sultanate's capital, el-Fasher, Zubayr's slave caravans had to pass through the territory of the Rizaygat, a Baggara tribe of the steppes. In 1873, secretly incited by the Sultan, the Rizaygat attacked and looted several of his caravans. Zubayr decided to teach them a lesson. The Rizaygat were pugnacious and aggressive fighters, but Zubayr had a secret weapon – his seven-thousand-strong private army of *bazingers*: the first body of drilled, trained and disciplined slave-riflemen ever seen in Darfur.

Zubayr, as brilliant a general as he was an organizer, had an instinctive grasp of guerrilla tactics – night operations, surprise attacks, ambushes. The Rizaygat, accustomed to cowing their enemies by fierce cavalry charges and fighting face to face in broad daylight, found themselves suddenly outclassed. Desperately, they called for support from the other Baggara tribes. Among the volunteers was the *feki* 'Abdallahi, whose ability to write charms warding off *bazinger* bullets was now at a premium. That his skills failed to tip the balance, though, is clear, for at the battle of Shakka in August 1873 he was captured along with other Baggara tribesmen, and condemned to death.

That might have been the end of 'Abdallahi – and incidentally the end of the Mahdiyya – had it not been for a dozen *'ulama* or Islamic elders acting as Zubayr's counsellors. They advised the slave-trader that, as a *feki*, 'Abdallahi was a non-combatant. His execution would only enrage the tribes. 'For this reason I refrained from putting the man to death,' Zubayr wrote in his memoirs, 'and I wish to God I had done so, for he only lived to become one of the scourges of the Sudan.'[3]

Sometime after his narrow escape from execution, 'Abdallahi had a vivid dream in which Zubayr appeared to him as the Mahdi, the Messiah his great-grandfather had come looking for in the

Sudan. He promptly had a letter written to the slaver. 'I saw in a dream that you are the Expected Mahdi,' he wrote, 'and I am one of your followers; so tell me if you are the Mahdi of the Age, that I may follow you.'[4] Zubayr, an orthodox Sunni Muslim, was horrified. The suggestion amounted to heresy. He wrote back asking 'Abdallahi not to repeat such a preposterous idea. His plans extended in the opposite direction. He was shortly to be recognized as Turco-Egyptian governor of Bahr al-Ghazal, and to invade Darfur in the name of the Khedive.

In November 1874 Zubayr defeated and killed Sultan Ibrahim in battle, and occupied el-Fasher, Darfur's capital. He was joined shortly by the governor-general of the Sudan, 'Ayyub Pasha, who declared the former sultanate a new Turco-Egyptian province. Zubayr had expected to be appointed governor, but was never to enjoy the fruits of his victory. Jealous of his power, 'Ayyub ordered him back to Bahr al-Ghazal. Instead, Zubayr headed for Cairo to demand his just deserts from the Khedive. Once he was there, Isma'il Pasha made sure that he never returned to Darfur.

In the disturbances that followed the invasion, 'Abdallahi and his ageing father, Torshayn, decided to leave the province. They would complete the hajj, the pilgrimage to Mecca, that 'Abdallahi's great-grandfather had cut short decades before. They got as far as Shirkayla, in the territory of the Jimi' – a Baggara tribe of Kordofan – where they were welcomed as holy men.

It was while living among the Jimi' in the late 1870s that 'Abdallahi sensed a feeling in the air that confirmed his own expectations. Everywhere there were rumours of unrest in Egypt, of the revolt of 'Arabi Pasha against the Ottoman regime. It was clear that Egyptian grip on the Sudan had loosened. If there were ever a chance to throw off the Turco-Egyptian yoke, it was now. There was also talk of the Expected Guide or Mahdi, whose coming was predicted before the year 1300 of the Hijra – the year AD 1880. There was a groundswell of feeling that the time for the Mahdi's emergence had arrived.

It was probably at this time, also, that 'Abdallahi first heard of Mohammad Ahmad, an adept of the Sammaniyya brotherhood who had a growing reputation on the White Nile. He wondered if this man might be the Messiah he sought. When Torshayn died in late 1880, he felt free to go and investigate the sage for himself.

4

By late 1880 or early 1881 – the actual date is uncertain – 'Abdallahi had tracked Mohammad Ahmad down to al-Masallamiyya, a village lying not far south of Khartoum in the Jazira, the wedge of land between the Blue and White Niles. All he possessed in the world by then was tied on a donkey with a back so galled he was unable to ride it. Apart from the clothes he stood up in, he owned a water-skin, a bag of grain, and a cotton shirt, or *jibba*, draped over the animal's flanks. He was now thirty-six years old, a spare, intense, wiry man of middle height, with a face marked by smallpox and a slight limp.

'Abdallahi had had a hard journey. The Baggara were detested by the tribes of the White Nile. They spoke the same language, Arabic, but their cultures were poles apart. When he asked after a Sufi elder named Mohammad Ahmad, he was told that the sage would not demean himself even by pronouncing the name of 'Abdallahi's tribe. Almost everywhere he had been abused and jeered at. Only the gift of food from a few generous souls had saved him from starvation.

At al-Masallamiyya, he was shown to a graveyard, where a gang of men were building a mud-brick dome. One of these men was Mohammad Ahmad. He was tall and powerfully built, about thirty-four years old, with a chocolate brown complexion and a beguiling smile that showed the V-shaped gap in the middle of his front teeth. This was considered a sign of attractiveness in the Sudan. His face displayed three vertical scars or *shluk* on each cheek – the ancient mark of his tribe, the Danagla. Mohammad Ahmad was working on the dome's scaffolding like a labourer when 'Abdallahi arrived, but the Ta'ishi was not the only spectator. Slowly groups of people gathered to hear him speak. When he finally addressed the crowd, 'Abdallahi was profoundly impressed. His voice seemed to come from somewhere deep in the earth. His message, that men should forsake the material for the divine, was unequivocal. Mohammad Ahmad was a mesmerizing preacher, and his words held the conviction of absolute sincerity. 'Abdallahi knew at once that this had to be the Messiah he had come to seek.

At first he was too overawed even to approach him. He was a simple nomad from the west, a holy man who could not even read the Quran. Mohammad Ahmad was evidently a man of great learning. 'Abdallahi felt out of place and self-conscious, remembering the warnings of the White Nile people. He hung back, observing the sage, soothed by his voice. When the crowds had thinned a little, he found the courage to introduce himself. He begged to be taken on as a disciple.

The master revealed none of the disdain 'Abdallahi had been warned about. Instead he immediately instructed the Ta'ishi to bring water and a prayer rug. When they were brought, he entwined 'Abdallahi's hands with his own in the manner of a bride and groom at a Sudanese wedding. He asked if 'Abdallahi was ready to turn to God with repentance. The Ta'ishi said he was, and kissed the master's hand. He then repeated an oath, pledging loyalty to the sheikh for as long as he lived.

It was in this act of personal submission that the Mahdist movement was born.

5

There have been many Mahdis in Islam, but as Mohammad Ahmad must already have known, there is no reference to the idea in the Quran. Several contrasting concepts of the Mahdi are to be found in the *Hadith* or Traditions of the Prophet Mohammad. The common elements of these traditions are summed up by the Arab historian Ibn Khaldun in his book *al-Muqaddima*.

First, the Messiah would be called the 'Mahdi'. Second, he

would be a descendant of the Prophet Mohammad, through his daughter, Fatima. Third, he would support the faith, reinstate justice, and restore the unity of Islam. Fourth, his appearance would herald the coming of the Day of Judgement. Although we have nothing but circumstantial evidence, it is generally accepted, even by the *Encyclopedia of Islam*, that it was 'Abdallahi who first acclaimed Mohammad Ahmad as the Mahdi. Certainly, the Mahdist revolt followed closely enough on the encounter at al-Masallamiyya to suggest that this was the spark that set the smouldering embers aflame.

Being addressed as 'the Mahdi' was the first requirement of the prophecy. The second was fulfilled by Mohammad Ahmad's pedigree – he believed that he was descended from the Prophet Mohammad's daughter, Fatima, through both his paternal grandparents and his maternal grandmother. As for asserting the faith, restoring justice, and Islamic unity, these had always been his aims. The Day of Judgement was continually imminent, and as an ascetic, Mohammad Ahmad had preached incessantly against the material temptations of the world, and proclaimed the necessity of preparing for the afterlife. He had always shunned material wealth. His self-discipline, exaggerated humility, and self-mortification, however, were manifestations of a militant rather than a pious spirit. His view of Islam was narrow and doctrinaire: discussion or interpretation of the Quran was forbidden. Later, even the Sufi orders would be banned.

Though the Turco-Egyptian government was Muslim, and subject to the Khalifa of Islam – the Ottoman Sultan – the Mahdi regarded the Turks and Egyptians as apostates. They might call themselves Muslims, but in his view they were hypocrites who had turned their backs on the Holy Law. They had espoused the manners and customs of infidels, and had connived with Jews and Christians against fellow Muslims. This was a practice forbidden in Islam from its earliest days. Mohammad Ahmad felt it his destiny to lead a return to authentic Islam. This required the immediate removal of apostate governments, including the so-called Khalifa – the Ottoman Sultan in Constantinople.

Apostasy was Islam's most venal sin. While unbelievers still had a chance of seeing the light, apostates had known the light and rejected it for the sake of worldly advantage. No human authority could forgive such an offence. Only God could absolve apostasy after death. Apostates must therefore be killed out of hand. By Islamic law, to fight against apostasy was one of only two legitimate reasons for declaring a holy war or jihad.

The man who was to become the Mahdi was born in 1844 on Labab, a tiny island in the Nile near Dongola al-Urdi, capital of the Sudan's Dongola Province. His tribe, the Danagla, were a Nubian folk of mixed Arab and African ancestry. Their mother-tongue was one of the two distinct Nubian languages spoken in the region. They had inhabited the palm-groves of the Nile from time immemorial.

Between Aswan in southern Egypt and Khartoum, the Nile is about twelve hundred miles in length – the distance is much shorter as the crow flies, because between ed-Debba and Abu Hamed the river twists back north in a sweeping hairpin – the famous Nile 'question mark'. Though the Nile's bed is in most places deep and floored with silt and clay, this stretch is broken by six cataracts, where hard, igneous rocks of the basement complex thrust up through the bedrock and emerge in jagged shoals, shallows, gorges and islands. At low Nile, some of these cataracts make the river unnavigable for part of its length. They have proved an effective obstacle to easy invasion for thousands of years. This stretch of the Nile is referred to as Nubia, and it shares with Egypt an unbroken history of literate culture that spans six millennia. The Nubian people from whom Mohammad Ahmad sprang were very different from the unlettered Baggara nomads of the west. They were the lineal heirs of a civilization that existed here when Rome was a village and London a swamp.

Mohammad Ahmad's father, 'Abdallah, was by trade a boat-builder. When Mohammad Ahmad was five years old, he moved his family south to Kerreri, a village twelve miles north of Khartoum, where timber was more abundant. Mohammad Ahmad took up his father's trade but also showed early scholastic promise. He was sent to study in a series of traditional Islamic retreats or *khalwas*.

Instruction in the *khalwa* consisted solely of the Quran. Students might be as young as four years old. They would copy out *suras* of the holy book on a *loh*, wash them off, and inscribe them again and again until they could do it automatically. They would also repeat Quranic *suras* orally, in unison, until they had committed them to memory. The regime was strict. The teacher would rap the boys' knuckles severely to revive poor concentration. The ultimate object was to recite the entire Quran by rote, and to be capable of this by the age of ten or even younger was not considered a particular distinction. The Prophet Mohammad had himself been illiterate, and the Quran had been memorized long before it had been written down.

The institutionalized Islam of the *'ulama*, introduced by the Turco-Egyptians, was alien to the Sudanese way. Islam in the Sudan had traditionally been disseminated by lone Sufi ascetics – holy men who had something of the shaman and the mystic about them. Sufis employed methods that varied from whirling dances to endless repetition of a mantra, to communicate directly with the divine. It was this mystical aspect of Islam that drew the man who would become the Mahdi. He enrolled as the pupil of a Sufi elder, Mohammad Sharif, sheikh of an order named the Sammaniyya. The sheikh was the grandson of the order's founder, a Sudanese who had studied in Arabia at a time when Islam was undergoing one of its bouts of self-purification.

Mohammad Ahmad remained with his master for seven years, emerging a fully fledged sheikh with a reputation for asceticism. In 1870, his father now dead, his three brothers decided to relocate their boat-building business to Aba, a forested island on the White Nile. The newly established sheikh accompanied them, and made Aba his headquarters for frequent peregrinations through the nearby regions as a wandering ascetic. Celibacy was not part of Muslim asceticism, and Mohammad Ahmad married a young cousin of his father's while on Aba. For much of the time, though, he was to be found in a hollow by the Nile bank. He acquired few possessions beyond the necessities of life. His reputation for piety and self-renunciation soared, gaining him a large following, especially among the Kinana and Dighaym – Arabic-speaking cattle-nomad tribes of the White Nile.

In 1872 he encouraged his revered master, Mohammad Sharif, to join him on Aba. This was to prove a momentous mistake. There were now two Sufi masters on a small island that was evidently only large enough for one. Tension grew between them, and erupted into street fighting between their rival supporters. The final break came when Mohammad Ahmad censured his mentor for permitting dancing, feasting and music at his son's circumcision, contravening the *Shari'a* or Islamic law. In response, Mohammad Sharif expelled him from the order. According to legend, the sage repeatedly asked for his master's forgiveness in vain.

Mohammad Ahmad offered himself to another elder of the Sammaniyya, Sheikh al-Qurayshi, who lived near al-Masallamiyya on the Blue Nile. The sheikh, already advanced in years, welcomed him with open arms. When his new master died, in 1878, he took over as sheikh of the chapter. Later, he journeyed to al-Qurayshi's home village to build a shrine to his memory. It was thus in al-Masallamiyya rather than on Aba that his fateful meeting with 'Abdallahi wad Torshayn took place.

6

When Mohammad Ahmad returned to Aba island in early 1881, his new disciple, 'Abdallahi, went with him. Within weeks of his arrival there, he had undergone a series of visions that confirmed 'Abdallahi's insight. In one such vision he found himself in the company of both the Prophet Mohammad and Jesus Christ, and heard the Prophet tell Christ that he, Mohammad Ahmad, was certainly the Mahdi. The Prophet also informed Mohammad Ahmad directly that he should fear neither the Turks nor the *'ulama*, and that the twelve virtues supposed to be manifest in the Mahdi were to be found only in Mohammad Ahmad himself.

In March, he revealed to 'Abdallahi and his inner circle that he was indeed the Expected Mahdi. He made his second visit to Kordofan shortly afterwards, probably to find a safer refuge than Aba to retire to when the storm broke. On his return he wrote letters to pious notables all over the Sudan, signing himself 'Mohammad al-Mahdi'. These letters invited those who accepted his call to rally to him at once.

Mohammad Ahmad was aware that in declaring himself the Expected One he was issuing a direct challenge to the Islamic establishment. He knew that they would not be long in striking back. Fortunately for him, he had been preparing himself for this situation all his life, by his study of Islamic military history.

The first Muslims had suffered persecution from the infidels in Mecca. They had emigrated to Medina, where they had set up the original Islamic state. This exodus, known as the Hijra, is the point from which the Islamic calendar starts. Already the Mahdi had begun to model his movement on that of the first Muslims. He decreed that his disciples would no longer be called dervishes (a word of Persian origin) but *Ansar* ('helpers') after the original adherents of the Prophet Mohammad. He also planned a Hijra to Jebel Qadir in the Nuba mountains of Kordofan. This was not simply a matter of imitation. The Mahdist movement was a conscious attempt to relive and renew 'authentic' Islam. The use of such traditional archetypes, with their many layers of association for Muslims, spoke directly to the subconscious. They tapped a rich vein of meaning and power.

The Mahdi drew genuine inspiration from the early Muslims. Like all fundamentalists before and after him, though, he believed that religious ideals were contingent not on historical conditions but on eternal and immutable truths. In reality, a return to 'authentic Islam' was not feasible, because the world that had given birth to Islam – a world without steamships, railways, the printing press, firearms or telegraph – no longer existed. If, for instance, the original Muslim army had been an army without firearms, then a Muslim army *with* firearms was *ipso facto* not 'authentic'. To use this technology – which was of course the work of unbelievers –

would be to admit that artefacts developed without divine inspiration were superior to those created with the help of God. The Mahdi's reluctance to allow his men to use firearms, and his deployment of mostly pagan Jihadiyya battalions as his main rifle units, indicates his acute awareness of this problem.

The Hijra to Jebel Qadir was strategically planned. The Mahdi gave his followers four weeks to assemble, which meant that the emigration would take place during Ramadan. This was the month of fasting in the Islamic world, when government departments traditionally hibernate. In 1881, Ramadan also happened to fall at the height of the rainy season. Travel in the *goz*, while it presented no obstacle to lightly equipped tribesmen, would be impossible for a modern army weighed down with baggage and artillery.

All might have gone without the slightest hitch had his declaration not reached the ears of the Egyptian authorities in Khartoum, through his bitter rival, Mohammad Sharif. His former master informed the governor-general, Ra'uf Pasha, of the subversive developments on Aba island. Ra'uf, the son of an Egyptian father and an Abyssinian mother, had been governor-general of the Sudan since 1880, when he had replaced Charles Gordon. He had previously served in Gondokoro Province under Sir Samuel Baker, who had thought him incompetent. Under Gordon, he had been governor of Harar in Abyssinia. Gordon had dismissed him without trial on charges of tyranny and corruption, but he had quickly returned to grace after Gordon had left office.

At first Ra'uf put the stories down to the rivalry between two sheikhs of the Sammaniyya. He was concerned enough, though, to wire the Qadi at al-Kawa, the nearest telegraph station to Aba, instructing him to visit the adept with two learned elders. The Qadi returned with copies of documents that made the Sufi leader's claim unequivocal. There was also a personal message to Ra'uf that amounted to a threat. Mohammad Ahmad informed him that he was the Expected Mahdi, and that his acts were directly inspired by the Prophet Mohammad. He could not be defeated, he said, as he now enjoyed divine protection: anyone who did not accept his divinely appointed mission would be 'purified by the sword'.

The implied challenge to the might of the entire Ottoman Empire by a handful of fanatics must have appeared ludicrous at first. Ra'uf decided to send a representative to talk to Mohammad Ahmad. He chose as his envoy his deputy, Mohammad Bey Abu Sa'ud, a former Egyptian slave-merchant and scion of the company Aqqad & Co., who had been jailed both by the Khedive Isma'il and by Gordon. After Gordon's departure, Abu Sa'ud had become Ra'uf's deputy, but remained universally despised. This was the man, representing all the worst aspects of Turco-Egyptian rule, whom Ra'uf had selected to confer with a Sufi holy man. He was to be accompanied by a few of Mohammad Ahmad's relatives from Khartoum.

The government steamer dropped anchor off Aba on 7 August 1881. Abu Sa'ud and his party were granted permission to enter the Mahdi's retreat. After rising to greet them in the Arab manner, the Mahdi and his counsellors, including 'Abdallahi, shook hands. Mohammad Ahmad invited them to sit on the mats of palmetto fibre covering the floor.

When they were settled, Abu Sa'ud adopted an ingratiating tone that Mohammad Ahmad must have seen through immediately. He said that the governor-general had heard of his declaration, and rejoiced in it, but would like to see him in Khartoum. When Mohammad Ahmad refused to go, Abu Sa'ud argued that it was his duty to obey the summons of the governor-general. According to legend, Mohammad Ahmad replied sharply that since he was now the ruler of the entire Muslim community on earth, he was not obliged to answer the summons of anyone but God. Some sources say he put his hand on his sword at this point. Others say he leapt up and beat his chest. According to the 'official' Mahdist version, though, he spoke kindly to the former slave-trader, realizing that the man was totally out of his depth.

Seeing that the sheikh was unlikely to be persuaded, Abu Sa'ud dropped his act. He told him that he must give up his claim to be the Mahdi. He could not hope to fight the government with his handful of men. The Mahdi pointed calmly at 'Abdallahi and his other close companions, and told Abu Sa'ud that if necessary he would take on the government with only the men in that room.

Abu Sa'ud and his escort returned hastily to their steamer.

In Khartoum, Ra'uf received Abu Sa'ud's report with some consternation. He realized that the Mahdi would have to be brought in by force, and dispatched troops within a few days. By the time the arrest-party landed on Aba on 12 August, though, the Mahdi and his small band were ready for them.

7

Abu Sa'ud had no military experience, but Ra'uf Pasha again entrusted him with the mission. He then muddied the waters by also informing the senior military officer, an artillery captain named 'Ali Effendi, that he was in charge. This was a recipe for disaster. Abu Sa'ud and 'Ali Effendi began arguing almost as soon as they had boarded the steamer. They had with them two companies of Egyptian soldiers – about two hundred men – and a mountain-gun. The soldiers were quartered on an iron barge towed astern of the steamer *Isma'iliyya*.

It took fifteen hours to get back to Aba. They arrived off the island about sunset and moored the boat about a quarter of a mile from the Mahdi's village. 'Ali Effendi wanted to launch an attack immediately, but Abu Sa'ud argued that they should wait until first light next morning. The Mahdi should be given the chance to surrender and go to Khartoum voluntarily, he said. Force should only be used as a last resort. 'Ali Effendi disagreed, and ordered the men ashore.

The rest of the story reads like a black farce. The captain had recruited some local guides – a group of merchants who knew the island. As they marched to the village, it began to bucket down with rain. The advance party arrived well ahead of the main body of troops. 'Ali Effendi asked his guides which was the Mahdi's hut, and barged in abruptly. Finding a dervish inside, he reproached him in a loud voice for claiming to be the Mahdi, and shot him dead. The dervish was not Mohammad Ahmad, but a visitor to his house.

The Mahdi himself, forewarned of the attack, was hiding with his men in the dense bush outside the village. When 'Ali Effendi emerged from the hut, thinking his task easily accomplished, the Mahdi, 'Abdallahi, and their followers set upon him and his troops. The dervishes were armed with sticks, stones, hoes and palm-knives, and a very few spears and swords. What they lacked in weapons, though, they made up for in zeal. They were also assisted by the muddy ground, which gave the advantage to bare-footed tribesmen over boot-shod soldiers. The Egyptian advance party, outnumbered and taken by surprise, was cut down on the spot.

The main party, stumbling suddenly on the mêlée, was also taken unawares. They did not have time to get in formation before the dervishes fell on them. A hundred and twenty were killed or wounded outright. The rest fled back to the *Isma'iliyya*. Nine were taken prisoner. The dozen dervishes who were also killed became the first martyrs of the Mahdiyya.

When the fiasco was reported to Abu Sa'ud, he ordered *Isma'il-iyya* to steam abreast of the Mahdi's village, with the intention of shelling it. Once there, he saw Mohammad Ahmad and his dervishes standing on the shore, waving their spears and jeering, daring the Egyptian troops to land. No one took up the challenge. Abu Sa'ud ordered the gun-crew to open fire. The gun was being towed on a second barge astern of the first barge, and he had to shout himself hoarse to be understood.

The artillerymen fumbled about, trying to locate powder and shot, then trying to remember how to lay the gun. After what seemed like an age, there was a deafening clap and a shell burst on the bank. It missed the dervishes by about twenty yards. Some of the soldiers opened a random fire. The dervishes, knowing their bluff had worked, simply walked back to the village out of range. The fight was over, and the Mahdi had won. *Isma'iliyya* remained at anchor in midstream until the following morning to pick up survivors, but there was none. At first light she headed for al-Kawa, the nearest telegraph station. Here Abu Sa'ud informed Ra'uf Pasha of the defeat.

The battle of Aba – retold and embellished – was the first great legend of the Mahdiyya. It seemed an awesome achievement to have defeated a well-equipped government force with so-called 'white weapons'. Mohammad Ahmad himself had been hit by a bullet in the fight, and wounded in the right shoulder. Thinking that the wound would undermine the leader's credibility, 'Abdallahi had secretly dressed it and advised his master to keep quiet about it. The official Mahdist biography, though, claims this as one of the five miracles manifest at the battle of Aba.

After the encounter, the Mahdi deliberately drew parallels with the battle of Badr, the Prophet Mohammad's first military victory. These enriched his own drama by giving it yet more levels of association with the struggles of the first Muslims, twelve hundred years earlier. One such parallel was the number of fighters involved. At Badr the Prophet Mohammad had been supported by 313 *Ansar*. At Aba, the Mahdi's comrades were said to have numbered just over three hundred. The fact that both battles took place on the 17th Ramadan was also considered highly significant. The Prophet Mohammad had himself been wounded at Badr, lending a miraculous interpretation to the Mahdi's wound at Aba. The uncultured 'Abdallahi had evidently been unaware of the propaganda value of this revelation when he had advised his master to conceal the injury in the heat of battle.

The Mahdi claimed later that he had been informed of the troops' imminent arrival by the Prophet. Whether it was this, simple intuition, or a more prosaic force at work is difficult to say. It is at least possible that Abu Sa'ud might himself have aided the dervishes in the fight. 'The failure [to capture the Mahdi] may have been pre-arranged,' wrote Reginald Wingate. 'Anything is possible with Abu Sa'ud.'[5] The former slaver, who had been thrown into jail by the Khedive, maligned by the tyrannical Baker, suffered a defeat in court, and been dismissed by Gordon, had every reason to support the rebels. The Mahdi's success would mean the reinstatement of the slave trade from which Aqqad & Co. drew its main profit.

Whatever the case, Mohammad Ahmad's victory at Aba was

hailed by his followers as proof that he was truly the Mahdi. It was also the signal for the Hijra to start. The Mahdi knew that Ra'uf Pasha would soon follow up the defeat, sending overwhelming numbers of troops. The die was now irretrievably cast. The following day he and his followers slipped away from Aba and began their exodus to his chosen refuge – Jebel Qadir in Kordofan.

It was here, in the remote fastness of the Nuba mountains, that the Mahdi consolidated his power. It was here, too, that 'Abdallahi showed his true mettle, helping to weave an alliance between the warlike Baggara horsemen – the 'Red Indians of the Sudan' – and the settled Arabs of the Nile Valley, the *awlad al-bilad* or 'Sons of the Soil'. It was this unique balance between farmers and nomads – between two of the most powerful elements in Sudanese society – that laid the foundation of the Mahdi's later success. The dervish army grew steadily, defeating every government force sent against it. In January 1883 Mahdist troops captured el-Obeid, the provincial capital, and put the governor to death. In the two years following the battle of Aba, the Mahdi took prisoner or killed sixteen thousand Egyptian troops. He captured seven thousand rifles, eighteen field-guns, a rocket-battery, and half a million rounds of ammunition. The rebellion culminated in the massacre of the Hicks Pasha column on 5 November 1883, and a week later in the Mahdi's triumphal entry into el-Obeid.

8

Despite Colonel Henry de Coetlogon's fears, the Mahdi had no immediate plans to attack Khartoum. First of all, he could not indefinitely maintain the large army he had collected for the attack on Hicks. Of all the Mahdi's followers, only the true *Ansar* – the religious disciples who had been with him on Aba – were with him for purely religious motives. These were a tiny minority. The Baggara were, like most nomads, only loosely religious, and had joined his cause for two reasons. First, because military operations offered a chance of plunder, and second, because they hated authority and were apprehensive about the trend to strong central government that had taken place under the Turco-Egyptians. Some of them may quickly have realized that they had only exchanged a foreign tyrant for a home-grown one, for after Shaykan, many Baggara squadrons simply melted away on their little ponies back to their huts in the *goz*.

The second powerful element in the dervish army – the sedentary tribes of the Nile – was with the Mahdi mainly for political and economic reasons. Many had been involved directly or indirectly in the slave trade, and all had been subject to the Khedive's crippling taxes. They were prepared to veil their true motives under the mask of Islam, but their main objective was the return of the slave trade and their old way of life.

Apart from the instability of his force, the Mahdi had another reason for not wanting to fall on Khartoum at once. The large and powerful province of Darfur (actually divided into three provinces) lay behind his rear, and was still loyal to the government. The Mahdi knew he had little to fear from the pocket-sized Darfur garrisons, now cut off from the capital, but he was a meticulous man, and wanted to ensure that Darfur was his before advancing to the Nile.

It took seven weeks for news of the Hicks disaster to percolate to the Turco-Egyptian garrison at Dara, in southern Darfur. Three days before Christmas 1884, the provincial governor, twenty-seven-year-old Rudolf Carl von Slatin, assembled all his officers and informed them that their last hope of relief had gone. Two days earlier, an Egyptian messenger whom Slatin had sent to the Mahdi had arrived back from el-Obeid, dressed in the patched *jibba* of a dervish. This was, in itself, news enough. The messenger confirmed the massacre of Hicks at Shaykan in early November. In case Slatin was inclined to disbelieve it, the Mahdi had thoughtfully sent him a sheaf of documents, including the personal diaries of the *Daily News* man, Edmund O'Donovan, and Major Arthur Farquhar, Hicks's chief of staff.

This was a devastating blow to Slatin. His garrison had been fighting hostile tribes for four solid years – long before the Mahdi had come into the picture. Slatin had personally survived no less than thirty-eight engagements since taking over the running of the province. He had even converted to Islam, and adopted the name 'Abd al-Qadir to retain the loyalty of his troops. Now, his garrison was down to 510 regular Egyptian soldiers, with five cartridges apiece. Slatin gave his men the choice of resistance or submission to the Mahdi. That evening, the senior officer, Faraj Effendi, told him that the officers had all voted to surrender. Slatin said he would sleep on it and give them his final decision in the morning.

That night he lay awake in his hut considering the situation. The idea of admitting defeat was bad enough. Slatin knew that since he had adopted Islam, he would, as a prisoner, be obliged to act out a charade. He reflected on the possibility of an honourable suicide, but rejected it. He was young, and even as a prisoner he would still have a chance of striking a blow at the enemy. 'God in his mercy had spared me almost miraculously in this constant fighting,' he wrote, 'and perhaps He would still spare me to be of use to the Government I had tried to serve most loyally.'[6]

Born near Vienna, in 1857, Rudolf von Slatin was the son of a wealthy Viennese merchant of Jewish origin. His grandfather had converted to Roman Catholicism, but the family were not pious. Conversion had not changed the disdain with which they were treated. Rudolf had been educated at Vienna Commercial School, but had fared poorly, and had left aged sixteen, having secured a job with a Cairo bookseller. After working in Egypt, he had quit and travelled south to the Sudan, where he had spent some time in the Nuba mountains.

He had been fascinated by the country. Back in Khartoum he had met Eduard Schnitzer, a German doctor who would one day become famous as Emin Pasha, governor of Fashoda Province. Schnitzer had advised him to write to Charles Gordon, who was then governor of Gondokoro, asking for a position. Slatin did so, but received no reply. He returned to Austria and joined the army. It was while serving as a sub-lieutenant in the Archduke Rudolf's 19th Hungarian Infantry, in 1878, that he finally had a letter from

Gordon offering him a post. He left the army the following year, and made a beeline back to Khartoum, where Gordon was now governor-general. Gordon appointed him inspector of finances, and a year later made him governor of Dara, one of the three sub-provinces of Darfur. Under Ra'uf Pasha, he had been made provincial governor of all Darfur.

By the time the first light of dawn came flooding through his window of the Muderiyya at Dara, Rudolf von Slatin had decided that surrender was his only choice. 'I must become, so to speak, the slave of those I had governed,' he wrote, 'I must be obedient to those who are in every respect my inferiors, and I must, above all, be patient.'[7] He rose and donned his uniform for the last time in many years. Shortly after dawn he learned that his Jihadiyya troops had all deserted to the dervishes: this made surrender inevitable.

That evening he saddled his horse, and accompanied only by his servants, a few Arab chiefs, and the provincial *qadi*, rode to the village of Hillat Shieriyya. Here he surrendered to the man who was to take over as Mahdist governor of Darfur, the Mahdi's cousin, Mohammad Bey Khalid. This was particularly hard for Slatin, because Khalid had been his own deputy for several years, and this made him a traitor. Slatin was an expert at concealing his true feelings, though, and the surrender was amicable. Since Slatin was already a Muslim, the Mahdi had 'pardoned' him and agreed to spare all his soldiers and their wives and children.

Slatin returned with Khalid to Dara, where the local civilian officials had already donned the patched *jibbas* of the dervishes. As a gesture this was wasted, for Khalid immediately ordered all the inhabitants out of their houses. He had the whole town ransacked for treasure. Those who he thought were concealing their riches he had flogged or suspended head-first over a well. Slatin protested in vain. Male and female slaves were divided up amongst the dervishes, and the most beautiful girls earmarked for the Mahdi's personal harem.

The garrison at el-Fasher was still holding out, under an Egyptian officer named as-Sayyid Bey Jum'a. A week later he surrendered, and Khalid obliged Slatin to accompany him to the capital. The town, situated on the banks of a perennial lake known as the *fula*, was the traditional base of the Khayra sultans of Darfur, and the southern terminus of the great *Darb al-Arba'in*, the Forty Days Road, a caravan route to Egypt across some of the most arid desert on earth.

Khalid quickly ordered a repeat performance of his actions at Dara, turning the inhabitants out of their houses and torturing them until they gave up their treasure. One of the Egyptian officers, Hamada Effendi, declared that he had no money, but was betrayed by a female slave. Khalid called him an infidel dog. Hamada, a devout Muslim, was outraged at being addressed in this way by a man who had been a fellow officer and had betrayed his oath to the Khedive. Unable to control his rage, he poured out a string of invective against Khalid. Khalid had him marched outside and flogged repeatedly – for the next three days he was given a thousand lashes a day. Every stroke made Hamada more determined not to yield. He did not even bother to deny that he had hidden his gold and silver. 'Yes, I have concealed money,' he told his tormentors, 'but it will remain buried in the ground with me.'[8] After three days, Khalid ordered the lashing stopped and had Hamada's ruined body handed over to his jailers. When Slatin went to see him, he found the officer in agony. His guards had poured a solution of salt-water and chilli pepper over his open wounds at intervals, in the hope that Hamada would confess. The pain, Slatin wrote, must have been unbearable, but still Hamada refused to reveal where his money was hidden. Slatin begged Khalid to allow him to take care of Hamada. The new governor consented only after Slatin had kissed his feet.

Slatin had Hamada moved to his own house, but it was clear he was dying. When Hamada tried to whisper where his treasure was concealed, Slatin silenced him with a gesture. Moments later, Hamada died. 'As I gazed at this poor mangled corpse, my eyes filled with tears,' Slatin said. 'How much was I still to suffer before it came to my turn to enter into everlasting rest?'[9]

Not long afterwards, Khalid showed Slatin a letter that had come from Cairo, addressed to him, and burst out laughing. Unaware that Darfur had fallen to the dervishes, the Egyptian government had ordered Slatin to concentrate all his troops at el-Fasher. He was to await the arrival of a Fur prince named 'Abd ash-Shukkur, whom the Khedive Tewfiq had just appointed the new Sultan of Darfur. He was now at Dongola, in the northern Sudan, but had left Cairo on 26 January, in the company of Major General Charles Gordon.

Part Three

1

Gordon's train steamed into Cairo station on the evening of 24 January 1884. Kitchener, who was there to meet him with Gerald Graham, did not know Gordon, but was a close friend of his Military Secretary, Lieut. Colonel John Donald Hammill Stewart, of the 11th Hussars. The two had worked together in Turkey. Kitchener was too junior to play much part in Gordon's forthcoming whistle-stop, but there can be little doubt that he was deeply impressed. Gordon was to remain his hero for the rest of his life.

Charles Gordon was a thickset man of five foot five. He had curly hair and brilliant blue eyes that held almost hypnotic power. Normally he spoke quietly, but would sometimes gesticulate as he talked, as if his mouth could not quite get out what he wanted to say. When he got excited, he would speak too fast and stammer. There was a quality of authority about him, though, that caused people to obey him almost without thinking. His own father had described him as a 'powder keg'. He carried with him the air of power under restraint, like an explosion waiting to go off. Sometimes it did go off. Gordon was notorious for his fits of violent temper, and had been known to cuff and punch servants. On at least one occasion he had stabbed a waiter's hand with a fork. He was also a prodigious smoker of cigarettes and drinker of strong liquor. This was probably a self-imposed cure for his short fuse.

Gordon came of a military family, with four generations of service to the crown. His father, Henry William Gordon, was an officer of the Royal Artillery, who became a lieutenant-general. Born in Woolwich, London, in 1833, Charles was Henry's fourth son, one of five brothers and six sisters. Their mother, Elizabeth Enderby, was the daughter of a London ship-owner.

Charles Gordon's father was a genial, humorous man, with strict standards of honour. He believed that the British army was the finest institution in the world, and did not hold with officers who entered foreign service. It is significant that his son Charles spent much of his career in the service of foreign potentates. Perhaps this was an unconscious attempt to escape his father's influence.

Gordon was educated at Taunton School, and entered the Royal Military Academy at Woolwich when he was fifteen. Woolwich trained officers of supporting arms, particularly the artillery and engineers. As a cadet Gordon was quick-tempered and intimidating. He was intolerant of petty injustice, and was frequently involved in protests and fights. He once butted a cadet corporal over some trifling rule in the dining-hall, sending the boy skittering downstairs and through a glass window. When carpeted for this action, Gordon hurled his epaulettes contemptuously at his commander's feet. He was reprimanded again for beating a junior cadet with a hairbrush, and lost six months' seniority. He also lost his chance of entering the Royal Artillery, and had to be content with the Royal Engineers. He was commissioned in 1852, at the age of nineteen.

In 1854 Gordon served in the Crimea. He fought with distinction at Sevastopol and was commended for his coolness under fire. He perfected a technique that would today be accorded a special forces role. He would crawl up close to enemy lines, sketching and mapping their positions and defences. Sometimes this involved standing in full view of the enemy to draw their fire, noting their position from the puffs of smoke. His encyclopedic knowledge of enemy dispositions allowed him to predict their movements in a way that seemed almost uncanny.

After the Crimea, he was given a spell on surveying duty in Armenia and Bessarabia. Here he became devoted to a young Armenian boy called 'Ivan', with whom he would read the Bible. Ivan was the first of a long line of young male companions in Gordon's life, whom he referred to as his 'Kings'. In 1860 he was transferred to China, which had then been in the grip of the Taiping Rebellion for nine years. Led by a Hakka peasant named Hung Hsiu Ch'uan, who claimed to be Jesus Christ's younger brother, the rebellion was largely the result of European influence carried to China by foreign missionaries. Hung, the so-called 'Heavenly King', sought to overthrow the dynasty of the Manchu emperors, themselves foreigners of Tartar origin. It turned out to be the bloodiest civil war in human history.

With an eclectic creed mixing Old and New Testaments with Buddhism, Taoism and Confucianism, Hung raised a peasant army millions strong. He claimed to have restored the Ming dynasty, the last indigenous line of emperors. His disciples wore Ming dress and grew their hair long in Ming style. In 1853, his horde of 'long hairs' sacked the old Ming capital of Nanking, and massacred twenty-eight thousand people. Two months later the Taipings advanced on Beijing, but were routed by the Imperial army. The tide began to turn. By 1859, Hung's army was itself besieged by the Emperor in Nanking.

At this point, Beijing was captured by an Anglo-French expeditionary force. The 'foreign devils' were intent on implementing the Treaty of Tientsin, signed in 1859, forcing the Chinese to buy opium from European traders. Gordon was among the officers serving in the expedition. The fighting was over by the time he arrived, and his first act was to help demolish the Emperor's Summer Palace, a two-hundred-building complex housing priceless treasures.

The Taipings soon recovered the ground they had lost. In 1862, Gordon joined a British force under Major General Charles Stavely, charged with defending the city of Shanghai against the rebels. Shanghai had a large community of foreign merchants, mostly involved in the opium trade, who had raised and financed their own private army. Known as the 'Ever Victorious Army', it was composed of Chinese soldiers with foreign officers, mostly criminals and fugitives. It was commanded by Frederick Ward, a twenty-nine-year-old American.

Ward, who led his men into battle wearing a frock-coat and

carrying nothing but a baton, was a skilled guerrilla fighter. When he was killed in action, though, his place was filled by Henry Burgevine, another American, notorious for his drunkenness and dishonesty. He was eventually sacked for assaulting and looting the house of the EVA's paymaster, Shanghai merchant Tai Chi, and joined the rebels in a fit of pique. Major General Stavely proposed Major Charles Gordon to take Burgevine's place.

Gordon was not a combat officer and had no experience of battle except in the Crimea. He knew nothing of infantry tactics and less of military administration. The EVA was largely dependent for transport on a flotilla of armed steamers, and Gordon had no knowledge of amphibious warfare. He did not know a word of Chinese. Though there were other contenders, including Major Garnet Wolseley, Stavely had an excellent reason for recommending Gordon: he was married to Gordon's sister.

Nepotism or not, the appointment proved thoroughly justified. Gordon had an instinctive grasp of irregular warfare. Over the next two years he fought sixteen actions against the rebels, putting to use the techniques he had learned in the Crimea. He would creep up on an enemy town and survey its strong and weak points. Then, during the night, he would have his guns brought up and punch a hole through the mud wall. When the breach was satisfactory, he would lead his men in a frontal attack. He was usually to be seen striding along with a cigar in his mouth, weaponless except for his baton, 'The Wand of Victory' – a habit picked up from the previous commander, Ward.

The Taipings would either run away or surrender. Those who surrendered were conscripted into the EVA. During this period Gordon chose six handsome Chinese boys as his personal servants, and later he collected scores of male orphans, whom he fed and clothed.

The EVA fought for loot only, and there were constant problems with discipline. Twice Gordon was obliged to have mutineers shot in front of the ranks to keep order. In December 1863, his army and an Imperial force commanded by General Ching captured Soochow, capital of the silk industry. Gordon had contacted the Taiping generals and bribed them to leave the city's gates open. He gave his word that they would not be harmed. When Ching's forces entered, though, they put the Taiping generals to death. Gordon was so incensed at the loss of his honour that he retired to barracks and brooded for two months.

On 11 May 1864 Imperial forces recaptured Nanking. Among the dead they found Hung Hsiu Ch'uan, 'Jesus Christ's Younger Brother', who had hanged himself along with all his concubines. Gordon played no part in the final act. By then the British government had withdrawn permission for its officers to serve with Chinese forces. For the significant part he had played in suppressing the rebels, though, the Chinese Emperor promoted him to Ti Tu – the equivalent of field marshal. On his return to Britain he was awarded a somewhat less exalted lieutenant-colonelcy, a CB, and was lionized by the public as 'Chinese Gordon'.

Thereafter he was quickly forgotten by press and admirers. He languished for six years as a fortifications officer at Gravesend, building forts he knew no one would ever use. During this period he concentrated on religion, and his 'Kings' – mostly poor urchins he found on the docks. He devoted himself to these boys, turning his house into a school, hospital and church for them, finding them jobs and berths on merchant-ships.

Gordon had not been religious as a child. He had experienced a conversion to Christianity as a subaltern, through the influence of a fellow officer named Captain Drew. Many have suggested a close parallel between Gordon and the Mahdi, yet the comparison does not hold up to close analysis. In fact, while the Mahdi was in some ways a soldier masquerading as a mystic, Gordon was in a sense a mystic masquerading as a soldier.

Few prominent figures of his time understood Gordon, dismissing him as 'cracked' and 'unstable', a 'dangerous lunatic' or 'a religious fanatic' with 'a bee in his bonnet'. In fact, he was none of these things. His contemporaries were unable to understand him, because they were locked in a mentality in which rigid rules must be followed, and in which integrity meant acting in a consistent manner, and in accordance with these rules. Most of

Gordon's peers paid lip service to individuality, but had been reared in a milieu that was conformist in the extreme.

Gordon had passed beyond conformity. He was perfectly aware that his superiors were suspicious of him simply because he looked on things differently. He had absolute faith in a higher power, but was not a 'fanatic' or a radical, which implies partisanship of a particular dogma. He never claimed that his view was the only one. He belonged to no established church, bowed to no priesthood, and believed that no mortal could mediate between man and God. He had a profound respect for all religions, including Islam, and believed in acceptance rather than control. He was neither a sentimentalist nor a romantic. His view was that all individuals were part of God's unfolding, and that all actions should be taken in humility rather than arrogance.

In 1872, during a visit to Constantinople, he had encountered Nubar Pasha, who was already a statesman of some note in Egypt. Nubar was looking for a replacement for Sir Samuel Baker as governor of Gondokoro Province in the Sudan. Gordon recommended himself for the job.

Gordon, then forty-one years old, met and became an admirer of the Khedive Isma'il, whom he considered a man of outstanding ability. He spent much of the next three years in the humid, malarial swamps of Gondokoro with a close-knit bunch of adventurers. These included the Italian Romolo Gessi, the American Charles Chaille-Long, the Frenchman Linant de Bellefonds, two Sapper subalterns, Charles Watson and William Chippendall, and the notorious Abu Sa'ud, whom he had sprung out of jail.

Although Isma'il had ordered him to halt the slave trade, Gordon realized that he could do no more than window-dressing. The White Nile could be policed, but this only meant that the slavers shifted to the periphery. The big merchants started moving their slaves along the desert caravan routes. The worst of it, though, was that most of Isma'il's civil servants in Khartoum were themselves involved in the trade. This included the governor-general, 'Ayyub Pasha himself.

Gordon remained loyal to the Khedive Isma'il, but came to loathe the Turco-Egyptian officials. He found them corrupt, dishonest, hypocritical, greedy, stubborn, unreliable, inflexible and lacking in professional skill. Weary of the climate, the privations, and most of all of the hostility and duplicity of the officials, Gordon resigned in 1876. Isma'il refused to accept his resignation: Gordon was far too valuable as a bulwark against European criticism. Gordon agreed to rescind it, but only on condition that he was made governor-general in Khartoum, with authority over the entire Sudan.

Isma'il stalled, knowing that to commission a European Christian as *hikimdar* would cause great resentment, not just among the locals, but among his own officers. At this point, though, the British consul-general in Cairo, Vivian Hussey, gave the Khedive an ultimatum. Unless he eliminated the slave trade in all his territories forthwith, Britain would cease financial, political and moral aid. Hussey added that the British government informally supported Gordon's application for the governor-generalship. They believed he could eradicate the slave trade. Gordon was installed as governor-general on 5 May 1877.

As governor-general Gordon spent much of his time on extensive journeys by camel, ceaselessly crossing and recrossing the *goz*. On one occasion he rode into the camp of three thousand armed rebel slavers entirely without an escort, and survived. Gordon supported Isma'il Pasha during the debt crisis in 1878, suggesting that Egypt's creditor-powers should simply waive the Khedive's debts. This was a reasonable solution, but the move was met with fury by men like Baring, who accused Gordon of naïveté.

Gordon found Baring pretentious, grand and patronizing. 'When oil will mix with water, we will mix together,' he commented.[1] Baring regarded the Sudan as a largely useless territory that should be abandoned as soon as possible. Gordon believed that the government had a duty to consider the needs of the local people, and to help them attain a better standard of living. And yet from their own points of view Baring and Gordon were remarkably similar. Baring believed that his destiny in life was to save Egypt: Gordon believed that his mission was to save the Sudan, which essentially meant saving the Sudan *from* Egypt.

When Isma'il was deposed in 1879, Gordon was out in Darfur, chasing slave-traders. He had never lost his admiration and respect for Isma'il, but soon fell out with Tewfiq, whom he called a 'deceitful little creature'. His resignation, in 1880, had been a cause for celebration by Turco-Egyptian officials and European diplomats alike.

2

That was four years earlier. Now, Gordon was returning to the Sudan for the third and final time. In fact, he and Stewart had not been expecting to visit Cairo at all. When their ship, the P&O steamer *Tanjore*, put into Port Said that morning, HMS *Carysfort* was waiting in harbour getting up steam, ready to take them directly to Suakin. Before they were able to board her, Sirdar Sir Evelyn Wood and his ADC, Lieut. Colonel Charles Watson, came alongside *Tanjore* on a steam-launch. Wood found Gordon and Stewart on the poop-deck.

Wood and Gordon had not met since they were subalterns in the Crimea thirty years earlier, but they recognized each other instantly. Wood probably knew that he owed his position as Sirdar to Gordon, who had suggested his name to Lord Granville two years before. With his ragged moustache, bald head, and beagle-eyes, the forty-six-year-old Sirdar did not look much like a hero. Yet he had been a man of remarkable ability. At fourteen, he had run away from school to join the navy, and had served in the Crimea as a midshipman with the Naval Brigade. At the Redan, where he had first met Gordon, he was the only man out of an entire naval column to survive an attack on a Russian embankment. Wounded badly in the elbow, Wood managed to crawl back to his own lines.

After being invalided back to Britain, Wood transferred to the army. Later, with the 17th Lancers, he fought in the Sepoy Revolt in India. He learned to speak fluent Hindi, led patrols mopping up mutineers, raised an irregular cavalry unit, and won the Victoria Cross rescuing a local merchant from a gang of dacoits by whom he and his men were heavily outnumbered. He had achieved all this by the time he was twenty years old.

Wood explained that he had been sent to persuade Gordon to make a diversion to Cairo, and presented him with letters from both Baring and Graham. In any case, he went on, Gordon stood very little chance of getting from Suakin to Khartoum. The road through Berber had been shut by 'Osman Digna. He would be far better off going up the Nile Valley instead.

Colonel Charles Watson knew Gordon better than anyone else present. As a young lieutenant in the Royal Engineers, he had been on Gordon's team at Gondokoro, in the 1870s. It was probably mainly due to Watson's insistence that Wood had put pressure on Baring to accept Gordon for the current mission. Watson sensed that Gordon was reluctant to relinquish the idea of sailing directly down the Red Sea. He had a scheme, Watson wrote, for making overtures to the tribes near Suakin that he thought might assist Valentine Baker. In fact, Gordon had two proclamations addressed to the sheikhs of the Beja, asking them to allow the besieged garrisons to withdraw, and to come for a parley with him at Suakin. Gordon did not know that Baker's force had already left for its fateful encounter with 'Osman Digna at et-Teb.

His real reason for wanting to bypass Cairo, though, was to avoid meeting the Khedive Tewfiq, whom he had publicly criticized. Only a few days earlier he had written to Lord Northbrook, First Lord of the Admiralty, that it was Tewfiq he feared rather than the Mahdi. In a recent newspaper interview, he had referred to the Khedive as a 'little snake'. 'Must I see the Khedive?' he asked Wood. 'It is essential,' Wood replied.

Finally, the newcomers joined Wood and Watson on their steam-launch. In the five hours it took to reach Isma'iliyya, the Sirdar gave Gordon and Stewart a detailed rundown on the current state of affairs in both Egypt and the Sudan. At Isma'iliyya they went directly to the station and boarded the special train Baring had laid on. In the carriage, Gordon was delighted to meet his old secretary from the Sudan, Mohammad Bey Tuhami, but dismayed to find he had recently gone blind. Gordon gave him a present of £100.

When the train arrived at Cairo at nine, half an hour early, Gordon was relieved. It meant that he was able to dodge the official welcome from Nubar Pasha, who was still on his way to the station. Though Nubar had given Gordon his first posting in the Sudan, he had come to detest the Armenian, whom he thought greedy and indolent, interested only in filling his pockets at the expense of the state. Gordon had never forgotten that Nubar had once demonstrated his disloyalty to the Khedive by suggesting that Gordon should declare himself monarch of an independent Sudan. Gordon had rejected the idea furiously. He had called Nubar 'a gangster and double-dealer'.[2] Though he would have to modify his views now to suit Baring, he did not regret having missed the welcome ceremony. In any case, he detested such pomp.

He was happy to see Graham instead. 'It was a great sight,' wrote a witness to their meeting, E. A. Floyd of the Telegraph Department, 'as tall Graham, some inches over six feet, grasped both Gordon's hands with "Charlie, dear boy, how are you?" and "Gerald, my dear fellow, how are you?" answered the little man joyfully.'[3] Graham joined Gordon and Stewart as they drove in a carriage to Evelyn Wood's residence, where they were to stay. A squad of Egyptian syces trotted on foot before them to clear the way.

Gordon and Stewart had sailed on *Tanjore* from Brindisi, but their journey proper had begun on 18 January at Charing Cross station in London's Strand. Here, according to legend, an eccentric little tableau had been acted out. Their train, the 7.45 night-mail bound for Calais, had been delayed for fifteen minutes, while Adjutant General Lord Wolseley had gone in a hansom cab foraging for cash in the gentlemen's clubs of St James's. Gordon, in his hurry to be away, had apparently forgotten to bring any money with him.

When Wolseley returned with £300 in gold sovereigns he handed the money over to Stewart, whom Gordon referred to as his 'wet-nurse'. Wolseley then carried Gordon's carpet-bag down the platform. His chief, the Duke of Cambridge, C.-in-C. of the British army, opened the carriage door for Stewart and Gordon. In other versions of the scene, made famous by popular prints, Foreign Secretary Lord Granville buys Gordon's ticket, and Secretary of State for War, Lord Hartington, arrives to wish him god-speed.

It is an endearing, dream-like portrait. Here, in a single motif, we have the prelude to a drama of world-shaking import acted out on a common railway platform in the heart of London. Here are four of the world's most powerful men – the British Empire's two top generals, and her foreign and war secretaries – sending off the hero and his sidekick to the furthest reaches of the earth, to pull the Empire's irons out of the fire. The picture emphasizes the childlike unworldliness of the hero, Gordon – qualities that are supposed to highlight his cerebral genius. Like a child, Gordon cannot be entrusted with money. It has to be given to the 'sensible and worldly' Colonel Stewart, whom Gordon himself characterizes as his 'nurse'. The image is also redolent of the cosy 'clubbiness' of Victorian London. Here, everyone who is anyone knows each other, but, conversely, the most powerful of men, engaged in the most significant of imperial dramas, involving the lives of millions, are lost in a crowd of pinstripe suits, top-hats and greatcoats. They are just another group of well-heeled chums seeing a friend off on the night train for France.

Like many episodes of Gordon's life, this one is partly mythical. It is true that both Wolseley and the Duke of Cambridge were at Charing Cross that night. Wolseley was an old friend of Gordon's from the Crimea, and the Duke of Cambridge had known him as a child, when the Gordon family had been his neighbours on Corfu. Neither Granville nor Hartington were there, though, and Gordon does not mention Wolseley having gone hunting for cash. Whatever the case, at eight o'clock the whistle blew. The doors slammed shut. The night-mail steamed out of the station, taking

Major General Charles 'Chinese' Gordon to his rendezvous with destiny.

3

Only eleven days previously, Gordon had resigned his commission in the British army. He had been offered a job as governor-general of the Congo by King Leopold II of the Belgians, and had agreed to take it. For the past year he had been living quietly in Jerusalem, fulfilling a lifelong ambition to track down the actual sites of the Crucifixion and the Holy Sepulchre.

On 1 January 1884, Gordon had arrived in Brussels. His sabbatical was over, and he had come to finalize the details of his employment in the Congo. At his hotel he found waiting for him a letter from Sir Samuel Baker, urging him to lend his hand to the evacuation of the Egyptian garrisons in the Sudan. Gordon, now eager to get his teeth into the slave trade in the Congo, ignored it.

He was aware that he could not take up his new appointment and remain on full pay in the British army. There was no alternative but to resign. Concerned by the potential loss of his pension, though, he wrote to his old friend Adjutant General Garnet Wolseley, asking for his help in the matter. He told Wolseley that he would be back in London in a few days to deal with his resignation: Wolseley – the hero of Tel el-Kebir, author of *The Soldier's Pocketbook*, the very embodiment of the late Victorian army, and Gilbert and Sullivan's 'model of a modern major-general' – was horrified at the thought of Britain losing such a man as Gordon. 'I hate the idea of your going to the Congo,' he wrote back. 'Our very best man, burying himself among niggers on the Equator.'[4] Since Gordon was going to be in London presently, Wolseley asked him to come to the War Office on 15 January for a chat about his future.

Wolseley and Gordon had fought at Sevastopol together as junior officers. Even then, Wolseley had felt himself immensely drawn to Gordon. He admitted that Gordon was one of the few men who made him feel inferior in 'all the higher qualities of character'.[5] Wolseley, not a man habitually given to self-abasement, said later that he considered himself unworthy even to 'pipe-clay Gordon's belt'. He thought Gordon the only man he had met who came up to his ideal of the Christian hero. 'He absolutely ignored self in all that he did,' Wolseley said, 'and only took in hand what he conceived to be God's work.'[6]

In China, Wolseley had almost been offered the job that had gone to Gordon. It is interesting to speculate whether, if he, not Gordon, had become commander of the 'Ever Victorious Army', he would have become as great a hero. Wolseley himself thought not. He wrote later that had he been given the command he would have succumbed to the temptations of power, and ended up by making himself the 'Emperor of China'. Though they rarely met after their service in China, they remained in each other's thoughts, and followed each other's careers closely. Wolseley had the honour of being one of the people for whom Gordon regularly prayed.

As early as 1882, when the Mahdi had first laid siege to el-Obeid, Gordon's name had been suggested as the officer best suited to bring the Sudan to order. In December the same year Queen Victoria herself had opined that either Gordon or Samuel Baker could settle the Mahdi's revolt within two months. By the beginning of 1883, no Englishman had been appointed, and Lieut. Colonel Sir Charles Wilson, British intelligence chief in Cairo, had sent Lieut. Colonel John Hammill Stewart to report on the situation in the Sudan.

Gordon's name had not cropped up again until the news of the Hicks Pasha massacre. Then, a letter that had originated from Colonel Bevan Edwards, a former Sapper officer who had known Gordon in China, ended up on the desk of Hugh Childers, Chancellor of the Exchequer. The letter passed through the hands of Major General Sir Andrew Clarke, another Sapper, who was currently Director of Fortifications. Edwards simply named 'Charlie Gordon' as 'the one man who is competent to deal with the question'. In Clarke's covering note, however, Gordon had already acquired mystical status: '. . . if the Mahdi is a prophet, Gordon in the Sudan is greater.'[7] This concept of Gordon's mystical power over the Sudanese tribes, equal or superior to that of the Mahdi, is the secret thread running through the Gordon story. The idea had its origin in precisely the same Messianic archetype that had brought the Mahdi to power. Before this story reached its conclusion, some of the most rational and lucid of men were to be seduced by its spell.

The Edwards–Clarke letter landed on Lord Granville's desk two days before Baring wired that the Sudan should be abandoned. Granville thought Gordon might be useful. The public were clamouring for action. Neither Gladstone nor Granville wanted to waste money on the Sudan, and Gordon had the great advantage of being cheap. 'He has an immense name in Egypt,' Granville told the Prime Minister, unwittingly opening up a crack in the door to Gordon's apotheosis. 'He is popular at home. He is a strong but sensible opponent of slavery. He has a small bee in his bonnet.'[8]

It took a week to obtain Gladstone's approval. The Prime Minister was one of those who refused to be taken in by Gordon's mystique. According to his private secretary, G. W. Smalley, Gladstone actually hated him. There was something about Gordon that instinctively put his hackles up. But better one man than a British division, Gladstone thought, bee in his bonnet or not.

On 1 December Granville had wired Baring asking whether Gordon would be of any use to the Egyptian government. Baring replied with an unequivocal negative. Since the Mahdist revolt was Islamic in nature, handing over the governor-generalship to an ardent Christian would only inflame matters.

This was the official excuse. Actually, Baring was another of those who had not fallen under Gordon's spell. He remembered what he regarded as Gordon's 'unstable' character from the debt crisis days, and felt he could do without someone who treated orders as a basis for discussion, and habitually consulted the Prophet Isaiah before giving his approval.

On 8 January, the day after posting his resignation, Gordon arrived back in England. He reached the home of his sister Augusta

– a spinster twelve years his senior – at Rockstone Place, in Southampton, at eleven o'clock that night. There he found a message from William T. Stead, the editor of the *Pall Mall Gazette* – a popular evening paper, noted for its jingoism. Stead asked for an interview. Gordon slept on it, and wired Stead the next morning that his views were immaterial as he was off presently to the Congo. Stead came down anyway.

Gordon saw him in the drawing-room at Rockstone Place, in the company of Captain John Brocklehurst of the Royal Horse Guards, a friend from the Sudan, who was there as a witness. The room was full of antiquities and mementoes from Gordon's travels. Stead sat on a leopardskin-covered sofa and drank tea while Gordon spread a map on the floor. To Stead's dismay, it was a map of the Congo. Gordon was inclined to talk about how he intended to rid the Congo of slavery. Not to be deterred, Stead cut him off by reminding him that he was one of Britain's leading experts on the Sudan, and that was the country of the moment.

Gordon then cleared his throat and held forth for two hours. He asserted that the Mahdist revolt was the result of Turco-Egyptian mismanagement, and that the Mahdi had little following as an Islamic leader. He claimed that during his time as governor-general he had taught the natives to expect something better, and that when he had departed, the old oppression had returned. He deplored HM Government's policy of evacuation and abandonment, and declared that Egyptian Prime Minister Nubar should appoint a governor-general in Khartoum to relieve – not evacuate – the garrisons.

The revolt had to be stopped, he said, as it was likely to inflame the entire Islamic world. After it had been put down, a new constitution should be introduced and all Turks excluded. Evacuation was, anyway, he declared, totally unworkable. Once the rebellion had been dealt with, there could be an amnesty for the rebels, and the government should be entrusted to a man who kept his word.

Gordon's declarations to Stead reveal a significant underestimation of the Mahdi's power. Gordon clearly sympathized with the

Sudanese people in their bid to throw off the Turco-Egyptian yoke, which is why he suggested an amnesty for the rebels once the revolt had been put down. Although it is clear that he overrated the extent of his personal influence over the Sudanese tribes, his contempt for Mohammad Ahmad is understandable. He saw that what the Mahdi offered – compliance or death – was simply the blueprint for a new tyranny to replace the old tyranny of the Turco-Egyptians. To Gordon, the Mahdi's dictatorship was a retrogressive step that would result only in more bloodshed, hardship, and suffering for the Sudanese.

He never suggested directly to Stead that he himself should be sent out to the Sudan, but Stead picked up the subliminal message. His piece was published that evening under the headline *Chinese Gordon for the Sudan*. 'We cannot send a Regiment to Khartoum,' Stead wrote, 'but we can send a man who on more than one occasion has proved himself more valuable in similar circumstances than a whole army. Why not send Chinese Gordon with full powers to Khartoum, to assume absolute control for the territory, to treat with the Mahdi, to relieve the garrisons, to do what he can do to save what can be saved from the wreck of the Sudan?'[9]

The article caused a sensation. The chattering classes suddenly remembered Chinese Gordon. The interview was reprinted in almost every other newspaper, including *The Times*. Public interest became public furore. Suddenly the great and good began to stand up and take notice. Among them was Queen Victoria, who had been pushing for Gordon or Sam Baker to go to Khartoum for the past two years. The Queen nudged the Secretary for War, Lord Hartington, who was still sitting on Gordon's resignation.

On 8 January, the day Gordon returned from Brussels, Baring had confirmed the resignation of Egyptian Prime Minister Sharif Pasha and his replacement by Nubar. Hartington thought the change might ameliorate Baring's attitude to Gordon. He asked Granville to inquire again if the Egyptian government would be able to use him. Since no one had yet asked Gordon directly if he was prepared to go, Granville also mentioned intelligence chief Sir Charles Wilson as a possible substitute.

Once again, Baring turned them both down. Nubar Pasha had a candidate of his own for evacuating the garrisons. He had decided to send 'Abd al-Qadir Pasha, the Austrian-educated Egyptian civil engineer who had been governor-general of the Sudan up to February 1882. 'Abd al-Qadir was confident that he could pull the troops out, as long as he was given a year and ten thousand camels. He quickly backtracked when he was told that the British intended to announce the abandonment of the Sudan. Not only was this a blow to Egyptian national pride, it could not be done. 'Abd al-Qadir was canny enough to predict that as soon as the policy of abandonment became public knowledge in the Sudan, the tribes considered 'neutrals' would have no choice but to join the Mahdi. This would create a wholly hostile environment, in which it would be impossible to withdraw the remaining troops. 'Abd al-Qadir's assessment was perfectly correct. He had put his finger on what was very soon to become Gordon's dilemma.

On 15 January Gordon turned up at the War Office in Whitehall, expecting to talk to Wolseley about his pension. Wolseley had another agenda. While Gordon had been on his way, he had turned the matter over carefully in his mind and come up with a master plan that would force the government to reverse its policy of abandoning the Sudan. It would inevitably involve the use of British troops, a policy vehemently opposed by the government, but if all went according to plan, it would result in a British occupation of the Sudan and glory for Wolseley and his 'disciples'. The kingpin of this conspiracy would be Charles Gordon.

The previous day he had discussed Gordon with Granville. They had agreed that Wolseley would ask Gordon 'as a friend' what his views were on being sent to the Sudan. If Gordon replied that he could not go, or that he could not go without a large force (an idea Gordon had mentioned in a letter to *The Times* the previous day), all well and good. Granville would at least have an excuse for the public. If Gordon thought he could use his influence over the tribes to escort the Khartoum garrison and inhabitants to Suakin, then, Granville thought, 'a little pressure on Baring might be advisable'. Granville had given a précis of this plan in a letter to

Prime Minister Gladstone, who was then at his country house at Hawarden. Despite his distaste for Gordon, Gladstone approved.

Wolseley approached the subject obliquely, by telling Gordon that though he personally had never liked the idea of his being 'wasted' in the Congo, the government had removed its objection. This meant that he could withdraw his resignation. Having cleared this out of the way, he then asked him what he would do to solve the problems in the Sudan. Gordon answered without hesitation that he would dispatch himself out there immediately, sailing directly to Suakin without calling at Cairo. Wolseley asked if he would be willing to go to Suakin to 'enquire into the condition of affairs in the Sudan'. Gordon said he would, but added that he could not say, until he had examined the situation on the ground, whether he would recommend evacuation, or the appointment of himself as governor-general.

Having obtained this verbal agreement, Wolseley asked Gordon to write down his own instructions to himself for the mission. Gordon wrote that he would proceed to Suakin, report on the military situation in Sudan, and return. He would be under Baring for orders and would communicate through him. He added that he understood it was his duty only to report, and agreed that the government would be in no way bound by his advice.

What Gordon outlined for himself, in fact, was a reconnaissance mission. It was a long way from Granville's image of his inciting local tribes to escort the Khartoum garrison to the coast. The brief was passed to the Foreign Office, to Baring, and to the Prime Minister.

What happened next remains a mystery. The following day, Baring sent an official wire to Granville, reporting that 'Abd al-Qadir had reneged on his promise to go to the Sudan. He asked for 'a well-trained British officer, who would go to Khartoum and be given full civil and military powers to conduct the retreat'.[10] Why Baring did not mention Gordon is not clear. Gordon's proposal that he should go to Suakin on a reporting mission had been sent the previous day. Either Baring had not received it, or he had chosen to ignore it. Perhaps he did not wish it to be on record that he had officially requested Gordon – the first move in a series of 'buck-passing' exercises that marked all parties involved in the Gordon story.

It is clear that Baring *did* get the telegram about Gordon at some stage, for in his second message to Granville that day – a private one – he responded directly to it. He agreed that Gordon would be the best man for the job, if he would pledge himself to carry out the policy of withdrawing from the Sudan as quickly as possible. Baring added that Gordon must accept that his instructions would come from Cairo – that is, from Baring himself.

Baring, who never liked or trusted Gordon, lived to regret his capitulation. He wrote later that Gladstone's government made two major mistakes in dealing with the Sudan. The first was in failing to stop Hicks Pasha's expedition to Kordofan; the second was in sending Charles Gordon to Khartoum. 'Looking back at what occurred after a space of many years, two points are clear,' he wrote. 'The first is that no Englishman should have been sent to Khartoum. The second is that if anyone had to be sent, General Gordon was not the right man to send.'[11]

4

After meeting Wolseley, Gordon returned to Brussels, still unsure whether he would be going to the Congo or the Sudan. He knew that Baring held the whip hand and would probably turn him down. While boarding his ferry at Dover with his friend Brocklehurst, he dashed off a note to Wolseley telling him, if any hitch arose, to 'bury' the whole matter. No one knew about it but themselves, he said. 'I would not have the very slightest flutter of hurt on subject and would never mention it.'[12]

On arriving at the Hotel Bellevue in Brussels that afternoon, though, he was handed a wire from Wolseley. The message instructed him to return to London at once and report to the Adjutant General as early as possible the next morning. Gordon was suddenly flushed with excitement. His mission to Khartoum was on, and he sensed he had turned the great corner of his life.

He made his apologies to King Leopold II, whom he reported to be 'furious'. He and Brocklehurst took the overnight ferry, and were on English soil again by dawn on 18 January. Gordon went directly to the Household Cavalry barracks in Knightsbridge, where he washed and shaved. Then he took a cab to Wolseley's office at Horse Guards in Whitehall. Wolseley explained that Baring had accepted him: there was no further obstacle to his going to the Sudan.

He told Gordon that he had arranged a meeting with the cabinet at three o'clock that afternoon. Gordon, feeling tired but elated, went back to the barracks to sleep. Wolseley came for him at half-past twelve, and together they took a cab back to the War Office. An icy wind swept the City but inside the antiquated building it was warm, with the smell of furniture polish and an air of sepulchral calm. Wolseley asked Gordon to wait in the anteroom while he entered Lord Hartington's office. There was a coal fire burning in the hearth, and Gordon moved towards it. He suddenly turned to Hartington's secretary, and asked: 'Do you ever tell a lie?' The man stared back at him, astonished, but at that moment Wolseley returned and called him over.

'HM Government want you to understand that they are determined to evacuate the Sudan,' Wolseley told him, 'for they will not guarantee future government. Will you go and do it?'

'Yes,' Gordon said.

Wolseley gestured to the door. 'Go in,' he said.

Inside, three prominent members of the cabinet were waiting to see him. Sixty-nine-year-old George Leveson Gower, the 2nd Earl Granville, Eton and Oxford, had been Secretary of State for the Colonies and was now Foreign Secretary for the second time. His colleague and protégé, fifty-year-old Spencer Cavendish, Marquess of Hartington, later to be the 8th Duke of Devonshire, Axminster and Cambridge, had served previously as Secretary of State for India. Fifty-eight-year-old Thomas Baring, Lord North-brook, had been both Under-Secretary of State for War and Viceroy of India. He was now First Lord of the Admiralty. A fourth member turned up late. This was Sir Charles Dilke, President of the Local Government Board, at forty-three the youngest member of the cabinet. A legalist, traveller and author, with radical notions, Dilke was the heir to a newspaper fortune, and MP for fashionable Chelsea.

There is no official transcript of this meeting, but there are two distinct versions of what was said. According to all four of the cabinet ministers present, Gordon was dispatched to the Sudan only in an advisory capacity. When Granville wired to Baring after the meeting he did not mention that Gordon was being sent 'to evacuate the garrisons', only that he would *report* on the military conditions. He did add, however, that he would be under Baring's orders and would perform such other duties as Baring might entrust to him.

These words were reiterated by Baring's cousin, Northbrook, who wrote to him the same day: '. . . he leaves by tonight's mail for Suakin to *report* on the best way of withdrawing the garrisons, settling the country, and to perform such other duties as may be entrusted to him by the Khedive's government through you.'[13] Northbrook explained that Gordon did not believe in the 'great power' of the Mahdi, and did not think that the tribes supporting him would leave their own territories. He thought there would be no difficulty in evacuating the garrisons. 'He does not seem at all anxious to retain the Sudan,' Northbrook concluded, 'and agreed heartily to accept the policy of withdrawal.'[14]

This was certainly curious, because only nine days earlier Gordon had told William Stead of the *Pall Mall Gazette* that he deplored the idea of evacuation, and believed the garrisons in the Sudan ought to be relieved, not evacuated. According to Wolseley, Gordon referred to the policy of abandonment at their earlier meeting as 'weak' and 'silly'.

Hartington made a précis of the gist of Gordon's conversation with Wolseley on the 15th and sent a copy to Gladstone. This confirmed that Gordon was to go out to Suakin only to report back. When the chips were down later, Gladstone was thus able to claim officially that, as far as he knew, Gordon had not been sent to the Sudan to do anything other than 'report'.

One thing Granville went to some trouble to instil in Gordon, though, was that retention of the Sudan was not an option. 'It appeared in his conversation with Wolseley on Tuesday (15th),' Granville wrote to Dilke later, recapitulating the conversation Dilke had missed due to his late arrival, 'that he was as likely to recommend one course as another when on the spot. I told him that we would not send him out to re-open the whole question [of retaining the Sudan], and he then declared himself ready to go out merely to help in the evacuation . . . He is not remarkably precise in conversation, though I found him much more so than Wolseley had led me to expect.'[15] All four ministers agreed that Gordon left with a clear understanding that there would be absolutely no question whatsoever of sending a British relief mission to the Sudan.

Gordon's version is significantly different. In the meeting with Wolseley a few days earlier he had suggested that he should go out to Suakin and, having observed the situation, should advise the government on future strategy. He had himself specified that the government would not be bound by his advice. During his briefing with the cabinet, however, his role – at least according to two private letters he wrote shortly afterwards – had been changed to an executive one. The ministers, he said, had asked him to go to the Sudan, not simply to report, but to 'evacuate the garrisons'.

As to which of the two versions is correct, Granville's phrase 'help in the evacuation' and Northbrook's mention of 'settling the country' are giveaway clues to a secret subtext not revealed fully in their messages. The lack of an official transcription was itself probably no accident. Gordon was an unknown quantity urged on the government by Wolseley. If he succeeded, they could claim triumphantly that it had been their achievement. If things went wrong, they could claim he had exceeded his orders – or that his instructions had been 'perverted' by Baring in Cairo. The 'semi-official' version of the meeting was almost certainly the second gambit in the game of evading responsibility that had begun when Baring had ignored Gordon's self-imposed brief a few days earlier. The cabinet wished Gordon to evacuate the garrisons, but

none of those who had sent him – least of all the Prime Minister
– was willing to admit the fact.

5

Wolseley had good reasons for wanting a popular success in the
Sudan. Cunning, ambitious, snobbish, egotistical, he was the most
capable soldier of his generation, and knew it. One of a tiny
minority of officers who had reached senior posts on merit, he had
sidestepped the purchase system as a youth of fourteen by appealing
directly to the Commander-in-Chief of the era, the Duke of
Wellington.

Like Kitchener, Wolseley was an Irish-born Englishman, the
eldest of four brothers and three sisters. His father, the descendant
of old Anglo-Saxon aristocracy, had retired from the army as
a major with twenty-nine years' service in the King's Own
Borderers. He had died when Garnet was seven, leaving the family
in poverty. Garnet had attended a day school which he had been
obliged to leave at fourteen to work in a Dublin surveyor's office.

In 1852, after a number of appeals from Wolseley's mother, the
Iron Duke had granted him a commission without purchase, on
the strength of his father's record. He still had to pass a stiff entrance
examination to the Royal Military Academy, Sandhurst, in algebra,
history, geography, fortification and a foreign language. He
crammed for these subjects while working as a surveyor. He was
accepted for the Academy aged sixteen, and was later gazetted as
an ensign in the 12th Foot. Wolseley promptly asked for a transfer
to the 80th – the South Staffordshire Regiment – because they
were on active service. He had realized very quickly that, lacking
the funds to buy promotion, the only way to get ahead was to put
his life on the line on every possible occasion.

His first war, in Burma, was in at the deep end – a Victorian
Vietnam without the helicopters, medical assistance, or jungle
equipment. It was redcoats against dacoits – lightly equipped
bandits, who knew the area intimately. Wolseley's regiment had

been obliged to endure a terrible march up the Irawaddy river, in phenomenal heat and humidity, and had been decimated by cholera. That Wolseley lived through the campaign was no less than incredible. He led an attack on the headquarters of a dacoit leader named Myat Toon, and on the first assault fell into a man-trap pit full of spikes. Clambering out, unhurt, he led a second assault and was hit in the thigh by a *jingall* bullet as big as a prune, which severed a vein. His comrade, Lieutenant G. C. Taylor, also hit, bled to death, but Wolseley was rescued by a medical orderly who staunched the bleeding in time. Evacuated down the Irawaddy by boat, he contracted cholera but, amazingly, recovered.

The Burma campaign was a walk through hell. Afterwards nothing looked quite the same again. The experience made Wolseley impervious to the horrors of war. Later, in the Crimea, where he lost an eye, he was serving as an assault pioneer when he saw a sapper's head blown off and the man's jawbone embedded in another soldier's face. Wolseley was close enough to be spattered with blood, but looked on impassively.

He became a general twenty years ahead of most of his contemporaries, and regarded himself as the Imperial fixer par excellence. The Queen found him an opinionated egotist, but Wolseley was popular with the public and the cabinet: the press had dubbed him 'our only general'. He was that *rara avis*, both a reformer and a chauvinist. Raised to the peerage by Gladstone, who needed a spokesman for army reform in the House of Lords, he detested Gladstone's foreign policy. Indeed, Wolseley came to despise Gladstone as a traitor who believed his office more important than the nation's honour. His most earnest hope was that the 'Grand Old Man' would be turned out ignominiously by the Conservatives, who he believed would deal with problems on more patriotic grounds.[16] Rumour had it that he had trained his dog to bark at the mention of Gladstone's name.

Wolseley was perfectly aware that Gladstone was desperate to abandon the Sudan. He considered this policy 'the worst of ignorant, cowardly folly'. He had no time for politicians in general, but had attained an ascendancy over the Secretary for War, Lord

Hartington, whom he admired as 'a patriot more than a party politician'. Hartington consulted him daily on every issue. Through the Secretary for War, Wolseley was able to manipulate the government and leapfrog over his nominal chief, the Duke of Cambridge.

Cambridge loathed Wolseley and the feeling was mutual. Wolseley thought Cambridge's ideas on war 'childish in the extreme'. 'He was at Alma and Inkerman [in the Crimean War],' Wolseley wrote, 'but he lost his head on both occasions . . . after Inkerman he went off his head altogether and retired . . . forever from all the excitement of war's alarms.'[17] Their enmity went back to Wolseley's attempt a few years earlier to make himself Commander-in-Chief of British forces in India. What the Duke particularly disliked was the fact that Wolseley ran his own mafia within the army – the notorious 'Ashanti Ring', which operated as an unofficial 'General Staff'. The 'Ring' was a secret society of special service officers, many of whom had worked together on the Ashanti campaign. Their loyalty was to Wolseley himself rather than to the Queen. Naturally, officers of the 'Old School' (Wolseley called them the '*very* old school') viewed it as a sinister development – such informal organizations threatened the status quo. The status quo was itself a network of informal relationships based on family ties between land-owning aristocrats.

The Duke of Cambridge had managed to keep Wolseley out of India. By manoeuvring him into an office job as Quartermaster General, he had clipped his wings. Without its leader in the field, the Ashanti Ring fared badly. Its most able strategist, Major General Sir George Colley, was defeated at Majuba Hill in the First Boer War, due to poor planning. He was killed in action. Evelyn Wood had taken over, and had been obliged to accept an ignominious surrender. This humiliating debacle was ultimately to be laid at the door of Wolseley, who had underestimated the Boers, predicting that they would not fight. The Ring itself had a rival whose power was growing in India. This was the 'Roberts Ring', a cabal centred round Major General Sir Fred Roberts, VC, the hero of Kandahar. Small and endearing as Wolseley was tall and incisive, 'Bobs'

Roberts was beloved both by the rank and file, and by the traditionalist element among the officer class.

Wolseley had fought hard to maintain his position. His triumph at Tel el-Kebir had put him back in the running, but he still had many enemies – including the Queen. What he needed was a decisive operation that would raise his profile once more, resurrect the glory of the Ashanti Ring, and establish his name as the great British general of the late Victorian era. He was one of the few men shrewd enough to understand that Gordon's idea of integrity entailed following his own inner voice rather than any rigid loyalty to Queen and country. He was also aware of Gordon's true feelings about the Sudan from the *Pall Mall Gazette* article, and they happened to dovetail closely with his own.

He knew Gordon would not succeed in evacuating the garrisons without a British military force. This much is clear from a memorandum he wrote Hartington on 8 February, before Gordon even reached Khartoum. He predicted that Gordon would be cut off and surrounded once he established himself in the capital. When this happened, he said, there would be a popular outcry in Britain. Gladstone would have no alternative but to send out a relief force of British troops to take over the Sudan. From that point the country would cease to be a Turco-Egyptian colony. It would have become part of the great and benevolent British Empire, of which Wolseley was an ardent supporter.

Any operation that involved Gordon would be sure to meet the approbation of Queen and public. What was more, a military action in the central Sudan would almost certainly be given to Wolseley. That the Gordon mission was a Wolseley conspiracy on one level or another is almost certain. It is not likely, though, that Gordon connived with him in the plot. It became fashionable after Lytton Strachey's biography of Gordon in *Eminent Victorians* (1918) to deprecate him as an ambitious charlatan. Gordon never denied that his ambition sometimes got him into hot water – he was aware of its power and sought constantly to balance it. On his return from China, for instance, he refused to be publicly received or thanked, and even destroyed his diaries of the Taiping campaign in case they should be regarded as vainglorious. But Gordon was no charlatan – his desire to help the oppressed and to make a difference in the world was entirely genuine. He had an intense sympathy with suffering wherever he found it. The love and empathy that flowed from him was sensed instinctively by many of those who knew him. Gordon was not a 'stage mystic' or a poseur eccentric, and felt no need to live up to some currently fashionable ideal of perfection. He had his rages, his off-days, his moods and humours. While Evelyn Wood had actually enjoyed killing as a young man, Gordon – a far more capable general – wrote that war was an inglorious round of 'murder, pillage and cruelty', in which the chief victims were usually women, children and old people. Many of those who despised Gordon – among them Gladstone – did so out of an unconscious realization that among all the paper heroes, Gordon was the 'real thing'.

Gordon believed that the people of the Sudan deserved to be liberated from the misgovernment they had been subjected to for sixty years. As he had told Stead, he thought he had introduced a new perspective to the country during his time as governor-general: justice, honesty, loyalty, sympathy and the development of a genuine community spirit. He had proved that it was possible for the Sudanese to live honest and honourable lives without suffering the oppression of the Turco-Egyptians.

He had also told Stead that the Mahdist rebellion had come about as a result of his resignation. This hint of egotism in Gordon's perspective may be explained by his years of exposure to Sudanese culture. The traditional Sudanese ethos exalts reputation rather than material wealth, and is thus a milieu in which a man can quickly become a legend in his own mind. His six years in the Sudan may have convinced him that he really was the saviour the people hungered for. Gordon had told Wolseley that once he reached the Sudan he would decide on the best course. The cabinet had made it clear that they would not tolerate any course but abandonment. Gordon had accepted this, but knew that the situation in the Sudan was too complex and fluid to lend itself to easy resolutions made in a London office. This does not mean that he made a conscious decision to ignore his orders. On the contrary, he went to great efforts to carry out the instructions he had been given. He was wise enough, however, not to become enslaved by consistency, knowing that in the fluid situation of war, rigidity could mean death. To Gordon, integrity did not mean kowtowing to the hierarchy of the British Empire, but remaining consistent with his own deepest intuitions.

That Wolseley genuinely admired Gordon is beyond doubt. 'He is infinitely superior to every man in our Cabinet,' he wrote, 'both as a patriot and a high-minded man of honour, and I hope our people may be able to distinguish between the dross of our party politicians and the honest pure metal of which he is made.'[18] Wilfred Scawen Blunt was one of many observers who later believed that Wolseley and Gordon had cooked up a plot between them to turn what was supposed to be a reporting mission into a conquest. It is more likely, though, that the plot was Wolseley's alone. He simply pointed Gordon in the right direction and let the inevitable unfold.

After the meeting with the cabinet representatives, Wolseley inquired whom Gordon would like as his assistant on the mission. Gordon requested Lieut. Colonel John Hammill Stewart, the officer whose 1883 report on the Sudan he had read. Stewart was fetched from his club, and met Gordon at the War Office that afternoon. He had not been expecting the job, and did not even have his uniform with him, but he agreed to leave on a moment's notice. Stewart was, as Baring put it, a man of 'shrewd common sense' who would 'act in some degree as a corrective to the impulsiveness of his wayward chief'.[19]

While Gordon had been reassuring everyone that the threat from the Mahdi was overrated, and that they would have no trouble in carrying out their task, Stewart kept his feet firmly planted on the ground. 'I will not disguise from you [that this] is a very dangerous mission,' he wrote to a friend. '. . . if we come to grief, it will be in a good cause.'[20]

The morning after Gordon arrived in Cairo, he donned his full-dress uniform and was marched off with Baring to an audience with the Khedive Tewfiq at the Isma'iliyya Palace. It was the thing he had least been looking forward to. Biting the bullet, though, he presented himself to the stubby, flabby-faced, dark-bearded young man in tarboosh, Stamboul coat, waistcoat and string tie. The setting was familiar. It was the same audience room in which he had been appointed governor-general of the Sudan by Tewfiq's father seven years earlier. Gordon apologized formally for having called Tewfiq 'a little snake' in the *Pall Mall Gazette* interview. Tewfiq, seated on the same divan Isma'il Pasha had sat on in 1877, smiled and accepted the apology. He then handed Gordon a firman appointing him governor-general of the Sudan for the second time.

There was no mention at the royal audience of Gordon having been sent on a 'reporting' mission. All talk of this had now vanished. Within twenty-four hours of his arriving in Egypt, Charles Gordon had once more been granted supreme authority in the Sudan. Baring was later berated by the press, the public and the government in London, for having deliberately 'waylaid' Gordon en route to the Sudan and 'perverted' the course of his mission. Significantly, it was Wolseley who shouted loudest, saying that Baring had brought Gordon to Cairo and had him appointed governor-general, 'a distinct departure from the terms on which he left England and the consequence [*sic*: presumably 'cause'] of all subsequent troubles'.[21]

Not only was this hypocritical, it was entirely untrue. Before Gordon had even crossed the English Channel on 18 January he had whipped off a memorandum to Granville, proposing that the Khedive should appoint him governor-general of the Sudan for the 'time needed to accomplish the evacuation'.[22] Granville had approved the request, and relayed it to Baring four days later. The following day, Baring had received a long screed from Gordon, recommending that authority in the Sudan should ultimately be handed back to the sheikhs and sultans who had held it before Mohammad 'Ali Pasha had invaded the country in 1820.

Baring wrote that it was something of a shock to him to find himself later accused of having modified Gordon's objectives without authority. As Gordon's letters show, he had already been tasked to evacuate the garrisons by the cabinet. The idea that he should be made governor-general had come from himself. Baring never believed that Gordon had had any intention of going to the Sudan to 'report' in the first place. 'No one who knew anything of [Gordon's] character,' he said, 'would have supposed for one moment that he would confine himself to mere reporting.'[23]

Wolseley's accusations against Baring for deflecting Gordon from his real mission were mere eyewash. The re-establishment of himself as governor-general had been on Gordon's agenda from the very beginning. As Baring commented, since Gordon was not a man who paid any attention to instructions, it mattered very little what instructions he was given anyway.[24] Gordon had arranged with Tewfiq that one of the sons of a previous Sultan of Darfur should return with him to become Darfur's new chief. This was in line with his idea of reinstating the authority of the traditional leaders who had reigned before Mohammad 'Ali Pasha's invasion. The prince, 'Abd ash-Shukkur – the new 'Sultan of Darfur', whose appointment Slatin would learn about too late – was the first such recruit. At the initial interview, though, the youth seemed unenthusiastic. Taken by surprise, he requested a few days to collect his family. 'Look,' Gordon said, 'you want a throne. Throne first, family afterwards.'[25]

After the audience with the Khedive, there was a conference between Gordon, Stewart, Wood, Baring and Nubar Pasha at Baring's house. Funds of 100,000 Egyptian pounds were granted. Later, Gordon paid his respects to General Sir Frederick Stephenson and to Sharif Pasha, the recently deposed Prime Minister. It was while passing through the reception room at Sharif's house that he noticed a tall Sudanese in a white *jallabiyya* and skullcap – a very black man with a striking face, 'like a death's head tenanted by a demon'. There was an unmistakable aura of gravitas around this man, and Gordon asked Sharif who he was. Sharif answered that he was Zubayr Pasha.

Gordon was fascinated. For a second their eyes met, and in that moment Gordon had an epiphany. He knew that Zubayr was the natural ruler of the Sudan. He knew it intuitively, exactly as 'Abdallahi had known a decade earlier that Zubayr was the Mahdi. They passed a few words, and Gordon decided that he must talk to him more extensively.

There was a major obstacle, however. Though they had not met previously, Zubayr reportedly held Gordon responsible for the death of his son, Sulayman. During his first term as governor-general, when Zubayr was already in exile in Egypt, Sulayman, officially a 'Bey' of the Egyptian government, had joined the slave-traders' rebellion in Darfur. He had attacked and wiped out a military post manned by 200 Jihadiyya in the Bahr al-Ghazal. Gordon, who had been elsewhere at the time, had dispatched his truculent Italian assistant Romolo Gessi to hunt him down. Gessi had captured Sulayman and had him tried, condemned and shot. Gordon suspected that Zubayr had incited Sulayman's revolt, and had confiscated Zubayr's property in the Sudan.

Gordon believed that Zubayr blamed him for the death of his son. One of the many telegrams he had fired off on his way to Cairo was a suggestion that Zubayr should be exiled to Cyprus, out of harm's way. Baring had rejected this. Cyprus was part of the Ottoman Empire, and the British had no authority to make Zubayr stay there.

There can be no doubt that Gordon's epiphany was right. If any man could challenge the Mahdi for control of the Sudan, it was Zubayr. Ten years earlier, even the *feki* 'Abdallahi had sensed his power. As a general and administrator he far outshone anyone else in the Khedive's camp. What was more, he was a hero who had fought bravely for the Ottomans in the Turco-Russian war, and had been wounded three times. The chance encounter had convinced Gordon that their meeting was pre-ordained.

Back at Wood's house, Gordon launched straight into a memorandum explaining why Zubayr ought to go with him to the Sudan.

He wrote that many of the Mahdi's chiefs had once worked for Zubayr and were still loyal to him. He felt instinctively that Zubayr would be accepted by all sides and would finish the Mahdi in a matter of months. It all seemed to fit into place perfectly, and came out in a single rush, ending on a note that must have sounded bizarre to men like Baring: 'I would willingly take . . . Zubayr up with me, if after an interview with Sir E. Baring and Nubar Pasha, they felt the mystic feeling I could trust him, and which mystic feeling I had tonight when I met him at Sharif Pasha's house . . . I cannot exactly say why I feel towards him thus, and I feel sure that his going would settle the Sudan affair.'[26]

That they met after lunch the next day at Baring's house is certain: what actually happened at the meeting is not clear. Zubayr strode in scowling, and when Gordon offered his hand, Zubayr placed his own behind his back. According to one observer, a momentary expression of fury crossed Gordon's face. They sat down facing each other on the divan, with their interpreter between them. Around them, watching with interest, were Baring, Wood, Nubar Pasha, Watson, Stewart, and Gordon's old deputy from Khartoum, the ginger-bearded German Giegler Pasha, now living in Cairo. According to their own testimonies, there were also two ADCs, Lieutenant Eddie Stuart-Wortley, Royal Rifles, Wood's Military Secretary, and Captain Reginald Wingate, Royal Artillery – a fluent Arabic speaker. An English secretary, Samuel Davies, took shorthand notes.

Gordon started by asking Zubayr what complaints he had. Zubayr asked why Gordon had confiscated his property back in 1879. Gordon replied that it was because a letter had been found in his son's belongings, implicating him in the slave-traders' revolt. Zubayr denied that there had been any such letter. Soon the two men were raging at each other.

It was quickly clear that Zubayr was consumed with grief over the death of his son. Sulayman, he claimed, had been only sixteen years old, and, as a Bey in Egyptian service, had been under Gordon's protection. 'He was as your son,' he told Gordon, 'but you killed my son whom I entrusted to you!'[27]

'Well, well,' Gordon is supposed to have answered. 'Then I killed my own son. There is an end of it.'[28]

Zubayr continually challenged Gordon to produce the letter that implicated him. Stuart-Wortley (in Wingate's version it was Wingate) was sent to the government archives for the court files, but the letter could not be found. In fact it never was found. Baring claimed to have seen a copy of it years later, but even he was not convinced that the document he saw was genuine. It is quite possible that the letter never existed in the first place, which would explain Gordon's apparent feeling of guilt in regard to Zubayr.

According to the official version, the meeting ended inconclusively on this note. Reginald Wingate, however, recorded in his diary that when the letter could not be found, Gordon apologized. Zubayr then shook hands and told Gordon he was 'his slave for life'. (Baring, though, does not mention Wingate in his list of those present.) The Baron de Kusel, a Liverpool-born merchant, now head of the Egyptian Customs Service, who spoke to Zubayr a few days later, claimed that the former slave-trader told him he no longer held Gordon responsible for the death of his son.

Still, when Zubayr finally left, only Gordon and Baring were in favour of his being sent to the Sudan. As a realist, Baring knew that if Gordon was to pull out the garrisons successfully, he would need to establish some sort of authority. Such an authority could only be secured by strong men like Zubayr. Both Wood and Watson had been warned by Gordon's blind scribe, Tuhami, that if Gordon and Zubayr left for the Sudan together, only one of them would reach Khartoum alive. The tradition of *tha'r* – the vendetta – is sacred among Sudanese tribes and, according to Tuhami, Zubayr would have been duty bound to kill Gordon in revenge for the death of Sulayman. How far Zubayr really held Gordon responsible, though, is open to question. Even in the recorded discussion, he seems only to have blamed Gordon for allowing Sulayman to be executed while under his protection. The fact is that it was Gessi rather than Gordon who was directly accountable for Sulayman's death.

On the other hand, Baring had already been prevented by the anti-slavery lobby from using Zubayr in Suakin with Valentine Baker. He doubted whether Granville would allow it. He felt that Gordon himself was motivated by a feeling of guilt, and could not forget that, only days before, Gordon had asked him to deport Zubayr to Cyprus.

Baring did not place much faith in mystical feelings. While Gordon used intuition as a tool, Baring followed the more prosaic warrior's logic of cause and effect. The way he saw it was that Gordon had a tendency to act on 'wild impulses'. Though he did not rule out the idea of using Zubayr in future, he decided to let it mature a little in Gordon's head. He told Gordon that he had decided against employing Zubayr Pasha. Gordon was furious, and at his farewell dinner with Sir Evelyn Wood that evening remained silent and aloof. Afterwards, Eddie Stuart-Wortley helped Gordon pack his bags. He had very little luggage, but among it Stuart-Wortley was surprised to see a tin uniform-case containing the full-dress uniform Gordon had worn for his audience with the Khedive.

'But General,' Stuart-Wortley said, 'why are you taking this up to Khartoum?'

'Because, my dear boy,' Gordon answered, 'when the British army arrives in Khartoum to relieve me, I wish to receive it properly dressed.'[29]

Afterwards, Gordon and Stewart were escorted to Bulaq station on the Nile, where they met the fledgling Sultan of Darfur, 'Abd ash-Shukkur. The prince had been told to bring one or two people with him, but had arrived with an entourage of twenty-three, including wives, relatives and servants, and mountains of baggage. (Stewart's claim that he was accompanied by twenty-three *wives* is unlikely to be true: Muslims are allowed a maximum of four wives.) Gordon had to arrange for more carriages to be added to the special train so that they would not be left behind. At the last moment 'Abd ash-Shukkur discovered that he had lost the special gold-lamé gala uniform presented to him by the Khedive for his glorious arrival in Darfur, complete with 'the largest decoration that could be found'. There was a furore on the platform until it was retrieved. When the train shunted off into the darkness at 2200 hours, it carried not only Gordon, Stewart and 'Abd ash-Shukkur, but also Major General Sir Gerald Graham, who would accompany Gordon as far as Korosko, forty miles north of the Sudanese border.

After watching the train go, Baring returned to his house and telegraphed Granville that Gordon was safely on his way to the Sudan. The consul-general had been suffering from a throat infection for the past few days, and felt that it had affected his judgement. Gordon's strategy seemed sound enough, but at close quarters Baring had found the man himself even more odd than he remembered. 'However,' he wrote, 'the die was cast. A comet of no common magnitude had been launched on the political firmament of the Sudan. It was difficult to predict its course. It now only remained for me to do my best to help General Gordon, and to trust in the shrewd common sense of his companion, Colonel Stewart.'[30]

The next morning the train arrived in Asyut, where Gordon's party transferred to a Thomas Cook Nile steamer. 'Abd ash-Shukkur, gorgeously turned out in his gala uniform and large decoration, immediately acquired the main deck cabin. He was ignominiously expelled by Gordon, who was, after all, governor-general. Afterwards, the prince took to quaffing vast quantities of gin, in a sulk. He was virtually poured out of the steamer at Aswan, saying that he would accompany Gordon no farther. It was a great relief to Gordon and his party. 'Abd ash-Shukkur never did reach Darfur. He got as far as Dongola in the northern Sudan, remained there a few months, then returned to Cairo for ever.

They reached Korosko on 1 February, where they were met by a squad of 'Ababda camel-men who were to escort them across the Nubian desert to Abu Hamed. The caravan was led by two sons of the governor of Berber, Hussain Khalifa, both carrying Beja swords and elephant-hide shields, as well as old double-barrelled flintlock pistols.

Before he left, Gordon presented Graham with a silver-plated *kurbash* – a hippo-hide whip much beloved of the Bashi-Bazuks. Gordon was taking with him no arms, but accepted Graham's white umbrella instead, having lost his own. He told Graham that he was giving him the whip as a symbol of the end of the 'age of the *kurbash*' in the Sudan. Graham climbed a ridge and with field-glasses watched Gordon's party getting smaller until it merged with the desert, completely out of sight. It was the last he was ever to see of his old friend.

7

Two weeks later, in the course of a leisurely voyage back to Cairo on a steamer, Graham received a message informing him that Valentine Baker had been routed by 'Osman Digna at et-Teb. Sinkat had fallen and Suakin was threatened. Graham had been appointed commander of a British expeditionary force being sent to relieve Tokar in the eastern Sudan.

Baker's defeat created a huge outcry in Britain. The Conservative opposition lost no time in using the situation in the eastern Sudan as ammunition against the Liberal government. At the War Office both Wolseley and the Duke of Cambridge pushed for a punitive expedition. Egged on by the press, cabinet members Dilke and Hartington proposed that their suggestion should be at least debated. Gladstone, fighting a desperate rearguard action, argued that sending in British troops would alter the whole basis of their involvement in the Sudan. In Cairo, Baring was alarmed that public opinion might push the Prime Minister into assuming more responsibility than he could cope with. He told Granville that he was entirely opposed to sending troops to Suakin. 'I trust,' he wrote, 'that in spite of the panic that appears to prevail in London, Her Majesty's Government will not change any of the main points of their policy.'[31]

This time Baring was altogether outgunned. On 12 February the Queen herself added her ordnance, insisting that Gladstone take action. Her opinion was unequivocal. 'The Queen *trusts* Lord

Wolseley's plan will be considered,' she wrote, 'and our whole position remembered . . . we must not let this fine and fruitful country [the Sudan], with its peaceful inhabitants, be left a prey to murder and rapine, and utter confusion. It must be a disgrace to the British name, and the country will not stand it.'[32]

The news of the fall of Sinkat, and Tewfiq Bey's heroic attempt to break out, was received the same day. It caused a swell of indignation. Granville, seeing the way the wind was blowing, thought it better not to mention Baring's reservations. After a heated debate the fateful decision was made. Gladstone had lost. British troops would be sent to the Sudan after all. 'You might as well try to stop a mule in a snaffle-bridle,' Granville informed Baring ruefully, 'as check the feeling here on the subject.'[33] The Queen was delighted that the government had at last shown some spirit. 'May it not be too late to save other lives!' she wrote to Gladstone. 'The fall of Sinkat is terrible!'[34]

Orders were relayed to Lieut. General Sir Frederick Stephenson, the sixty-three-year-old GOC, British Army of Occupation in Egypt. He was to send a force selected from his seven-thousand-strong Cairo garrison to relieve Tokar. Rear Admiral Billy Hewett, whose tiny troop of Marines and bluejackets were still holding Suakin, was told to expect a British fighting force of two infantry brigades and one cavalry brigade within a week. In addition to Stephenson's contingent, part of the force was to come directly from Britain, and part from Aden, en route from India.

When Gerald Graham arrived back in Cairo on 15 February, he found that Stephenson was already in the process of dispatching the spearhead unit, the 1st Battalion, the Black Watch. They were shortly to be followed by the 1st Gordon Highlanders, the 3rd King's Royal Rifles, the 19th Hussars, a composite Mounted Infantry unit, the 26th Field Company, Royal Engineers, and a camel-mounted Royal Artillery battery.

The British end of the expedition had been organized with all the efficiency Adjutant General Wolseley could muster. His Confidential Mobilization Committee had met in London before Graham had even learned he had been appointed commander.

The committee arranged for the dispatch of ammunition, stores, equipment, clothing, boots, tents, artillery, camels, horses and field hospitals with medical staff. There were three months' rations for six thousand men, including 180,000 lb of preserved meat. The Royal Navy assigned two condenser-ships to the Red Sea so that the force would never be short of water.

Gerald Graham landed at Suakin on 22 February and was met by acting consul in Jeddah Augustus Wylde, who informed him that he was too late. Tokar had already been taken by 'Osman Digna. This was a blow. Graham's troops had preceded him and were about to land at Trinkitat, with full logistic support. Billy Hewett, wiring the news of Tokar's fall to Cairo, suggested that they should still go for it, as a decisive victory would 'restore order among the local tribes'. Stephenson agreed, and wired Lord Hartington that Graham should be ordered to continue. Baring's was the only dissenting voice. He telegraphed Granville that this 'useless effusion of blood' should be stopped. Charles Gordon, asked his opinion, wired from the Sudan that no action against Tokar would be of any advantage to him. His object was to hand the country back to its hereditary chiefs. There had already been plenty of blood-lettings, and another one would achieve nothing.

Graham himself was raring to go, and though Baring dis-approved, he understood the political logic of the situation. 'To have landed a force at Trinkitat,' he wrote, 'and then have brought it away without achieving anything whatever, would have rendered the Government ridiculous, and would have exposed them to further attacks in Parliament.'[35] By 0935 hours on 26 February 1884, Gerald Graham had concentrated 3,970 soldiers and bluejackets at the beach-head at Trinkitat. It was the first all-British fighting force ever landed in the Sudan.

8

For Graham and his staff, it was as much about military honour as political expediency. The army that had been slaughtered here three weeks earlier had been Egyptian, but its officers and its commander had been British. Queen Victoria had understood this as well as anyone when she had pointed out to Gladstone that both Hicks's and Baker's expeditions had been led by Englishmen. 'A blow must be struck,' she had written, 'or we shall never be able to convince the Mohammadans [*sic*] that they have not beaten us.'[36]

Graham believed he was the right man to strike that blow. A fifty-three-year-old blond giant of a man, six foot six, broad-shouldered and massive, he was everyone's idea of what the Victorian soldier should be – big, brave, brawny and unimaginative. The son of a Cumberland doctor, he was married to the widow of a clergyman and had six children. Despite his VC, Graham had actually been on the unemployed list when Garnet Wolseley had picked him to command the 2nd Infantry Brigade of the 1st Division at Tel el-Kebir, and to lead the advance from Isma'iliyya.

Graham had distinguished himself twice in the battle against 'Arabi Pasha. The first was when his men had defeated an Egyptian force outnumbering them five to one. The second was at Tel el-Kebir itself, when they had advanced through withering fire to capture 'Arabi's trenches. Graham had been mentioned in dispatches five times, awarded a knighthood, and officially thanked by both Houses of Parliament. Wolseley had caused some mirth among Graham's messmates by referring to him as having 'the heart of a lion and the modesty of a young girl' – a description that did not sit comfortably on the giant bruiser's frame.

Valentine Baker was very much in evidence at Graham's side. Baring had been all for having him sent back to Cairo, but Burnaby had intervened, persuading the British agent that his defeat had been 'bad luck'. 'We all feel for him, and like him so much,'

Burnaby had written. Baring had relented and appointed him Intelligence Officer.

It brought a lump to Baker's throat to see his old regiment, the 10th Hussars, among the cavalry contingent. They had not been part of Stephenson's army in Egypt, but had been diverted on their way home from India. They were only three hundred strong, and at Suakin had taken over the mounts of Baker's gendarmerie. Later, Baker sent their CO, Lieut. Colonel Edward Wood, a proprietorial note saying that he hoped to see them in action. Burnaby himself, still armed with his shotgun and a pouchful of boar-shot, was riding with the Mounted Infantry.

Transport ships clustered in the still seas around Trinkitat on the morning of 26 February – *Hecla*, *Dryad*, *Briton*, and Billy Hewett's flagship, *Euryalus*, *Orontes*, *Teddington*, *Jumna*, the fast gunboat *Sphinx*. The condenser-ships *Tor* and *Teb al-Bahr* were also in evidence, producing twelve thousand gallons of drinking water per day. British Tommies stripped to their shirt-sleeves to help the bluejackets unload the endless stream of stores. The Black Watch and the Royal Irish Fusiliers accompanied patrols of the 19th Hussars and a camel-mounted artillery battery, in securing the country as far as Fort Baker. The fort was refurbished with barbed-wire entanglements and protected by a Krupp gun.

Two of Wolseley's Ashanti Ring, sent from Britain, disembarked at Trinkitat from the Egyptian steamer *Damanhour* on 27 February. They were Brigadier Sir Redvers Buller, VC, King's Royal Rifle Corps, and Brigadier Herbert Stewart, 3rd Dragoon Guards. Forty-five-year-old Buller was a beefy man with virtually no neck, and an impassive manner that concealed a savage temperament. As a child he had been irretrievably traumatized by the sudden collapse of his mother on a railway platform. She had suffered a massive haemorrhage, and could not be moved. Buller had looked after her for two days on a bench at the station before she died in his arms.

Known in his youth for his uncontrollable rages, Buller had been expelled from Eton, and almost expelled from Harrow. Since then, he had learned to keep his anger hidden under a poker face, so perfectly that it hardly ever showed ... until he was on the battlefield, when it emerged in a berserk appetite for killing 'savages'. Letters written to his wife after battle demonstrate that combat brought him relief from a lust for which he felt shame. 'Noticed' by Garnet Wolseley during the Red River Campaign in Canada in 1861, he passed through Staff College and served as Wolseley's Intelligence Officer during the Ashanti war. He had won his Victoria Cross in 1879 in the Kaffir war in South Africa.

Buller led by the force of his physical presence, but was at his best only under an avuncular authority like Wolseley's. Given lone command he collapsed with indecision. He had a poor grasp of strategy, and little competence in logistics and administration. He was also an alcoholic. Partial to rich food and endless magnums of Veuve-Clicquot, he was essentially a loud-mouthed but inarticulate tough who might have made a competent sergeant, but should never have been promoted to high command. In Graham's show, Buller was given charge of the 1st Infantry Brigade, which had sailed with him from Britain. He was also to be Graham's second-in-command.

Buller had always been jealous of Herbert Stewart, who was in many ways his opposite. 'Stewart [is] much the better man of the two all round,' Wolseley wrote, 'though Buller has some excellent military qualities. Buller never loses a chance of crabbing Stewart's ability and making out that he [is] constantly wrong.'[37] Wolseley had met Stewart by chance on the battlefield in South Africa during the Kaffir war, and, charmed by his personality, had appointed him his military secretary. The son of a Hampshire clergyman, educated at Winchester, Stewart had been gazetted with the 37th Foot in India in 1863. After a decade of service with the infantry, he returned to Britain to attend Staff College and transferred to the cavalry. He served with the 3rd Dragoon Guards in the Zulu war in South Africa, and later, in the First Boer War, was Chief of Staff under Wolseley's favourite major-general, Sir George Colley. During the war against 'Arabi Pasha in 1882 he was on the staff of the cavalry division, and personally led the advance on Cairo. For his brilliant action in capturing the city and the citadel, he was awarded the CB, made a brevet-colonel, and appointed ADC to the Queen. 'It is a comfort to have such a man to work with,' Wolseley wrote of him. 'He is always cheery, always prepared to take on any job no matter how unpleasant it may be, and the very best staff officer all round I have known since poor old Colley died . . .'[38] Stewart was appointed commander of the Cavalry Brigade, most of which had come with him from Britain.

En route to Suakin, Graham had worked out his plan. His instructions from Stephenson were to concentrate at Trinkitat and advance on Tokar. He was to evacuate the Tokar garrison and escort the Egyptian troops back to Suakin. At Gordon's request, he was to give 'Osman Digna a chance to disperse his army voluntarily, and to ask the Beja sheikhs to confer with Gordon at Khartoum. He had brought with him a proclamation to that effect. When the dervishes opened fire on the officer trying to carry it to them, under a white flag, he had it nailed to a post beyond Fort Baker.

Graham had decided to stick to the square formation. It had become outdated in conventional wars, due to the increased fire-power of machine-guns and quick-firing rifles, but it still had its advocates. Graham thought it useful when a relatively small body of men had to advance protecting a large amount of equipment. It was the best formation for neutralizing the effects of a shock attack – the favourite stratagem of 'Osman Digna's 'fuzzies'.

In any case, Graham's men were not reluctant Egyptian conscripts but professional British soldiers, who were, in Baring's words, 'like greyhounds straining at the leash'.[39] They were among the toughest and most resolute fighting men in the world, who had saved the reputations of their amateurish and frequently incompetent com-manders countless times. After Waterloo, Napoleon had called them 'lions led by sheep'. Wilfred Scawen Blunt's view of them was typical of the disparaging way they were regarded by the civilian upper classes in their own country: 'What are they?' he wrote. 'A mongrel scum of thieves from Whitechapel and Seven Oaks . . . without beliefs, without traditions, without other principles of action than just to get their promotion and have a little fun.'[40]

This was not only unfair, it was also incorrect. Although some were illiterate, and many under age, there were no deserters or convicted felons among them – men of bad character were excluded from the ranks. Most came from the unskilled labour class, the majority from large cities, and most were unmarried. About 80 per cent had joined the army as a last resort, because of unemployment. Others were on the run from a bad marriage, or wanted to escape from a life of manual drudgery. A few joined for glamour and excitement, and there were a handful of 'gentlemen' in the ranks, who had enlisted because of hiccups in their career. It was not the case, though, that the army accepted any applicant uncritically, since as many as 50 per cent of volunteers were rejected. Contrary to popular myth, too, the vast majority of soldiers in the British army at this time were Englishmen: only 8 per cent were Scottish and 13 per cent Irish.

Daily Telegraph correspondent Bennet Burleigh, a man of no mean experience who had fought with the Confederate army in the American Civil War, was perceptive enough to disagree with the popular perception of the British Tommy. While soldiers under the rank of lieutenant were rarely accorded much respect in Victorian society, he wrote, they laboured and fought with discipline and pride. Their reward was often 'death and a nameless grave in a strange land . . . The latter fate befell a good many before we left the Sudan.'[41] Blunt's attitude, though, was not shared by their officers. British officers might have been poorly trained in battle tactics, but they were often loved by their men. The mutual affection between officers and other ranks manifested itself frequently during the Sudan campaign, when they repeatedly risked their own lives for each other.

Enlisted men in English, Scottish and Irish regiments had all undergone at least twelve weeks' training at their depots. The course included drill, physical training and an eight-day musketry course, in which they practised firing deliberate and rapid volleys and independent fire. They had also been trained in infantry tactics, attack and defence, patrol and reconnaissance, bayonet fighting, and route-marches in fighting order of up to sixteen miles.

While Baker's gendarmes had been equipped with the Remington – a US-made weapon excellent in its own way – the British infantry had state-of-the-art Martini-Henry breech-loaders. This weapon was a milestone in the history of the rifle, combining Alexander Henry's seven-groove barrel design with the Austrian von Martini's breech mechanism. The Martini was accurate up to a thousand yards, and at 8 lb 12 oz was not a heavy weapon. Fitted with a bayonet it became a lethal pike almost six feet long. Among the weapon's drawbacks were its smoky ammunition, its vicious recoil, and its proneness to jams and stoppages in dusty conditions. It fired a .45 calibre slug with a brass cartridge case that was ejected by a lever under the trigger. The lever also cocked the striker for the next shot, opening the breech for a round to be fed in by hand. British infantrymen could fire a round every five seconds, and each man in Graham's force carried a hundred rounds. Many of the soldiers, warned about the shock tactics of the 'fuzzies', had filed the heads off their cartridges, creating a 'dum-dum' round – a practice imported from India. It flattened out on impact, making a huge entry-wound, with more effective stopping power. It was barbaric, but useful against attackers whose momentum and morale would carry them forward despite being wounded.

Cavalry training took longer than that of the infantry. Over a period of six months they underwent about 120 hours of riding drill. Junior officers were trained alongside the enlisted recruits. 'Mounting and dismounting from a barebacked horse, at the trot or canter,' wrote one subaltern, 'jumping a high bar without stirrups or even saddle, sometimes with hands clasped behind one's back; jogging at a fast trot with nothing but the horse's hide between your knees, brought their inevitable share of mishaps.' They were also trained in stablework, packing, saddling, fencing, and the use of arms on horseback. They received the same musketry course as the infantry, though the acceptable standard of shooting was lower.

The artillerymen were among the most professional soldiers in the British army. They had drilled with their field-guns for at least 150 hours in practice, handling shells, mounting and dismounting, laying, aiming and constructing gun-pits. Every gun was worked by two NCOs and eight privates, and commanded by the senior NCO, who was designated 'No. 1'. Their primary role was to initiate the attack by silencing enemy guns. Artillerymen were equipped with the Martini-Henry carbine – a short version of the Martini rifle – and trained to engage the enemy in defence of their guns at two hundred yards. At et-Teb, some of the gunners would be obliged to engage the enemy at much closer quarters, with much less effective weapons. Although Graham's Scottish battery, commanded by Major Frank Lloyd, had been ordered to take over Baker's Egyptian camel-mounted Krupps, Lloyd had begged eight seven-pounder naval guns instead. These could toss a seven-pound high-explosive shell three thousand yards.

Graham had three Gatlings and three Gardners. These machine-guns were manned by Rear Admiral Billy Hewett's bluejackets, who regarded their guns with the same reverence that Caesar's Praetorian Guard had reserved for their spears. The sailors, said Bennet Burleigh, 'patted and fondled these dread weapons of war as if they had been living things'.[42] The Gardner was a multi-barrelled volley-firing gun with multiple breeches and bolts, operated manually by crank-handles. Its .45 calibre ammunition was fed in from hoppers. The Gardner's big fault was that it was mounted on a fixed carriage, and could not be easily traversed. It had a range of two to three thousand yards, but it was eight hundred pounds of solid brass, and likely to overheat and jam in Sudanese temperatures. The .45 calibre Gatling also worked on a crank-handle, though on a different system – with a single bolt and breech around which the several barrels revolved in turn. It was also prone to stoppages in hot and dusty conditions. The machine-guns were not carried on mules or camels, but manhandled forward fully assembled by their bluejacket crews.

On the night of 28 February, Graham's force bivouacked at Fort Baker. At 2000 hours that night the men were roused by the sound of tramping feet and rose to witness the arrival of the 1st Battalion, the York & Lancaster Regiment. They had been in Aden on their way back to Blighty after a thirteen-year tour in India, and had been diverted to Trinkitat on *Serapis* to join the fray. They were still dressed in their tropical khaki drill and wore the outdated white pouch equipment of the Indian army, with their bedrolls slung across their shoulders. The rest of the force cheered as they marched in.

In his proclamation, Graham had given 'Osman until first light to disperse his troops. The Beja, though, were well entrenched in earthworks at et-Teb wells, and were not going anywhere. They had already defeated two expeditions sent against them, and had no reason to suppose this occasion would be any different. They had three thousand Remingtons and Baker's Krupps and Norden-feldts. The British bivouac was not pleasant. There was a wan new moon, and the sky was overcast. It drizzled at intervals in the night, and just before dawn there was a royal downpour. The men were glad to get up when the buglers sounded reveille at 0500 hours.

9

Just before nine o'clock on the morning of 29 February, dervish scouts saw Graham's square, already formed, emerging steadily out of the haze to their south. At first it looked unreal, like a mirage, trembling on the edge of their vision. To the front and flanks were fast-moving shadows – mounted vedettes of the 10th and 19th Hussars, riding easily in loose troops, their mounts raising a pall of pepper-coloured dust.

The dervishes opened fire with their Remingtons, but the enemy were still out of range. This new lot of 'Turks' looked at a distance very little different from the others they had sent packing. Like them, they would not stand up to the sheer ferocity of a Beja charge. Closer up, though, the tribesmen noticed that the troops in the front rank of the square wore green-coloured skirts instead of trousers, grey tunics instead of white, and bucket-like white helmets instead of tarbooshes. They also moved in a jaunty, loose-limbed fashion, almost as if they were enjoying themselves, carrying

1. Mohammad Ahmad, the Sudanese holy man who declared himself Islam's Mahdi or 'Expected Guide' in 1881. His Jihad against the Turco-Egyptians led to the establishment of the Sudan as the first independent Islamic state.

2. Lieut. General William Hicks. A British officer working for the Khedive of Egypt, Hicks led an 11,000-strong column into the wastes of Kordofan to recapture the city of el-Obeid from the Mahdi. Ambushed by the dervishes at Shaykan, he was killed and his column obliterated.

3. Khartoum, 1885. Standing at the point where the Blue and White Niles meet, Khartoum became important in the 1840s as the main entrepôt of the ivory trade. Most government buildings, as seen here, stood on the Blue Nile waterfront.

4. The Khedive Tewfiq, ruler of Egypt and the Sudan. Deposed by Colonel 'Arabi Pasha, he was restored to the throne by the British in 1882. The real power, though, lay in the hands of the British Agent and Consul-General, Sir Evelyn Baring.

5. Sir Evelyn Baring (later Lord Cromer). The de facto power in Egypt for more than twenty-five years, Baring was often regarded as a caricature British bureaucrat. In fact, he was a conscientious, honest and straightforward man whose ambition was to restore to Egypt a viable economy.

6. Suakin, the Sudan's main Red Sea port, stood on an island about one kilometre from the shore. Joined by a caravan route to the Nile at Berber, it became the base for all British operations in the eastern Sudan.

7. Lieut. General Valentine Baker. Once colonel of the crack 10th Hussars, Baker was cashiered from the British army in disgrace over a sex-scandal. Appointed commander of the Egyptian Gendarmerie by the Khedive, he led Egyptian forces against the Beja in the first disastrous battle of et-Teb in 1884.

8. Lieut. General Sir Gerald Graham, VC. Graham, a close friend of Charles Gordon, led British expeditions against the Beja 'fuzzy-wuzzies' in 1884 and 1885. Though his engagements were successful, they achieved no strategic goals.

9. Trinkitat Island, 30 January 1884. Valentine Baker lands his force of Egyptian Gendarmerie, Sudanese Jihadiyya and irregulars in a vain attempt to relieve the Egyptian garrison at Tokar and restore his good name.

10. Captain Arthur Wilson, R.N. Fighting with the Naval Brigade at the second battle of et-Teb, Wilson defends a gun-crew single-handed, using his fists when his sword is smashed. He is later awarded the VC.

11. The second battle of et-Teb, February 1884. In this first clash between British soldiers and 'fuzzy-wuzzy' Beja warriors, the British come off best. Both sides, however, acquire a lasting admiration for their opponents.

12. 'Osman Digna, dressed Haddendowa style. Although universally disliked, 'Osman was the most successful guerrilla fighter of all the Mahdist leaders. The great survivor of the campaigns, he was captured in 1900 but died a free man in 1926.

13. Tombs at et-Teb. After the second battle of et-Teb in February 1884, the Black Watch are given the task of burying the British dead. They also inter the fallen from Baker's force whose corpses have lain on the field since early January.

14. The battle of Tamaai, Eastern Sudan, 13 May 1884. Graham's 2 Brigade square is broken when the Black Watch launch an impromptu attack. Beja warriors pour into the gap, forcing the British into a fighting retreat and inflicting heavy casualties.

15. Burning 'Osman Digna's camp at Tamaai, 13 May 1884. By the time Graham's brigades arrive, the enemy has fled.

16. Lieut. General Lord Garnet Wolseley, 1884. Snobbish, opinionated and conceited, he was also a gifted manipulator, a brilliant innovator, and a soldier's soldier who had seen action many times. The Khartoum affair may have begun as a conspiracy hatched by Wolseley to force Gladstone's government to occupy the Sudan.

17. Major General Charles Gordon. Gordon was in a sense a mystic masquerading as a soldier. An individualist ready to die for his principles, he often chose to follow his inner voice rather than the orders of his political masters.

18. Major (later Field Marshal Lord) Herbert Kitchener enters Dongola disguised as an Arab. One of the most brilliant intelligence officers of his era, Kitchener spends the winter of 1884–5 criss-crossing the Sudan by camel with his guard of 'Ababda Bedouin, paving the way for the Gordon Relief Expedition.

19. Major General Sir Redvers Buller, VC. Buller was a savage fighter but an indecisive leader. One of Wolseley's favoured 'Ashanti Ring', he was Chief of Staff on the Gordon Relief Expedition but abetted its defeat by failing to provide enough camels for the advance.

20. Major General Sir Herbert Stewart. Wolseley's favourite officer, and another of the 'Ashanti Ring', Stewart was given command of the Camel Corps in the Gordon Relief Expedition. He commanded the British square at Abu Klea with cool professionalism, but was mortally wounded the following day at Abu Kru.

21. The Desert Column under Herbert Stewart sets off from Korti on 30 December 1884. Its objective is to march 176 miles across the Sudan's Bayuda desert on camels and horses, take Metemma, and rendezvous with Gordon's steamers sent down from Khartoum.

their rifles at the shoulder with bayonets fixed, marching to the strange skirling wail of pipes. These were the men of the 1st Battalion, the Gordon Highlanders – the Beja's first ever sight of British infantry.

At 0930 hours the naval guns on the gunboat *Sphinx*, in Trinkitat harbour, cracked out four shots. The shells burned air and dropped with flat thuds, a mile short of the dervish position. They fell so near the cavalry vedettes that the gunners were ordered to cease fire. The dervish scouts began to pull back, staying about twelve hundred yards in front of the cavalry screen. Suddenly the Mounted Infantry, Fred Burnaby among them, spurred their horses from behind and made a dash at the enemy, hoping to frighten them off. The dash had no apparent effect. The Beja stood their ground and showed every inclination to fight. The Mounted Infantry retired, joining the rest of the Cavalry Brigade under Herbert Stewart, nine hundred yards behind the square.

The Hussars continued to probe ahead. This was their speciality – they were light cavalry trained for a reconnaissance role, expert in eluding enemy fire. Sergeant Danby and three troopers of the 10th Hussars rode right up to the enemy position at et-Teb, finding trenches full of armed dervishes and Krupp guns. 'They commenced heavy fire on my . . . section, but were not clever enough to hit us,' Danby remembered. 'We moved a bit too fast for them. My troop soon joined us in support. We again advanced under their fire, not attempting to return it. At last we arrived on the right flank of their fort, right under the mouth of their guns, while the remainder of our army advanced in square.'[43] Within the square, Valentine Baker was helping direct the advance, making sure Graham avoided scrub-covered and broken ground that might conceal enemy ambush parties. Correspondent Bennet Burleigh, with another group of cavalry scouts, came across grisly mementoes of Baker's last encounter with the dervishes. 'The bodies studded the route to et-Teb,' he wrote, 'lying about in hundreds, polluting the air. Swarms of lazy carrion birds flew off at our approach . . .'[44] 'Most of the victims appeared to have fallen on their faces, as if they were speared or cut down from behind . . . of some only the bare skeletons were left, but for the most part the remains were unattacked by the vultures and wild beasts . . . Indignities of which one cannot write had been perpetrated on the dead by their ruthless slayers . . .'[45]

Both Baker and Moncrieff had advanced directly up the main track from Trinkitat to et-Teb. 'Osman Digna had expected this third force to do the same. His troops had set up their captured Krupps to fire directly down the track. They had also built a horseshoe-shaped pit and parapet around the wells, enclosing a derelict sugar factory, the mud-brick fort, and protecting, to the rear, a village of a few dozen palmetto-fibre huts. The defences were manned by six thousand Beja tribesmen from seven different tribes or sub-tribes – the Hassanab, Arteiga, Jemilab, Hendawa, Haddendowa, Ashrab and Demilab. Thanks perhaps to Baker's advice, Graham decided to outflank the enemy position and attack from the rear. This move took the dervishes by surprise. Eight hundred yards behind Danby's troop, Bennet Burleigh could clearly see the fort with its two guns, and the puffs of smoke as the dervishes popped off rounds at the Hussars.

Graham ordered the square to halt. The Hussars had performed their task perfectly, pinpointing the enemy positions. The British troops sat down, indifferent to the presence of the enemy a few hundred yards away. After a short breather, the buglers called 'attention'. The men stood up and began to move north again. 'As soon as the enemy saw us moving,' Burleigh said, 'they opened battle by sending a shell at us from one of the Krupps . . . It went wide over the square; but the next and the next were well aimed, bursting close to our men and wounding several. For savages the fire was astonishingly accurate.'[46]

The square advanced evenly to the stirring hum of the pipes. The Gordons in the front rank marched in step, their caps cocked, their rifles still at the shoulder as if on Sunday parade. The machine-gun crews of the Naval Brigade were tucked behind the front corners of the square, with the York & Lancasters and Marines on the left, the Royal Irish Fusiliers and four companies of the Rifles on the right, and the Black Watch bringing up the rear. The water, ammunition and baggage camels and mules were in the centre, with Graham and his staff, the Sappers, the camel-mounted artillery batteries, the medical staff, and elements of the Rifles and the Royal Marines.

Dervish rounds whipped and rasped past them as they came in range of the enemy Remingtons. A Highlander on Burleigh's right dropped suddenly, badly mauled. Then another and another. A Krupp shell smashed into the midst of the square, spraying dust and shrapnel. Valentine Baker collapsed with a lump of steel in his face. Brigade Surgeon Edmund McDowell rushed up to dress the wound. His medical orderlies and the stretcher-bearers ran about picking up the wounded. More and more dead and injured went down.

The square moved on without slowing, like a single cohesive organism. When the pipes ceased, there was no sound but the rumble and creak of the machine-gun carriages, and the crunch of boots on the hard ground. The infantry had now advanced a thousand yards without returning a shot. Even Graham admitted that they had performed a tricky manoeuvre. 'The first time the square came under fire was a very trying one for young troops,' he wrote later, 'as we were then moving to a flank – an operation at all times difficult, and especially so when in cramped forma-tion.'[47] They had passed right across the north face of the dervish entrenchments and had come abreast of the last enemy earthworks. Here, two Krupps and a host of dervish riflemen were entrenched behind a mound or gun-bank more than six feet high.

Suddenly Graham again gave the order to halt. The men threw themselves down. The York & Lancasters and Royal Marines on the left of the square were now the nearest to the enemy. They saw the scouts of the 10th Hussars riding back like furies, out of gunshot. Their horses left spurts of dust behind them as they galloped.

The sun was directly above them and there were no shadows. The air was as clear as a bell, and the light sea breeze carried off the gunsmoke. There was a plain view of the enemy positions. Major Frank Lloyd of the Scottish Royal Artillery battery ordered three of the seven-pounders assembled. The artillerymen couched the camels and unloaded the sections. They bolted the guns together with crisp movements of drill-like precision. Three machine-guns were run out in front of the square by bluejackets under the command of Rear Admiral Billy Hewett himself. A light pall of dust rose from beneath their wheels. For a few thrilling moments the British force waited, poised to strike. It was like that hiatus on the square at Horseguards Parade when the Household Brigade waited in perfect order to salute the monarch. 'There was dead silence . . .' said a navy gunner. 'The moment of action had arrived, and orders were awaited with eagerness. The black faces and glittering spears and swords could be seen in the distance.'[48]

The order to fire snapped out from beneath the headquarters flag. The Gardners and Gatling spat drumfire. The seven-pounders roared, sending shells wheezing into the dervish pits. The two Krupps entrenched there were silenced. Then the British riflemen opened fire.

They fired volley after volley, so fast and efficiently that shooting from the gun-bank almost ceased. Graham gave the order to advance. The bugles sounded. The infantry rose to their feet. The square moved again with steady, measured assurance. The troops fired as they came.

Now it was the turn of the Beja to demonstrate their own brand of élan. As the York & Lancasters and Marines in the front rank came within about two hundred yards of the gun-bank, a host of shock-haired warriors leapt over the top. '[They] were nearly naked and yelling fearfully,' wrote one of the naval gunners; '. . . most of them were tall, broad-chested fellows with the fierce glare of wild beasts in their black eyes.'[49]

The square halted. The front rank was given the order to kneel. To the amazement of the Beja, these 'Turks' showed no sign of running, but faced the charge with poker faces. Again they opened fire.

The dervishes bounded forward in loose formation with the speed and power of panthers, brandishing their spears and swords. The velocity of their charge was incredible; '. . . they came on, heedless and fearless of death,' said Bennet Burleigh. '. . . To the right and left they fell, but those who survived, even the wounded, rushed on.'[50] One fighter actually sprang right over the kneeling front rank, only to be impaled on the bayonet of a York & Lancs private behind. 'Howzat!' the Tommy asked his officer. 'Oh, well caught!' came the reply.

Other dervishes managed to get as far as the British guns and in among the artillerymen. Gunner Isaac Phipps, caught empty-handed, snatched a rammer and knocked one of the warriors clean off his feet. The dervish, already hit by a Martini round, tried to stand up but was stuck through by Highlanders' bayonets. Another gunner, Jimmy Adan, felled a dervish fighter by whacking him across the face with a seven-pound brass shell. A third was felled by a pistol-shot fired by Sergeant Treadwell of the Scottish Royal Artillery.

Meanwhile, the infantry had cleared the front. Now, they dashed towards the fort with a rousing cheer. The enemy entrenchment was slightly oblique to the front line, which meant wheeling a little to the flank. As they turned, some of the York & Lancasters outdistanced the Marines. Suddenly, there was a rupture in the front rank. In a few seconds it was thirty or forty yards wide. Just then there came another wild rush from the Beja. The York & Lancs fell back. The Marines spurted forward to close the gap.

One soldier, left out on a limb, was caught by a dervish spear-man. He fired at eight yards, and missed. It was a fatal error. The soldier hesitated, wondering whether to bayonet his attacker or retreat back to his comrades. 'It ended with his furtively looking over his shoulder,' said Bennet Burleigh, who witnessed the inci-dent, 'a caving in of his chest, swaying to the rear for a step or two, and the [dervish], who had not halted, bounded upon him, burying his lance in the . . . man's throat. Before the soldier had time to fall he was lanced again and again.'[51] At the same moment, the dervish was himself shot and bayoneted by two of the dead soldier's comrades.

By now the gap had closed. The front rank had reached the enemy gun-bank. British and Beja met in a hand-to-hand clash. It was sword against sword and bayonet against spear. Burleigh saw three or four soldiers cut down after missing shots at point-blank range. Others fired with deadly accuracy. The veteran warriors among the York & Lancs and Marines coolly parried spear-thrusts and sword-cuts, and riposted with their bayonets. Often the bayonets hit bone and buckled. Sometimes they made a wound so slight the dervish seemed hardly to notice it. When they struck soft flesh they sliced in deep and were hard to get out. Some of the dervishes grabbed hold of the bayonets with their hands and tried to push them aside. Others tried to wrench them off the rifles.

Beja swords and spears were sharp as razors, and cut through bone and muscle without the edges being turned.[52] By comparison, the British officers' swords were second-rate. Captain Littledale of the York & Lancasters cut at a dervish across the head, only to have his blade bend almost double. He fired his revolver and missed. A second later the warrior wrestled him down, almost severing his arm at the shoulder with his sword. The dervish was stopped by a British private, who rammed his bayonet up to the hilt in the warrior's back. Another comrade blew the man's head apart with a .45 calibre dum-dum fired at hard contact range.

On the left, Admiral Billy Hewett had unsheathed his sword. Determined that the Royal Navy should not be left out of the action, he ordered his bluejackets to charge with bayonets fixed. His machine-gun crew ran the Gatling forward with them as they advanced. 'The tars followed the admiral with a ringing cheer,' said one of the gunners. 'Some of the rebels planted themselves firmly at weak points of their defences, and there used their great, heavy swords with dreadful effect until shot down or bayoneted . . .'[53]

In the centre of the square Graham and Buller were directing operations. Graham tried in vain to persuade the severely injured Baker to return to base, but Baker had set his heart on seeing his revenge acted out, and refused to leave the field. Fred Burnaby left his horse and dashed forward on foot among the men of the York & Lancasters, conspicuous in his shirt-sleeves, without jacket or waistcoat. He carried his double-barrel shotgun with a brace of boar-shot shells in the chambers, determined to 'administer his reproof' at last. He clambered up the mound, seeing the two Krupps inside the trench, now silent. The crews had run away, but more dervishes were sheltering behind them. Burnaby fell prone, and let rip with both chambers. He broke the shotgun and rammed two more cartridges into the breech. Three or four dervishes ran at him whooping. He pumped off both barrels again, knocking a couple of them clean off their feet, inflicting terrible wounds. The others came so close that he had to slither down the slope to reload. The York & Lancs potted any dervish whose head popped up over the gun-bank. Burnaby scrambled back up the parapet but found himself surrounded by half a dozen Beja. He let rip with both barrels, then set about them with the butt of his weapon. A six-inch-wide spear blade embedded itself in his left arm, and Burnaby staggered. He would undoubtedly have been killed had a squad of Highlanders not arrived and finished off his assailants with their bayonets. Burnaby was later stretchered out, severely wounded. He had fired twenty-three shells and had brought down no less than thirteen of the enemy.

York & Lancs, Marines and bluejackets now poured over the gun-bank into the enemy position. Hayrick-haired fighters rose to meet them, like dark spectres out of a network of slit trenches. As the Gardner machine-gun was dragged across the mound on the right by men of the Naval Brigade, a pack of Beja ran forward. Captain Arthur Wilson, RN, commanding *Hecla*, sprang to defend the crew. He swept around frantically with his sword, keeping the whole group off. A dervish speared him in the side, but the giant, bearded sea-captain refused to be cowed. He cut at the warrior's head. His blade shattered. The dervish counter-attacked, slashing Wilson's head. Wilson held him off with only the hilt of his broken sword, then threw it away and fought with his fists. He was still boxing when the advancing York & Lancasters plunged bayonets into the dervish's stomach. Wilson was later awarded the Victoria Cross for defending his gunners single-handedly against the enemy.

To the left, Lieutenant Frederick White of the Royal Marine Light Infantry was attacked by two dervishes simultaneously. As he thrust at one of them with his sword, Private John Birtwhistle ran his bayonet so hard into the warrior's gut that the blade snapped off. He clubbed the man down with the butt of his rifle. His comrade, Private Frank Yerbury, grabbed the other dervish by the hair and swung him round. Sergeant-Major John Hurst shot him dead at point-blank range before he could use his spear.

At last, contesting every inch of the ground, the dervishes began to fall back. Their dead lay everywhere in dozens, the ground soaked with blood. It was 1220 in the afternoon. Since the buglers had sounded the advance, only twenty minutes had elapsed.

Brevet Major Tucker of the Royal Marine Artillery had his men seize the dervish Krupps and turn them round. In minutes the guns were laid. Tucker gave the order to fire. The Krupps blatted out deafeningly, and shells crumped into the next dervish position – the old sugar factory – only a few hundred yards away. The mud-brick building was crammed with dervishes, most of whom were killed instantly. The survivors, manning trenches outside, refused to budge. The British advanced inexorably. As they moved, wounded and dying Beja leapt out of foxholes to stab them. Burleigh saw a Highlander skewered in the back. 'The dying savages in their last throes, strove to thrust or cut with the keenest knives, lances, or swords,' he wrote. 'The troops had to shoot or bayonet all as they advanced, for the wounded often started up, killing or maiming soldiers, and a grim pleasure lit their faces whenever they could bury their weapons in a man's body.'[54]

Burleigh also saw a Beja boy of about twelve fighting with gritted teeth until he was shot and killed. The boy fell into a trench, grasping his small spear. Later, Beja boys as young as ten were found among the dead. Beja women were spotted dispatching the British wounded with hatchets.

It took another forty minutes to dislodge the dervishes from the second position. By 1300 hours, though, they had begun to withdraw. No sooner had they left the shelter of their trenches than the machine-guns mowed them down. Two companies of the Gordon Highlanders were the first into the vacated positions. They captured two Krupps, two brass howitzers, a Gatling, and two rocket-tubes that the Beja had taken from Baker's gendarmerie in early February. The enemy dead lay in heaps, but the Highlanders had to exercise great care in approaching them. Often they were shamming, and would jump up and try to knife their enemies before being shot.

Graham's men pressed the enemy as far as the wells at et-Teb. Here the dervishes turned to make a last stand. A few even made suicidal runs, only to be brought down by Martini fire. 'They seemed not to dream of asking for quarter,' Graham wrote in his report, 'and when they found that their retreat was cut off would charge out singly or in scattered groups to hurl their spears in defiance at the advancing lines of infantry, falling dead, fairly riddled with bullets.'[55] The village of et-Teb was taken by two o'clock that afternoon. The huts were found to be full of dead bodies.

Herbert Stewart, with the Cavalry Brigade, had hung back waiting for the infantry square to do its work. Now, he saw a column of dervishes withdrawing from et-Teb, making for Tokar. The warriors were moving fast, kicking up a mantle of dust. Graham had given him strict instructions not to attack until the enemy were completely crushed and retreating in panic. Stewart assumed that the Beja emerging from the village were the broken enemy: in fact they were the rebel reserve, some four thousand strong. They had not yet been engaged in any serious fighting.

Stewart gave the order to charge. The cavalry, with sabres drawn, thundered forward in three waves – the 10th Hussars leading, followed by a first line of the 19th Hussars led by their CO, Lieut. Colonel Arthur Webster, and a second line of the 19th, led by Lieut. Colonel Percy Barrow. Three lines of British light cavalry at full gallop should have been enough to terrify the most tenacious infantry. But the Beja refused to be intimidated. A squadron of dervish horsemen actually counter-charged. At the last moment they sprang off their mounts and, sheltering under the animals' bellies, tried to cut at the Hussars as they passed. As the 10th and the 19th sprang through the enemy ranks, the Beja footmen fell flat, where Hussar sabres could not reach them. As the horses cantered past, they leapt up hacking at the troopers with their broad-swords from behind. They hurled spears and boomerang-like throwing-sticks with deadly accuracy, knocking Hussars out of the saddle. Others cut at the horses' hocks, hamstringing them. Some squadrons failed to get through the dervish mass. Private Hayes of the 10th Hussars was attacked by a dervish spearman. Hayes tried to get at the man with his sword, but found his horse too nervous. He dismounted calmly. The dervish thrust at him with his spear, but Hayes parried the thrust and ran him through with his sword. Later, a legend arose that Hayes had put down his weapon and taken on the enemy with his fists.

Colonel Barrow got a spear through the left arm and into the gut. His horse collapsed under him and he went down into a mass of enemy warriors. He saw his Hussars sweeping past as if in a dream. Barrow saw the 'fuzzy' heads bobbing around him, and knew he was about to die. He extended his right hand in what seemed like a futile gesture of appeal. Miraculously, a strong hand gripped his own, and he felt himself wrenched to his feet. It was Quartermaster Sergeant Bill Marshall, who had dismounted purposely to defend his officer. Never had Barrow felt so pleased to see one of his NCOs. He was losing blood and hardly able to stand. Marshall, with one hand gripping the colonel and the other his sabre, hacked a path through the dervishes, parrying and thrusting like a madman. Fighting the enemy off with a dreadful defiance, he pulled Barrow to safety. Marshall was later awarded one of the two Victoria Crosses won at et-Teb.

The lines regrouped on the far side of the enemy and charged back again to rescue their comrades, in reverse order, the 19th leading and the 10th following. They smashed into the dervishes a second time, cutting around them frantically. The contact degenerated into a mêlée. More troopers were dragged from their horses and speared or hacked to death. The cavalry withdrew a second time, and were ordered to dismount. They began firing on the dervishes with their Martini carbines. Slowly the Beja melted away into the scrub. Twenty Hussars were killed and forty-eight injured in the double charge.

The second battle of et-Teb was over and Baker Pasha had been avenged. That night, Graham's force bivouacked at the wells. The next day, the Black Watch were detailed to bury the dead. Thirty British soldiers had been killed in all, and 150 wounded. The Watch counted 825 enemy dead. 'Osman Digna later admitted to losing fifteen hundred. Many of the bodies had been removed during the retreat. The burial parties also recovered the bodies of many of those who had been with Baker. These included the corpses of Surgeon General Dr Armand Leslie, and the former coastguard chief James Morice. They were buried with simple ceremony: Bennet Burleigh, who had known them both person-ally, saluted and moved on. Bloodshed and sudden death was not new to the forty-four-year-old *Daily Telegraph* man, who had been captured twice during the American Civil War and twice condemned to death by the Federal authorities.

The British had fought many kinds of 'savages' but had never encountered a braver enemy. 'I have been in a good many actions now, but it was one of the hottest,' wrote Lieutenant Percy Marling of the 3/60th Rifles, serving with the Mounted Infantry. 'I must say, they [the Beja] are the pluckiest fellows I have ever seen.'[56] What Marling interpreted as 'religious fervour', though, was simply fighting spirit. The Beja had never been religious fanatics. Survey-ing the enemy corpses, Bennet Burleigh found them surprisingly 'human' at close quarters. They had, he said, the look of 'enthusi-asts' rather than of 'blood-hunters or ferocious savages'.[57]

Both British and Beja had demonstrated equally admirable but startlingly different martial qualities. To the British generals, the greatest compliment they could pay their men was that they had been 'steady'. Their fighting style was marked not by savage charges, but by a methodical precision under fire. In fact, Graham was not pleased with Herbert Stewart, who he felt had ordered the cavalry to attack prematurely. The large number of casualties among the Hussars had been the result. Graham also criticized the Black Watch for breaking formation to fire at a house occupied by enemy sharpshooters. The Watch, he said, had been 'somewhat out of hand' – an ignominious label in British eyes.

The Beja rush was something the British had not seen before – not even those, like Buller, who had fought the Zulu impis. The Zulus attacked in heavy masses, making them easy targets for disciplined riflemen firing volleys from quick-loading rifles. The Beja, though, attacked in loose formation, with the unbelievable speed of lean, long-limbed men who were raised in the austerity of the desert. They were more difficult to hit. Thereafter, the 'fuzzy-wuzzy' would enter British folklore, emerging later as Kipling's 'first-class fighting man'. After et-Teb, British troops were instructed not to open fire on Beja warriors until they were within three hundred yards, to be sure of stopping them. From now on the Beja were to be treated not as infantry, but as 'honorary cavalry'. They should be met in the open, in tight square formation as if they were mounted men.

As for the Beja themselves, their sudden defeat had taken them by surprise. They had six thousand years of fighting tradition behind them, and were not used to being beaten by 'barbarians'. They had expected to put the 'Turks' to flight as usual. Instead they had found themselves outwitted and out-fought by 'fire devils' who had not thrown away their rifles and screamed in terror before them. These new 'Turks' had stood stoically shoulder to shoulder in the face of their most ferocious charge.

For now, though, the Beja's fighting spirit had momentarily deserted them. When the Hussars got within a mile of Tokar the following day, the dervishes fired a few perfunctory shots. Minutes later, four hundred of them were seen streaming out of the village towards Suakin. An hour and a half later, Graham occupied Tokar without a single shot being fired.

'Tokar expedition most successful,' Billy Hewett wired the Admiralty the next day. When Baring read a copy of the telegram seated at his desk in his office overlooking the Nile in Cairo, he reflected cynically that 'success' was a matter of opinion. Hewett and Graham had both been in combat and were flushed with victory. Baring, who had not been there, was less than impressed. 'It had been shown, not for the first time in history,' he wrote dryly, 'that a small body of well-disciplined British troops could defeat a horde of courageous savages. But no other important object had been obtained.'[58]

Graham and his force were back in Suakin by 5 March. They had brought out with them a thousand citizens from Tokar, including 129 Egyptian soldiers with their wives and children. From the beginning, strange tales had begun to emerge of how the garrison had surrendered to the dervishes. The story was that the Egyptian soldiers had agreed to submit, and to accept the Mahdi as the successor of the Prophet Mohammad, in exchange for their lives. Bennet Burleigh thought the account bogus. Many of the British officers with Graham, too, were certain that at least some of the Egyptian troops had fought with the dervishes at et-Teb. In particular, the accuracy of the dervish Krupps had looked like the work of Egyptian artillerymen. Although the true account never emerged, it was surmised that the Egyptians, in return for their lives and those of their families, had made a devil's pact to join the dervishes against the British who had risked everything to liberate them.

Graham's spies told him that 'Osman Digna was encamped at Tamaai, near Sinkat, only eight miles from Suakin. If the British force were to withdraw immediately, it would leave the port open to attack. If, however, Graham marched out to deal a decisive blow to 'Osman, it would not only secure Suakin, but would also make possible the reopening of the Suakin–Berber road – the task Valentine Baker had originally been sent to accomplish.

A dash by Herbert Stewart's cavalry across the three hundred miles of desert to Berber would then allow Graham's friend Gordon, in Khartoum, to evacuate the garrison as planned. On his arrival in Suakin, Graham wired the War Office for permission to march on Tamaai. Permission was granted. A few days later Graham's force left Suakin for what he believed would be a final showdown with the Beja chief.

Part Four

1

It took Gordon and Stewart eight days to cross the Nubian desert by camel, and it seemed to them that time was standing still. Each day passed in precisely the same way. The horizon remained the same distance before them, and their tiny caravan felt like a string of *nuggars* cast off in a vast ocean of rippling sand. As the heat of the day got up, the distant surface danced and shimmered insubstantially, so that the horizon itself melted into the haze between earth and sky.

The Nubian desert covers the whole of the Sudan east of the Nile, as far south as the great bend. It is bounded by the river on one side and on the other by the Red Sea hills. The town of Abu Hamed, situated at the point where the Nile turns abruptly west, was, in the 1880s, the natural terminus of the Nubian desert caravan trade. It lies 250 miles due south from Korosko on the Nile in Upper Egypt. The desert is an endless carpet of amber-coloured sand spreading to every skyline, where serried black peaks poke through the surface in rows, like the bad teeth of giants. In the whole of that vast expanse the eye seeks in vain for a tree or a green plant. In 1884, the desert had only two major water-sources in its entire length – Murrat and Gabgaba.

This desert was too arid even to support nomads. The only tribe who knew it well were the 'Ababda, a true frontier people. They were camel-breeders who lived half on the Egyptian side and half on the Sudanese side of the border. Claiming descent from the Kawahla, a pure Arab tribe, the 'Ababda were little distinguishable from the Beja in appearance, and the desert sections spoke the Beja language, Tu-Bedawi, rather than Arabic. Hussain Khalifa, whose eldest son, Salah, was in charge of Gordon's caravan, was one of the chief sheikhs of the 'Ababda and currently the governor of the combined provinces of Berber and Dongola – the kingpin of the northern Sudan.

Their day was regulated by the steady tread of the camel. In the *goz* previously, Gordon had trotted his animals. Here, in the real desert, they never travelled at more than a gracious walking pace, sometimes making sixteen hours a day. They would be up before sunrise, walking a little to ease the cold out of their bones. As the sun grew hotter they would mount their camels, riding until noon. As it was still the cool season they would not linger long at midday but would press on after a brief rest into the afternoon, and often long after sunset, until it grew too cold for the camels to carry on. Desultory conversation soon flickered out. They were overwhelmed and mesmerized by the vast magnificence of the desert. At night they would cover themselves in blankets and lie down on rugs on the desert floor. Above them, in the clear cold fathoms of the desert night, lay the boundless mystery of the stars.

On the eighth day they sighted the palm-groves around Abu Hamed in the far distance. The village was no more than a cluster of mud-built houses set above palm-groves by a narrow island called Moghrat. But it was civilization. When Gordon and his party rode into the settlement the townsfolk gave them a stirring reception. Messengers had been sent from Berber, and Gordon was expected. Dozens of bright young men sought him out to ask for employment. Tribesmen in white *jallabiyyas* and *'immas* crowded round him and kissed his hands. Women in rainbow-coloured *tobs* ululated. The contrast between the town and the eternal silence of the desert was complete.

In the desert they had met no one but occasional caravans of the 'Ababda, who were mostly loyal to the Egyptian government. But Gordon had been apprehensive of his first contact with the river people. The welcome he received gave a sharp fillip to his confidence. He wrote a letter to Baring, saying that he need not have 'the slightest anxiety about the Sudan'. He predicted that order would be established in a month, and everything settled within six months. The country, he said, was far less disturbed than de Coetlogon had reported.

On the five-hundred-mile voyage by train and steamer from Cairo to Korosko, Gordon had bombarded Baring with memoranda, representing a bewildering array of ideas and insights. Though neither Baring nor Granville were men of inflexible temperament, they could not cope with the breathtaking panoply of intellectual fireworks Gordon's messages displayed. Gordon's problem, as Stewart noted, was that he tended to fire off ideas as they struck him, without taking time to reflect. Stewart advised Baring privately never to act on his messages immediately, but to regard them simply as opening gambits.

Gordon's original idea had been to hand the Sudan over to the old sultans and chiefs who had run it before the Turco-Egyptian invasion. The loyalty of the river people, though, apparently convinced him that Egypt should remain the suzerain power. The essential thing was to get rid of the insidious Turco-Egyptian ruling class and replace them with native Sudanese administrators. Total abandonment would lead to anarchy and bloodshed, and this would itself be a threat to the stability of Egypt. In his letter from Abu Hamed, Gordon changed his tune – not for the first or last time – to a policy of evacuation without abandonment. It was the same policy, incidentally, over which Baring had forced Sharif Pasha and his ministers to resign.

To Baring, such inconsistency was a flaw. But Gordon's genius lay in his refusal to be fettered by consistency. As Bernard Shaw would write later, 'A reasonable man adapts to conditions, an unreasonable man tries to change them; therefore all progress depends on the unreasonable man.'

Gordon now turned his thoughts to the Mahdi. His first instinct was not to deny or challenge him, but to deflect his aggression. Upriver from Abu Hamed, two days later, he had a letter penned to Mohammad Ahmad, appointing him 'Sultan of Kordofan'. He told him that he had brought no soldiers with him, and explained that there was no need for war between them. He suggested that the Mahdi should release his European prisoners, allow the telegraph line to el-Obeid to be reinstalled, and encourage trade with Khartoum. He had the letter sent to Berber for forwarding to the Mahdi, accompanied by the gift of a scarlet robe and a red tarboosh, representing his new status.

Five days out of Abu Hamed, he arrived at Berber. It was a longitudinal settlement consisting of two broad streets of mud-built houses, roofed with palm fibre or acacia wood, stretching about seven miles along the side of a seasonal water-course. Between this wadi, inundated only in the rainy season, and the Nile itself, lay a fertile tract of arable land on which the local economy was based. Berber did not lie in a particularly rich area, but it was of crucial strategic importance. It stood just below the confluence of the Nile and its only major tributary north of Khartoum, the seasonal 'Atbara river. It also straddled two major caravan routes – east to Suakin on the coast, and north to Korosko via the Nubian desert. The population was about twelve thousand.

Gordon and Stewart were welcomed by the provincial governor, Hussain Khalifa, whose son, Salah, had escorted them from Korosko. Sixty-four-year-old Hussain was not only a notable of the 'Ababda but also a veteran administrator who had first been appointed governor of the northern Sudan in the 1870s. Before that, he had held the government concession for camel transport across the Nubian desert. He had returned to office after a ten-year gap as governor of the combined Berber and Dongola provinces, in 1883. The fact that he had accepted the post encouraged Gordon. A man who had suspected a dervish takeover, he thought, would have shied from office – Hussain owned extensive lands in Upper Egypt and could easily have retired there out of harm's way.

Gordon had showered Hussain with telegrams since leaving Cairo, announcing the evacuation of Egyptian troops. Now, face to face at the governor's mud-built Muderiyya, Hussain said that he was mystified by the Khedive's decision to pull out his forces. He was equally bemused by Gordon's insistence that all Turco-Egyptian officials should be replaced by Sudanese. Gordon had announced the remission of taxes for 1883, a halving of taxes for the coming year, and that the Mahdi would be appointed Sultan of Kordofan. Hussain, a man who had remained loyal to the Khedive all his life, stared at Gordon as if he had taken leave of his senses. Gordon left his presence troubled. After lying awake all night, he woke Stewart up at five in the morning and told him that he intended to reveal his secret agenda to Hussain.

When the governor entered his quarters that morning, together with his civil judge, Gordon showed them his secret firman from Tewfiq, proclaiming the abandonment of the Sudan. Hussain was astonished. The following day Gordon issued a public proclamation declaring that the province was now independent of Egypt, stating his tax concessions, and making clear that the slave trade, banned by the Anglo-Egyptian convention of 1877, would now be permitted to continue. In the evening he again produced the secret firman at a meeting of local headmen, and had it shown round.

Gordon and Stewart were later informed privately – perhaps by Hussain – that they had made an enormous faux pas. Rumours that the Sudan was to be abandoned had already arrived from Cairo, but no one had believed them. Hearing the news from the horse's mouth was bound to spread alarm. Gordon's sole hope of success had lain in pulling the garrisons out before the Mahdi sensed his weakness. His revelation could only have the effect of driving into the Mahdi's camp the key riverain tribes he needed on his side – the Ja'aliyyin, the Manasir, the Rubatab, the Danagla and the Shaygiyya. In one fell swoop, he had pulled the rug from beneath his own feet. The tribes were not likely to offer loyalty to a government that had decided to desert them: Gordon had just made the gravest political mistake of his career.

How Gordon came to commit such an elementary blunder is open to speculation. Certainly his *idée fixe* during the six years he had already spent in the Sudan was that the Turco-Egyptian officials who ran the country were its true enemies. Gordon had come to admire the Sudanese, who had a grace and dignity contrasting markedly with the venal pettiness of the ruling elite. He detested the Turco-Egyptians' corruption, cowardliness and dishonesty, their constant squabbles over status, their shallow imitation of European ways. He may have thought his revelation would force the Sudanese to establish their own authority in opposition to the Mahdi. Since he believed the rebellion was essentially a revolt against the mismanagement of the Turco-Egyptian ruling class, the removal of that class lock, stock and barrel would surely take the wind out of the Mahdi's sails.

In particular, he laid the present situation at the door of the man who had replaced him as governor-general in 1880 – Ra'uf Pasha. 'Ra'uf it was who did all the harm here,' he wrote. 'I had turned him out of the Equator and out of Harrar and had protested about his being set up there. However, thank him and the Mahdi, the Sudan has got its independence.'[1] Gordon, a brilliant and perceptive man in many ways, had not understood that local leaders would be loath to set themselves up as Aunt Sallies to be knocked down by the dervishes the moment the protecting military force pulled out. He had also believed in his own legend – that his name alone would be enough to inspire confidence among the wavering tribes.

After Gordon had left Berber and was sailing up to Khartoum on the steamer *Tewfiqiyya*, the enormity of his error began to dawn on him. The tribes had received him with delight only because he had announced an end to the ban on the slave trade. Once it was generally known that his intention was to remove the garrisons and abandon the Sudan, they would join the rebellion. The evacuation route would be blocked, the telegraph line would be cut, and he would be isolated in Khartoum. He had opened Pandora's box.

Gordon's faith in the power of his name already lay in ruins. He could not control the key tribes. The only way to prevent them linking up with the dervishes at once was was to install a Sudanese ruler in Khartoum as an alternative to the Mahdi. His thoughts returned to the only man who had the power and authority to bring this off – the former slave-trader, Zubayr Pasha.

2

On the morning of Monday 18 February 1884, Frank Power joined Colonel Henry de Coetlogon and the Turco-Egyptian officials on the landing stage outside the *hikimdar*'s palace in Khartoum. They were there to watch Charles Gordon's steamer cruise into harbour. The weather was cool, and the Blue Nile low. The water was dirty brown and chunks of sun-dried mud lay exposed along its banks like giant blocks of chocolate.

Tewfiqiyya rounded Tuti island at about nine o'clock, and hove to at the jetty. The wharf was thronged with citizens in their best brilliant white *jallabiyyas* and layered turbans. As Gordon stepped off the boat, resplendent in his gala uniform and scarlet tarboosh, a band played. A company of Jihadiyya from the 1st Sudan Brigade presented arms. Gordon returned the salute and waved to the cheering crowds. He shook hands with the officials who had come to greet him, including de Coetlogon, Power, and the Austrian consul, Martin Hansall, wearing his Ruritanian uniform complete with massive gilt epaulettes.

Gordon's first stop was at the Muderiyya, opposite the palace. After coffee and *sharbaat*, he and Stewart took their places by a large table covered in red velvet. Stewart, still dressed in his civilian clothes, felt slightly self-conscious. A member of the local *'ulama* named Hassan al-Majdi then read out the Khedive's firman declaring Gordon governor-general of the Sudan. Gordon said a few words, introducing Stewart as his 'brother' and deputy. He explained that the officer had left in such a hurry that he had come without a uniform. Then he made a speech, deprecating the way the Sudan had been allowed to drift into a miserable condition since his departure four years earlier. He presented himself as a saviour in the name of God. 'I have come here alone, without troops,' he declared, 'and we must ask Allah to look after the Sudan if no one else can.'[2] As he crossed the short space from the Muderiyya to the palace, more than 1,000 people mobbed him. Women brought their children, hoping he would cure them with a touch. Gordon was credited with the possession of *baraka* – the same mystical force the Mahdi was believed to hold.

Gordon climbed the stairs to the upper storey, feeling that he was home. The view from the terrace was comfortably familiar. The day was clear, and he could see the buildings of Qubba on the opposite bank – the open fields, the palm-groves, and the arid savannah beyond. *Sagiyyas* rumbled mesmerizingly at intervals along the bank, driven by blindfold oxen. There were *nuggars* riding at anchor, and almost naked black human figures on the mudflats below the northern shore. A school of kites wheeled above, now soaring high, now skimming the waters, forming and reforming in endless configurations.

After a breakfast of turkey, lager and Bass pale ale prepared by Frank Power's Dinka cook, Gordon started work in his upstairs office. His first act was to dash off a message to Cairo. He told Baring that even if he was successful in evacuating 'the Egyptian element' from the Sudan, his final withdrawal would still result in anarchy, which would be 'a misfortune and inhuman'. He suggested strongly that Her Majesty's Government should appoint a successor to himself as governor-general. This successor would not exercise authority by dint of British troops or money, but would have Britain's 'moral support' – of the same type currently enjoyed by the ruler of Afghanistan. As for the man himself, Gordon repeated that only one choice was possible: Zubayr Pasha. 'He alone has the ability to rule the Sudan and would be universally accepted by the Sudan,' he wrote.[3]

Gordon knew that it was only a matter of time before the news of the abandonment permeated the entire length of Nubia. He himself could not prevent the northern tribes joining the Mahdi simply out of personal charisma, but Zubayr Pasha could. A notable of the Ja'aliyyin, one of the most powerful tribes north of Khartoum, Zubayr would undoubtedly be able to exert authority over the waverers. The more he considered it, the more convinced Gordon became that, other than direct military intervention, Zubayr was the only solution. He was the one man who could hold the country together long enough for the evacuation to take place.

From now on, Gordon was careful to keep the firman announcing the abandonment under wraps. After he had sent off his message he started hearing petitions and going through piles of papers, almost as if he had resumed his post after a brief holiday. Power was deeply impressed. '[He] is a most lovable character,' he wrote in a letter home, 'quiet, mild, gentle and strong; he is so humble too. The way he pats you on the shoulder when he says, "Look here, dear fellow, now what do you advise?" would make you love him.'[4] The euphoria that greeted Gordon in Khartoum convinced Power that the legends were true – that Gordon really did exert a prophet's influence over hundreds of thousands of people.

Power thought the Mahdi's sway had been shattered once and for all by Gordon's arrival. He wired Baring that the reception Gordon had received was 'wonderful'. His coming, Power said, 'gives every promise of the speedy pacification of this portion of the Sudan'.[5] Gordon's aura of quiet humility filled him with hope. 'He is indeed, I believe, the greatest and best man of this century,' Power wrote.

That afternoon, Gordon had the old tax records, *kurbashes*, stocks and instruments of torture used by the Bashi-Bazuks burned in Muderiyya Square. He sent Stewart to the prison to strike the irons off all prisoners except murderers. 'I cannot express what pleasure it gave me to set these poor people free,' Stewart commented. 'It was quite worth coming up here just to do so.'[6] That night the *souq* was festooned with bunting and coloured lamps, houses were decorated and there was a firework display. There was a carnival feeling in the town: Gordon was being openly addressed as 'Saviour' and 'Father of the Country'.

On the 20th he checked the inventories of the various government stores, and found that food stocks were plentiful. There were, among other items, twenty-three thousand five hundred ardhebs of dhura, sixty thousand okes of Indian rice, and a million and a quarter okes of biscuits. (An ardheb was equal to five and three-fifths bushels, an oke to three and a half pounds.) Gordon reckoned that the garrison could hold out for at least six months on these reserves. So much, he thought, for de Coetlogon's claim back in

November that Khartoum and Sennar only had food enough for two months.

Unlike Power, Henry de Coetlogon saw through Gordon's supposed ability to influence the tribes. The distrust was mutual. Gordon gave de Coetlogon permission to return to Cairo in a letter full of hidden barbs, saying that his 'services here in a military capacity would be wasted' and that there 'was not the least chance of any danger being incurred in Khartoum'. For the man who had for months been predicting doom and despondency, this must have been a slap in the face, especially when Gordon asked him to tell the authorities in Cairo that Khartoum was 'as safe as Kensington Park'.

De Coetlogon, lily-livered though he might have been, believed correctly that the laugh would eventually be on Gordon. He decided to remove himself forthwith, and tried to persuade his friend Power to go with him. Gordon, he thought, was a dangerous crackpot who would get everyone killed. The romantically in-clined Power refused indignantly. He was now HM Consul, and he would, he declared, stay while Gordon was here, and see it out till the end.

De Coetlogon sailed downriver with his staff, several govern-ment officials, and the first batch of sick Egyptian troops, wives, widows, and children on 22 February. Gordon watched with his telescope from the roof of the palace as *Tewfiqiyya* steamed down the Blue Nile that morning. De Coetlogon took a last look and turned his back on the city he had feared might become his grave. He was never to see Gordon or Power again.

Gordon did not miss him. He walked the four miles of the city's defences from Burri to the White Nile, examining them with the eye of an expert. They were nothing but crude ramparts of piled earth, with a ditch, strengthened by forts. De Coetlogon had improved them as well as he could, and had had two of the three gates closed. The third gate – the Masallamiyya – was open, but entry was forbidden without a police pass. Gordon decreed that all three gates should be open during daytime, and that entry should be free. This meant that the tribesmen from the outlying villages could bring their fruit, vegetables and livestock daily to market in the city. Market tax was abolished, and food prices dropped by half. At the end of December the Fashoda garrison arrived in Khartoum on a steamer and thirty barges, doubling the number of soldiers there. Another two thousand men came in later from ed-Duem and Qana in the Jazira. Gordon inspected the troops at their emergency stations and adjusted the number at each post. He ordered the 1st Sudan Brigade to stand down, leaving only a skeleton guard, and instructed the artillery to return most of the guns to the arsenal. Keen to divide the 'white' forces from the Jihadiyya as a prelude to their evacuation, he sent the Egyptians and Bashi-Bazuks to man the fort across the White Nile at Omdurman.

The task that now faced Gordon and Stewart was a colossal one. There were about six thousand Turco-Egyptian troops, government officials, wives and families to be sent home. This number included a handful of Europeans, mostly Greeks. Although Gordon was not responsible for civilians, he felt morally bound to evacuate anyone who wanted to go. This raised the number of potential evacuees to as many as twenty thousand. Since the Berber–Suakin route was still closed, his initial plan was to transport them north to Abu Hamed by steamer. From there they would be taken across the Nubian desert by camel, under the watchful eyes of the 'Ababda.

Gordon had ten steamers available – seven in Khartoum, two north of Berber, and one at Sennar. There were two others in sections at the Moghran dockyard, but these would take too long to assemble to be of any immediate use in the evacuation process. He also had at his disposal 120 *nuggars*, each of them capable of carrying about sixty passengers. Two *nuggars* could be towed behind each steamer. If all went without a hitch, it would take twelve lifts to evacuate everyone. Since it was fifteen days to Abu Hamed and back, the entire operation would require at least six months to complete.

The Mahdi was still at el-Obeid, though his sojourn there was becoming less comfortable daily. The local wells could not provide enough water for his twelve-thousand-strong army, and the frequent fights at the wellhead were undermining its morale. He decided that he would move shortly to er-Rahad, a day's journey away, where there was a perennial lake.

For now, he occupied a large white pavilion in a vast city of tents and grass huts outside the town. The camp was a constant flux of noise and movement: the braying of asses, the neighing of horses, the continual throb of drums, the shouting and banter of tens of thousands of men, women and children. There was a daily market, where people brought fruit, vegetables and meat, setting up makeshift stalls of cotton cloth slung on the tips of leaf-bladed *shalagais*. At night, when cooking fires were lit outside each hut, it became a galaxy of glittering stars stretching on and on as far as the dark horizon.

Following his victory at Shaykan, the Mahdi had dispatched letters to various countries, invoking his success as proof of his divine status and summoning all Muslims to rise up and overthrow the Ottoman Turks. He saw himself as leading no longer a local revolt, but a universal jihad that would leave him the unchallenged master of the Muslim world. He sent letters to the people of the Jazira threatening to put them to the sword unless they joined him, and to the inhabitants of the native quarter of Khartoum, urging them to rebel.

When news of Slatin's surrender reached him in January, the Mahdi felt free at last to move to Khartoum. He sent a force under his general Abu Jirja' – a former Nile boatman who had commanded the cavalry at Shaykan – to lay siege to the capital. Abu Jirja's army was a small one, but the commander expected to recruit a large number of volunteers along the way.

In mid-February, spies brought the news that Gordon had arrived at Abu Hamed. The Mahdi knew of Gordon as the former governor-general, a devout Christian who had aggressively sup-pressed the slave trade. According to Father Joseph Ohrwalder, one of the Austrian Catholic priests held prisoner at el-Obeid, the revelation that Gordon had returned came as a shock. 'The Mahdi, who thought the Sudan was actually in his grasp, was thoroughly upset,' Ohrwalder wrote, 'for it was generally believed that [Gordon] had brought [British troops] with him.'[7] Mohammad Ahmad considered his arrival serious enough to halt Abu Jirja's expedition until he was able to assess Gordon's strength.

Ohrwalder and his fellow prisoners saw a gleam of hope in Gordon's advent. The Father, and the other members of his mis-sion, including several nuns, had been held by the Mahdi since September 1882, when their station at Delen, near Dilling in the Nuba mountains, had been captured by the dervishes. They had been taken in front of Mohammad Ahmad, who had tried to convert them to Islam. Seeing that he was wasting his time, he had passed them to his more truculent deputy, 'Abdallahi wad Torshayn. The *feki* told them that if they did not accept Islam, they would be executed. They adamantly refused, and spent a night in prayer, preparing themselves for martyrdom. In the early hours of the morning they witnessed an unexpected sight – a brilliant comet with a golden tail, streaking across the sky. The dervishes named the comet the Mahdi's Star.

When the sun was up, they were dragged in chains before the entire dervish army and forced to kneel. '[We were] ordered to bend our necks to receive the death-blow,' Ohrwalder wrote, 'and without the slightest hesitation we did so. But our hour had not yet come. We were summoned before the Mahdi who was riding on a magnificent white camel . . . As we approached, he turned round to us and said "May God lead you in the way of truth," and then rode on.'[8]

At first they were confined in a hut, where two of the nuns and an Italian carpenter had died of fever. The corpses were at first left to rot next to the survivors, as none of the dervishes wanted to bury them. Later, the missionaries were adopted by George Stambouli, a Christian Syrian merchant of el-Obeid who had converted to Islam, and who was a favourite of the Mahdi. With his help, they earned a pittance by making dervish *jibbas* from the uniforms the Mahdists had stripped off the bodies of Hicks's dead troops. 'Most of the clothing was stained with blood,' Ohrwalder recalled, 'which we were obliged to wash out; but what bitter thoughts occupied our minds in this sad task!'[9] One day they cut up a mackintosh that the deserter Gustav Klootz, who was with them, identified as having belonged to Edmund O'Donovan of the *Daily News*. Shortly, however, Stambouli fell from grace when 'Abdallahi raided his house and found his small daughter wearing a crucifix. The Syrian was obliged to beg for his life.

'Abdallahi wad Torshayn, the cattle-nomad from Darfur, was second only to the Mahdi in power and authority. Known as the *Khalifat al-Mahdi* – the Mahdi's official successor – he was Commander-in-Chief of the dervish army. The Mahdi had appointed three *Khalifas* – 'Successors' or 'Deputies' – following the practice of the early Muslims, but to the irritation of his relatives he had passed over his son-in-law, Mohammad ash-Sharif, who ranked second to 'Abdallahi.

'Abdallahi was also in charge of one of the three divisions of Mahdist forces, each named after its flag. His division, the Black Standard, the largest, was made up mostly of Baggara nomads from Darfur. The Red Standard division was composed of tribesmen from the Nile Valley, including members of the Mahdi's extended family and his original adherents, the *Ansar*. It was commanded by the Khalifa Mohammad ash-Sharif. The third group, the Green Standard, was the smallest division, made up of members of the Dighaym and Kinana, nomad cattle-tribes of Kordofan and the White Nile. Its chief was the Khalifa 'Ali wad Helu of the Dighaym, who had been with the Mahdi since the battle of Aba.

Each division had its own kettle-drum – a traditional symbol of chieftainship among Sudanese tribes. 'Abdallahi's Black Standard was unique in also having an *Umm Baya*, a trumpet made from an elephant's tusk.

The news that Gordon had arrived at Abu Hamed was followed

a few days later by his letter from Berber, together with the robe of honour and tarboosh. The arrival of the letter caused great excitement in the dervish camp, but when the Mahdi read it, he exploded with laughter. Gordon was offering him what he already possessed – the Sultanate of Kordofan. What interested him most, though, was the fact that Gordon had brought no troops with him. This at once soothed his initial fears – it meant that Khartoum was already his. 'He remarked,' Father Ohrwalder reported, 'that the very ground on which Gordon was standing was virtually in his hands.'[10]

4

Gordon had quickly begun to grasp his perilous situation. On the day de Coetlogon left, he was informed by a traveller from el-Obeid about Abu Jirja's aborted offensive. The Mahdi was not interested in a peaceful solution, but had halted the advance only until he could assess British strength. It was his first direct indication that the political means he had hoped to employ were doomed. Not only were there no British troops on their way to Khartoum, but he had gratuitously told the Mahdi as much, in the letter sent from Berber on 11 February. Gordon understood finally that he had underestimated and misunderstood the Mahdi. 'What holes do I not put myself into!' he wrote shortly to his sister, Augusta, 'and for what? So mixed are my ideas. I believe ambition put me here in this ruin. However, I trust, and stay myself on the fact that not a sparrow farts without our Lord's permission.'[11]

Gordon also started to regret his policy of opening the gates and allowing free access to the city. The effect of this had been to enable the Mahdi's agents provocateurs to foment rebellion more easily. Two-thirds of the population of Khartoum, who were loyal, were now, he believed, being terrorized by the third who supported the Mahdi. Instead of protecting the majority, he was expected to withdraw the Egyptian troops and leave the loyal inhabitants in the lurch. His fear of an uprising in Khartoum became so real that he ordered six hundred of the Egyptian troops he had already posted to Omdurman back to the city.

On 22 February Gordon received a telegram from Baring, passing on a message from Lord Granville. The message was an answer to his request that the government should appoint Zubayr as his successor. Granville said that he could not authorize Gordon to appoint *any* successor as governor-general. British public opinion would certainly not tolerate the appointment of Zubayr. Gordon was devastated. He wired back to Baring moodily that Granville had two choices: Zubayr or the Mahdi. Zubayr was a risk, certainly, but he was a known risk, while the Mahdi was an unpredictable fanatic. Though Baring did not consider the decision to bar Zubayr final – and in fact Granville wrote to him privately that the cabinet were still secretly debating it – Gordon felt it was the end. Zubayr had been the last chance of preventing the key river tribes from joining the revolt. Without Zubayr, the evacuation could not be carried out.

A few days earlier, Gordon had insulted the commanders of the 1st Sudanese Brigade and the Bashi-Bazuks when they had suggested that the Egyptian troops should not be evacuated. Now it was clear that Zubayr would not be allowed to come, Gordon found himself agreeing with them. Without Zubayr, the evacuation of Khedival troops would be fatal. Within a few days of their departure the people of Khartoum would ask for the Mahdi – not because they wanted him, but because, without the soldiers to protect them, there would be no other hope.

The city was already on the brink of revolt. Gordon begged Baring to send a small Indian force – say a couple of companies – to Wadi Halfa on the Sudanese border. He also asked for a British officer to visit Dongola, ostensibly to look for 'quarters' for a large number of troops. Dervish spies would pick up these developments, and the Mahdi would be convinced that Gordon was to be joined by British forces after all. It might give him the chance to get out the sick, the wounded and the civilians. At the same time, he told Baring that, ultimately, the Mahdi would have to be 'smashed up'. To do it now would be comparatively easy. If the government waited until the Mahdi took over Khartoum – which Gordon believed was inevitable unless Zubayr were sent up – it would be a great deal harder and more expensive. His words were to prove prophetic.

The jubilation that had surrounded his arrival had now evaporated. On 27 February, only nine days after he had been greeted in the city as a saviour, Gordon was obliged to threaten its inhabitants with dire reprisals, and to announce quite untruthfully that British troops were on their way.

In London the cabinet were horrified by this sudden volte-face. Gladstone claimed he was still under the impression that Gordon had been sent out on a 'reporting mission'. Here was the same man telling him that the Mahdi ought to be 'smashed up'. The cabinet had believed that Gordon could solve the problem by his presence alone. Now, it seemed that they had handed the Sudan over to a lunatic, who was dragging them towards the precipice of escalating military involvement. They did not have a clear idea of the fluid situation in the Sudan, nor the steps that had led to Gordon's latest suggestions.

At the beginning of March, Stewart and Power returned from a six-day reconnaissance on the White Nile with bad news. They had steamed upriver observing the normally placid villages of thatched huts and mud-brick dwellings that lay among palm-groves. Everywhere along the banks, tribesmen in the patched *jibbas* and baggy trousers of dervishes had hurled abuse at them, or regarded them with silent hostility. Stewart concluded that the country up to fifteen or twenty miles south of Khartoum was occupied by hostile elements. He was convinced that they would have been fired on had they put in at the bank.

Back in Khartoum, Stewart wired Baring directly that he believed the dervishes were poised to strike at the capital. He confirmed the conclusion Gordon had already reached – that the Mahdi was only holding back until he saw whether Gordon would be supported by British troops. Once he knew for certain that no British force was on its way, he would attack. Aware that Gerald Graham was at that moment fighting the Beja in the eastern

Sudan, Stewart saw that there remained only one hope. After dealing with 'Osman Digna, Graham must open up the Suakin–Berber road.

5

On 13 March, at Tamaai, on the edge of the Red Sea hills, dawn came at exactly six o'clock. Bars of light spread like the points of a star through a bleary haze of sea-mist. The crests and peaks of the Aulib took shape slowly, like crouching giants, out of the shreds of dark. The mist, chased away by the spears of light, gave way to a clear, bright morning.

Most of Gerald Graham's two infantry brigades had spent a sleepless night inside their zariba of acacia thorn. For one thing, it had been freezing cold, and many of the British troops had lain down without blankets on the desert floor. For another, the dervishes, who had crept to only thirteen hundred yards away, had kept up a constant fire from their Remingtons. One man, Private Sheldon of the York & Lancaster Regiment, had been shot in the head while lying down. The Beja had taken a particular pride in shooting at the two hospital wagons, whose bulky covers presented an easy target. Several of the medical orderlies on Graham's staff had had narrow escapes. Lulls in the firing had been filled with spectral voices croaking out jeers of abuse. At midnight, both brigades had been stood-to in anticipation of an attack. Fortunately, the Beja did not like to attack at night.

At 0530 hours the buglers sounded reveille. The men, glad to get up, rolled away their greatcoats and lit fires. They drank coffee and tea, and filled their bellies with hard tack biscuit. As soon as it was light enough to range the guns, a crew of Royal Navy blue-jackets let rip with a Gardner and a Gatling. The staccato rat-tat-tat of the machine-guns cut through the morning like a knife. Seconds later there was the whoff and boom of a nine-pounder, fired by the men of M Battery, Royal Artillery – a new addition to Graham's force, under Major Edmund Holley. The salvo sent the 'fuzzies' packing immediately, back to their main position around the wells of Tamaai.

Half an hour later, Herbert Stewart arrived at the head of his two Hussar regiments and the Mounted Infantry, riding in close columns. They had spent the night nearby at 'Baker's Zariba' – an enclosure Valentine Baker had built when carrying out his decoy raid here in late January. The horses thundered past, hoofs clicking on gravel, and the brigade divided, squadrons peeling off to reconnoitre enemy positions.

The village of Tamaai, 'Osman Digna's current headquarters, lay on broken, rocky ground a little less than two thousand yards to the south of them, but hidden by the hills. Behind them stood a fractured inselberg known as Tesela Hill. There was high ground on the right front, and before them a shallow depression lined with acacia scrub. Beyond that lay Khor Gwob, a steep ravine with rocky sides. It was twenty to sixty feet high, and had a sandy floor, covered with boulders and blocks of stone that had, over the millennia, fallen out of the sides. Graham knew from a captured dervish that the main Beja force were concentrated inside the khor. Twelve thousand strong, they outnumbered him by at least three to one. The enemy were out of sight there, and had good cover. Graham's plan was to march his men up to the rim of the wadi, and open fire with all weapons down into it. Assuming they got that far, it would be like shooting fish in a duck-pond.

Graham had divided his two infantry brigades, each forming a separate square. By 0730 hours Stewart's cavalry vedettes had returned, reporting to Graham that numbers of the enemy were retiring into the hills. Graham ordered the men to fall in immediately. By 0800, 2 Brigade, commanded by Major General John Davis, a fifty-two-year-old ex-Indian army officer, had formed up and were raring to go. The front rank was made up of three companies each from the Black Watch and the York & Lancasters. The rest of the Watch formed the left flank, and the remainder of the York & Lancs the right. The Royal Marines formed the rear. Some nine-pounder guns of M Battery were up on the right. Three machine-guns of Billy Hewett's bluejacket brigade, under

Commander Edward Rolfe, RN, were up on the left. Both batteries were just behind the front rank. Gerald Graham was himself riding with John Davis inside the square.

When 2 Brigade started to advance, 1 Brigade, under Redvers Buller, were not ready, and by the time they had got moving were six hundred yards behind 2 Brigade, slightly to its right. Buller's square was made up of the King's Royal Rifles, the Gordon Highlanders, the Royal Irish Fusiliers, Major Frank Lloyd's battery of the Scottish Royal Artillery, and some Royal Marines. The main body of Herbert Stewart's cavalry lay to the rear.

2 Brigade crossed the depression, and Graham ordered Holley's nine-pounders out of the square on its right. The square advanced towards the edge of the khor. The sea-mist was long gone. The sun was already baking, and the sky had turned a spotless methylene blue. The light was so intense that it seemed to magnify everything, making the great red and black humps of the hills seem almost unreal. The soldiers could see thousands of dervishes ranged ominously among the rocky outcrops to their front and right. The dark silhouettes stood out clearly – barefoot men clad only in white loincloths with plumes of hair contained by strips of leather. Most of them were over a mile away, but some were nearer. Skirmishers were hidden among dense thorn-scrub on the lip of the khor, at little more than a thousand paces.

There was dead silence but for the crunch of boots and the rumble of gunwheels. Suddenly, the Mounted Infantry spurred forwards, cantering past the squares towards the dervish skirmishers hidden in the brush. Close up, they slipped out of the saddle and engaged the enemy with their carbines. It was as if they had disturbed an ants' nest. Hundreds of dervishes appeared abruptly over the edge of Khor Gwob and opened fire at close range.

Lieutenant Percy Marling's Mounted Infantry section on the right bore the brunt of the fire. Captain Humphreys, Welsh Regiment, commanding the MI, sent Lieutenant F. Dodd Thornton with another section – mostly men of the Royal Sussex Regiment – to support Marling. 'I found the fire of the enemy was very hot,' Thornton recalled, '. . . and as it gradually became hotter, and the square was by this time close up, within about two hundred yards, Lieutenant Marling gave the order to the men, "to your horses".[12]

Dervishes were pouring out of the ravine, and Marling fired his revolver at them until it was empty. Private Morley of the Sussex Regiment was hit and went down. The enemy were advancing, firing from the hip as they came. Morley was still alive but unable to move. Private Joseph Clift crouched by his mate, determined to defend him to the death. Dervish bullets charred the air, whizzing and thumping around him. Marling, who had seen Morley go down, turned his horse and went back for him. Private George Hunter of the King's Royal Rifles, also mounted, followed him. The dervishes were getting uncomfortably close, but the little knot of Tommies remained cool. 'Hunter dismounted,' Clift recalled, 'and we put Morley on the horse, in front of Lieutenant Marling, but he slipped off almost directly. Seeing this, Lieutenant Marling dismounted, and we put him across Lieutenant Marling's saddle. Lieutenant Marling and myself held him on, and Private Hunter led the horse.'[13] With enemy bullets cracking into the gravel at their feet, they led the wounded man sedately back towards their own lines.

At that moment, a horde of Beja fighters leapt over the edge of the ravine. Snarling like tigers, they hurled themselves towards the front rank of the square which had now almost reached the edge. The Jocks and Tommies had seen a Beja attack before and knew what to expect. Instead of simply halting and laying down a barrage of fire, though, the Black Watch, in the front rank, suddenly launched into a screaming counter-charge of their own. Who gave the order, if anyone, is uncertain. With their bayonets and white helmets glittering, their kilts swept back, the Jocks smashed straight into the dervish mass. 'We charged and we were just rushing to our deaths,' said Private James Hope, 'for the smoke from our big guns and the firing from our right completely blinded us, and we could not see more than three yards in front of us. The enemy were advancing on their hands and knees and cutting our men down like rabbits.'[14]

Later it was said by some that Graham himself had ordered the attack. Others said that the officer commanding the Black Watch,

Lieut. Colonel Bill Green, had asked Graham for permission to charge, which had been granted. Another view was that the rank and file, incensed that Graham had impugned the honour of this old and revered regiment after et-Teb, had charged spontaneously. The truth will never be known for sure.

The charge of the Highlanders unsealed the square. The York & Lancasters had either not been ordered to charge, or had not heard the order, and were left behind. The dervishes had been waiting for just such a chance. Instantly a second horde of them seethed like a whirlwind through the gap, a blur of black bodies, frizzed hair, elephant-hide shields, curved sticks, and razor-sharp swords and spears. They crashed into the York & Lancasters and the remains of the Black Watch from behind. The unthinkable had happened – the dervishes had got inside a British square.

Daily Telegraph correspondent Bennet Burleigh, who had been riding next to Colonel Bill Green, noticed suddenly that the right flank was giving way. He galloped over to see what was happening. 'The [dervishes] were all over that side and corner of the square,' he said, 'bounding like deer out of the khor by hundreds, and running at us through the thick smoke. With hair on end, eyes glistening, and their white teeth, more like infuriated demons than men, they seemed to bound out of the battle smoke upon the soldiers like figures in a shadow-pantomime.'[15]

The Beja carried their shields and steel weapons in their left hands, and their curved throwing-sticks in their right. About ten yards from the front rank, they hurled their sticks at the enemy, replacing them with a sword or spear as they came in for the kill. In a few seconds the ordered British lines had fractured into small groups. The fate of the entire force hung in the balance. For a moment it looked as if this might be a second edition of the Hicks massacre. Colonel Bill Green of the Black Watch was hit on the ear by a ricochet, and a dervish spear struck his holster. Captain H. G. W. Ford and fifteen men of the York & Lancasters stood their ground, but the Beja hit them with such ferocity that they were all cut down or speared in moments. Gerald Graham, who had been directly behind them, was himself surrounded by dervishes, one of whom struck at his horse. The rest of the battalion were forced back against the Marines, throwing everything into chaos. 'Back everybody was borne,' wrote Burleigh, 'in a confused mass, men and regiments being inextricably mixed up.'[16]

The Black Watch who had charged were cut off and surrounded by dervishes. 'They were upon us in masses in a minute,' one private said. 'I had only fired one round when it came to a hand to hand fight. My right-hand man was killed at my side, my left hand one fell wounded by a spear thrust from a huge [dervish] over six feet in height. I thrust my bayonet into this fellow up to the hilt, and in trying to get it out his body fell on me and knocked me down, and striking my head on a stone, I was stunned and became insensible. How long I remained so I do not know but on coming round I felt a heavy weight on me. It was the body of the this [dervish] lying across my chest and the body of a dead comrade lying across my legs and stomach. I raised myself on my elbow, when to my horror and dismay, I saw our chaps in full retreat, and between them and me some hundreds of the enemy.'[17]

Another Highlander private, James Hope, was kicked accident- ally by a Marine as he retreated and fell sprawling in the face of the enemy. 'Five of the blacks came running past me,' he said. 'They must have taken me for dead, for I never got a scratch. I jumped up just in time to save myself, for two were running towards me. I shot one and bayoneted the other, and got into the square again.'[18]

On the edge of the ravine, one platoon of B Company of the Black Watch were wiped out except for three soldiers, all badly wounded. Monkey-running on hands and knees to avoid the rifle- fire, the Beja cut at the Jocks' bare knees with their swords. They would stab at the soldiers' hands with their spears to make them drop their rifles before going for the body with a thrust. Some ripped the Highlanders' kilts clean off. Two Black Watch officers fought with their basket-hilted claymores, which proved more effective than the swords of the English units. Burleigh saw them run the blades into enemy bodies several times, right up to the basket.

Major Aitken, surrounded by slashing dervishes, held them off until Sergeant Donald Fraser and Lance Corporal Percy Finlay rushed up to help him. Aitken was shortly speared to death. The two Highlander NCOs charged clear over the edge of the ravine and found themselves so closely pressed by the dervishes that there was no time even to reload their rifles. Between them, using bayonets and even the butts of their weapons, they killed more than a dozen tribesmen. When the rifles were torn out of their hands they used their fists, until both collapsed and died from multiple spear-thrusts and sword-cuts.

Private George Drummond, of the same section, found himself facing a rare dervish horseman – it was 'Osman Digna's cousin, Mohammad Musa, the dervish field commander. The Beja cut at his head with his sword, but Drummond was saved by his white helmet. Momentarily stunned, the Highlander drove his bayonet right through Mohammad's body. As he struggled to pull it out, Mohammad's steward rushed at him with a spear. He was shot dead by Drummond's mate, Private Kelly. A split second later, Kelly himself was speared. Drummond managed to get away, losing blood from three spear-wounds.

Percy Marling of the Mounted Infantry and his small party managed to get Private Morley back to their own lines without being hit. For his coolness under fire, Marling was to win one of the battle's two VCs. In his diary, he expressed indignation that Clift and Hunter had not been honoured with the same award. Marling, who had now re-entered the fray, saw another Black Watch sergeant, wounded and blinded by the blood in his eyes, crawling away from a dervish at the base of an acacia tree. The Bejawi, also wounded, was on hands and knees, stabbing at the sergeant's legs with his spear. He changed direction and came at the Highlander from the front. The sergeant fired instinctively straight into the warrior's face.

The British were retiring with their faces to the enemy, firing and thrusting with their bayonets. 'Here and there the Marines and Highlanders retired slowly,' Burleigh said, 'firing steadily at the rushing [dervishes], whom they bowled over like ninepins, though . . . these were instantly replaced by others.'[19]

The sudden retreat had left the machine-gun battery high and dry. In a second the Beja were in among them cutting, stabbing and chopping the crews to bloody rags. The bluejackets managed to remove the sights and lock their guns before they were slaughtered. Lieutenant Houston Stewart off *Dryad* and Lieutenant Bill Montresor off *Euryalus* were slashed and stabbed to death. Lieutenant Walter Almack, off *Briton*, had been serving in the Royal Navy for twenty years, but had never seen action on land before this campaign. In charge of No. 4 gun, he and a bluejacket tried to defend it against the avalanche of black bodies. Private Tom Edwards of the Black Watch, who had been assigned to the battery as a mule-driver, was bringing up ammunition on two mules. He was suddenly surrounded by half-naked warriors. Edwards fought his way to No. 4 gun and joined Almack and the sailor in defence of the Gatling.

The bluejacket was speared in the stomach next to Edwards, and collapsed in a gush of blood. Almack was fighting off the dervishes frantically with a sword and revolver. Edwards saw a dervish cut at the lieutenant with his broad-sword. The razor-sharp blade almost severed Almack's arm from his body. Almack slumped over the gun, and Edwards vaulted forward to defend him. Three dervishes sprang in front of him and gouged at the officer repeatedly until he was dead. White with rage, Edwards hurled himself on the Beja. He rammed his bayonet into the belly of one, withdrew it, and stabbed the other in the side. He dimly registered the enemy going down. The third dervish thrust at him with his spear, and Edwards took the blade across his fingers, which were almost sheared off. His hand pouring blood, he withdrew, grabbed the halter of his mules and led them back to his own lines. Lieutenant Ballard, in charge of transport, urged him to leave the field, but Edwards stayed despite his wound. He was to receive the second VC awarded at Tamaai.

Ten bluejackets had been killed and seven wounded. The Beja had captured the guns. 'Their success,' wrote Burleigh, 'maddened them with joy. In the excess of triumph a sinewy [dervish] leapt upon one of the machine guns, and capered and yelled in glee not

more than thirty yards from us. In a moment he wilted like a green plant before the leaden hail, and fell headlong to the ground.'[20] The Beja turned the machine-guns on the withdrawing British, but could not make them fire.

Gerald Graham rode up to the line and shouted at the ranks to close up and fire steadily. Burleigh, forgetting for a moment that he was an observer, rode back and forth among the York & Lancasters yelling at them to aim and fire carefully. He saw a friend, Captain Rutherford of the York & Lancs, facing the enemy almost alone, his company dead, wounded, or retreating. Rutherford, his helmet gone, was waving his sword at the enemy, bawling hoarsely at his own troops, 'Men of the 65th! Close up!'

Burleigh saw one Black Watch private take on a huge dervish who was slashing right and left with a broad-sword. The Highlander shoved his bayonet into the man's abdomen so violently that his rifle muzzle stuck in the wound. He was forced to drag the dervish's body with him for some distance until he could get the rifle out.

'It was not a rout, but a retreat,' Burleigh said, 'for our soldiers kept loading and firing, although there was no semblance at the time of an orderly military line; but in place thereof, facing and fighting the enemy, were an irregular body of men in rather ope order on what was the west face of the square.'[21]

Bluejackets, York & Lancs, Black Watch and Marines were mixed together now. Layers of dust and smoke drifted a the battlefield, stinging their eyes. The blast and crash o nine-pounders, the whinnying of horses, the continuous c of musketry, the clack of Martinis being recocked, the ag screams of dead and dying, the defiant roar of the enemy, t of steel on steel, deafened and maddened them. A few ra though, stood shoulder to shoulder, letting rip round af at the leaping, bounding dervishes.

As warrior after warrior went down, the British la cheered. 'One almost ought to be ashamed to write said, 'but truth telling is above *mauvaise honte*.' As de dust, the Tommies crowed, 'That's the way! Giv

men!' But still the enemy came on, raging with berserk battle-fury. 'A savage gleam shone in their faces,' Burleigh remembered, 'defiant, unrelenting, hating, as they gathered all their strength . . . to make their last blow at us.'[22]

Even dum-dum rounds seemed to have no effect on the enemy's terrible impetus. Individual charges were only halted when a round shattered a leg, or struck the heart or head. 'I saw [dervish] after [dervish],' Burleigh said, 'through whose bodies our bullets had ploughed their way, charging down . . . with blood spouting in pulsating streams from them at every heart-throb. Down they bore on us; some with two or three bullet wounds, reeling like frenzied, drunken men, but still pressing onwards, to throw themselves, without attempt at parrying, upon our bayonets.'[23]

Others, shot down before they reached the British, would hurl their weapons – swords, sticks or spears – at the enemy in their dying seconds, as their blood soaked into their native soil. Another mounted chief, urging his men on from horseback, was skewered by a private of the York & Lancs, who rushed shrieking like a madman out from the retreating ranks.

The faster 2 Brigade withdrew, the greater the disadvantage to the Beja, who had to cross more open ground in the face of rapid fire. M Battery with their nine-pounders had been left exposed on the right flank without infantry support. The artillerymen stood firm, loading, laying, ranging and firing with mechanical care. The dervishes who got in among them were fought off and repulsed. The nine-pounders crashed out, slapping shell after shell of case-shot into the enemy lines. The gunners fought the Beja with anything they could lay their hands on – carbines, swords, revolvers, and even rammers. Through the whole onslaught, Holley's guns never ceased.

Still the dervishes came on. British soldiers who went down were doomed. Any soldier showing the slightest sign of life was stabbed instantly. 'A dozen of them just round me were engaged in spearing every wounded man of ours they came across,' said the Black Watch private trapped under two dead bodies. 'It struck me instantly my only chance of escape was to feign death. One of the

wretches was then just finishing off poor Tom, my comrade. Had they once seen there was life in me I was done for, I felt certain; so I laid quite still, but oh! The agony I suffered no tongue can tell. I silently prayed then as I had never prayed before. They passed over me two or three times, one stepped with his naked foot right on my cheek as I lay with my head on the sand.'[24]

The rapidity and discipline of the British retreat threw the dervishes. They had seen the Egyptian gendarmerie hurl away their weapons and run, but this kind of fighting withdrawal was new. The line was already reforming eight hundred yards from the abyss. Buller's 1 Brigade, on the right, had also come under attack, but had pushed the enemy back, and now moved up quickly. Buller's men, still in perfect formation, began to lay down steady volleys of covering crossfire. The Mounted Infantry galloped up on the left flank. The men swung out of the saddle, threw themselves down, and opened up withering fire with their trusty Martinis. Herbert Stewart ordered a squadron of Hussars up from nine hundred yards in the rear. They too dismounted and added their salvoes to the fire.

Buller's 1 Brigade halted in square formation, seven hundred yards from the lost machine-guns. 2 Brigade under John Davis was now in line, with the remains of the York & Lancs in the centre, the Black Watch on the right, and the Marines on the left. At once, they began to advance. The dervishes had lost the momentum – their 'innings', as Bennet Burleigh put it, was over. Incredibly the whole action, from the moment the Black Watch had charged, had lasted no more than five minutes.

Davis's brigade moved forward dressed by the right, firing as they came, fifteen hundred bayonets glittering. Jock, Tommy, Bootneck and Jack Tar advanced in tight formation. Calloused fingers shoved rounds into chambers, and worked cocking levers with the speed of mechanical claws. Aimed and deliberate fire created a deadly screen through which no enemy could penetrate. The dervishes had never encountered such deliberate or rapid fire. They fell back, or attacked in small sorties that were shot down easily. Cheering, Davis's men now quickened pace. 'We kept up steady fire,' said James Hope of the Black Watch, 'and we could see them falling as thick as snow.'[25]

As they neared the machine-guns there was another cheer and, in a sudden charge, the battery was retaken. 'We made a rush and once more got our guns,' Hope recalled. 'Then you should have heard the cheer, it struck terror into the hearts of the blacks, and as they were retiring down the ravine, we were shooting them down . . . at the bottom there were thousands of [dervishes].'[26] Commander Rolfe and Lieutenant Graham RN quickly took charge of the guns. They were intact, and in a second the remaining bluejacket gunners were turning the handles, wreaking revenge on the retreating enemy for their fallen comrades. The rattle of drum-fire was added to the cacophony of noise. One of the guns had been pushed over the edge of the ravine, but the bluejackets managed to haul it out.

The Beja were in retreat. The battle of Tamaai was over. In a radius of sixty yards around the place where the original right corner of the square had been, Burleigh counted a thousand dead dervishes and a hundred dead British soldiers. The sand was red with blood. There were no British wounded on the field.

Dervish wounded were approached with extreme caution. They would lie still, feigning death, but grab any opportunity to strike at the enemy. It was, Burleigh said, 'like walking among wounded vipers'.[27] He described how a British party led by a bluejacket approached a Beja warrior whose knee had been shattered, but who was still grasping his spear. Forbidden to fire, one soldier hit the Beja from behind with a stone, stunning him long enough for the bluejacket to stick his cutlass up to the hilt in the dervish's belly — so hard, in fact, that the blade bent almost hoop-shaped. A small Beja boy found by the medical staff, and bandaged, promptly tore off the bandage and went for a Tommy's bayonet. He had to be tied up, but later, given water by an army chaplain, he spat it in the padre's face. Not long after, he struggled free and managed to grab a spear before being stunned with a rifle butt. Later that evening he died of blood loss, still cursing his enemies.

Davis's Brigade halted on the edge of the ravine. His men

covered Buller's Brigade as they descended. The Beja were retreating sullenly, making for the hills. Some stood watching from the peaks of the ridges, well out of range. Buller's point companies of the Gordon Highlanders kept up a ceaseless fire in their direction. It was answered only weakly now. They toiled down into the khor and up the rocky hillocks on the opposite side, moving warily. Any number of dervishes could be concealed in the folds of the hills. The Gordons shot down any fuzzy head that bobbed up. Eventually they reached the ridge overlooking the khor, where the scores of tents and huts of Tamaai village lay in a depression 180 feet below them.

At 1140 hours, Graham rode into Tamaai. It was full of goats, donkeys, and a few camels. The ground was scattered with Remington rifles, belts and pouches that had been captured from the various Egyptian expeditions the Beja had massacred. There were also water-skins, saddles, swords, knives and spearheads that had been hastily abandoned. Of human beings, it was deserted except for a slave woman who had been stabbed in the shoulder by a dervish. She was leaning on the prop of a hut door, losing blood, when Bennet Burleigh found her and gave her water. Later, she told him that 'Osman Digna himself had retired into the hills before the start of the battle, 'to pray for its success'.

Afterwards Burleigh caught up with Gerald Graham and asked him if he was going to advance any further. The blond giant said that they had reached the objective. Graham wrote a hurried dispatch with a rough estimate of the dead, and gave it to Burleigh to take back with him to the telegraph station. The *Daily Telegraph* man turned his horse's head towards Suakin, and rode off in a bolus of dust towards the Red Sea.

6

The main force retired to the zariba in which they had spent the previous night. This time, though, there was no shooting or jeering, only the wailing of dervish widows seeking their dead on the battlefield. The following morning, Graham took the cavalry back to the village. They carried the ammunition and rifles they found there down to the khor and made a huge bonfire of them. Finally, they set fire to the huts and tents of Tamaai before heading back towards Suakin.

There, they were received with astonishment. Sixteen Egyptian camel-drivers of the Carrier Corps had bolted back to the port on the first sign of 2 Brigade's withdrawal and had told tales of a British defeat. Admiral Billy Hewett later condemned them all to death for desertion, causing a furore among the hundreds of other Egyptian troops at Suakin. Refusing to guard the captives, they demanded to be returned to Cairo. Thirty-eight of them were arrested for mutiny, and awarded two dozen lashes apiece and a year in prison. Billy Hewett told their officer that if he were found guilty of mutiny he would be shot. Gerald Graham commuted the camel-drivers' death sentences to lashings. They were tied to wagon-wheels and flogged by men of the Provost Corps, with a thick-looped rope. Under the lash, the Egyptians howled and begged for clemency, writhing and weeping. As Bennet Burleigh pointed out, these men were supposedly 'volunteers', who in Cairo had begged and pleaded with equal desperation to be included on the expedition.

The final death-toll at Tamaai was reckoned at 109 British soldiers killed, and 112 wounded. The Black Watch had lost sixty men killed in action, the York & Lancasters thirty. 'Osman Digna later admitted having lost two thousand dead and about the same number of wounded. He had suffered two resounding defeats and had lost the best part of four thousand warriors in all. He had not been crushed, though. The Beja had simply retired into their hills as they had always done over their six-thousand-year history, and were waiting for the enemy to go away.

After Tamaai, Graham renewed his pressure for a march on Berber. He suggested sending a 'flying column' of Herbert Stewart's cavalry. His superior, Frederick Stephenson in Cairo, though, felt that sending a small force would be dangerous. The route across the desert was also too poor in water-resources to support a larger one. The British cabinet agreed. They believed that Gordon was already out of hand, and determined to drag them into war in the central and western Sudan. Gladstone was adamant that he was not going down that road. Granville wired Graham that he was not to undertake any operations beyond the coastal plain. After a few more local skirmishes and reconnaissance missions, Graham's men packed up and left. The entire field force was out of Suakin by 7 April.

Graham had won two major victories over the dervishes, but achieved nothing. He had not captured 'Osman Digna, had not relieved Tokar, had not opened the Suakin–Berber road, and had not saved Gordon. Ten thousand men, British and Sudanese, had died in vain. It was not, as Baring commented, '[an episode] to which any Englishman can look back with either pride or pleasure. Many valuable lives were lost. A great slaughter of fanatical savages [*sic*] took place. But no political or military result was obtained at all commensurate with the amount of life and treasure expended.'[28]

The Beja had inhabited these hills since before the pharaohs had ruled in Egypt: the British had come and gone like ghosts in the night.

7

Three days after the battle of Tamaai, Lieut. Colonel John Hammill Stewart arrived by steamer at Halfaya, eight miles north of Khartoum, to witness a ghastly sight. The dead bodies of two hundred Egyptian soldiers and Bashi-Bazuks lay strewn across the battlefield – almost all of them had been stabbed in the back. Twenty or so wounded lay in pools of blood at a nearby fort known as the Eastern Palace, unattended by medical staff. All had multiple wounds from swords or spears. Stewart had them transferred to his steamer and taken to the hospital in Khartoum.

Four days earlier, tribesmen loyal to Sheikh el-Obeid wad Badr, an influential holy man, had cut the telegraph wire between Khartoum and Berber. The same day, Gordon had been informed that a dervish force five thousand strong was marching up the Nile. They had attacked Halfaya and dislodged or captured eight hundred irregular cavalry of the Shaygiyya tribe. Some of the dervishes advanced as far as Gubba, opposite Khartoum, and fired at the palace itself. That night, they had ambushed a patrol of three hundred Jihadiyya on the north bank of the Blue Nile, and killed a hundred of them. They had now set up camp north of Gubba, and were taking regular pot-shots at the palace. Gordon sat in front of his window, as usual, ignoring them.

What had disturbed Gordon much more than pot-shots was his intuition that the Mahdi's men intended to turn Halfaya into a permanent post. The village dominated the Nile, and all craft heading north or approaching from the north would from now on have to run the gauntlet of dervish fire. Without the telegraph, river transport was Gordon's only major means of contact with the outside world. It was also his only means of implementing the evacuation he had been ordered to carry out.

Gordon had the feeling that the noose was tightening around him. On the day the wire was cut, two thousand tribesmen of the Fetayhab and Jammu'iyya tribes who had been living in Khartoum had deserted to the Mahdi. They had been accompanied by a large number of men from the Mahdi's own tribe, the Danagla. Mostly armed with Remington rifles, they were now on the west bank of the White Nile, just south of Omdurman. There were another two thousand dervishes loyal to Sheikh el-Obeid opposite Halfaya, on the west bank at Khor Shambat. There were three thousand south of the village of Kalakala, just outside Khartoum's southern defences. The chiefs of these forces had sent Gordon a message declaring Mohammad Ahmad the Mahdi, and urging him to surrender. Gordon had written back refuting Mohammad Ahmad's claim, and assuring them that he would never surrender.

After dashing off the letter, Gordon had called out the 1st Sudan Brigade. He had inspected the fortifications once more from horseback, and ordered a hundred rounds issued to each soldier. He instructed Faraj Pasha, commanding the Brigade, and Sai'd Pasha, of the Bashi-Bazuks, to detach companies on steamers to

Halfaya. They were to take with them a mountain-gun and try to flush the dervishes out. Gordon and Power, who had watched the engagement by telescope from the roof of the palace, were aware that something had gone wrong, but were too far away to make out what had happened. Gordon sent Stewart to find out.

From the Eastern Palace, Stewart telegraphed that two of the Turco-Egyptian generals, Hassan Pasha and Sa'id Pasha, had betrayed their own men. Several witnesses told Stewart that both pashas had broken up their own ranks, and had murdered troops under their command. The Egyptians and Bashi-Bazuks were already crying out for vengeance.

The next day, Gordon ordered the pashas tried by court-martial, presided over by Jihadiyya commander Faraj Pasha. The trial was long and tedious, but the result was inevitable. Sai'd and Hassan were found guilty of treachery and murder, and were taken outside and shot. Gordon later regretted the executions, evidently not entirely convinced that they had turned traitor, but the incident caused a wave of despair among the townspeople. If they could not trust the generals commanding the soldiers who were meant to be defending them, who could they trust? A mutinous spirit spread through the army. Many more citizens defected to the rebels. Gordon had soldiers patrolling the streets day and night, and ordered a curfew. Anyone found outdoors more than two hours after sunset would be shot on sight, and their property confiscated.

The significance of the loss of Halfaya became very obvious a few days later, when *Tewfiqiyya* returned from her run to Berber. By this time the dervishes had erected forts along the banks on both sides of the Nile. As *Tewfiqiyya* steamed past the new fortifications, she was fired on and her rudder destroyed. Gordon, watching from his roof, ordered *Abbas* and two other steamers to help her out. When *Tewfiqiyya* finally put in at the jetty beneath the palace, Gordon received the mail she had brought. After reading it, he announced confidently that all his requests had been granted. 'Troops will soon arrive,' he told the people. 'Take courage and be happy.' This was another invention on Gordon's part. The day before the telegraph line had been cut, he had received a message from Lord Granville, relayed through Baring. The message had not only given a second and very final 'no' to Gordon's request for Zubayr, it had also made clear that under no circumstances would Britain send troops to the Sudan. Graham's force in Suakin had been deployed only to secure the Red Sea ports and was already being sent home.

Gordon shared this news with no one, but Frank Power, in the next room, guessed that all was not well. 'I know he [Gordon] suffers fearfully from low spirits,' Power wrote. 'I hear him walking up and down in his room all night.'[29] Gordon had good reason to be restless. The mission he had been sent to carry out had failed. Khartoum was now surrounded by the dervishes, defended by soldiers whose own officers had betrayed them, and almost completely cut off from the outside world.

8

On the same day that Gordon's pashas turned traitor at Halfaya, Lord Randolph Churchill, a Conservative, stood up in the House of Commons and roundly condemned Gerald Graham's failure to open the Suakin–Berber road, despite the slaughter of some four thousand dervishes. 'We know that General Gordon is surrounded by hostile tribes,' he said, 'and is cut off from communication with Cairo and London . . . the House has a right to ask Her Majesty's Government whether they are going to do anything to relieve him. Are they going to remain indifferent to the fate of the one man on whom they have counted to extricate them from their dilemmas . . . and not make a single effort on his behalf?'[30]

To the Tories, the Khartoum issue was convenient. Gladstone's current political hot-potato was the Franchise Bill – a proposal that would extend the electorate far beyond its current confines. The Tories opposed the bill, but were chary of criticizing it in public. They knew that they would be cutting their own throats by alienating potential voters. The Khartoum question was an ideal substitute. It gave them the opportunity to undermine Gladstone's credibility without even mentioning the Franchise Bill.

Gladstone's evasive answers only fuelled public fury. There were letters to newspapers, vitriolic editorials condemning his dishonesty, and madcap rescue proposals. Baroness Burdett-Coutts, a friend of Gordon's, appealed in *The Times* for donations to finance a mission by a sort of 'league of extraordinary gentlemen' – a gang of big-game hunters who would 'go a thousand miles to shoot a lion'. They would snatch Gordon from Khartoum. Another proposal was that a hunter named Curly Knox should go to Khartoum alone disguised as a dervish and whip Gordon out from under the Mahdi's nose. Wilfred Scawen Blunt, the well-known Arabist, offered to go to Kordofan to negotiate with the Mahdi. Granville vetoed the idea, considering Blunt even more cracked than Gordon. In early May there was a protest meeting at St James's Hall, and there were mass meetings in Hyde Park and Manchester. A vicar suggested that daily prayers should be offered in every church in the country for Gordon's delivery. Gladstone was hissed in public.

Through all this, though, the Prime Minister remained apparently unmoved. To Gladstone the situation had taken on the trappings of a needle-match between himself and Gordon. Gordon, the *soi-disant* Christian hero, was attempting to manipulate him, the elected leader of the nation, and he would not have it. Across the three thousand miles that separated them, it seemed to him, they were playing a game of bluff. Wolseley had duped him, and Gordon had pulled the wool over his eyes. Gordon had, as one minister put it, 'done everything he said he wouldn't do and nothing they told him to do'.[31] He had played the mild and compliant servant in London, but the moment he had boarded that train at Charing Cross he had begun to show his true colours.

Throughout the summer of 1884, Gladstone was harassed by the opposition and by the press. In the Commons, questions were asked daily. Gladstone's evasions only made his enemies' attacks more determined. The Grand Old Man was being swept away by a deluge that was being orchestrated by the Tories for their own political reasons. It had tapped into deep stirrings of a people who believed in their own destiny as masters of the world.

After the Easter Recess, Parliament opened to a Motion of Censure from Her Majesty's Opposition. It was tabled by Sir Michael Hicks-Beach, shadow Chancellor of the Exchequer. The motion asserted that the government had done nothing to help Gordon carry out his mission, and had even delayed steps necessary to ensure his personal safety. After a long and bitter debate, the vote was taken. The government lost by twenty-eight votes. Gladstone remained poker-faced, but by the second week in May a chink appeared in his armour. He told Sir Charles Dilke that he would raise the question of Gordon's relief at the proper time.

Weeks passed and the 'proper time' did not materialize. Finally, on 31 July, Secretary for War Lord Hartington decided that enough was enough. He wrote to Foreign Secretary Granville that he could no longer accept Gladstone's inactivity over the Gordon issue. 'I, with you and Northbrook,' he wrote, 'are more responsible than any other members of the cabinet for sending out Gordon, but I consider that I had the largest share of the responsibility.' Granville sent the letter to Gladstone, who realized at once that Hartington was obliquely threatening to resign. Hartington was the leader of the aristocratic Whig faction in the Liberal party, and was widely regarded as a man of integrity. His resignation could bring down the government.

Gladstone's reply was typically ambiguous. He still did not believe, he said, that Gordon's position justified military interference. He added, however, that certain *preparations* could be made, which would 'entail expenditure of money but would not involve a change of policy'.[32]

Hartington would not be put off this time. Both he and Home Secretary Lord Selbourne threatened to resign if nothing was done. Finally a face-saving compromise was reached. No relief expedition would be sent out immediately, but the government would ask Parliament for the sum of £300,000 so that they could undertake operations for the relief of Gordon *if they became necessary*.

Part Five

1

In mid-April the Mahdi moved his entire army to er-Rahad, where the shore of the lake was transformed into an ocean of *tukuls* stretching in every direction as far as the eye could see. After the fasting month of Ramadan, Mohammad Ahmad declared publicly that he would shortly march on Khartoum.

The Mahdi had reverted to repressive measures to maintain discipline among his frequently changing tribal forces. The drinking of alcohol – traditional in the Sudan even among Muslims – was punishable by eighty lashes. Smoking tobacco was considered even more heinous, and was allotted a hundred lashes. Traditionally, Baggara women dressed scantily, often wearing only a loincloth, and were relatively free compared with most townswomen. To curb licentiousness, the Mahdi decreed that from now on all women must cover their hair, and any parent allowing a girl over five years old to go bareheaded would be flogged. No woman was allowed to visit the marketplace, and a hundred lashes would be doled out to any man who spoke to a woman not of his family, even in answer to a greeting. The traditional wailing of women at funerals and lavish expense at wedding feasts was forbidden. Flogging became such a frequent punishment that the young braves of the nomad tribes took to lashing each other with hippo-hide whips, to see who could take the most strokes – a custom continued among some tribes until the present day.

The dervishes pulled out of er-Rahad on 22 August, with kettle-drums beating and the Umm Baya honking. According to Father Ohrwalder, there were more than two hundred thousand people on the move – fighting men armed with spears, swords and shields, Jihadiyya riflemen, Baggara cavalry, camel-men, artillery batteries, wives, children, camp-followers, baggage-trains, donkeys, herds of cattle and flocks of sheep. The force was so vast that the Mahdi ordered it to travel by three separate routes to spare the water-sources. The camel-mounted tribes went north, the Baggara horse-men south, and the Mahdi, his *Khalifas* and *Ansar* took the central road to ed-Duem. With the Mahdi was his Commander-in-Chief, 'Abdallahi wad Torshayn, among whose retinue was Rudolf Carl von Slatin, now known as Khalid and dressed in turban and patched *jibba*.

Though 'Abdallahi had overall command of the army, the actual planning and execution of the siege of Khartoum was to be left to Abu Jirja', Abu Anja, and wad an-Nejumi, the Mahdi's three most gifted field commanders. While Abu Jirja' had been a simple boatman before the revolt, Abu Anja came from an even more modest background – he belonged to the Mandala, a Darfur tribe made up mostly of former slaves of the Ta'isha, the Khalifa 'Abdallahi's folk. Abu Anja himself was a half-caste, the son of a Ta'isha tribesman and a Mandala woman. He had served as a rifleman in the *bazinger* army of Zubayr Pasha back in the 1870s, and was one of the few Mahdist leaders with military training. Abu Anja had been a famous giraffe- and elephant-hunter in his youth, and now commanded the Mahdi's Jihadiyya.

'Abd ar-Rahman wad an-Nejumi was probably the Mahdi's single most brilliant soldier. A tribesman of the noble Ja'aliyyin tribe from the Nile Valley north of Khartoum, he claimed direct descent from the Prophet Mohammad's uncle, Abbas. Like 'Abdallahi, wad an-Nejumi had been a *feki* before the revolt, and had joined the Mahdi in the early days at el-Obeid. He owed his ascendancy both to the severity of his religious principles and to the victory at Shaykan, which had been largely due to his planning. He had a reputation as a severe but fair commander and a man of honest and abstemious character.

The Mahdist army mustered at ed-Duem on the White Nile, the place from which Hicks had set out a year earlier. Here, the Mahdi held a review of his forces. Then, he turned to the north.

With his divisions swollen daily by recruits who flocked to join him from the Jazira and the Nile Valley, he began his slow encroachment on Khartoum.

2

The day after the Mahdi's army left er-Rahad, Garnet Wolseley was having breakfast at home in London when a note arrived from the War Office. It was from Lord Hartington, telling him that Gladstone had given him command of the Gordon Relief Expedition. Wolseley raised an eyebrow in surprise. He had always known that the Prime Minister would eventually be forced to send him to the Sudan – what startled him was that Gladstone had made up his mind so quickly. He had not yet officially accepted that an expedition was necessary. The appointment was to remain secret, and in any case, it was not until the following Tuesday that Queen Victoria gave her reluctant consent. When he heard about it, the Duke of Cambridge had an attack of gout.

Wolseley was content that his plans had at last fallen into place, but perturbed by the delay. He had devised a contingency plan for snatching Gordon from Khartoum as early as April. Since then, there had been a major change in the strategic situation. On 27 May the dervishes had captured Berber, closing off the route from the coast. The Relief Expedition would have been a difficult and dangerous operation even four months earlier. Now it threatened to be a Herculean task.

The immense and unique difficulties of the terrain were Wolseley's first consideration. The northern Sudan was almost all desert or semi-desert, through which the Nile snaked like a single tortuous oasis. Seven separate routes to the objective had originally been mooted, but only two had presented themselves as feasible. Either Khartoum could be approached from the east, from Suakin, across the eastern desert to Berber, and then up the Nile. Or, the relief force would approach from Cairo, via Wadi Halfa, upriver all the way. Of the two routes, the eastern one was by far the shorter. It was only 245 miles from Suakin to Berber. Cairo lay 1,060 miles away.

Wolseley had always favoured the Nile route. This was not because he thought it was easier, but because it would allow him to use the experience gained on the Red River Campaign in Canada in 1870. It had been one of his outstanding early successes. The GOC in Cairo, Sir Fred Stephenson, had disagreed passionately, condemning Wolseley's plan as ludicrous. He had plumped for the Suakin–Berber route, even though he had argued against Graham using it in February. This route was now dismissed as impractical by the loss of Berber, leaving Wolseley's proposal the only option. Since Stephenson could not be expected to lead an operation he did not believe in, command had fallen like a ripe fruit into Wolseley's palm.

Wolseley's plan was bold and original in concept. His entire force would be ferried up the Nile, not by steamers, but in six hundred wooden boats, powered by oar and sail, small enough to navigate the notorious cataracts. Camels would be used to 'track' them on ropes through the more difficult shoals. The boats' specifications had been worked out weeks earlier by Major General William Butler, one of Wolseley's Ashanti Ring. They would be similar to the ones he and Wolseley had used to carry troops from Lake Superior to Lake Winnipeg on the Red River Campaign. Then, they had made sixteen miles a day in conditions Butler claimed were 'very much more unfavourable than those of the Nile'.[1]

The boats would carry some of the force as far as Korti, near ed-Debba, below the fourth cataract, on the Nile's 'question mark'. Korti would become Wolseley's forward operating base. Here, the expedition would be divided into two. The first section, the Desert Column, would dash on camels across the Bayuda desert – the peninsula of land enclosed by the Nile bend. This would be the crucial phase of the operation. They would rejoin the river at Metemma, opposite Shendi. A flotilla of Gordon's steamers would be waiting there to carry the final assault party to Khartoum.

Meanwhile, the rest of the force, the River Column, would continue in boats up the Nile. They would knock out Abu Hamed and Berber, before joining up with the Desert Column for the final assault on Khartoum.

The Desert Column was an innovation. British troops had never operated on camels before, and there was no repository of expertise in the British army on which to draw. Wolseley had thought long and hard about what kind of troops would be needed for the desert march. They would have to be men who were extremely fit and adaptable, preferably with combat experience. They would be deep inside hostile and unfamiliar territory, facing a fanatical enemy of unknown, but vastly superior strength. The difficulties of the terrain would favour the dervishes. One false move would result in the same situation that had done for Hicks.

The question was where to find such men. It was clear to Wolseley that they were not to be found in any single unit. In his day, a 'crack' regiment was one that drew its officers from the highest social strata – notably the Guards and cavalry units such as the Hussars. Wolseley thought this idea medieval 'bosh'. His force would be taking on a massive army of irregulars in which every man was 'either a crack shot or a born warrior'. It became clear to him that the solution was to select a small number of the best men from every regiment and corps in the British army. The special forces concept had been born.

It would be another thirty-two years before T. E. Lawrence developed modern guerrilla warfare, and another sixty before the special forces idea would come into its own. In 1884 it was no less than revolutionary. It had the 'very old school' in fits of apoplexy, raving about regimental traditions and *esprit de corps*. The Duke of Cambridge called it 'outrageous', and succumbed to another attack of gout. 'I believe he would prefer us to fail,' Wolseley said, 'as long as we adhered to the old traditions in preference to success arrived at in defiance of all those cherished ideas of his childhood.'[2] He felt that any British general these days had to begin his campaign by fighting the Duke.

One thing Wolseley did not reveal was the true objective of

the mission. It was named the Gordon *Relief* Expedition, but Wolseley's instructions were only to get Gordon out of Khartoum. He must have been aware that this was impossible. He knew Gordon well enough to understand that he would never leave the city unless everyone he considered himself responsible for went with him. Wolseley may have believed that once British troops were installed in Khartoum, the occupation of the Sudan would be a fait accompli.

Wolseley left England amid cheering crowds on 27 August, telling his wife, Louisa, that he would be shaking hands with Gordon at Khartoum in about five months' time.

3

Wolseley arrived in Cairo on 9 September and immediately began to collect officers and inspect troops. The main pillars of his staff would be his Ashanti Ring. These would include Sirdar Sir Evelyn Wood, who would control the vital lines of communication. Brigadier Herbert – now *Sir* Herbert – Stewart would command the Desert Column. Brigadier Sir Redvers Buller would be Chief of Staff. Two of Wolseley's favourite officers, Major General William Butler and Major General Henry Brackenbury, would go with the River Column. As his intelligence officer, Wolseley wanted Valentine Baker.

Baker was still living in his suite at Shepheard's Hotel, where he had been nursed back to health by his wife, Fanny, and daughters, Hermione and Sybil. The elder, Hermione, a seventeen-year-old beauty, had fallen in love with the aloof but handsome Major Herbert Kitchener, who knew Baker from his time as military attaché in the Balkans. He occasionally visited the family in the hotel. Marriage to the daughter of a social outcast would not have been advantageous to his career, but he returned Hermione's devotion. Baker and his wife certainly believed a future union was on the cards.

Baker had not given up his quest to restore his good name, and was keen to accompany Wolseley as intelligence chief, but he had had his last chance at the second battle of et-Teb. Hartington barred the appointment. He suggested instead Baring's former military adviser, the forty-nine-year-old Sapper, Lieut. Colonel Sir Charles William Wilson FRS – the man who had almost been given Gordon's job.

The son of a Quaker family from Liverpool, Wilson was a 'thinking man's soldier'. He did not have any combat experience, and had never held field command. Later to lay the foundations of British geographical intelligence, he was a brilliant cartographer and surveyor, with the kind of analytical mind that was ideal for intelligence work. He also had a more subtle grasp of the true strength of the Mahdi than any other man in the field, including Gordon. An intellectual who was more at home excavating archaeological sites than mixing in 'polite society', he was not exactly Wolseley's cup of tea. Wolseley accepted him because he had been recommended by his partisan, Hartington. Wilson's second-in-command, with the ponderous title of Deputy Assistant Adjutant General of Intelligence, was to be Herbert Kitchener, who had already established himself as Sir Evelyn Wood's eyes and ears among the desert tribes.

Kitchener had come to love the desert life. He operated his own small army, the fifteen-hundred-strong 'Ababda Frontier Force. His second-in-comand, Salah Hussain, was the man who had escorted Gordon and Stewart across the desert. Salah's father, Hussain Khalifa, the former governor of Berber, was now a prisoner in the Mahdi's camp.

Kitchener dressed in Arab clothes and let his beard grow long. He had a bodyguard of twenty braves mounted on the finest camels. They had been sworn to fealty on a blood oath administered by a holy man. After seeing a dervish prisoner beaten to death, he kept a phial of cyanide in his headcloth in case he was ever captured alive. All through the sweltering summer, he had been leading his 'Ababda ceaselessly back and forth across the Sudanese border. He had learned to travel fast and light, as the 'Ababda did, eating their poor desert fare, drinking tainted water from a goatskin, and sleeping at night on a rug on the hot desert ground. This was the kind of life he had dreamed of on his first trip behind enemy lines in Egypt. It was perfectly suited to his aloof and solitary character.

In July he rode to Dongola along the east bank, following a tortuous road through rocky country that wove in and out of the palm-groves. He and his camel-men were ferried across the river on *nuggars* at Akasha. In Dongola, a straggling town of mud-brick houses on the west bank of the Nile, Kitchener made contact with the Mudir, or governor, a Circassian named Mustafa Yawar, whose loyalty was suspect. Mustafa, a small man with piercing black eyes and a hooked nose, received Kitchener in his whitewashed Muderiyya, sitting on a bentwood chair, dressed in a Stamboul coat, white alpaca trousers, and a wool cap. He had begun life in Egypt as a slave, and was an enthusiastic exponent of rule by the *kurbash* and the Bashi-Bazuk – exactly the kind of official Gordon detested. Gordon had, in fact, sacked him on his arrival in the Sudan in February, but the Egyptian government had reinstated him, knowing he would be a key man in holding off any dervish advance on Egypt. It was proposed in Cairo that he should be recognized as independent ruler of the province. Kitchener advised against it, reporting to Evelyn Wood that the Mudir was a fanatical Muslim, an intriguer, and a liar. He was, Kitchener thought, interested only in exploiting the British and filling his pockets. Kitchener's advice was rejected.

Still, both Wood and Stephenson were highly impressed with Kitchener's tact, energy and devotion to duty. Stephenson recommended him for promotion, telling Wolseley that there was no other officer in either the Egyptian or the British armies who could have performed the frontier duty so well.[3] Wolseley was less than convinced. He had crossed swords with Kitchener while serving as High Commissioner on Cyprus, when Kitchener was carrying out his survey for the Foreign Office. Wolseley had wanted a rough military job, Kitchener an elaborate scientific one. Kitchener's repeated insubordination had infuriated Wolseley. He had reminded him that he was the superior officer, and that his orders must be obeyed. He had never forgiven him, and, before leaving London for Cairo, had vetoed his promotion. He relented later, realizing that Kitchener was performing a unique service, but he wrote spitefully in his private diary, while steaming up the Nile, that he had 'never placed much reliance on Kitchener's reports'.[4]

After Dongola, Kitchener and his bodyguard rode south to ed-Debba, a small town sitting on the sharp eastward sweep of the Nile. Ed-Debba was occupied by a troop of Bashi-Bazuks, who were still playing 'ferret in the rabbit warren' and terrorizing the local population. It was vital as a market town for nomads from the desert to the west, and a junction of caravan routes south across the Bayuda and north along the Nile. It was also the end of the telegraph line.

The first task set Kitchener was to survey the possible routes between ed-Debba and Khartoum. The job would mean entering enemy territory, and would be highly dangerous. Wood wrote specifically that he did not expect Kitchener to carry out the surveys himself. Kitchener, laughing off the risk as always, disguised himself as an Arab and traversed the Bayuda desert with a group of 'Ababda, riding to within three days' march of Khartoum. On arriving safely back in ed-Debba, he telegraphed Wood that the Bayuda route was likely to be the most suitable for the Relief Expedition. In fact there were already accurate maps of the area, showing the key wells. It had been suggested as a possible course for a railway by Isma'il Pasha, and had been surveyed thirteen years earlier by a British engineer working for the Khedive.

Kitchener's principal task at ed-Debba was to establish communication with Gordon. He ran a group of couriers working the routes to Khartoum by desert and river, carrying letters and telegrams to the beleaguered town. Some returned, others did not. Those who did were carefully debriefed by Kitchener in fluent Arabic. Slowly, he built up a detailed picture of the situation in Khartoum, and his admiration for Gordon soared. At the end of August, Wood wired him that the time factor for Gordon's relief was now critical. He asked his opinion on the quickest way of reaching Khartoum. 'My opinion,' Kitchener answered, 'is decidedly, send up your troops.'[5]

In September the Bashi–Bazuks in ed-Debba were deployed by the Mudir of Dongola upriver at Korti, near the ruined town of Ambikol. Here, they met with a Mahdist force sent to oust the Mudir and replace him with the Mahdi's own man. The dervishes were crushed. Despite his misgivings about Mustafa, Kitchener was impressed. He asked Wolseley for permission to lead the Mudir's troops against Berber. Wolseley wired back that he was needed in ed-Debba as link man with Gordon. He must remain there until British troops arrived, and until his chief, Charles Wilson, had reached Dongola. On 21 September, Kitchener sent a message by courier to his friend John Hammill Stewart in Khartoum, confirming that the relief mission was on its way.

The message crossed with one from Gordon to Kitchener, which arrived the next morning. Stewart was no longer in Khartoum. On 10 September he and Frank Power had left the city on a steamer hoping to reach Dongola. They had been carrying all Gordon's files and letters. Kitchener was alarmed. He wired for permission to ride to Berber and escort Stewart and his party across the desert. His request was refused. He began to bombard Cairo with appeals for native troops, and even for a steamer to go to Stewart's aid. All of these were rejected. Instead, he dispatched his most trusted courier to intercept Stewart's steamer before it reached Berber. The messenger was to tell Stewart to leave the boat and make for Dongola by camel – on no account should he attempt to pass through the Abu Hamed reach, where the hostile Rubatab and Manasir tribes were now aware that British forces were on their way. It was too late. By the time the messenger arrived at Berber, Stewart's steamer was long gone.

Stewart, with Frank Power and the new French consul, Henri Herbin, had left Khartoum on the steamer *Abbas*, at the dead of night. They hoped to be able to steal past the dervish defences at Halfaya in the darkness. As luck would have it, *Abbas* broke down just abreast of Halfaya and had to be repaired in sight of the dervish positions. She finally got away the following night.

Morale in Khartoum was then at its lowest ebb. The Mahdi's advance force had arrived, with his artillery. Eleven days earlier, Gordon had suffered his greatest reverse of the entire defence when a thousand Egyptian soldiers and Bashi-Bazuks had been 'Hicksed' near the village of Umm Dubban on the Blue Nile. Sent on three steamers to deal with a dervish build-up there, they had been lured into a forest, ambushed, and wiped out.

All that is known about the evacuation of Stewart, Power and Herbin comes from Gordon's journal. After Umm Dubban, Gordon wrote, all three had felt the situation was desperate. Gordon clearly agreed with them, because he decided to send *Abbas* to Dongola with his journal and his files and documents concerning the defence of Khartoum. First Herbin had asked to go, then Power, then Stewart. They had tried to persuade Gordon to go with them, but he had replied over and over again that this was impossible, and that he intended to die there. All of them had argued that they would not go unless Gordon went. Gordon pointed out that if they stayed they would inevitably be taken prisoner. They would be of much more use to him if they escaped.

How much of this is true, and how much of it Gordon's attempt to absolve himself from guilt after subsequent events, is impossible to say. It does indicate, though, that at this stage Gordon thought Khartoum was doomed, and that he was prepared to die in its defence.

The truth is that he had wanted to send Stewart out even before the Umm Dubban reverse. He considered his assistant brave, just and upright, and in a telegram earlier in the year had recommended him for a knighthood. Privately, though, he thought Stewart's heart was not really in the work. His insistence that every official order should be respected jarred against Gordon's notion that they were 'a basis for discussion'. Much worse in Gordon's eyes was the fact that Stewart had 'supreme contempt for the Sudanese people and for their courage, which I do not share'.[6] He had called Gordon's Sudanese soldiers 'cowards'. Gordon, who looked on them almost as his children, admitted that they were not heroes, but thought they could fight well enough if given a modest chance of success. He had felt the same way about the Chinese.

In Stewart's case, the question of his evacuation involved a thorny problem of personal honour. He could go only on the condition that Gordon exonerated him from the charge of desertion. He wanted a written order instructing him to leave, but this Gordon refused to give. He wanted to make it clear that Stewart was going of his own free will.

Power, Gordon said, though chivalrous, brave and honest, was tarred with the same brush as Stewart. The Irishman believed that when it came to the crunch, the soldiers would simply throw in the towel. Gordon's only comment about Herbin, the French consul who had replaced Marquet and who doubled as correspondent for the *Bosphore Egyptien* – a Cairo daily – was that he liked him and thought him 'very sharp'.

In the end Gordon wrote an official letter covering both Stewart and Power: '*Abbas* is going down; you say you are willing to go in her, if I think you can do so with honour – you *can* go in honour, for you can do nothing here, and if you go you do me service in telegraphing my views.'[7] It was true that all three men could do more for him if they reached Egypt than they could in Khartoum. Power's reports in *The Times* would galvanize public support at home, while Herbin's in the *Bosphore* would stir things up in Egypt. Stewart would be able to explain the situation to the government in their 'own language', and carry arguments that they would not accept from Gordon himself. The night before he left, Gordon dictated to Stewart a list of questions he thought the government likely to ask, and pencilled his answers in the margin.

Gordon also sent his telegraph ciphers off with Stewart. This meant he could no longer read encoded messages even if they did arrive. Why he did so remains a mystery – Garnet Wolseley considered it an 'inexplicable act'. Probably it was an oblique statement of disgust at the government's inactivity, and a symbol that he now considered himself a sacrificial lamb. He did not, of course, know about the Relief Expedition. Kitchener had sent him a message on 31 August mentioning the possibility, but Gordon did not receive it until long after Stewart had gone.

On the other hand, Gordon had no doubt that *Abbas* would get through. She was the smallest of his steamers, with the shallowest draught, which gave her an advantage in the cataracts. She was riddled with no less than 970 bullet-holes from her many engagements, but she had now been equipped with bulletproof parapets of hard wood and boiler-plating. She had bulletproof turrets fore and aft and a bulletproof crow's nest on the masthead. She had buffers sunk a foot into the water to prevent her from being holed by rocks. She also carried a complement of fifty soldiers, and a mountain-gun. She towed two *nuggars* carrying nineteen armed Greeks whom Gordon had paid to support Stewart in case of any sign of mutiny on the part of the crew. He assigned to Stewart his best interpreter, Hassan Bey Hassanayn, an Egyptian who had arrived in Khartoum in 1883 as a telegraph clerk, and whom Gordon himself had promoted to the rank of lieutenant-colonel. Hassan spoke English and French as well as Arabic.

Gordon had taken great care when briefing *Abbas*'s captain, ar-Rais Mohammad ad-Dongolawi. He was to anchor only in midstream, and not take on wood except in carefully selected spots. *Abbas* would be escorted by the steamers *Safia* and *Mansoura* past the places where trouble was anticipated. They would stay with her as far as Junaynetta, two days upriver from the Fifth Cataract, to make sure she got clear of Berber. Once she entered the sparsely inhabited Abu Hamed reach, Gordon thought she would be home free. 'That the *Abbas* could be captured by force,' he wrote, 'seems impossible.'[8]

The Nile was in spate, though the flood was lower than usual this year. The steamers chugged steadily down the smooth golden brown stream, keeping to the centre of the river. Magnificent groves of date-palm rose suddenly along the banks, alternating with austere desert panoramas. Mud-brick villages stood amid dusty fields of brown sand. The steamers passed wild jungles of *sunt* acacia and tamarisk, inhabited only by exotic birds and mobs of goats. Occasionally they passed expanses of rich black soil, neatly divided into postage-stamp-sized plots by low bunds and feeder channels. There were cattle in the fields, their backs dotted with the white flashes of Nile egrets. Dozens of *sagiyyas* were working along the banks, powered by matched pairs of bulls, dipping earthenware pots into the Nile and splashing the water into channels. Farmers in their white robes could be seen toiling in the fields, most of whom took little notice of them.

They sailed through the Sixth Cataract – the Sabaluka Gorge – without a hitch. Then, at Shendi, they were suddenly fired on. Stewart ordered his gunners to open up with the mountain-gun, and followed the shelling with a volley of rifle-fire. *Abbas* raced past the town without a scratch. At ed-Damer, near the mouth of the 'Atbara, the dervishes were well entrenched. Stewart landed troops, who attacked the enemy positions and killed fifty men. All the way past Berber they ran the gauntlet of enemy guns, and fired back. The three steamers came through intact, and once clear of Berber, Stewart ordered *Safia* and *Mansoura* to turn round.

When it was reported to the dervish commander at Berber, Mohammad al-Khayr, that *Safia* and *Mansoura* were steaming back upriver, he realized that *Abbas* must be on her own. This meant that she was making a run for Dongola, which was still held by the government. He knew about Kitchener in ed-Debba, and that British troops were on their way. He decided that whatever *Abbas* was carrying, she must not reach her goal.

He sent off in pursuit the steamer *el-Fasher*, captured in the dervish assault on Berber in May. *El-Fasher* was larger and faster than *Abbas*, and caught up with her at Junaynetta. There was an exchange of fire, but *Abbas* outran her to the Fifth Cataract, which was too narrow for *el-Fasher* to enter. Unfortunately, Stewart was obliged to cast adrift the two *nuggars* she was towing, carrying most of the Greeks. The boats were captured by *el-Fasher*, and all their passengers taken prisoner.

Just before dawn on the morning of 18 September, *Abbas* was approaching the island of Umm Dwermat, which divided the Nile into two channels. Suddenly an argument broke out between the skipper, ar-Rais Mohammad ad-Dongolawi, and his assistant, 'Ali al-Bishtili, as to which channel to take. Stewart peered out in the starlight and noticed that the water in the left-hand channel seemed to be running as fast as a mill-race. He agreed with ar-Rais Mohammad that they should follow the right-hand channel, and instructed him to shoot it at full steam. Before *Abbas* could enter the channel, though, she swung round at seventy-five degrees to the island. Suddenly there was a crash that shook the whole boat. Then another. The paddles stopped.

The crew examined the hull and found that she had struck a gigantic submerged rock. She was seriously holed. After desperate attempts to get her off, Stewart decided to abandon her. A boat was unwinched and the crew began transferring equipment to Umm Dwermat nearby. Stewart had the mountain-gun spiked and thrown overboard, with spare boxes of ammunition.

As day broke, hordes of excited men and women of the Manasir tribe, from the nearby village of as-Salamaniyya, gathered on the bank. One group of men appeared under a white flag. They were led by Sulayman Na'iman wad Gamar, a Manasir chief who was also the local governor. He was dressed in his official Turco-Egyptian uniform of Stamboul coat and trousers. Stewart ordered his interpreter, Hassan Bey, with two other Egyptians, ashore to confer with him. At first they refused to go, saying they would be murdered, but Stewart pointed his revolver at them and threatened to shoot them unless they obeyed his commands.

They rowed ashore in the boat and conferred with Sulayman, who assured them that he was still loyal to the Khedive. He offered to provide the party with camels to reach Merowe – the nearest town held by the government. He spoke soothingly, pointing out that both his father and his grandfather had served the Turco-

Egyptians. He offered to guide the 'Turks' to Merowe personally, and begged them to come ashore and rest while the camels were found.

When Hassan brought the news back to Stewart, he was wary. He, Power and Herbin discussed the situation. On the one hand, Gordon had warned them against possible treachery. On the other, they were now stuck, and camels were what they needed. As far as they knew, anyway, the Manasir were still pro-government. They decided to take a chance and trust Sulayman. It turned out to be the biggest mistake of their lives.

They crossed over to the bank in the boat, with Hassan Bey as interpreter. Sulayman greeted them graciously, and Stewart began to negotiate for the camels. They agreed that half the amount would be paid in advance, and the rest when they reached Merowe. Though the bank was bustling with tribesmen clad in white *jallab-iyyas* and turbans, there was no sign of hostility. Patched dervish *jibbas* were noticeable by their absence, and Stewart began to feel more confident.

Meanwhile, the soldiers had begun to bring equipment across in the boat. When the camels arrived, they started to couch and load them. Sulayman had disappeared in the company of the steamer's captain, ar-Rais Mohammad. When the work was under way, Stewart asked for Sulayman in order to pay him, but received instead an invitation to visit him in a house nearby. The house was owned by a blind holy man named 'Atman Fakri. Unknown to Stewart, the blind man was a fanatical dervish supporter, and the real power in the district.

On his way there, with the consuls, Hassan Bey, and a military escort, Stewart was met by another messenger. This man told him that Sulayman requested him not to approach with arms or troops, as it would frighten his people. Perhaps because no hostility had been evident up to then, Stewart agreed. The escort was left behind. None of the four men in the party was armed except for Stewart himself, who had his revolver in his pocket.

At the holy man's mud-brick house, they were made welcome. They sat on *angarebs* near the door, and were served coffee and dates. When they were settled in, Sulayman took a copper water-pot and said he was going out to get water, leaving them with the blind man. A second later they heard a shout. Suddenly forty or fifty Manasir rushed into the room with swords, axes and spears, yelling, 'Become Muslims, you infidels, and you will be spared!' Stewart leapt up and drew his pistol, but realized that he was cornered. He gave his revolver to the enemy. As soon as it was out of his hand, the Manasir fell on Herbin and Power, smashing in their heads with axes in front of him. Blood splashed across the mud walls and floor. With a roar of rage, Stewart charged forward and set about them with his fists. He too was quickly dispatched. Hassan Bey was stabbed in the arm with a knife and speared in the leg, and fell unconscious. When he came round, the bodies of the other three were being dragged out of the room. Sulayman wanted to finish him off, but his brother pleaded for Hassan's life, saying he was 'sick to the stomach' from the bloodshed and treachery. Possibly because he was a Muslim, Hassan was spared.

The soldiers were still loading the camels when the horde of armed Manasir came hurtling towards them from the village. They were taken completely unawares. Many were killed where they stood. Others hurled themselves into the river or crammed into the small boat. The boat overturned. The Manasir shot the swimmers dead from the bank, and speared those who tried to pull themselves out of the water. In minutes all the Turco-Egyptian soldiers were dead and the Jihadiyya and Sudanese crew taken prisoner. When the Manasir boarded *Abbas* they found on board only the wife of one of the Greeks, who shot three of them before she was speared to death. Her body, together with the bloody corpses of Power, Herbin and Stewart, was thrown into the river. Stewart's journal and Gordon's precious files, messages, seals and ciphers were packed in boxes and sent to Berber.

Hassan Bey was made to work as a shepherd for his captors for some weeks, and was then sent to Berber, where he was imprisoned for four months by Governor Mohammad al-Khayr. He was eventually sent to Omdurman. He alleged later that the trap had been sprung with the collusion of the *Abbas*'s skipper, ar-Rais

Mohammad ad-Dongolawi, and his assistant, 'Ali al-Bishtili, whom Stewart threatened to shoot for having wrecked *Abbas*. According to Father Joseph Ohrwalder, however, it was Hassan Bey himself who arranged the trap. Since he was the only survivor, we only have his word for it that he was wounded. Ohrwalder claims that when Hassan reached Berber he demanded a reward from Mohammad al-Khayr for 'having secured Colonel Stewart's death'.[9] The murder of Stewart, Power and Herbin was a disgrace by any standards, but especially by those of the Sudanese, for whom a guest is sacred.

When Kitchener received the news of Stewart's murder he was devastated. At first he would not accept that his friend was dead. He prayed that he and his party had been taken prisoner. For days he lay awake all night turning the matter over in his head. Every morning he wired for permission to leave ed-Debba and go in search of survivors from *Abbas*. He asked leave to deploy the Mudir's Bashi-Bazuks. He asked for the loan of a British officer who could take over his post while he went to look for Stewart. He suggested a surprise attack on the Manasir. He suggested using diplomacy and bribery. All these appeals were refused.

The shrillness of his telegrams led to complaints from his top chief, Buller, that Kitchener was trying to fight a 'private war'. His immediate superior, Sir Charles Wilson, disagreed. He maintained that Kitchener's requests did him honour. Wilson wired Kitchener for a précis of all the telegrams he had sent. Kitchener complied, writing apologetically that he was alone at ed-Debba without any brother officer to discuss the matter with. He added that he had been motivated only by a desire to help his friend Stewart. 'I can only say I did my best according to my lights,' he wrote, 'and that I would not go through that eight days again, from 2nd to 10th October, for a fortune.'[10]

Wolseley heard of Stewart's death in a wire from Kitchener, and was shocked. 'Poor Stewart,' he wrote, 'his loss at this moment is a national one. A fine, chivalrous fellow to die at the hands of a murderer! May that murderer fall into my hands.'[11]

Sulayman Na'iman never did fall into Wolseley's hands. He was killed two years later by Salah Hussain, chief of Kitchener's 'Ababda raiders. Salah had known Stewart well, having been his companion and guide for eight days across the Nubian desert.

5

Stewart's murder convinced Wolseley that his task of getting to Khartoum upriver would be even harder than he had thought. If the Manasir had gone over to the Mahdi, his River Column would have to pass through the Fifth Cataract in full strength. The entire operation had become more urgent.

Wolseley had left Cairo by steamer on 27 September, and was on his way up the Nile. The news of Stewart's death had reached him at Wadi Halfa – known to the troops as 'Bloody Halfway' – on the Sudan–Egyptian border. A message from Gordon arrived via Kitchener on 4 November, informing him that the Mahdi himself was just across the White Nile, near Omdurman. The dash across the Bayuda desert by the Desert Column was now imperative. Wolseley was working on Gordon's suggestion that if he could get even a small number of troops in red jackets into Khartoum, it would be enough to convince the townspeople the British were on the way. It would hold the rebels off until the main force got there.

Wolseley's forward operating base at Korti lay four miles outside the mostly ruined town of Ambikol, a little upstream from ed-Debba. He had chosen it because it lay due north from Metemma – his Desert Column's objective. Metemma was 176 miles away, but it lay across a desert of gravel and rock. There were several key wells on the way, the most important being at Abu Tulayh (called Abu Klea by the British) and Jakdul. Water would be the deciding factor in any advance across the desert. The Camel Corps' first action would be to secure these wells.

Wolseley arrived at Korti on 16 December. It had taken him seventy-nine days to steam upriver from Cairo. Brigadier Sir Herbert Stewart had arrived there the previous day with his Guards

Camel Regiment and a squadron of the 19th Hussars. Stewart had set up a camp of blankets, sheets and makeshift shelters a thousand yards away from the Nile, on cultivated ground. The fertile strip was not wide here, and extended to sparse palm-groves on the bank. From his cabin, Wolseley could hear a *sagiyya* groaning ominously.

A host of officers had gathered on the bank to greet his arrival. Wolseley wanted to know if Kitchener was there. Kitchener, now back in uniform, Arab robes and cyanide laid aside, beard shaved off, was called forward to board the steamer. Wolseley, who had not seen him since the contretemps in Cyprus, shook hands with him and asked for the news. Kitchener gave him a full briefing. He had kept in touch with Gordon. He had collected supplies and camels, and gathered intelligence on the local tribes and conditions. He had completed surveys, drawn maps, and selected sites for base camps and field hospitals. Acting quite alone, he had become the undisputed pioneer of the expedition. As he listened, Wolseley must have realized what outstanding work Kitchener had done. Without his local knowledge the expedition would literally have been 'a leap in the dark'.

Kitchener was anxious to ask permission to go with the advance guard across the Bayuda. Wolseley had forbidden this a few weeks earlier, and Kitchener had concluded he was still nursing a vendetta for what had happened on Cyprus. Now, he found that the Com-mander-in-Chief had changed his tune. Wolseley said that he had done remarkable things here, and gave him permission to go with the Camel Corps. He even invited him to dinner the following night.

It was the cold season and exactly the right time for a desert operation. The sun was still hot at midday, but a refreshing wind cooled the air. Unfortunately the wind was downstream, and was likely to slow the progress of Wolseley's four hundred small boats, christened 'whalers'. They were still strung out along the Nile, and the river was already falling. To speed them on, Wolseley offered a prize of £100 for the first unit in. He hoped to have his entire desert assault force assembled at Korti by Christmas Day.

He had seen the Gordon Relief Expedition as a last chance to lead from the front. Right up to the last minute he had expected to take personal command of the historic sprint by camel across the Bayuda. The River Column would be led by Major General William Earle, a favourite of the Duke of Cambridge, who had previously commanded the garrison at Alexandria. Wolseley liked Earle, but considered him inexperienced and incapable of inspiring the men under his command. He could not refuse him, since he was senior to any member of his Ashanti Ring.

Wolseley's hopes were dashed when he received a message from Lord Hartington at Korti forbidding him to go with the advance guard. Instead, command would devolve on his protégé, Herbert Stewart. Stewart was competent and cool in action. Despite his less than perfect performance at et-Teb, Wolseley still believed him the finest soldier under his command.

Wolseley's other Ashanti Ring man, Sir Redvers Buller, his Chief of Staff, proved a constant thorn in the side. Buller was now far gone in alcoholism. He hired forty-six camels just to bring to the front his supplies of Fortnum & Mason delicacies and magnums of Veuve-Clicquot champagne. Wolseley opined that Buller thought 'all the world are fools and he alone is wise'. He vowed that he would never again employ him as Chief of Staff. Buller argued constantly with his subordinates, including Kitchener, whose pleas for a chance to investigate Stewart's death Buller had thrown out.

How much time, if any, Wolseley had spent considering who would take over from Stewart if he became a casualty is unknown. Buller was a good fighter, and had plenty of combat experience, but he was a born second-in-command, and lacked decisiveness alone. Colonel Fred Burnaby, now recovered from his wounds at et-Teb, had inveigled his way once more on to the staff. Wolseley liked and admired Burnaby mainly because the Duke of Cambridge hated him. Burnaby had a reputation as an adventurer and a swashbuckler, but was a loose cannon with no experience of field command.

The other senior officer with Stewart, Lieut. Colonel Sir Charles

Wilson, was an intelligence officer who had never been under fire. Neither he nor the chief of the Naval Brigade, Captain Lord Charles Beresford, RN, was really qualified to take charge in the field. The senior colonel of the Camel Corps was the Honourable Edward Boscawen of the Coldstream Guards. He was an unknown quantity. Wolseley hoped for the best, but admitted that he dreaded the thought of Stewart being killed or injured. 'It would be extremely difficult to replace him as leader of the advance guard,' he wrote.

His plan was to send the Camel Corps across the Bayuda desert on 28 December. They would be accompanied by a Royal Artillery camel battery carrying three two-and-a-half-inch screw-guns, firing seven-pound shells. A Naval Brigade of bluejackets with a Gardner, half an infantry battalion of the Royal Sussex Regiment, and a squadron of the 19th Hussars would also be on the orbat. They would be supported by transport personnel, including camel-men imported from Aden, Somalia and Egypt, Royal Engineers, a field hospital, bearer corps and medics. The desert force and their gear and provisions would be carried on the best part of three thousand camels. The Hussar detachment would be mounted on horses, and would act as scouts.

Hitting the Nile near Metemma, they would capture the town as a forward base, then rendezvous with Gordon's steamers. A small force of the Royal Sussex Regiment, with three selected officers, Sir Charles Wilson RE, Lieutenant Eddie Stuart-Wortley of the Royal Rifles, and Major Dickson of the Royal Dragoons, would go up to Khartoum as quickly as possible. The spearhead would be reinforced by the River Column under Earle, which would by then have mopped up dervishes along the Nile and taken Abu Hamed and Berber. It would also be backed up by a second Desert Column under Brigadier Sir Redvers Buller.

It was a daring plan, but blemished by the fact that there were not enough camels to go round. The total of three and a half thousand camels earmarked for the assault force was not adequate for the two thousand men with their equipment and rations. 'It was an easy problem to solve,' wrote Alex MacDonald, a *Daily*

News correspondent with the expedition, '. . . if a dash across 170 miles of desert . . . is necessary, how many riding, and how many pack camels will be required for so many men and so many tons of stores?'[12] Chief of Staff Sir Redvers Buller, who was responsible for logistics, had evidently failed to do the arithmetic. He had secured enough camels to carry his vital supply of Veuve-Clicquot, but neglected to ensure there were enough to do the job.

Wolseley was showing signs of strain when he arrived at Korti. After talking to Kitchener, he spent a day resting in a houseboat, suffering from conjunctivitis. Over the next few days the camp expanded around him. Tents arrived on *nuggars* and neat military lines sprang up. Troops came in on whalers in dribs and drabs – volunteers from the Black Watch, the Gordons, the Essex Regiment, the South Staffordshires, and the Duke of Cornwall's Light Infantry and others, to serve with the Mounted Infantry Camel Regiment. The Heavy and Light Camel Regiments came loping into camp on their new mounts. Another squadron of the 19th Hussars arrived. Commissariat, transport, medical and engineers stores were unloaded. On 26 December Billy Hewett's Royal Marines marched in, as smart as paint in spotless white helmets and pipe-clayed belts. They had been redeployed from Suakin to form a company of the Guards Camel Regiment, the fourth element in Wolseley's elite Camel Corps.

The four regiments of the Camel Corps totalled about eleven hundred men. The Heavy Camel Regiment was made up of troops from heavy cavalry units – the Blues and Royals, Dragoons and Dragoon Guards, Lancers, Queens Bays, and Royal Scots Greys. The Light Camel Regiment had been formed exclusively from the nine regiments of Hussars. The Guards Camel Regiment consisted of volunteers from the Coldstream, Grenadier and Scots Guards, and Royal Marines. The Mounted Infantry Camel Regiment was a mixture of picked men from line infantry battalions. Wolseley considered the Camel Corps the cream of the British army. Alex MacDonald thought the Mounted Infantry the cream of the Camel Corps.

Wolseley's idea of creating the first 'special forces' unit had been a brilliant innovation, but it was flawed in execution. The main problem was the time element, which had been beyond his control. The men were, as the press put it, 'a mixed salad' from different backgrounds, and had only had six weeks to gel together as a coherent force. Some of the Mounted Infantry had not yet seen their camels. None of them had any idea of how to ride or handle the beasts. The camel did not form part of their cultural heritage, and was widely regarded in ethnocentric terms as a 'horse designed by a committee'.

This ignorance was shared at all levels. Not realizing that camels' soft pads are custom-made for walking on sand, the army had actually sent out a number of cavalry shoeing-smiths. They were unable to see the beast through Arab eyes, as a magnificent animal perfectly adapted to desert conditions. They did not know its capabilities or limitations. They did not know that the word 'camel' itself was derived from the Arabic word for 'beauty', *jamaal*. Even if they had known, they would have laughed – few British soldiers got past the idea that the camel was a joke.

Though the rank and file were picked troops, they were spoiled by their officers. The number of 'honourables' tells its own tale. There were six hereditary members of the House of Lords among the Camel Corps officers, at least four lords' sons, one Count, and untold numbers of friends and relatives of people in high places. Typical of these was the third son of the Duke of Cambridge, Major Augustus Fitzgeorge of the 11th Hussars, whom Wolseley referred to as his chief's 'diseased offspring'. Lieut. Colonel Stanley de Astel Clarke, another Duke of Cambridge nomination, was given command of the Light Camel Regiment, against Wolseley's wishes. Clarke, equerry to Edward, Prince of Wales, like many of the 'swells' in the corps, had never been on active service. Wolseley considered him 'useless' and commented that 'any old woman from the court circle could have done as well'.

These men were brave almost without exception, but as Wolseley himself knew, courage was the small change of war. Efficiency and the ability to achieve tasks in the heat of battle was a far rarer quality. Wolseley had struggled all his career against this problem, but there was only so much he could do. The special forces concept would eventually rid itself of the dilemma by eliminating officers almost entirely from the battlefield. That revolutionary idea would take almost another century to come to fruition. For now, the Camel Corps was 'in with the in crowd', and Wolseley had to accept that everybody who was anybody in high society wanted a part in it.

Elements of the Camel Corps had first encountered their transport at Wadi Halfa in early November. After being issued with their saddles and equipment, they were turned loose among a herd of thousands of camels of all shapes and sizes, and told to take their pick. Since Egypt raised few camels of its own, most came from the northern Sudan. A handful came from Arabia, and these were considered the fastest and most reliable beasts. The first problems came as soon as the would-be cameleers approached the animals. Anyone who stood in front of an irritated camel was likely to get splattered by evil-smelling vomit. Contrary to myth, camels do not spit saliva. When annoyed, they void the contents of their several stomachs on anything standing nearby. They would gnash their teeth and make snapping attacks on those who grabbed their headropes. They would roar like lions, raising their tails perpendicularly and spraying everything in the vicinity with pellet-like droppings. Camels' eyes are sited so that they can see backwards as well as forwards. A man approaching too abruptly from the rear ran the risk of getting his leg smashed with a kick. At least two broken legs were reported.

The first rash of 'croppers' occurred when they tried to mount up. They were using British-designed saddles that incorporated stirrups – a device never used by the Arabs. Invariably the camel would leap up as soon as it felt the weight on the stirrup, and throw the rider sprawling into the dust. Eventually the troops discovered that it was best to ignore the stirrups and simply throw the leg over the saddle in the Arab way. The only drawback here was that they had been issued with special Namaqua rifle-buckets for carrying their weapons, slung from the saddle. The rifles were inserted butt-first, and got in the way whenever they tried to fling their legs over. The solution was to sling the rifle from the left wrist as they mounted, and slot it into the bucket once they were up.

A mad circus of roaring, spinning, kicking camels spun across the plain in spirals of dust. NCOs bawled out orders that even they themselves could not follow. The men clung to saddle-pommels and headropes for dear life. They quickly found out that, unlike horses, camels were able to turn their heads and bite their riders' knees. They could also butt with the back of the head, kick the rider's calves with their back legs, wriggle out of their headstalls, and even drop and roll over to throw the riders off. Young camels were unable to bite because they only had teeth on their lower jaws, but dominant males had canines the size of sharks' teeth that could shear off a man's arm. '[The] camel is the most awkward and ill-conditioned beast you can tackle,' recalled Private Bill Burge, of the Guards Camel Regiment. 'Ride him once and you will never forget it; be bitten by him and you will give his mouth a wide berth forever.'[13]

Another spate of 'croppers' came when they attempted a canter. Camels roll their backs while cantering, and any novice who tried it was likely to end up in a sorry heap on the sand. Even those who clung on tenaciously were betrayed by rotten girths that snapped and precipitated them to the ground. All over the plain, men hit the earth with resounding slaps. The place was dotted with soldiers picking themselves up and cursing. Everywhere there were men jogging frantically after their beasts.

They were given orders not to try anything more than a walk. The animals were, in any case, carrying loads of about 350 lb, including the rider, rifle and ammunition, about twenty litres of water in a goatskin, forage, rations, gear and saddle. To have ridden them fast would have meant needlessly tiring them out.

These troops were breaking new ground. There was no standard camel drill-book for the British army. The Mounted Infantry drill of one man holding four horses, while the other three men skirmished, was soon scrapped. Every senior officer who had a role in the Camel Corps added his own two-pennyworth of advice, which was nearly always useless. The counsel of the few camel experts like Kitchener was, as usual, ignored.

By the end of November, Herbert Stewart had thought out a modus operandi. The objective of the Camel Corps was to attain freedom of action as infantry, combined with defence of their transport. Dismounted on the battlefield, they would knee-hobble the camels in a mass, and form defensive squares at opposite corners. If they had to operate at a distance from their mounts, they would deploy a rearguard to defend them, and go into action as infantry. At Shabadud on their way to the forward base, the units already formed practised this drill for a solid nine days, until, in the words of one subaltern, 'we were as nearly perfect as we ever expected to be'.[14]

The Camel Corps made use of the time at Korti to master their drills. They practised incessantly in the desert, about a mile from the river, where the ground was hard gravel or flat sand. 'We were brought to a fair state of perfection,' wrote twenty-one-year-old Count Albert Gleichen, a subaltern of the Grenadiers, serving with the Guards Camel Regiment. 'The quickest time on record from the word of command, "Close order," to "Prepare for cavalry" being just one minute thirty seconds.'[15] The steadiness of the camels was tested by exposing them to a charge by the 19th Hussars, which had no perceptible effect. 'Everybody expected [the camels] to break their ropes, and career wildly over the desert,' Albert Gleichen wrote. 'The only result was that one camel struggled to his feet, looked round, and sat down again; the others never moved an eyelid.'[16]

Still the corps did not know what their objective was. The rumour for a while was that they were being sent into Manasir country to avenge John Hammill Stewart. Christmas Day passed and was marked with do-it-yourself plum puddings, and a concert on packing cases by two huge bonfires in the desert. Afterwards there were cheers for the generals, first Wolseley, then Stewart, then – to his astonishment – Kitchener, who was still only a brevet major. He considered this the greatest honour he had ever been given. The fact that he had been cheered before Brigadier Sir

Redvers Buller, VC, can have escaped the notice of neither. Still, there was no sign of any orders being issued. Wolseley was raring to go, but his camel battery had not yet turned up. It came on 27 December. Next morning, Wolseley told the spearhead troops that they would march in two days.

Herbert Stewart and Charles Wilson reported to Wolseley's tent for final orders. Wolseley instructed Stewart to move with half the force to Jakdul wells, about a hundred miles to the south. He had wanted the whole force to march to Metemma in a single movement, but the shortage of camels ruled this out. The actual amount of water available at Jakdul was an unknown factor. The water-sources there were not artesian wells but rainwater cisterns of the type the Arabs called *geltas*. These cisterns held water for two years after a heavy rain, but were not replenished from underground aquifers. The volume of water depended on the temperature and the number of animals that had recently watered there. Once at Jakdul, Stewart and his Sapper chief would calculate the amount. If it proved insufficient for the entire force, Stewart's orders were to press on directly to Abu Tulayh and Metemma. If it was thought sufficient, he would return to Korti with the camels to bring on the other half of the expedition.

The Guards and Mounted Infantry Camel Regiments would march with the first group. The Lights' and Heavies' camels would be used to carry their gear. Provisions would be dumped at Jakdul. The Guards would be left holding the wells, while the camels were taken back to bring the Heavies up. The Lights would be held in reserve. The force would muster at Jakdul and move forward en masse first to Abu Tulayh, then to Metemma. Whether they would be opposed or not was still unknown, but Wolseley hoped Stewart would get clear to Metemma without firing a shot. Metemma itself would have to be captured. Herbert Stewart commented that he could deal with it by taking out 'five hundred or so of the poor devils'.[17] As Albert Gleichen noted, a superstitious person would have said that he was tempting fate.

Once at Metemma, a line of communication would be established across the Bayuda desert. Stewart would remain in charge of the desert force. Charles Wilson would embark on Gordon's steamers for Khartoum with his two officers. He would take with him two dozen infantrymen of the Royal Sussex Regiment, who would be dressed in red jackets. On arrival in Khartoum, he was to march his red jackets through the streets, and confer with Gordon. He would then withdraw to Metemma, leaving Dickson and Stuart-Wortley in the town to assist Gordon until the Relief Force arrived. Captain Lord Charles Beresford, RN, commander of the Naval Brigade, was not at the briefing, but Wolseley explained that his role was to take over Gordon's steamers at Metemma, and sail Wilson and his small force to Khartoum.

The spearhead watered their camels on the afternoon of 30 December, then saddled and loaded amid a crescendo of noise – camels vomiting and roaring, leaping up and throwing off their loads. Tails went perpendicular and ordure was sprayed everywhere. There were raucous shouts, curses of the vilest nature, and the crack of whips liberally applied. Saddles were fitted, greased girths pulled tight. Double saddle-bags of canvas and leather were slung, bedrolls on one side, tents on the other. Rifle-buckets were buckled, water-skins and bags of camel-feed draped from pommels. Finally saddle-blankets and covers were fitted. No extra equipment was allowed. Every trooper was limited to 40 lb, in addition to his rifle and ammunition. In his saddle-bag he carried a valise with a spare jacket, tinted sun-goggles, a face veil, spare shirts, spare boots, socks, housewife (sewing kit), washing and shaving kit, and prayer book. His daily rations – tins of bully beef, biscuits and tea – were carried in a haversack.

The Camel Corps were dressed in grey serge tunics, known as 'jumpers', with corduroy riding breeches of yellow ochre. They wore spirals of cloth or 'puttees' round their lower legs, and ankle-high brown boots. The most vital item of their equipment was the pith helmet – also known as a 'Wolseley Helmet' – with a broad brim and high crown. Originally white, the men dyed them brown with a mixture of mud and the boiled bark of acacia trees. The helmet was embellished with a strip of cloth wound around the centre, known as a 'pugaree', which was also dyed. Herbert Stewart himself wore a steel Horseguards helmet, and an orange pugaree for quick recognition – a small but hazardous vanity. Officers wore the same kit as the ranks, except that most had high field-boots instead of puttees. All ranks were issued with cummerbunds, known as 'cholera belts', which their commanders fondly believed would ward off cholera and other diseases. This bit of superstition was the British equivalent of the dervish *hejab* for warding off knives and bullets.

The men were equipped with standard Martini-Henrys with 120 rounds carried in a pouch, and a leather bandolier worn across the left shoulder. They had sword bayonets slung in a frog from their leather belts. Each man carried a wooden water-bottle as well as a leather water-bottle of Egyptian design, known as a *mussak*. Officers carried swords and Webley revolvers in holsters. According to Private Bill Burge of the Guards, the clothing itself was not oppressive. 'The one thing that seemed to grow in weight and tightness . . . was the bandolier,' he wrote. 'The belt became a positive vice around your chest and shoulder in the course of a long, hot desert march.'[18]

One by one the men flung themselves into the saddle. The beasts rose snorting and honking, tussling at the headropes. The riders headed for the mustering point on the nearby desert plateau in a cloud of dust. At 1500 hours Wolseley inspected them. He was intensely moved by the magnificent sight of over a thousand British soldiers mounted on camels. He saluted Herbert Stewart and wished him luck. Herbert saluted again and gave the order to move out. 'Wolseley's Commandos' – the first ever camel-mounted expedition of British troops – wheeled into columns of forty and set off jauntily into the desert, determined to save Gordon or die.

Wolseley watched them go. 'It is the beginning of the first scene in the last act of this Khartoum drama,' he wrote in his diary. 'May God bless this expedition, and grant that it be in every aspect a complete success.'[19] It was, as Wolseley knew, the high point of an advance of astonishing boldness, fourteen hundred miles through some of the most difficult country on earth. 'I think those engaged in it,' he wrote, 'are now beginning . . . to feel they have the honour of taking part in an operation the like of which has never been undertaken before.'[20]

The next day his sanguine mood was shattered. He had the first news from Gordon for six weeks. A messenger he had sent in October had returned with a piece of paper the size of a postage stamp, inscribed 'Khartoum all right 14/12/84' in Gordon's hand-writing. The man also had a long and rambling oral message to impart. The gist of it was that the dervishes were investing Khartoum, and Wolseley's force must come quickly and in strength. The news threw Wolseley. He went to bed that night depressed, and could not sleep. He had calculated his entire oper-ation on Gordon's repeated assertion that only a small force of British troops was needed to frighten the dervishes off. The timbre of Gordon's latest communiqué changed everything. Instead of a dash to Khartoum from Metemma, he would have to concentrate forces there before he advanced. Another slow build-up like the one here at Korti would cost him days.

Before dawn he got up and told Buller to cancel the dispatch of the 19th Hussars earmarked to escort the River Column at Merowe. They would now go across the Bayuda instead. He would have to set up another forward base at Metemma, and leapfrog supplies there via the desert wells on relays of camels. Wilson's small force would act as a stop-gap. The knowledge that the British were on their way would hold off the Mahdi's offen-sive until his main force reached the capital. He would garrison Metemma with one camel regiment, and send the other three with the Hussars and ten guns to Khartoum.

Once he had thought it out, he realized that the situation was not as bad as it had looked. It would be, after all, a safer plan to advance in force than to execute a mad rush. By the time the sun came up on New Year's Day 1885, his depression had passed. He believed he still had a chance of being in Khartoum by the end of the month.

6

The Bayuda desert was bathed in the last iridescent light of sundown. The light lay on the gravel plains and jagged hills like liquid gold. The sun was a vast globe sinking on their right, throwing great gangling spider shadows of camels and men on their left flank. That so many camels could move with no perceptible sound was almost disturbing to the British soldiers. They talked and joked together as if to fill the vacuum. They had become a floating island in the emptiness. The force that had seemed so large when mustered at Korti was reduced to nothing by the infinite vistas of the landscape.

It is often said that the Bayuda is not a 'real' desert, but this is untrue. It may not be an 'idealized' desert of rolling sand-dunes, but it is as arid as almost anywhere on this latitude in the Sahara, of which it is but an eastward extension. It is a stony, sandy wilderness relieved only by the occasional seam of stunted thorn-trees. Endless wastes of wind-graded *sarir* stretch on, punctuated by grey plains of cracked clay, wrinkled and fissured like old weathered hide. Everywhere, razor-peaked buttes burst through the stony surface like chunks of polished coal. Rainfall is scant. When the rain comes, though, it runs quickly off the hills, creating an intricate network of wadis or khors. The rain is held for days by the clay plains, and the nomads and semi-nomads of the area move their makeshift settlements and congregate with their camels and sheep around the pools. Moving south, the Bayuda becomes a chequerboard of black and amber – gloomy gravel plains interspersed with areas of rippling fish-scale dunes. The plains are dotted with thorn-trees, growing hundreds of yards apart, but gradually coalescing further south into seams of vegetation whose verdure is only rich by comparison with their stark surroundings.

The sun set at about 1700 hours. Night came and with it a three-quarter moon, brighter than most of the men had ever seen. The moonlight was clear enough for them to make out the hills around them, rising sheer out of the desert, looking like lopsided pyramids and warped dark blades. In places, there were patches of thorn-trees and *tabas* – a hardy species of esparto grass the nomads used to make huts and mats. The British referred to it as 'savas'.

As the night came on the men's laughter petered out. Many would have fallen asleep and dropped from their camels but for the constant stoppages caused by the baggage-train. There was a shortage of handlers – another omission by Buller. The pack-camels were tied head to tail in strings of three, with one handler. If one stopped, the others would continue, snapping headropes or getting hopelessly tangled, sitting, rolling and throwing their loads. Then all the camels in the string would have to be couched and reloaded over again. This was awkward, even in moonlight, and often poorly executed. Many of the camels developed galls. The constant halts were agonizing to Stewart, but they gave the men a chance to snatch some rest before the buglers sounded the advance.

Kitchener and his 'Ababda escort had raced ahead. The Hussars formed a protective screen a mile or more in front. The main column was led by native guides from Ambikol, who had been press-ganged into service by Herbert Stewart. He had had the local chiefs brought to him and showed them a box full of money. He had informed them that they could either accept the money to guide him to Metemma, or go for nothing, lashed on to their camels with rope. Even in the field he was taking no chances. The guides had a close escort of Hussars, who had orders to shoot them if they tried to bolt.

Dawn came up like a miracle, in blood-red streaks and a wing of fire-edged dark cloud. It seemed as if the darkness had fractured into shards, slowly burned up by the power of the new day. The buglers sounded reveille. It was a typically English ironic joke, and the men responded with a jeering cheer. They were crossing a hard plain of cracked clay, sloping up to a wadi between two hills. The wadi was full of acacia trees. The expedition rode into the trees and Stewart gave the order to halt. Gratefully the men couched their camels, and stretched their legs. They ate bully beef out of new-fangled tin cans, with hard tack biscuits, and drank tea.

Then they slept under the guard of vedettes and pickets until woken by the mosquitoes and flies.

They were off again at 1500 hours, the Hussars disappearing into the foreground until they became specks on the distant hills. Stewart commented on the excellence of the 19th Hussars, telling Albert Gleichen that they were the 'very acme of light cavalry'. The scouts riding with Stewart were commanded by Lieut. Colonel Percy Barrow – now recovered from his wound at et-Teb – and Major John Denton French, a future field marshal. At midnight that night, still padding doggedly onwards, the men broke into a spontaneous round of 'Auld Lang Syne' to mark the New Year. Not long afterwards they came to the wells of al-Hawayat, where they halted. The horses were given a bucket of water each and the men slept. Stewart posted a company of the Sussex Regiment here to secure the wells.

The men slipped quickly into the routine of the desert march. After a couple of days, it seemed that they had been here for ever. It was difficult to believe that another world existed beyond this. Of the enemy there was no sign. On New Year's Day the Hussars picked up a tribesman of the Hassaniyya – a nomadic people of the Bayuda. Stewart's Ambikol guides identified him as 'Ali Lulah, a notorious robber of caravans, and called for his immediate execution. Seeing his worth, though, Stewart spared him and pressed him into service, bringing him along together with his wife and baby. The next night the Hussars spotted a fire in the distance, and surprised a dervish supply caravan. They captured a number of dervishes and scattered the rest.

Within two days it had become clear that the equipment issued to the Camel Corps was defective. They had been given standard native water-skins, an item of great antiquity in northern Africa. Though the skin kept the water deliciously cool, it was porous and lost water by evaporation. Like the camel, it was superbly adapted to the desert, but only effective in the hands of experts who knew its strengths and limitations. Desert-dwelling Arabs serviced their skins almost constantly, and never laid them on the hot ground, knowing the water would vanish by osmosis. They had their own way of plugging leaks, with twigs and camel-dung, and would cover the skins with woven cloth in high winds. They used a special tar made from the crushed seeds of wild melons for waterproofing.

The British knew none of this. They would stitch up all apparent leaks, grease the leather over and over, but still find that at the end of the day half the water was gone. 'The worst of all privations was the lack of water,' said Private Bill Burge of the Guards Camel Regiment. 'We carried as much as we could . . . but the skin bags in which it was carried leaked badly, and the precious, priceless fluid was lost . . . It was terrible to see the fierce struggling for a drink as soon as a so-called well was reached – a drink of foul and muddy concoction which would make you ill to look at in ordinary times.'[21]

Another major problem was the saddles. Many had been made of unseasoned wood, and were not robust enough for the expedition. If they broke or warped, they would inevitably end up chafing the camel's skin and causing a gall. Camels were among the most enduring pack-animals alive, but a bad gall could be a death-sentence. Even the local saddles, however, were not suited to British-style baggage in boxes and tin trunks. Desert Arabs always used sacks and bags that would mould themselves to the camel's shape, and had no abrasive edges. By the time they arrived at Jakdul on the third day out, many of the camels were already suffering from poor handling and bad treatment.

The expedition reached Jakdul in the early morning. It lay inside a wedge of dense black hills that ran right across the desert horizon. After heavy rains, run-off from the hills poured down a *siq* or steep-sided watercourse into a vast stony-floored amphitheatre, hemmed in by sheer scarps and littered with copses of thorn-trees. During the rains the whole area would be flooded, but when the flow ceased, a chain of pools was left scattered along the course of the *siq*, and through the valley itself. These pools gradually dried up throughout the hot summer, leaving water in only the deepest cisterns. The entrance to Jakdul lay through a narrow opening in the sheer rock wall, and was not easy to find. It would have been impossible for the column had Kitchener not ridden forward with his 'Ababda and showed the way. Kitchener was now back in Arab dress, having obtained special permission from Wolseley. According to Private Bill Burge, he could have passed as an Arab. 'I often saw him walking about,' Burge recalled, 'and believed him to be a real son of the desert.'[22]

They found only three pools currently full, the largest at the base of the cleft in the rocks, where the *siq* opened into the valley. Here, at the water's edge, protected by sheer cliffs on two sides, they set up their base. Another cistern lay in the *siq* itself, and could only be approached by a stiff scramble up the escarpment. Climbing up there later, Albert Gleichen was amazed to find what he described as a 'beautiful, large, ice-green pool, deepening into black as I looked into its transparent depths. Scarlet dragonflies flitted about in the shade; rocks covered with dark green weed looked out of the water; the air was cool almost to coldness. It was like being dropped into a fairy grotto.'[23] Stewart inspected the pools carefully with the chief of the Sapper detachment, Major Dorward, who calculated that there were about half a million gallons in the existing pools – enough to water twenty thousand camels. This turned out to be an underestimation, but Stewart could not refute it, and knew he would have to return to Korti to bring up the rest of the force. The Royal Engineers set up half a dozen pumps and a hose to convey the water to troughs for the camels and horses.

The camels got no chance to rest. By midday the stores had been unloaded and dumped. After dark, the entire baggage-train set off back to Korti under Stewart. The Guards Camel Regiment, the Sappers, and a section of six Hussars remained to defend the water. Kitchener and his 'Ababda stayed with them. Kitchener began to send off his men in twos and threes to gather intelligence on the way ahead.

After the caravans had left, it seemed uncannily quiet in the camp. Major Dorward began to organize his pumps, hoses and troughs into a more efficient system, so that, when the caravans returned, up to eighty camels could be watered at a time. Men of the Guards Camel Regiment laboured up the scarps and began work on the construction of three sangars. The Hussars manned the high ground near the entrance. A chain of sentries was posted around the pools, and a heliograph station was set up outside the cul-de-sac to signal any unusual occurrence. The mornings were intensely cold, and the men would stamp about and brew tea or coffee to warm themselves. A tin of bully beef and a biscuit was breakfast, lunch and dinner. During the day, sentries would occasionally spot natives crossing the plain. Kitchener and the handful of Hussars would shoot out after them on horses. Several times Kitchener's party captured caravans carrying dates and grain to Metemma. On one occasion a terrified tribesman offered Kitchener a dollar to let him alone.

7

Gordon's latest message had reminded Wolseley that maintaining close communication with Khartoum was vital. For this he needed Herbert Kitchener, whom Gordon had come to regard as a lifeline. Gordon wrote in his journal that Kitchener ought to be the Sudan's next governor-general. As it turned out, he would be, but fourteen long years would pass and tens of thousands of lives would be lost before it occurred.

For now, Wolseley regretted having allowed Kitchener to go with the Camel Corps. When Herbert Stewart arrived back at Jakdul at noon on 12 November, with the Heavy Regiment, he found Kitchener in Gleichen's 'fairy grotto'. Kitchener's 'Ababda scouts had returned. He told Stewart that the latest intelligence suggested that Metemma was held by between two and seven thousand dervishes, but the road was clear. He had already sent the scouts off again, and they would return shortly with more up-to-date information.

What Kitchener did not know was that Stewart had already lost the element of surprise. It had taken him ten days to get back to Jakdul, and in that time the British presence there had been spotted.

Desert Arabs are keenly observant and have superb memories for detail. They also have a grapevine system that is highly efficient. The desert grapevine had been buzzing. Reports of dervish spies had reached 'Ali Sa'ad Farah, the Mahdist agent at Metemma, that the British were already committed to the Bayuda desert. There could be no doubt as to their objective. The dervishes moved quickly. Before Stewart had even arrived back at Korti, the Mahdist force at Metemma had been joined by a force from Berber under Mohammad al-Khayr – the man who had sent the steamer *el-Fasher* after *Abbas*.

The Mahdi himself had been aware of the Relief Expedition since October. On 13 January, the day his dervishes captured Omdurman, he dispatched part of the Green Standard division to Metemma. It was led by Musa wad Helu – brother of the Khalifa 'Ali wad Helu. The force was composed mostly of tribesmen from the Kinana and Dighaym, the Baggara cattle-nomads who had been with the Mahdi from the beginning, and the Hamr, a tribe of settled and semi-nomadic cattle- and camel-breeders from Kordofan. The Metemma and Berber garrisons were made up of dervish regulars, including captured Jihadiyya riflemen, and levies from the local riverain tribe, the Ja'aliyyin, and its desert-dwelling sub-section, the 'Awadiyya.

The Mahdist chiefs at Metemma were aware that Stewart would have no choice but to water at the wells of Abu Tulayh. The joint Metemma–Berber contingents occupied the wells on 12 January, the day Stewart arrived back at Jakdul. The Omdurman force under Musa wad Helu would rendezvous with them there five days later. Together, the three dervish contingents numbered between twelve and fourteen thousand men. When the British arrived at Abu Tulayh, exhausted and thirsty after their long march, they would find there a dervish force, fresh, well armed, and outnumbering them by at least six to one.

Stewart thanked Kitchener for his news, and informed him that Wolseley wanted him back at the forward base. He had brought with him Kitchener's chief, Lieut. Colonel Sir Charles Wilson, who would take over his role as expedition intelligence officer. Kitchener was furious, but kept quiet. His part in the advance was over, but his reputation was assured. The press contingent had got hold of his story, and he had been headlined in every British newspaper as the 'intrepid hero' of the campaign. Within six months he would be a brevet lieutenant-colonel, and within three years Adjutant General of the Egyptian army.

A day earlier, the stores and ammunition had come in on a train of a thousand camels led by Lieut. Colonel Stanley Clarke – Wolseley's least favourite battalion commander. The camels were now in very bad shape. Albert Gleichen noticed at once that their humps had turned flabby. Many had developed galls from bad saddles and poor loading, and some had foundered under their loads. More than twenty had expired on the way back to Jakdul.

Both camels and men had had a hard time of it on the second trek. On 8 January there had been an unseasonal turn in the weather, of the kind that sometimes occurs in the desert of the northern Sudan in winter. The nights remained freezing cold but the daytime temperature soared. In Korti, the change did not go unremarked by Wolseley. 'Oh this dreadful tropical heat,' he fretted, 'how I dread the long sick list which it foretells! This is the enemy I dread.'

The men had been rationed to a litre of water a day. They could only drink from their water-bottles at prescribed times. Skins were not supposed to be touched as they carried the communal water for cooking and making tea. In all, the men were consuming not more than two and a half litres a day, and this was inadequate. Even in the cool season four litres were barely enough to maintain the body's moisture balance. At the time, the word 'dehydration' did not even figure in the medical dictionary, and its symptoms were listed under 'sunstroke'. It would take another half century before medical knowledge grasped that fluid loss was a far more insidious enemy than the sun. In fact, a loss of only 5 per cent of a man's body moisture can cause coma and eventual death. The worst aspect of dehydration was that it sneaked up unexpectedly.

A man could be seriously affected before he had even realized that he was thirsty.

Morale had taken a massive slump. The Egyptian camel-men had begun stealing water from each other and from their officers. The enterprising Aden camel-men had started to sell it at a dollar per one-and-a-half-litre bottle. The situation had become so bad that Stewart had sent Lieutenant Eddie Stuart-Wortley ahead to Jakdul to bring back water.

The camels were receiving half rations of sorghum grain, and the grain made them thirsty. On arrival at Jakdul they drank massive amounts, and it took the entire night to water them. The noise, wrote Gleichen, was 'fiendish': 'Native drivers jabbering, camels bellowing, Englishmen swearing all night through.'[24] By dawn the pools had almost run dry and the watering had to be suspended. Stewart had intended to march out the following day, but the water situation compelled him to postpone the advance for another twenty-four hours. He had brought with him half of the Naval Brigade under Lord Charles Beresford, with their Gardner machine-gun, carried in sections on four camels. When they had mustered at Korti, the sight of fifty-eight naval ratings in grey uniforms and straw hats, and officers in blue frock-coats, mounted on camels, had struck Wolseley as bizarre. 'This is certainly a strange episode in our Military History,' he wrote. Beresford himself, whom Wolseley counted as 'a really first rate man', was riding a huge white Nubian donkey.

The bluejackets gave their 'ships of the desert' the same care they lavished on their men-of-war. They had brought oakum, a caulking material of rope fibre laced with tar, which Beresford thought might salve camel-galls. Buller had laughed at him when he asked for it, but it turned out to be highly effective. Not a single camel of the Naval Brigade was lost. They had also had the foresight to make their own rubber water-bags. These proved far better at retaining water than those issued to the army. 'I wish the government would have gone to the expense of providing everyone with them,' Gleichen complained. 'It would have saved an enormous amount of pain and privation.'[25]

The camel battery with their screw-guns had also come in with Stewart. Due to the lack of camels, they had brought only a hundred shells per gun. The Naval Brigade were even worse off, with only a thousand .45 calibre rounds for their Gardner. At a fast rate of fire these would be used up in ten minutes. Two hundred and fifty-eight men of the Royal Sussex Regiment had been brought up to secure the wells after the column had departed.

The next day the sun came up on a merciless sky. The day was hot and windless. From dawn till dusk the men laboured, working pumps, hauling buckets, filling water vessels, watering camels and horses under a furnace sun. There was not a breath of air. 'It was like working in the stoke-hole of a steamer,' wrote correspondent Alex MacDonald. The condition of the water-skins was now terrible. Gleichen reckoned that only one in five held its full complement of water. As much water as possible was poured into fantasses – 160-litre steel tanks carried two to a pack-camel. Even these were battered out of shape and leaking almost as badly as the water-skins.

By the end of the day, the entire column was ready. It was a far smaller army than the one that had been slaughtered at Shaykan with Hicks the previous November – nineteen hundred assault troops, 340 camel-men, three guns, one machine-gun, 2,880 camels, and 157 horses. The column was accompanied by a herd of cows for fresh meat.

The next morning a caravan of a hundred camels came in carrying grain from Korti. It was led by Lieut. Colonel Fred Burnaby, conspicuous in his blue astrakhan-lined 'pilot jacket' and hessian boots. He had ditched his shotgun after complaints about 'bad form' from fellow officers. In its place, he had an almost equally vicious Lancaster four-barrelled 'British Bulldog' pistol, known for its stopping power. Burnaby dismounted from his horse near the pool at the base of the *siq* and lit a cigarette. 'Am I in time for the fighting?' was the first thing he asked.

Burnaby had arrived in Korti the day after Stewart had left. Having heard good reports on his work along the lines of communication, Wolseley had decided to send him with the Desert Column. He needed someone to take over the forward base at Metemma after the column's two senior officers, Stewart and Wilson, had left. Burnaby was elected. His progress so far had not been marked by fortune: on his way to Jakdul, he had lost an officer – a Captain Gordon, who had left with him from Korti, carrying dispatches. Gordon had wandered into the blue with a Greek servant and vanished off the map for ever.

The Desert Column formed up that afternoon. The laughter and high spirits that had accompanied its departure from Korti were all gone. Though there were still no reports of enemy on the road ahead, the atmosphere was solemn. The men felt in their bones that they were in for trouble. 'I do not know what mysterious force is at work in time of war to tell opponents that a fight is coming on,' said Private Burge, 'but that force was in operation.'[26]

As the mass of men and camels surged forward in military formation, Alex MacDonald was struck by its heroic aspect: '. . . the march out into the desert displayed under all its circumstances a courage and dash worthy of our best military traditions,' he wrote. 'Here was a handful of our soldiers standing resolved, in the face of all the difficulties anticipated or unknown which must harass and endanger them, to carry out their order to save Gordon.'[27]

They rode over an undulating plain of gravel, with jagged hills hanging like ghosts in the sand-mist far off to the east. Not far out of Jakdul, Major John French and his Hussars came across horse tracks. The tracks were fresh: the Hussars thought they had been made only that day. If there was any doubt as to the identity of the horsemen, it was dispelled by the discovery nearby of a Remington rifle. When French brought the news to Stewart, he feared that the column was being watched by the enemy, but still hoped that the road to Metemma would be clear. That day they made only ten miles, pitching camp on a hard sandy slope scattered with *tabas* grass and acacia bushes. The units were carefully positioned in defensive formation around the camels.

The next morning they tramped ceaselessly across the Bayuda's black gravel plains towards a conical hill, Jabal an-Nus, 'Half-Way Hill'. There were constant stoppages from the baggage-camels. 'The way the brutes toiled on was something marvellous,' wrote Albert Gleichen; 'you would see one go slower and slower, till the tail of the animal in front he was tied to seemed nearly coming off; then he would stop for a second, give a mighty shiver, and drop down stone dead.'[28] Scores of dead and dying camels were left strewn across the desert as the column marched.

The force passed Jabal an-Nus at 1300 hours, and camped that night near another landmark, Jabal Sarjayn. At two o'clock on the morning of 16 January, Stewart sent off a party of Hussars under Percy Barrow to reconnoitre the way as far as Abu Tulayh. An hour later the buglers sounded reveille. The column started before daybreak, hoping to make Abu Tulayh wells by the afternoon. They were moving through a valley of black clinker rock, with hills a mile off on both sides that converged some way in front of them. By 1100 hours they had reached the end of the valley, from which a narrow track led up through a pass between the hills. Abu Tulayh wells lay on the other side of the pass, about three miles away.

No sooner had the column halted than a shout went up, and Percy Barrow's Hussars were spotted riding hell for leather down the perilous track. Barrow cantered up to Stewart, saluted, and reported breathlessly that they had found the enemy in force. Thousands of dervishes were deployed between them and the wells. One of his sections had encountered a troop of dervish scouts, and had chased them right up to the wells. The commander, Lieutenant Craven, had actually managed to grab one of the enemy. He was preparing to bring him back as a present for the Intelligence Department, when a host of dervish spearmen had suddenly sprung out of the tall grass and bounded towards him. Craven had jumped on his horse and he and his men had ridden for their lives.

The news went round the column like wildfire, and was greeted with a surge of exhilaration. 'At last we were actually coming to blows with the enemy,' Gleichen said, 'that so many had regarded as a phantom.'[29] The Desert Column were about to engage in the bloodiest action ever fought by British troops in the Sudan.

8

To Herbert Stewart the news was a jolt. He had not expected to find the enemy in force at Abu Tulayh. He realized that the dervishes had played their hand well. Shortage of water meant that retreat was now impossible. The only option was to drive the enemy off the wells.

He urged his horse a little way up the escarpment and surveyed the heights with his field-glasses. He saw that the cliffs overlooking the pass were alive with dervishes waving their weapons. Their white robes stood out brilliantly. Spearheads the size of masons' trowels flashed in the morning sun. He estimated there were about two thousand enemy on the hills.

He wanted to get his force on to high ground as soon as possible, but decided against trying the pass. Instead, he ordered the expedition to advance straight up the escarpment in line of columns, with the baggage-train in the rear. They reached the top without hindrance and pressed forward down a rocky slope covered in stony hillocks. Stewart gave the order to halt. He, Charles Wilson, the newspaper correspondents, and some of the staff, went to look for the enemy.

They rode to the edge of the plateau, from where he had a magnificent view of the Abu Tulayh valley. It was a serpent of green threading through black desert, waves of patinated shingle, undulating like a frozen sea. The wadi was wide and sandy, and full of *tabas* grass and trees – white-spined acacias and the larger *talh* trees from which the place took its name. Their great bushy heads stood out against the sombre hues of the desert like giant green versions of 'fuzzy-wuzzy' hairstyles. The entire plain was circumscribed by low rocky ridges in all directions but the south. The wells were marked by a line of fluttering green and white banners, and Stewart could also make out a large tent. The sound of dervish tom-toms came faintly from the direction of the enemy camp. Beyond the wells the plain flattened out into browns and greys until it melted into the pastel sky towards the Nile.

Stewart told the press contingent that he intended to attack at once, and sketched out a rough plan in the dust with his stick. Alex MacDonald, who had been at the rear, saw the staff gathered on the salient, and rode towards them to find out what was happening. He passed the assault force, who were already dismounted and drawn up in battle order. Their Martini-Henrys were being inspected by officers and NCOs. It looked to MacDonald as if they were about to advance to contact, and he was impressed by their morale. 'Had they been going to a sing-song instead of into a life and death struggle with a savage force,' he wrote, 'they could hardly have evinced more cheerfulness.'[30]

On his way to the staff group, MacDonald met Fred Burnaby, riding a donkey. The big man, he thought, looked worried. Burnaby told him that if any disaster happened, none of them would ever see London again. MacDonald, surprised by the note of pessimism in his voice, told Burnaby he was the last man he would have suspected of anticipating disaster. He asked what he meant. Burnaby shrugged and said that he rated their chances of getting past the enemy at about twenty to one. 'Perhaps he was chaffing me or taking my pulse,' MacDonald wrote, 'but I think not.'[31]

There was plenty of activity in the valley. Fifty dervish horsemen were riding in single file across a ridge along the far side of the wadi to the left. Enemy footmen with rifles were scampering towards a conical hill on the right. They were about two thousand yards away. Shortly, puffs of smoke from the dervish positions told Stewart that they were being fired on. The shooters were well out of range, and Stewart decided not to return fire. It was now after 1500 hours, and Burnaby reminded him that they only had three hours of daylight left. He suggested postponing the attack until the following day. Stewart agreed, and rode back to the column. He moved the force forward to a lying-up place on a stony plateau just out of sight of the wadi, and gave the order to halt.

Hussar vedettes were detailed to occupy the hills to the left. The bluejackets unslung the pieces of their Gardner from the four camels that had lugged it from Korti. They assembled it in four minutes, and ran it up a hill overlooking the left of the lying-up place. Semaphore flags began to wave from the Hussar forward pickets, announcing that the dervishes were still coming.

At the lying-up place, outpost sentries were detailed from the Sussex Regiment and the Heavy Camel Regiment. The rest of the force, both officers and men, piled arms and set to work to build a defensive zariba. The ground was scattered with loose boulders, but there were not enough for a proper parapet. The troops did the best they could, and by sunset had built a wall two feet high. A fort was constructed on the left of the zariba from dozens of boxes, trunks and sacks from the baggage-train. This was to be Stewart's command post, and he had his red flag planted there. The stone wall covered only three sides of the area. At the rear were some oval pits about fifteen feet deep, where the camels were hobbled in tightly jammed lines, and the rest of the stores unloaded. The open side of the pits was protected by hedges of cut thorn-bush and a hastily erected barbed-wire entanglement. A stone sangar was constructed as a hospital post.

The sun was going down to their right, a gleaming egg-yolk dissolving into a miasma of blue and pink dust. The sound of tom-toms eddied towards the British ranks eerily from the low ground. Suddenly there was the crackle of musketry from less than a mile away, and the whizz of .43 calibre bullets scorching air. Several camels in the baggage-train, and a camel-man, were hit. The men got down behind their low wall. The host of dervishes Stewart and Wilson had spotted advancing on the right before sunset had now crept up a hill within twelve hundred yards. The fire was dropping on the camp from an elevation of about seven hundred feet.

The dervish riflemen were building a sangar on their hilltop. In the last glimmer of sunset, Alex MacDonald watched them running up and down like ants carrying stones for its construction. He was just wondering what had happened to the screw-guns when two

22. The Desert Column waters at Jakdul Wells in the Bayuda desert. Enclosed in a perfect amphitheatre of rock, Jakdul's water-pools are crucial to the advance, but by lingering there for ten days Herbert Stewart's Camel Corps loses the initiative.

23. The Desert Column marching towards Abu Klea. At this stage, commander Herbert Stewart is unaware that the dervishes are occupying the wells in force, making an engagement inevitable.

24. Building a stone zariba above Abu Klea. Although under fire by dervish skirmishers, Stewart orders the Camel Corps to construct a defensive position, hoping to draw the enemy into the attack the next day at first light.

25. Lieut. Colonel Sir Charles Wilson of the Royal Engineers. Wilson, officially Chief of Intelligence on the Gordon Relief Expedition, took command when Stewart was mortally wounded at Abu Kru. Wilson was blamed by Wolseley for the failure of the mission, but eye-witness accounts show that he behaved with uncommon bravery.

26. Lieut. Colonel Fred Burnaby of the Royal Horse Guards. A giant of a man, Burnaby was a soldier and adventurer much loved in the ranks of his own regiment. Not everyone, though, was impressed by his facetious approach to war: at et-Teb he carried a shotgun as if on a 'grouse-shoot'.

27. The mêlée at Abu Klea. The confused hand-to-hand fighting lasted only ten minutes but was remembered as the bloodiest engagement the British ever fought in the Sudan.

28. 'The Gatling's jammed and the colonel dead' – Lieut. Colonel Fred Burnaby lies mortally wounded on the field of Abu Klea. Posterity has remained largely silent about the fact that he jeopardized the British square by wheeling out a company of the Heavy Camel Regiment without orders.

29. Bird's-eye view of the battle of Abu Klea. The dervishes suddenly switch their main attack to the rear left-hand corner of the square, where Burnaby has opened the ranks to protect the Gardner machine-gun. By chance, the enemy meets the Heavy Camel Regiment, the least experienced foot soldiers in the square.

30. The British square at Abu Kru. Charles Wilson pushes his men on under heavy fire, determined to reach the Nile that night. A glance at their resolute faces fills him with pride: this is the British soldier at his very best: steady, stubborn, ready to sell his life dearly.

31. Evacuating Herbert Stewart. After the failure of the Gordon Relief Mission, Stewart is evacuated with the other wounded to Jakdul Wells, where he dies. His grave is still to be found there today.

32. The death of Charles Gordon. An eye-witness account by Gordon's ADC, Orfali, suggests that he did not wait for death passively but killed and wounded several of the enemy before being over-whelmed.

33. Charles Wilson's gunboats arrive at Khartoum, 28 February 1884. Paddle steamers *Bordain* and *Talahawiyya* run the gauntlet of dervish guns and rifles for no less than four hours, only to discover that Khartoum has fallen and Gordon is dead.

34. Rudolf von Slatin (*left*) and Reginald Wingate. Slatin, once Turco-Egyptian governor of Darfur, escaped from Omdurman in 1895 after twelve years' captivity. Sent for debriefing by Egyptian army intelligence chief Major Reginald Wingate, Slatin and Wingate became close friends.

35. The battle of Tushki, August 1889. The Khalifa 'Abdallahi launches an invasion of Egypt under star Mahdist general Wad an-Nejumi. The dervishes are defeated for the first time by the Egyptian army, newly trained under British officers, and an-Nejumi is killed.

claps of shellfire bent the air. There was the drone of seven-pound shells flying, and two thumps as they exploded among the enemy. Twenty-seven dervishes were killed at a blow. The dervish fire halted momentarily. Soon it was too dark for the gunners to see their targets and the guns quit.

There was no moon and the night was very dark. Soon after sunset enemy fire started up again, and MacDonald saw their hill sparkling all over with jets of fire. In the zariba the troops were served with water and a pannikin each of lime juice. Then they manned the wall in double ranks. Whenever a light was shown there was a salvo of fire from the dervishes hidden in the darkness. A medical officer performing an operation on the wounded camel-man in the hospital sangar had to extinguish his lamp promptly when bullets started pinging off the walls. The fire was kept up most of the night. 'The whistling of the bullets overhead was too near to be pleasant,' said Charles Wilson, 'and the vagaries of the tom-toms in the valley, which now approached and now retired, kept us constantly on the alert.'[32] At one point Albert Gleichen thought the tom-toms were no more than three hundred yards away, and heralded an imminent attack – '. . . it was very jumpy listening to them,' he said.[33]

It was a great tribute to their trust in the alertness of their sentries that the men slept at all. Gleichen admitted that he fell fast asleep, only to be woken up with a shock when one of the men jumped up with a heart-rending yell after a bad dream. At 2100 hours, and again at midnight, the troops were stood to when the sentries came running in. MacDonald was unable to sleep for the whine of the bullets overhead. '[They] sounded like a cloud of giant mosquitoes bent on a foraging mission,' he wrote. After midnight there was a lull in the firing, but by that time seven of the British force had been hit. Two hours later, MacDonald saw fires suddenly flare up on a ridge and witnessed the dervishes performing a wild dance.

It was a long night. Stewart expected an attack at sunrise, and as the morning star, Venus, came up, he ordered the men stood to. They waited in silence, lying prone behind their poor defences.

No attack came. Instead, the sun appeared over the eastern hills, a giant shimmering ball of fire, slowly breaking free from the dark horizon, pulsing out long sequences of reds and yellows. The jagged hills cast elastic shadows over the undulating plain, and darkness lingered in purple pockets on the sides of the low escarpments. Thousands of black heads could be seen on the hilltops peering over hastily thrown up sangars. It quickly became clear to Stewart that the enemy had both increased in number and come closer during the night. They had also found their range.

As daylight thickened, so did enemy fire. A solid barrage of Remington bullets was now raining down on the zariba. Suddenly, a troop of dervishes rushed downhill towards the British position. They did not attack, but threw themselves into cover and opened up from close range. Stewart sent skirmishers from the Guards and Mounted Infantry forward to take them out.

The heaviest fire was coming in from the right, and falling among the tethered horses. Several of the Hussars' mounts were hit, and one killed. A native groom who had been sent by a Hussar officer to bring his horse was unhitching the animal when a round passed through its nostrils, and through both of his thighs. The bullet hit arteries in both legs, and blood spurted in jets across the stony ground. Before the bearer company could get to him the man had bled to death in agony.

Moments later, Major George Gough, 14th Hussars, commander of the Mounted Infantry, was sent sprawling by a spent bullet that entered his helmet, but was deflected before it did any real damage. Gough was knocked out and remained unconscious. Alex MacDonald ran to Stewart's command post to find out what the general's plans were. A soldier of the Mounted Infantry in front of him was shot through the chest, the round bursting out of his back in a shower of blood and burned cloth. It zipped past MacDonald's ear. The soldier spun round, and fixed his eyes on the correspondent. 'I am badly hit, sir,' he gasped. He collapsed in MacDonald's arms. MacDonald laid him down gently, noticing a large hole in his grey tunic with a red and black ring around it. He screamed for a stretcher. A bearer team came sprinting up, keeping low. More bullets zapped past MacDonald's head, and he suddenly became aware of a dozen voices yelling at him to get down.

He crawled after the bearers to the hospital sangar, where he saw Major Dickson of the Royal Dragoons being carried in with a shattered calf. Dickson, who was serving with Wilson in the Intelligence Department, had been detailed for the final assault party on Khartoum. He was cheerful, but worried that the wound would deprive him of his chance of saving Gordon. Lieutenant Lyell of the artillery was brought in, gasping for breath. He had been shot in the back and the bullet was lodged in his lung. The hospital was quickly filling up as more and more casualties came in. Outside, MacDonald counted fourteen dead bodies lying in a row.

MacDonald wondered what Stewart was waiting for – it was obvious to him that they could not stay cooped up in the zariba for ever. 'It did appear high time for something to be done,' he said. A troop of Baggara horsemen was cantering up towards the right flank, riders in flowing white robes with spears flashing. The report of a seven-pounder cracked out suddenly, lobbing a shell into their midst. The horses reared and whinnied, throwing men out of the saddle. The enemy cavalry quickly dispersed.

Stewart had left the command post, and was giving instructions for the formation of a square. He and Burnaby were already mounted. Charles Beresford, who had brought the Gardner back down the escarpment, yelled at them to get down. An instant later Burnaby's polo pony – borrowed from a fellow officer – was shot in the fetlock and taken away limping. 'I'm not in luck today, Charlie,' Burnaby told Beresford. Stewart dismounted and went to sit quietly with the Camel Corps officers, who were tucking into bully beef and biscuits. When expectant faces were turned towards him, he explained that he was 'waiting to give the niggers another chance'.[34]

It was now almost 0900 hours and the men had been stood to since two hours before first light. It was evident that no attack was coming. Stewart perceived that the dervishes intended to keep up their harassing fire but were not going to risk an all-out assault.

Time was on the enemy's side because they had access to the water, and Stewart's thirsty column did not. At 0900 hours sharp, Stewart ordered his men to form a square.

The men moved out of cover and began to form up coolly in front of the zariba. The formation of the square had been carefully prearranged. The front face was made up of the Mounted Infantry and the Guards Camel Regiment. The Guards were also on the right face, and the Mounted Infantry and Heavies on the left. The rear face was made up of Heavies, Royal Sussex, and the Naval Brigade. Each face of the square was manned by a double rank of troops. According to the manual, when under attack the front rank would kneel, so that the rear rank could fire over their heads.

Stewart put his three screw-guns behind the middle of the front face, with the Gardner in the rear face. Medical orderlies and bearers were placed in the middle, and behind them 120 camels with their handlers. These would carry water and ammunition, and 'cacolets' – mounted double litters for the wounded. Herbert Stewart, Fred Burnaby, Charles Wilson and the staff were with the medical personnel in the centre. The rest of the camels and stores were left at the zariba, defended by a detachment of the Royal Sussex Regiment. The zariba was also protected by one troop of the 19th Hussars, while the other was ordered to skirmish along the square's left flank.

At exactly 1000 hours on 17 January 1885, the buglers sounded the advance.

9

Anyone who visits the site of the battle of Abu Tulayh (Abu Klea) today can easily follow the progress of Stewart's square from the zariba that morning. The foundations of the wall the men threw up so hurriedly on the evening of 16 January 1885 still remain, even though more than a century has passed. The wadi is still green, and the wells are in the same place, though due to changes in the environment, the *talh* trees have vanished. Pacing out the square's progress reveals just how difficult a task the British were taking on. There was – and still remains – a track leading down from the plateau towards the wells, and the dervishes had evidently been expecting the enemy to follow it. They had thrown up breastworks along it ready to repel the advance. Fred Burnaby, who remembered how Gerald Graham had outflanked the Beja at et-Teb, suggested moving across the high ground to the right instead.

Here, the desert is a series of stony folds up to six feet between peaks and troughs, falling across the direction of advance down towards the khor. These knolls, covered in clinker-like chunks, gave cover to the enemy even at close range, and made manoeuvring well nigh impossible for the British. The square was made the more unwieldy by the baggage-camels, which also found the rough ground difficult going. The camels could not keep up with the men, and strayed from each other, forcing the rear rank to balloon out dangerously. It was the worst possible surface for the square formation, and it had to be managed with absolute precision.

The British kept up a funereal pace. Dervish sharpshooters – most of them trained Jihadiyya captured in Kordofan – followed them, leaping from rock to boulder. A hail of lead hit the British from left and right as they advanced. Some snipers were hidden among the tall *tabas* grass on the edge of the wadi, only four hundred yards away. Bullets whanged and hissed into the ranks. Men staggered and fell. On the right, Colour-Sergeant Kakwich of the Guards was shot and badly wounded. On the left, Captain Lord St Vincent, adjutant of the Heavies, was also felled by a sniper's bullet. The square halted and the British replied with withering fire, loading, ejecting and shoving cartridges into breeches with manic determination. Dust and smoke wafted over the ranks. Transport camels were couched and the wounded loaded into cacolets by the bearer corps. Then the buglers again sounded the advance.

Stewart sent skirmishers from the Mounted Infantry's C Company, under Lieutenant Johnny Campbell of the King's Royal Rifle Corps, to deal with the snipers. The company peeled off from the square and moved unhurriedly into cover. Campbell's men were mostly from the KRRC and the Rifle Brigade, and were all picked marksmen. Their shooting was exceptional. They opened up a rapid and deadly fire, picking off dervishes at between six and eight hundred yards. The enemy fire quickly dwindled. One of Campbell's company was hit, and a medical officer, Surgeon Major John Magill of the Guards Camel Regiment, raced out to attend him. While he was working Magill was himself shot, a .43 bullet shearing the muscle off his calf. Campbell's men dragged Magill and the other wounded man back to the square with enemy bullets whacking into the stones around them.

On the rear right of the square, skirmishers from the Royal Sussex under Colour-Sergeant Kelly were suddenly confronted by a dozen dervish spearmen, who rose out of one of the folds in the ground four hundred yards away. They were distant enough to get off a volley. Snapping orders like a drill-sergeant, Kelly got his men kneeling. Their Martini-Henrys cracked out in unison, and seven of the spearmen hit the dust, dead or mortally wounded. Five seconds later, another volley took out three of the five survivors. The other two dashed for cover.

On the left, a squadron of Baggara cavalry were moving up fast out of the cover of the wadi, a shimmering mass of dark horses and men in flying white robes, kicking up a nebula of dust. The sun glimmered on the tips of their lances. Stewart ordered the square to halt. His artillerymen ran out the screw-guns from the front rank, and they belched fire. A shell crumped into the sand in front of the Baggara, scattering them. Before they could disperse, a second shell smashed right in their midst. Forty-eight dervish cavalrymen and numerous horses were killed. The screw-guns were run back into the square, and the slow march resumed.

The deadly firewalk had now covered a mile and a half and had gone on for more than an hour. For most of the soldiers present, it was the longest hour of their lives. The wadi and its wells were on the left, but the wadi was below them, and Stewart had been expecting an attack from the high ground on the right. For this reason he had put the Heavies – the least experienced infantrymen

– at the left corner. Stewart could make out the row of fluttering green and white banners he had spotted from the plateau's salient the previous day. Even Wilson could not tell him whether they marked the dervish command post, or something else. One officer claimed they were a graveyard. Stewart was informed that some of the camels carrying the wounded had been left behind, and he halted the square to wait for the handlers to bring them up.

Lieutenant Johnny Campbell, leading the Mounted Infantry skirmishers, had advanced to within four hundred yards of the flags among the *talh* trees. He sent a runner to Stewart asking permission to go and take them. Stewart was about to consent when Wilson drew his attention to scores more green and white banners that had suddenly arisen from a hidden depression on the left, eight hundred yards away. What followed was a sight no British soldier present would ever forget.

From the hidden ravine, thousands and thousands of black figures appeared. They were mostly shaven-headed in the dervish style, with white skullcaps, and brilliant white robes tied at the waist and thrown over the shoulder. A few were dressed in the patched *jibba* of the Mahdists. Many carried spears, swords and knives, which glowed like red gold in the sunlight. It was as if they had materialized from thin air. The left flank, a second ago dead, was now teeming with dervishes brandishing their weapons, as numerous as swarming wasps. They were moving towards the British fast, in three arrowhead phalanxes, each point led by a mounted chief with a banner. Charles Wilson gasped in admiration. He found the sight beautiful and striking, a vision dipping deep into the most romantic race-memories of the warrior tradition. His feelings were tinged with pity – the certain knowledge that warriors charging in close formation could not hope to survive the volleys of picked marksmen with Martini-Henrys. Within minutes he was proved wrong.

The dervishes moving so rapidly towards the square were mostly Baggara cattle-nomads and Hamr semi-nomads from Kordofan. This was the first time the British had come face to face with the Baggara, and though they admired the enemy's bravery, most believed it was born of religious fanaticism. The Kinana and Dighaym had been with the Mahdi since the beginning, and were certainly committed to his cause, but they were not inspired by martyrdom alone. What the British did not know was that these Arab tribes lived by a heroic code – a code that laid stress on physical courage as one of five cardinal virtues that together comprised 'ird or 'honour'. This was the quality Baggara warriors pursued when they hunted elephant and giraffe with spears. Without honour, a Baggara tribesman was nothing, no matter how many head of cattle he owned. Wilson felt a patronizing sense of pity for the enemy, considering them rather like brave but foolish children who knew no better than to charge Martini-Henrys and machine-guns. He did not understand that these men despised firearms, considering them the resort of the weak. To them, a true warrior fought with sword and spear, face to face with his enemy. Unlike the Beja, they did not even carry shields.

Most of the riflemen in the dervish army were Jihadiyya captured from the government. These were all pagan southerners or men from the Nuba mountains, whom the Baggara considered 'slaves', and therefore without honour. The Mahdi himself had advised his men against using firearms, which he considered the work of unbelievers, and thus the work of the devil. While the Jihadiyya were deployed to soften the enemy up with bullets, the hand-to-hand fighting was done by the 'real' warriors, with what they termed *asliha bayda* or 'white weapons' – cold steel. The men Wilson and Stewart saw rushing towards them were not doing so because they were ignorant of the danger, or because they were anxious to become martyrs. They were advancing to contact despite the threat of pitiless fire, because, in their culture, this was the only way an honourable man could fight.

Stewart reacted with admirable coolness. He did not want to be caught on low ground, and ordered the square to move thirty yards, to the top of the next ridge. It was an awkward movement, and a gap appeared at the rear corner of the left flank, manned by the Heavies. Some of the camels carrying the wounded had sat down and refused to budge. Their petrified handlers abandoned them and scrambled back to the square. Men from the Heavies jogged out and dragged the squealing camels into the ranks.

The British reached their new position only to find their targets obscured by Campbell's skirmishers, who were in a race to the death with the dervishes. One of the Mounted Infantry officers bellowed at them to get down. 'No, no, run like hell!' Campbell told his men. Some were only yards in front of the leading warriors. Most managed to tumble into the square, but one man was brought down by the enemy, who jumped on him and plunged their spears into his body.

This was the signal for the Mounted Infantry, Guards and Heavies, to open fire. 'The sides of the square literally blazed with fire,' recalled Bill Burge of the Guards Camel Regiment. 'The air was thick with flying bullets and deafening with the cries of man and beast.' The British poured volley after volley into the onrushing whirlwind. They squeezed triggers, ejected and loaded like men possessed. The shooting failed even to slow the Baggara assault. Wilson's face dropped as his expectations dissolved. The enemy were getting closer and closer. They were within eighty yards before the British fire had a visible impact. Then, its effects seemed speeded up. Within a few seconds so many dervishes had dropped and fallen over each other that a huge wall of dead was formed.

For a moment, Wilson was certain the attack would be broken off. Instead, he was amazed to see the dervish army wheel sharply to the right as if on manoeuvres. No drilled infantry could have executed a more elegant movement. The front ranks of the enemy rushed directly towards the Heavy Camel Regiment. Wilson, watching from the centre, remembered thinking, 'By Jove, they will be into the square!'[35]

The subsequent action at Abu Tulayh lasted only ten minutes. Celebrated by Sir Henry Newbolt in his poem *Vitae Lampada*, once known by every British schoolchild as 'the square that broke', it was to become the *sine qua non* of grit and tenacity – the qualities most admired in British military tradition. The action itself was so swift and confused that no complete reconstruction of the battle is now possible. As Bill Burge of the Guards Camel Regiment said, 'It was a furious and incredible turmoil . . . made all the more dreadful because it had come so suddenly . . . like an awful storm bursting on a calm sea.'[36]

What seems likely is that the short advance uphill had left a gap in the rear left of the square. Through this gap, Lord Charles Beresford gleefully ran the Gardner gun with a crew of eight bluejackets, thirty yards out of the ranks. Beresford was obsessed with the gun, regarding it virtually as his own private weapon. He was determined to get it into action, and intended to operate it himself. He later claimed that Stewart had authorized his move, but this is disputed. Fred Burnaby, now mounted on a fresh horse, had been sent to the rear by Stewart, to oversee but not command the rear rank. When Burnaby saw Beresford's intention, he did something unforgivable – he ordered 3 and 4 Companies of the Heavy Camel Regiment to wheel out of the square. At that moment the dervishes were still four hundred yards away, and it seemed that the impetus of their attack would fall on the Mounted Infantry at the front left-hand corner. The enemy's startling change of direction caught both Beresford and Burnaby by surprise.

Beresford had laid the gun before he realized that the Baggara were coming straight at him. 'They were tearing down upon us with a roar like the roar of the sea,' he wrote, 'an immense surging wave of white slashed black forms brandishing bright spears and long flashing swords; and all were chanting as they leapt and ran the war song of their fathers, *La ilaha illa-llah wa Mohammad rasul Allah.*'

In the seconds before impact, Beresford opened fire. The metallic rattle of the machine-gun sang out over the roar of the enemy. For a moment he had the satisfaction of seeing the leading figures bowled over like skittles. He stopped to lower the sights, and fired another six rounds. Then the gun jammed with an ominous click. An empty cylinder had stuck in one of the barrels.

Beresford and his crewman, Chief Bosun's Mate Bill Rhodes, began to unscrew the feedplate to eject the cylinder. In an instant they were surrounded by the Baggara. Rhodes took a spearhead in the stomach, and dropped the heavy feedplate on the crouching Beresford, who fell under the gun. Armourer Walter Miller was speared and hacked to death with an axe, spattering Beresford with blood. A dervish chopped at him with an axe, but missed, hitting him with the helve. Another thrust at him with a spear, but Beresford caught the blade and deflected it, badly lacerating his hands. Before the dervish could wrench it away, he was knocked down by a bullet. All seven bluejackets who had been with Beresford were cut to pieces in a matter of seconds. He staggered to his feet, only to find himself swept back by a tidal wave of enemy bodies.

The Baggara surged forward, smashing into the Heavies No. 4 Company like a battering-ram, screaming, hacking and thrusting with their ten-foot spears. The Heavies rattled off a few wild shots before the enemy hit them. A moment later they were jammed face to face with the foe, so tightly that neither British nor Sudanese could use their weapons. Beresford had the bizarre experience of finding himself thrust up against a dervish warrior whose long spear-shaft was trapped behind his back in the crush. Beresford could draw neither sword nor pistol.

The Heavies fell back fast facing the enemy. The Royal Sussex Regiment, behind them, were hurled back by the impact, but were brought up against the solid mass of baggage-camels to their rear. The Sussex riflemen were a little higher than the Heavies, and began to fire over their heads. For a moment their salvoes thinned the press of dervishes, freeing the Heavies to use their weapons.

That there must have been gaps in the line, though, is evident. Charles Wilson, who was on the other side of the camels, heard the uproar and felt the surge as the dervishes hit the square. He drew his pistol. Over the backs of the camels, he saw a dervish chief bound in on a horse and plant a banner in the middle of it. The chief was Musa wad Helu, commander of the Mahdi's force from Omdurman. He began to recite a verse from the Quran as if he expected it to protect him from bullets. An instant later Corporal Yetton of the Rifle Brigade shot him dead, and he fell on his banner. Almost at once, Wilson saw Baggara warriors creeping towards him on all fours beneath the camels.

As more dervishes appeared in the front part of the square, Lieutenant Percy Marling of the Mounted Infantry, the man who had won the VC at Tamaai, had the presence of mind to order his rear rank to turn about and engage them. It was a dangerous move, but a crucial one. Marling's thin double rank were now fighting back to back – the front rank bayoneting dervishes who had renewed their onslaught on the left front, and the rear rank firing at enemy warriors behind them. Their crossfire whipped across the square, bringing down both dervishes and British troops. Stewart's horse was hit and collapsed and Stewart was hurled out of the saddle. His bugler, who had been standing only a foot away, was shot and killed instantly. Almost at once three warriors with spears rushed on Stewart. Wilson, who had been standing behind him, gunned down the nearest at about three paces with his Webley, seeing a bloom of blood well from the dark chest. The others were blasted by Marling's Mounted Infantry.

The outer rank of Mounted Infantry were shooting, parrying spears, and jabbing with their bayonets. Half the rifles jammed. Wilson saw troops throwing down useless rifles in disgust and picking up those of fallen comrades. Many officers and NCOs were so busy clearing rifles for their men that they were unable to join the fight. The bayonets fared no better than they had at Tamaai, bending hoop-shaped on impact.

No. 3 screw-gun was left exposed in the frontal attack. Its commander, Lieutenant Guthrie, Royal Artillery, who was supervising the laying of the gun and had no weapon in his hand, was rushed by a spear-toting warrior. He would have been killed but for the prompt action of his young 'striker', Gunner Albert Smith. Smith, also unarmed, grabbed the gun's traversing handspike and parried the spear-thrust. The dervish staggered back, giving Guthrie time to draw his sword and run him through. As the warrior went down, he stabbed Guthrie in the thigh with a long knife. Before he could strike again, Smith smashed his skull with the handspike. He leapt over his officer's body and stood astride it, fighting off more attackers furiously. Guthrie died later, but Smith survived to win the battle's only VC.

Albert Gleichen, with his Guards company, on the right, had also felt the terrific impact of the assault, but could see nothing. He ordered his men to stand fast. Then he rammed his way through the turmoil and realized that the Heavies, Sussex, and camels were pressing back on his slim double rank of Guards and Marines. If his men had given way, all would have been lost. But Gleichen had ordered, 'Stand fast,' and stand fast they did.

On the other side of the camels, Gleichen saw 'swarms of [dervishes] in desperate hand-to-hand fight with our men, hacking, hewing, hamstringing and yelling like black devils on a ground literally piled with the dead and dying. On the right, the Mounted Infantry were pouring in their fire with deadly effect, the niggers falling in hundreds.'[37]

Wounded men lying helpless in cacolets on the baggage-camels were speared to death. Captain Lord St Vincent, who had been hit earlier, was toppled out of his litter when his camel was killed. The camel fell on him and knocked him out. The soldier in the opposite side of the cacolet was skewered. Wilson's deputy, Captain Charles Willoughby Verner of the Intelligence Department, though not among the wounded, was also stunned when a camel collapsed on top of him. Gleichen saw the medical officer in charge of the wounded, Surgeon Briggs, his helmet gone, a drawn sword in his hand, desperately trying to rally the men nearest to him. More crossfire wheezed across the square, rounds narrowly missing Gleichen's head. The rounds hit several of the camels carrying ammunition, setting fire to their pack-saddles. The ammunition started to explode, and frenzied camels began to leap, shrieking with terror and pain, among the thrusting and wrestling fighters.

Fred Burnaby had been stranded outside on his borrowed horse. Beresford got a glimpse of him riding back and forth, yelling at the men to fall back quickly. Nearby stood a naval lieutenant, Alfred Piggot, who had acquired Burnaby's penchant for the shotgun and was using a fowling-piece with great effect. 'The Arabs were crawling and twisting . . . in and out of the legs of the men,' wrote Beresford, 'whom they tried to stab in the back, and Piggot was loading and firing, and the bluejackets kept calling to him, "Here's another joker, sir!" I saw a bald head emerging from a pile of bodies, and as Piggot fired I saw the crown riddled like the rose of a watering-pot.'[38]

Piggot was soon speared, and another naval officer, Lieutenant de Lisle, had his face hacked clean off by a razor-sharp dervish sword. Burnaby, still mounted, shot down a Baggara horseman charging towards him. Almost simultaneously a warrior on foot shoved a trowel-sized blade into his throat. Burnaby reined in and tried to parry more spear-thrusts, but they were coming thick and fast from all sides now. Another spearman stabbed him in the right shoulder, but his assailant was immediately gutted by the bayonet of Private Laporte of the Heavies. A third Baggara gave Burnaby a neck wound, and as he tumbled off his horse, a dozen fighters fell on him like vultures.

Corporal McIntosh, of the Blues, determined not to let his hero die alone, rushed out and stuck his bayonet into one of Burnaby's assailants. A split second later a Baggara warrior cut McIntosh's throat, while another finished him off with a spear-thrust. Burnaby lumbered to his feet, gasping for breath, his huge body drenched in blood. He swung his sword twice and collapsed heavily on to the stones.

The front and right ranks of the square held steady. The camels in the centre had provided a providential buffer against which the dervish impetus had spent itself. The Heavies and Sussex Regiment in the rear face had also turned to fire inwards, at an enemy who were now trapped inside the square. Volleys fired with unbeliev-able speed bowled them over where they stood. Percy Marling, among the Mounted Infantry, was almost deafened when one of his own sergeants put his rifle over his shoulder and fired within half an inch of his ear. The British were shooting at close range with terrible accuracy. The Baggara ranks began to thin. Dead piled up. Soon there was not a single living dervish in what remained of the square. Not one of them managed to get out alive.

The enemy outside began to withdraw downhill. More volleys

poured after them, bringing down scores. '[The enemy] withdrew almost as swiftly, it seemed to me, as they had advanced,' wrote Bill Burge. 'I saw them drawing off in their thousands, and dotting the little hills about us just as they had dotted them before the frantic rush across the desert.'[39]

'A loud and long cheering broke out,' Wilson recalled. 'Our men had got somewhat out of hand – wild with excitement. It was for a few moments difficult to get them into their places; if the enemy had charged again few of us would have escaped.'[40]

Wilson saw a mass of Baggara hesitate out of range, and for a nasty moment thought they actually *were* going to have a second go. More salvoes from the British dissuaded them, and they made off. Many turned and shook their fists at the cheering troops. A few groups of four or five who had feigned death jumped up and charged deliberately at the square. A surge of fire brought most of them down, but several made it to the line, to be impaled on British bayonets.

Slowly the shooting petered out. A strange unearthly calm descended. The whole area was swathed in smoke and dust, and as it began to clear the men looked at each other, pale with shock. They were aware that they had just walked through the gates of hell and had emerged alive. Eighty-six of their comrades had been killed. Eleven hundred dervishes lay dead on the field. It had all come and gone with such intensity that it seemed almost like a dream.

Charles Wilson holstered his pistol, and looked about him, dazed. It suddenly hit him that he had killed at least one man, and probably saved his commanding officer's life. Major Lawrence Carmichael, 5th Lancers, of the Heavy Camel Regiment, had been shot in the face by the volley that had killed Stewart's horse. He also had a gaping spear wound in the neck. Another Heavy, forty-one-year-old Major Wilfred Gough, of the Blues, had been killed by the same gout of British fire, along with Stewart's bugler and several other men. Wilson kept asking himself how he had survived.

Stewart ordered the square to move fifty yards forward, away from the carnage. When it was reformed in the new position, officers and men hurried back to the dead baggage-camels to salvage the water and ammunition. The water was desperately needed. Many of the troops were in the last throes of thirst, their lips cracked, their tongues bloated and white with mucus. Several men who had stood steadfast in the face of the dervish attack fainted from dehydration.

Wilson walked back shakily with them to help distribute the water. On the way he witnessed a strange incident. A dervish who had played dead suddenly sprang up and went for an officer with his spear. The officer grabbed the spear in his left hand and ran the warrior through the guts with his sword, right up to the hilt. 'And there, for a few seconds they stood,' Wilson recalled, 'the officer being unable to withdraw his sword, until a man ran up and shot the [dervish]. It was a living embodiment of the old gladiatorial frescoes of Pompeii. It did not, strange to say, seem horrible; rather, after what had just passed, an everyday occurrence.'[41]

Wilson inspected the place where the square had broken. The reg (gravelly desert) was shiny with blood. Sixty-eight of the Heavy Camel Regiment had been killed or mortally wounded: many of the wounds inflicted by dervish spears had been horrific. The bodies looked wax-like, and were covered in sand and blood. The enemy dead lay in heaps, some of them smouldering from hard contact gunshot wounds. Weapons in hundreds – spears, swords, throwing-sticks, knives and broken banner-staves – littered the ground. Wilson wondered how the square had come to break. He surmised that the Heavies, fighting as infantry for the first time, had not grasped that the idea was to maintain a rigid line. Their instincts and training, he thought, had led them to move back in a fighting withdrawal under heavy attack.

As Wilson was examining the corpses, Charles Beresford appeared, intent on examining the effects of his Gardner fire. He was pleased to discover three enemy corpses whose craniums had been sliced off by his bullets as neatly as if by a butcher's cleaver. Able Seaman Jumno, a giant who had been helping Beresford to man the Gardner, was still alive, lying face down with no less than seventeen stab wounds in his back. When Beresford had him lifted up and told him he would be sent back to the zariba, Jumno remarked, 'Sent back, sir! I haven't done with the buggers yet.'[42]

Beresford had Jumno loaded on a cacolet, next to an injured dervish. The Arab immediately began chewing off the sailor's thumb. In a fit of indignation Beresford yanked the wounded enemy down and shot him. Suddenly another officer yelled, 'Look out, Charlie!' Beresford glanced up to see a dervish running at him with a long spear. He moved into a defensive posture, parried the spear, and held out his sword at arm's length. The spearman ran straight into it.

Fred Burnaby was lying face upwards in the blood-soaked desert where he had fallen, thirty yards outside the square, with a dervish spear across his body. Next to him lay his pony, Moses, dead from twelve separate wounds. Nearby were the scarcely recognizable corpses of McIntosh, Laporte, Piggot, De Lisle, Miller, Rhodes, and the other bluejackets who had died defending the Gardner. Burnaby was just alive when Private Wood, a young soldier of the Heavies, found him. The lad lifted his head, trying to support it on his knee, and offered him water. 'Look after yourself,' Burnaby croaked. They were his last words. Shortly, Lieutenant Lord Binning, of the Blues, Burnaby's own regiment, arrived. 'Oh, sir!' Wood told him. 'Here's the bravest man in England dying, and no one to help him.'[43] Binning took the big man's hand, realizing that he was past help. 'A spear had inflicted a terrible wound in the side of his neck and throat,' Binning recalled, 'and his skull had been cleft by a blow from a two-handed sword.'[44] A few moments later Burnaby was dead. So popular had he been among his own regiment that some of the Blues sat down and cried.

Back in the square, Stewart was still on his guard. There had been no sign of the dervishes on the high ground to the right, and he expected an attack from that direction any minute. Officers and NCOs bawled out orders to close up. The men licked their cracked lips, reloaded their Martini-Henrys, and grimly looked around for more enemy to shoot at.

No second attack materialized, but dervish snipers kept up a haphazard fire from behind rocks and trees. Private Ormiston, of the Guards Camel Regiment, was standing next to Albert Gleichen. He was handing his water-bottle to a comrade when a sniper's bullet smashed through his friend's hand and slapped into Ormiston's chest. 'He fell on to me, a torrent of blood gushing out of his mouth,' Gleichen said, '. . . he was dead in less than a minute.'[45] A few moments later, Gleichen saw a lone Baggara horseman galloping straight towards his company. The young Count drew his pistol and took aim, but was pre-empted by a Marine, who, to Gleichen's disgust, 'bowled him over an awful "crumpler" at an unfairly short range for a rifle'.[46]

Wolseley later laid the blame for the 'square that broke' on the Heavies, using the dreaded epithet 'unsteady' to describe their behaviour. This was an undeserved slander. If blame can be attributed, it must be laid firmly at the door of two of Wolseley's own favourites. Fred Burnaby might have been 'the bravest man in England', but he did for the men who hero-worshipped him by opening the square without orders. Captain Lord Beresford, Wolseley's 'really first rate man', was equally to blame for running out the Gardner. Burnaby is celebrated namelessly for posterity in Newbolt's poem, as the dead colonel. The Gardner gun that jammed is celebrated – much to its maker's relief, probably – as a 'Gatling'. This was the second time a Gardner had jammed at a critical moment since British troops had been deployed in the Sudan.

Once again, British honour had been jeopardized by the incompetence of officers who felt that the rules did not apply to them. It had been saved, as on so many other occasions, by the sheer professionalism of the enlisted men. Even Beresford, one of the major culprits, admitted that it had been 'a soldiers' battle' in which orders had been useless. '[Only] strength, determination, steadiness, and unflinching courage,' he wrote, 'could have stemmed the onslaught.'[47] Newbolt's tribute to the men at Abu Tulayh is no romantic overstatement. Not even Rorke's Drift in the Zulu war displayed more perfectly the resolution and tenacity of the British fighting man – men mostly off the streets of British cities, whom Blunt called 'a mongrel scum'.

Today, the bodies of Burnaby and the rest of the fallen still lie under cairns on the lonely hillside in the Bayuda desert where they were buried on that day, 17 January 1885. A monument with a brass plate, placed there later by the British government, is inscribed with the names of Burnaby and the other eight officers killed at Abu Tulayh. It had been a 'soldiers' battle' indeed, yet the names of the seventy-nine enlisted men who died there are not mentioned.

10

The 19th Hussars under Lieut. Colonel Percy Barrow dashed up to the square to find it was all over. They had been tasked with skirmishing to the left, but had been held up by a company of dervishes and had been obliged to fight their way through. Barrow was not even aware that the square had broken. Stewart ordered him to pursue the enemy, but Barrow said his horses were too thirsty for a pursuit – in fact, they were almost uncontrollable with thirst. Bill Burge probably spoke for more than just himself when he expressed pleasure that the enemy had got away unmolested. 'Of their kind they were the bravest of the brave,' he commented. 'They did not know the meaning of fear. I was glad, and relieved, too, and I do not think that there was either officer or man in the broken square who had not a feeling of thankfulness to see the backs and not the faces of them.'[48]

Water was now Stewart's main priority, and he sent the Hussars to look for the wells instead. They were almost impossible to locate without a guide. The wells were narrow sinkholes in the bed of the wadi, virtually invisible until one was on top of them. It took Barrow's scouts until 1700 hours to locate them, and by that time Stewart was already considering marching back to the zariba.

There were 106 wounded – far too many to carry on the cacolets. Instead, the Guards Camel Regiment, who had been least

229

involved in the fight, and had taken no casualties apart from Surgeon McGill, volunteered to carry them on stretchers. They were carried straight to the wells. After they had drunk, the force was ordered to water by company. The water turned out to be chocolate-coloured, with the consistency of mud, but it was cool and delicious to men dying of thirst. It took eight hours to water the entire force. By the time the watering was complete, night had fallen. An edge of cold air, as sharp as a razor, replaced the heat of the day. Stewart reformed the square on high ground overlooking the wells for the night.

The men had not eaten since breakfast, and had had no proper meal in two days. Stewart instructed three hundred volunteers from the Camel Corps to return to the zariba, load up all the baggage and stores, and return before first light. The men left in the square had no blankets or greatcoats, and, already ravenous with hunger, soon began to quiver with cold. Some tried to nuzzle up against the camels for warmth. Others passed around pipes or shared cigarettes. No one slept, and when the baggage-column arrived at 0700 hours the following day, the men were too weak and cold to cheer.

Wilson spent the next morning examining captured documents and interrogating prisoners. The papers suggested that the concentration of dervishes at Abu Tulayh had been possible because of Stewart's double journey to Jakdul. Had the Desert Column marched straight through, as Wolseley had originally intended, the road would have been open. A camp of grass huts, littered with refuse and smashed pottery, a little way from the wells, indicated that a force had camped there for some time.

Stewart was acutely aware that his delay had brought about the bloody confrontation at Abu Tulayh. This may have affected his decision to go for the Nile in a single march. The river lay twenty-six miles away, a short distance in relative terms, but an excruciatingly hard one for men who had just fought a bloody battle, had suffered thirst, cold and hunger, and had not slept properly for two days. Equally persuasive, though, was Stewart's fear of being caught without water. His experience at Abu Tulayh had taught him that

230

water was the one fundamental factor in desert warfare. If his men had not captured the wells, many of them would now be dying in agonies of thirst. He did not want to repeat this mistake.

The third point was the possibility that Metemma might be reinforced in massive strength by the Mahdi before his expedition got there. Prisoners had informed Wilson that a large back-up force had been dispatched from Omdurman. He had to get there before they arrived.

Stewart held an informal orders group and told his senior officers that his plan was to march within sight of Metemma that night, then turn right, striking the Nile about three miles upstream. He wanted to make sure that the next attack would be launched from a place where water was assured – the river. The expedition would have to be there before first light. Once there, having had no sleep for a third night, the troops would attack Metemma after breakfast. It seemed a tall order even for specially picked men, but Stewart believed that the dervishes had been shattered by their defeat at Abu Tulayh. He did not expect much opposition at Metemma.

One senior officer suggested falling back on Jakdul, to wait for reinforcements under Buller. Stewart received this proposal with a contemptuous stare. Withdrawing would mean the end of the mission, and would certainly be interpreted by the enemy as a victory. He must have felt the loneliness of command intensely at that moment. Had the telegraph line been run out after his force, he would have been able to consult Wolseley at once. As it was, he could expect no advice from the C.-in-C. before a week had passed. Whichever way he looked there were no easy solutions.

Several officers, including Wilson, asked him at least to break up the march into two legs to give the men a chance to rest. Stewart refused. He thought the men were 'in good spirits', and would do it cheerfully. He had made up his mind to take Metemma the following day, and to have Wilson steaming up the Nile to Khartoum by the 20th. He would not budge, even when 'Ali Lula, the bandit who had been picked up on the second day out, pointed out some difficulties. 'Ali had agreed to guide the expedition to the Nile, but told Stewart that there were thick forests of acacia trees within ten miles of the river. These thorny groves would be very hard going in the dark.

The column formed up at about 1600 hours. The wounded had been taken back to the zariba, where they would remain until the Relief Column arrived. The zariba and the wells would be held by the Sussex Regiment. Wilson had sent native runners with a bundle of dispatches to Wolseley in Korti, together with private messages and correspondents' reports. The 19th Hussars were sent off ahead to scout.

At about 1630 hours the men mounted their camels and began to move off. It was to be a tactical march. Orders were to be given in whispers from now on – Stewart wanted no bugles blasting out in the night to warn the enemy of their approach. This was a small but crucial change for the worse. The column stretched for six hundred yards. Front and rear were too far apart for whispered orders to be effective, especially after dark.

At first the march went well. The road was flat and open. Before long the camels emerged from the valley hemmed in by hills, and began to cross the undulating plain. The reg was hard, with fields of rust-coloured boulders and patches of twisted scrub, rolling on grey-green towards a horizon marked only by a thickening of greyness, hidden by the shimmer of heat. The heat quickly burned itself out, and the sheen of blue above them was torn by parallel gashes of molten gold, casting broad blades of light in radiating patterns. Gold edges brought into sharp focus the dust billows on the horizon, and a vibration of colours seeped across the sky, Prussian blue and salmon pink.

The men had been expecting to bivouac at dusk, and were looking ahead for possible camping places. The camels plodded on and on, but no halt was ordered. At sunset Charles Wilson rode to the front of the force with his deputy, Captain Charles Verner, the guides, including 'Ali Lula, and the commanding officer, Stewart. 'Ali Lula was to lead, while Verner, who had taken a bearing on Metemma, checked the position with map and compass.

As night came, the men drowsed, falling into silence as the harrowing experience of the previous day replayed itself in their heads. Soon there was only the groan of the camels, the creak of saddles, and the rhythmic slosh of water in the fantasses and water-skins. Darkness fell on them like a heavy black cloak. Once more, the temperature plummeted. There was no moon, but the track to Metemma was visible in the starlight, running straight as an arrow to the Nile. The going was still flat and firm underfoot, and Wilson began to think that Stewart's plan had been sound after all.

For the first two hours after dark there were no hitches. Then the surface changed abruptly from wind-graded reg to rocky hammada, and at once the camels began to stumble. Wilson noticed that the tall *tabas* grass that had dotted the plain since leaving Abu Tulayh was growing thicker. As the hungry camels passed, they stuck out their long necks to snatch a mouthful of green. For some a mouthful was not enough, and they stopped to have a good feed. As more and more of the animals halted, the rhythm of the march was wrecked. Camels and men got out of sequence, and there were continual stoppages. Orders to halt or catch up had to be passed from mouth to mouth, but it was soon impossible for the rear to communicate with the front unless an officer took the message in person. The regiments were now separated by yawning caverns of darkness. The grass gave way to thickets of *sallam*, *tundub* and *siyal* trees, and a little further on to the full-blown forest 'Ali Lula had warned Stewart about.

The trees loomed grey in the darkness like spectral skeletons. The bare, thorny branches looked like grasping talons. The units were split up by them, and got jumbled together. The men lacked the concentration to keep formation, dozing off and letting their camels wander away. At least two men vanished without trace, as if the forest had swallowed them. Percy Marling of the Mounted Infantry kept falling asleep, and twice led his company astray. The mounted camel-handlers at the rear continually fell asleep and let their animals drift aimlessly. One of them actually cut two of his camels loose so that he could sleep more easily. The Guards Camel Regiment, who had been given the job of escorting the baggage-train, got mixed up with their charges. It was, as Albert Gleichen noted, 'horrible confusion' – 'It was useless to try and find one's own men and camels,' he said, 'and transport, medical stores, regimental baggage, bluejackets, niggers, and commissariat all got hopelessly entangled.'[49]

Baggage-camels got stuck in the thorny branches and tried to force themselves through, only to have their loads torn off their backs. The loads were replaced carelessly. A hundred of the animals were lost completely in the darkness. By now the turmoil was complete. The men had given up trying to whisper: roars of abuse and strings of Anglo-Saxon epithets raved out of the darkness, preceded and followed by the shrieks of camels. Wilson began to realize that 'Ali Lula had understated the difficulty of the acacia forest – it would have presented a serious obstacle even in daylight.

Stewart called a halt at the point where he intended to turn off from Verner's bearing on Metemma, and make for the Nile. Verner calculated that they had covered almost sixteen miles, and had another ten to go. Wilson had a long talk with Stewart, trying to persuade him to build a zariba here. The scattered units would have a chance to catch up, and the men would get some rest. They could dump the baggage in the zariba with a rearguard, and advance directly on Metemma. It was a sound idea, but Stewart reiterated that they must reach the Nile before attacking, to be sure of their water-supplies.

Wilson knew that there was now little hope of getting to the river before first light. By the time the column began to emerge from the trees on to a gravel plain, Venus was already hanging over the horizon. The force's cohesion had been lost. There were baggage-trains on both flanks. The Camel Corps units were scattered and muddled up. Gleichen swore that the column had been going round in circles, and claimed that at one point the advance guard had turned up behind the rearguard. The line of march was south-south-west, but Gleichen maintained that he had once seen the Pole Star in front of them instead of the Southern Cross. 'Thank God there were no enemy about that night,' he wrote. 'If the column had been attacked, slaughter must have ensued.'

When Stewart halted the column again, clear of the woods, it was only half an hour to first light. Verner estimated that the Nile was three miles away, but 'Ali Lula disagreed, saying that it was nearer six. They moved on again, as streaks of scarlet spread like violent scratches across the black velveteen night. The sky became a layer-cake of shades, orange, lemon, magenta, aquamarine and pale blue. The sun appeared like the edge of a giant golden coin on the rim of the plain, with chevrons of rose-coloured vapour above it. The men could feel the latent heat in the air long before the sun rose – it was welcome after the freezing night. As the light thickened they peered ahead for any sign of the river, but the grey plain stretched monotonously on and on. After two more miles, Stewart dispatched Verner with a troop of Hussars to reconnoitre the way ahead.

Half an hour later they came trotting back across the gravel. Verner rode straight up to Stewart and saluted. He reported that he and his Hussars had been fired on by enemy scouts. They had seen Metemma and the town was buzzing like a disturbed wasps' nest. Tom-toms were beating, and thousands of dervishes were streaming out towards the British column. Stewart realized that he now had no alternative but to fight his way to the Nile.

11

Stewart blamed the camels for the failure of his bold gamble. As he must have realized, though, it was his own inclination to ignore 'Ali Lula's warning about the acacia forest that had led to this pass. Now his column was stranded in the open, with exhausted men, camels and horses and little water. The enemy were advancing to contact in force – exactly the situation he had wanted to avoid. 'Ali Lula had also proved to be right about another thing: the Nile was further than Verner had calculated. At the point where Verner had rejoined the column, the river was still four miles away.

Stewart instructed Percy Barrow to lead his Hussars in a feint against Metemma to distract the enemy. How effective Barrow's shattered mounts would prove in such a movement was open to question. A little further on, Metemma became visible on the left. After the long march across the Bayuda, it seemed vast and formidable to the troops, like a medieval castle set among thorn-groves and palms, magnified in the limpid light of early morning. Beyond it in both directions they could see the vegetation lying along the banks of the Nile, a layer of greyish-green squeezed narrow by the steel-blue weight of a cloudless sky.

There was a skirt of scrub running out as far as the gravel plain, and dervish sharpshooters were already crawling through it on hands and knees. The scrub was thin, but dense enough to provide cover. The crack and thump of rifles started up almost at once. Stewart looked around and saw a low knoll on the plain, two or three hundred yards clear of the scrub at its nearest point. 'I will occupy that position,' he told his staff. 'I intend attacking the enemy as soon as the men get something to eat.'[50] The ground was appallingly open, and the men did not like the look of it. Many grumbled that they had come this far, and would have preferred to keep going till they reached water. There was some-thing very alluring about that line of green along the Nile bank.

The camels were couched and knee-hobbled on the knoll, and the advance guard set to work to build a parapet of biscuit-boxes, saddles, and paraphernalia from the baggage-train. The sappers were dispersed into the brush to cut thorn branches. It was less a zariba than a miniature hill fort. Shortly the Hussars returned and tethered their horses. The bluejackets arrived with Beresford, then the artillery camels, then the Mounted Infantry, the Guards, the Heavies, and finally the Sussex Regiment.

By about 0800 hours, the dervish sharpshooters had crept to the edge of the scrub and opened close-range fire with their Remingtons. The British in the zariba, many of them standing up, presented clean targets, but the snipers were invisible except for the smoke-puffs from their weapons. Percy Marling of the Mounted Infantry had just finished giving orders to an NCO from his company, Lance Corporal Howard, when a neat black hole was stamped in Howard's chest and blood gushed from his mouth. Marling yelled at his men to get down. Two soldiers in front of him crumpled among the boxes and baggage. Remington bullets zipped and whizzed across the fort. Many slapped into the flanks of the helpless camels. Some Heavies were filling a kettle for war correspondent Alex MacDonald when a round smacked clean through the vessel. A trooper of the 16th Lancers was hit. Another Heavy of the Lancers grabbed the kettle and was trying to stem the leak when his head exploded in shreds of blood and grey matter.

Sometime after 0830 hours Herbert Stewart instructed a staff officer, Major Rhodes, to tell the men that they could grab a quick breakfast. The officers separated, and Stewart had gone about twelve yards when a bullet smashed into him. He dropped soundlessly, with blood pumping out of his abdomen. He was carried to the hospital area, gravely wounded – the bullet had lodged in his spine. Wolseley's worst case scenario had come to pass.

Despite much ado later by observers about 'who should have taken command' after Stewart was hit, there was, in fact, no room for debate on the battlefield. The military system of seniority exists for this very reason: command automatically devolves on the next in seniority, and the next in seniority in this case was Lieut. Colonel Sir Charles Wilson. Wilson, who was criticized scathingly later, did not want the hot seat, but had no choice. To have refused would have been an abnegation of responsibility, and a court-martial offence. He had asked Wolseley to appoint him political agent instead of staff officer. Combat was not his business. He was disliked by many in Egypt and at home – only a few like Kitchener appreciated his intelligence and loyalty. He was probably the most brilliant officer in the Sudan, and therein lay the problem.

Men like Wilson were regarded with suspicion at all levels in the Victorian army and outside it. Intellectualism was equated with effeminacy and even 'un-Englishness'. The popular officers were men like Burnaby, Buller and Graham – preferably big, beefy men, with a hearty manner and a gung-ho attitude, who were not too bright. These were the 'bravest men in England', whose appearance and manner made them the embodiment of what a Victorian officer should be. By comparison, Wilson – a Fellow of the Royal Society – with his star-gazing, archaeological digs, and classical references – was an 'old woman'.

Stewart had been highly popular, mainly because of his charming manner and his determination. His performance had not always been excellent, as his choice of a defensive position shows. Wilson's suggestion of building a zariba in the acacia forest during the night would have been a far better plan. It was Stewart's disregard of 'Ali Lula's warning about the forest that had led to the failure of his night-march. It was his own selection of a lying-up place – probably coupled with his small vanity in wearing a Household Cavalry helmet and an orange puggaree – that led to his mortal wound.

Wilson and the senior Camel Corps officer, Lieut. Colonel Edward Boscawen, went to see Stewart in the 'hospital' area. They found him cool and lucid. Wilson said he hoped that he would soon be better. Stewart's spine was injured and he was paralysed from the waist down. He said that his wound was fatal, and that his soldiering days were over. It sounded as though he had decided to die. Wilson asked what he had intended to do. Stewart replied that Wilson must either take Metemma or go for the Nile. Wilson told him that he would fight the dervishes as soon as possible, and if circumstances were favourable, would try to take Metemma. When Wilson left, Stewart was dictating notes to his private secretary, St Leger Herbert, a civilian who doubled as correspondent for the *Morning Post*. Moments later, Herbert went to get his water-bottle and was shot in the head.

Wilson set about preparations in his characteristically meticulous manner. His first priority was to defend the redoubt, so that work on it could be completed. He sent out a fighting patrol of the Mounted Infantry in company strength to occupy a low ridge fifty yards ahead. Their orders were to keep the enemy's heads down. The patrol dashed across the exposed ground, firing as they went. They dropped and crawled up the ridge as .43 calibre rounds whanged off stones and seared the air around them. The patrol found that the only targets they had were wisps of white smoke from enemy muzzles, or the occasional dark shadow flitting from bush to bush.

Albert Gleichen was among the officers leading another fighting patrol of the Guards, sent to occupy a ridge forty yards away to the right. Their orders were to build a miniature fort on the ridge. This meant they had to struggle across the intervening no man's land with boxes and saddles. As they were building the new fort, the snipers began to pick them off. Bullets whistled over their heads, and thunked sickeningly into flesh. Two were shot dead. The survivors threw themselves flat, hugging the surface, and began to fire back at anything that moved.

Gleichen was crouching, trying to focus his field-glasses, when he felt a biting pain in the belly. He staggered up and fell flat on his face. Captain Edward Crabbe, commanding the patrol, detailed two men to rush him back to the zariba. By the time they got him there, Gleichen realized that he had had a miraculous escape. A ricochet had hit a brass button on his uniform and had been deflected, causing him nothing more than a bad bruise.

The enemy had steadily increased in number, and according to Gleichen a British casualty was now being carried past on a stretcher every minute. The troops were so exhausted that instead of eating breakfast they fell asleep, despite the whizzing bullets. Percy Marling, who had paid a farewell visit to Stewart, simply lay down behind a camel and slept for an hour. Gleichen tried to sleep, but the two camels he was sandwiched between kept shifting position. Scores of them were shot, and rolled over without a sound. During the morning another war correspondent, John Cameron of the *Standard*, was killed while taking a tin of sardines from his servant.

Charles Beresford of the Naval Brigade had run out the Gardner earlier, but the gun was useless against concealed snipers. It became a liability when a sharpshooter partially disabled it by shooting out a spoke of its wheel. Beresford's weapon, the 'Jonah' of Abu Tulayh, now turned out to be a damp squib. Two of Beresford's bluejackets were shot dead by a single sniper while they were asleep, and another was hit so badly in the stomach that he writhed in agony until a medical orderly gave him laudanum. 'There we lay in the blazing sun, helpless,' Beresford recalled. 'The rattle of rifles all around, the thin, high note of the bullets singing overhead or ending with a thud close at hand; men crying out suddenly or groaning; camels lying motionless and silent with blood trickling from their wounds.'[51]

By early afternoon Beresford could stand it no longer and sent a message to Wilson, urging him to advance. The messenger was killed on the way, and Beresford handed the message to Sub-Lieutenant Edward Munro, RN, who was wounded seven times carrying it to Wilson. The message was the same kind of unnecessary stroke that had led to the shattering of the square at Abu Tulayh, and it was in any case redundant.

Wilson was perfectly aware of the necessity for action, but had been waiting in his scrupulous way for the zariba to be completed. When the work was done, at about 1400 hours, he started to give instructions for the formation of a square. Stewart had urged him to copy the strategy at Abu Tulayh, leaving the wounded, the baggage, and most of the camels in the zariba defended by the best part of the Heavies, some of the 19th Hussars, the Naval Brigade and the artillery. The zariba would be commanded by Lieut. Colonel Percy Barrow.

The square would march straight to the Nile. The Guards Camel Regiment would take the front and right positions, the Mounted Infantry the left. The Sussex Regiment and a few Heavies would form the rear. At each corner there were extra men from the Royal Engineers and the 19th Hussars in case of a sudden rush. There were about twenty camels inside the square, carrying cacolets, ammunition and water. Wilson, who was himself in overall command, handed what he called 'executive command' to Edward Boscawen, a Guards officer with no more combat experience than himself. This was presumably because Wilson had not been trained in infantry drills. Once again, Verner was to navigate. Gleichen estimated the square's fighting strength at about nine hundred bayonets. It was ready at about 1500 hours, and moved out of the redoubt to the south.

This was the second time in three days that the British had had to fight their way to water, and the men knew that it was a do or die gambit. Since leaving Jakdul they had had less than sixteen hours' sleep, had lived on only one and a half litres of water per day, and for the last few days had scarcely had a proper meal. The camels had been eight days without water and four without food. The horses had not drunk in fifty-six hours. 'I must say it looked as risky a business as it well could,' said Gleichen. 'We all felt it was exceedingly doubtful if the two halves of the force would ever see each other again, but yet it was the only thing possible to be done.'[52] Percy Marling admitted later that he was convinced none of them would come back. Beresford agreed. 'If ever a little British army looked like walking into certain death,' he wrote, 'it was that thin square of infantry.'[53]

Wilson fully realized how grave the situation was, but a glance at the men's faces filled him with pride. '[They] were set in a determined way that meant business,' he wrote, 'and I knew they intended to drink from the Nile that night.'[54] This was the British soldier at his very best: steady, stubborn, ready to sell his life dearly.

As soon as the men rose there was a crescendo of fire from the dervish rifles. Boscawen's adjutant, Lieutenant Charles Crutchley of the Scots Guards, was the first casualty – shot through the thigh as he handed a chit to a sapper officer for entrenching tools. Once again the British set off at a slow march to ensure that the camels could keep up. Men went down and were left on the gravel for the Heavies to collect later. One of Gleichen's men, Private Woods, was armed only with a shovel. He was holding it before his face, joking with a comrade that it would make a good shield, when it was shot out of his hand. Another Guardsman was knocked flat when a bullet hit his bandolier. Captain Edward Crabbe, who was next to Gleichen, jumped out of his skin when a bullet furrowed his beard and plopped over his shoulder. Percy Marling was advancing next to Lieutenant Charles Hore of the South Staffords at the left corner, when a bullet hummed between them and blew apart the head of a Marine in front. Blood and brains splattered their faces.

The fire became hotter and hotter as the British advanced.

Bullets soughed and groaned over them, and the troops got used to the dull thump as lead struck flesh. They were moving no faster than two miles an hour, and by the time they had made six hundred yards from the zariba the sun was already low. At this point, seven men were shot dead at once. For a moment it looked as if the whole force might be annihilated. Several officers thought that Wilson would order a withdrawal at this point. Wilson gritted his teeth, knowing that to pull back now would spell disaster. It was advance or die. He ordered the square closed up and they moved on steadily under intense fire.

Boscawen was directing the men left and right to stay on the open patches of gravel. Whenever they came to difficult ground, the square would halt. The men would fling themselves flat and lay down a volume of fire at the *tabas* grass, so devastating that the enemy had to stop shooting. Then they rose and advanced, with formidable determination. 'They moved in a cool, collected way,' said Wilson, 'without noise or any appearance of excitement.'[55]

The sun's heat had been sucked away. The plain had turned the colour of blood, and the shadows were grotesquely elongated in front of them. Wilson could see dervish banners ahead, and noticed that the enemy had begun to appear, collecting in masses to their front. His heart leapt. British steadiness had at last paid off. The enemy's patience had snapped. The men saw it too, and there were audible sighs of relief from the ranks. 'Thank God!' Gleichen muttered. 'They're going to charge!'[56]

Wilson gave the order to halt. The men went silent; the front rank sank to their knees with their rifles ready at their shoulders. This was the moment they had all been waiting for – the moment of truth. Their faces were set with grim resolve. All eyes were on the enemy in front. Wilson knew that his troops were going to hold steady, and would fight to the last bullet. The dervish shooting stopped abruptly. The British heard a bass growl, starting very low and rising steadily to a full-blown roar, as the enemy came rushing downhill like a whirlwind, black faces, white robes, weapons flashing like fire in the last of the sunlight. They came on shrieking defiance, in three prongs, exactly as they had at Abu Tulayh.

The British actually cheered when they saw them. This was soon stifled, one officer commented, 'as we were afraid the enemy would turn back without coming on'.[57] They let rip with volley after volley. As at Abu Tulayh, it seemed at first as if their rounds had no effect. Remembering his lesson from the previous battle, Wilson had the bugler sound 'Cease fire'. To stop firing in the face of an enemy charge required discipline of a rare order. Wilson himself was surprised that the men obeyed. Most of the Martinis went quiet. Cartridges were pressed into breeches. For a few agonizing seconds the British waited unflinching, watching the screaming, bounding warriors getting nearer and nearer. Five hundred yards. Four hundred yards. Three hundred yards. 'Continuous fire!' Wilson snapped to the bugler.

The clear trumpet-notes rang across the square. Fire seared out, a sheet of flame and smoke, and the din of hundreds of rifles spouting lead in unison, low and steady. The noise became a continuous roar. The dervishes went down in dozens. Shells from the screw-guns fired long range from the zariba behind them scraped air and plunged into enemy positions. The whole of the dervish front rank was scythed down like grass. A few survivors got within thirty yards and were blasted. One officer in the front rank commented that there seemed to be a 'death zone', like an invisible field, between a hundred and two hundred yards from the square, beyond which the enemy could not pass. Not more than half a dozen dervishes who entered that zone escaped. They and the rest of the enemy withdrew quickly towards Metemma, leaving three hundred dead comrades on the slope. Within five minutes the battle that would be known to the British as Abu Kru was over. Wilson knew they had won the Nile.

The men gave three resounding cheers. Boscawen saluted Wilson and congratulated him. Wilson complimented Boscawen on his handling of the square. It was only the second time either of them had been in action, but they had done remarkably well. 'Nor was ever a square better handled,' wrote Alex MacDonald.

Now, however, Wilson was bombarded by advice from every side. Boscawen suggested that only the front face of the square should march to the Nile, while the other three should return to the zariba. Wilson accepted this, but before the face had marched a hundred yards, Major George Gough, CO of the Mounted Infantry, now recovered from his knock on the head at Abu Tulayh, strode up to Wilson and, risking a charge of insubordination, told him that Boscawen's idea was ridiculous and would get them all killed. Wilson saw that he was right, and had the square reformed.

It was dark before they reached the river bank, and the water was visible only as a silver streak in the light of a crescent moon. The discipline of the troops never faltered. The men were allowed to drink in sections, three faces of the square covering while one drank from their helmets, and filled water-bottles. Sentries were detailed to cover the party. Once the men had drunk their fill, they simply collapsed where they were, and fell asleep.

12

At 0900 hours on 21 January, Sanjaq Mohammad Khashm al-Mus Bey heard the sound of artillery-fire coming from the direction of Metemma. He was aboard the steamer *Bordain*, a little downriver, in a four-steamer flotilla that also included *Talahawiyya*, *Safia* and *Tewfiqiyya*. All four steamers were carrying Egyptian soldiers, Jihadiyya, and mountain-guns. Gordon had sent *Bordain* from Khartoum on 14 December, while the other three vessels had been patrolling this stretch of the Nile since October, waiting for Wolseley's troops to appear.

Khashm al-Mus was about fifty-three years old, a short, powerful, dignified Sudanese with a stubbly grey beard and three horizontal tribal scars on each cheek. These identified him as a tribesman of the Shaygiyya, an Arabic-speaking tribe of the Nile Valley. Known as fierce irregular cavalrymen from the days of the Turco-Egyptian invasion, the Shaygiyya had first resisted, then joined the Turks. Many of them had remained loyal to the government. Khashm al-Mus had enlisted in the Shaygiyya cavalry as a youth, and had served as commander or Sanjaq of the frontier station at Fedasi. More recently, he had been at Halfaya, when Sa'id and Hassan Pashas had betrayed their own troops. Khashm al-Mus had been one of the officers who had desperately tried to rally the men. Since then, he had become one of Gordon's most trusted lieutenants.

The masts of the steamers, flying the Egyptian flag, came into view above the dhura stalks in the fields along the river at about 0930 hours. At that moment the British were formed up in a square and moving slowly around the periphery of Metemma, while Wilson and Boscawen tried to work out how to assault the town. The dervishes were keeping up a scattered fire from loopholes in the walls, and a company of skirmishers was shooting back, without much effect. Wilson had ordered the screw-guns into action, but the shells simply punched straight through the soft walls without detonating. It was the crash of the seven-pounders that had alerted the steamers.

The Expedition had spent all the previous day moving the men left at the zariba and the baggage-caravan to Gubbat al-Krumat – the village where they had first watered at the Nile, about two miles south of Metemma (the British referred to it as Abu Kru or Gubbat). Wilson had mustered them at 0400 hours that morning, for the march on Metemma. The few dervishes they had encountered outside the town had quickly skedaddled inside. Since first light, the situation had been stalemate.

A minute after the cry of 'Gordon's steamers!' had run like a ripple through the British force, Wilson heard a whizz of shot through the air and a heavy thud behind him. He looked around to see that an egg-shaped boulder, fired from a dervish Krupp, had buried itself in the ground near the square. Three more shots followed in rapid succession. One knocked off the lower jaw of an artillery camel. Another killed a camel and wounded a man. Wilson had the square form an open column and march out of range.

On *Bordain*, Khashm al-Mus ordered two hundred of his Jihadiyya ashore with two brass nine-pounder mountain-guns. The black troops scampered to the assistance of their allies enthusiastically. They were wearing tarbooshes and one-piece shirts with belts and bandoliers, and carrying Remington rifles, swords and spears. 'They were all fine men,' Albert Gleichen wrote.' . . . It was marvellous to see what good soldiers Gordon's genius had made out of this rough material.'[58]

Within three minutes the Jihadiyya had their nine-pounders firing. The riflemen fanned out and began peppering the walls with bullets. The British troops felt a surge of relief on meeting the Sudanese government troops, and morale soared. The British square was redeployed behind a ridge, and the guns bombarded Metemma for an hour, without achieving anything. The Guards Camel Regiment was ordered to give covering fire for the batteries. They suffered one casualty, when the officer commanding the Marines, Major W. H. Poe, was hit by a dervish bullet that smashed his thigh. Poe had insisted on wearing his red jacket, because his grey one was, he said, 'not fit to be seen'. He had also been standing up in full view of the dervish sharpshooters talking to his men, who were all lying prone. He could not have presented a better target had he launched into a song and dance routine.

At about 1500 hours Wilson withdrew to meet Khashm al-Mus, who gave him a note from Gordon reading, 'Khartoum all right, can hold out for years.' It carried Gordon's seal and was dated 29 December. This news was reassuring, but Khashm al-Mus's other intelligence was not. On the way down he had passed the Mahdi's relief force from Omdurman which Wilson had heard about from prisoners at Abu Tulayh. Khashm al-Mus estimated that it was three thousand strong and would be at Gubba within two days. Even worse, a second relief column from Berber was believed to have reached Sayal, a village downstream from Metemma. This meant that the British would soon be trapped in a pincer movement.

Wilson came to the conclusion that he did not need to capture Metemma. More of his small force would be killed and wounded, more rifle ammunition and scarce artillery shells would be wasted. He decided instead to establish his forward base at Gubba, and ordered the force to retire there immediately. Stewart, who was still lucid, agreed that Gubba was a better position to hold anyway.

Many of the men grumbled about the futile action that morning, and Percy Marling wrote that he wished Redvers Buller had been there – implying that Buller would have captured the town.

There is no doubt, though, that Wilson's decision was the right one. In military theory, the force required to take a defended position should outnumber the defenders by at least two to one. Wilson's men might have been able to capture the town against the odds, but not without serious casualties. As for Redvers Buller, when he arrived there weeks later he took one look at the situation and reported to Wolseley that 'it was not worth taking' – precisely the verdict Wilson had come to.

For the moment it looked as if Wilson's force was in a precarious position. It was small, and would soon become smaller when the supply caravan and its escort was sent back to Jakdul to collect stores. The men under his command had been trekking through the desert on poor rations and little water for three weeks, and were exhausted mentally and physically. They had fought two extremely bloody actions that had called for all the strength, skill and courage they could muster. They had lost 111 men, and 193 were wounded, many critically, when Wolseley had expected them to reach Metemma without a single casualty. The designated commander was *hors de combat*. The Royal Navy officers whom Wolseley had expected to man the steamers were almost all dead. Their commander, Charles Beresford, was now so incapacitated by a large boil on his behind that he could hardly walk.

Wilson had to do the jobs of at least three men. He was both commanding officer and intelligence officer, and also had all the responsibility for taking the steamers to Khartoum to relieve Gordon. The man who was supposed to take over at Metemma after he left, Fred Burnaby, was lying in a shallow grave at Abu Tulayh. Though the steamers carried a full complement of Egyptian soldiers with their wives and children, Gordon had sent a confidential note telling Wilson that on no account should they be brought back to Khartoum. Wilson was now burdened with the unexpected task of removing them from the steamers. The River Column, under Earle, which was eventually to rendezvous with the Desert

Column at Metemma, had not even crossed the Amri Cataract, a little upstream from Korti. Earle could not be expected until March. To cap it all, Wilson had superior enemy forces advancing on him from both north and south. Handling all this was a tall order for an officer who had never before commanded men in the field, and in the circumstances Wilson managed it with resolution, courage and considerable organizing skill. He was never to get the credit for any of this. Wolseley, who defamed his character in his journal, calling his action at Metemma 'silly', and claiming that he had lost his nerve after Abu Tulayh, had not seen the determination with which he had commanded the square at Abu Kru. Neither had Wolseley seen the dervishes in action. His claim that 'no amount of the Mahdi's troops could withstand the smallest of our columns' was, to use his own favourite epithet, 'bosh'.

Wilson's first priority was to dig in at Gubba. It was a collection of huts and mud houses founded on the shrine of a holy man, standing about a mile from the river. It was significant for its low gravel ridges. They were no more than fifty feet high, but they offered almost the only elevated position in the entire area. Wilson split the force into two, one to hold the high ground, and another to defend the river bank, where a zariba of camel-saddles and boxes would be built. Some of the mud houses in Gubba village were demolished and the rubble used to construct a fort on the gravel ridges. The Guards Camel Regiment was to occupy the fort. All other units were sent to the river to defend the zariba, which housed the hospital and the wounded.

While the work was going on, Wilson went through Gordon's papers, brought to him by Khashm al-Mus. They included the last volume of his journal, which Gordon had given to the safe-keeping of a Greek merchant. The final entry in the Journal, penned on 14 December, was ominous. 'NOW MARK THIS,' Gordon had written, 'if the Expeditionary Force . . . does not come in ten days, *the town may fall*; and I have done my best for the honour of the country. Goodbye.'

Gordon's ten days had expired almost a month earlier. The tone of the journal entry contrasted alarmingly with the note of

29 December, stating that Khartoum could hold out for months. Wilson suspected that Gordon had written the note on the assumption that its content would reach dervish ears. Wilson questioned Khashm al-Mus and the steamer captains carefully, and concluded that Gordon was still holding out.

He now had to wrestle with a dilemma – whether to leave for Khartoum immediately in the hope of preventing the catastrophe, or to secure the forward base at Gubba. The base was needed for the River Column, and the second wave of the Desert Column, from which the actual relief of Khartoum could be launched in March. Wilson's planned ascent to Khartoum was intended only as a propaganda exercise. Its purpose now was to convince the townspeople – and the enemy – that the British really were coming.

Wilson decided that the establishment of the base was his first priority. If his force at Gubba were crushed while he was in Khartoum, Wolseley's whole plan would have been shattered. There would be no forward operating base for the River Column, and no dump for the supply caravans that would soon be criss-crossing the Bayuda. There would also be no place for him to return to, whether or not Gordon was still holding Khartoum when he arrived.

Wilson discussed the situation with Charles Beresford, whom Wolseley had instructed to take charge of the steamers going up to Khartoum. Beresford was now in no state to go, but he advised Wilson strongly to carry out reconnaissance missions to the north and south before heading off. He may have hoped that his condition would improve in a couple of days, and that the delay would give him time to reclaim his role as one of Gordon's rescuers.

Wilson could not, anyway, have left that day or the next, as the steamers were almost out of fuel and a supply of wood had to be found. They were also so badly battered and holed from their long string of engagements that they needed overhauling. The run to Khartoum would be a perilous exercise. The river banks on both sides were occupied by hostile elements all the way to the capital, where they would undoubtedly run into dervish defences. To break down or run out of fuel would be disastrous. Wilson was too thorough a man to start off on the most important mission of his life on a wing and a prayer.

Against this was the advice from the steamer captains that if the mission was not carried out in the next twelve days, the Nile would be too low for the steamers to get back through the Sixth Cataract. Khashm al-Mus in particular was keen to get moving at once, but he had a personal stake in the matter – his family and all his worldly possessions were in Khartoum. Wilson decided that as Gordon had held out this long, another two days would make little difference. His reasoning was sound, but his conclusion was wrong.

The following day Wilson set off upriver in *Talahawiyya*, with *Bordain* and *Safia*, to reconnoitre the advance of the dervish force from Berber. The flotilla was engaged by guns from Metemma and Shendi on the opposite bank, and fired back twenty rounds from its two mountain-guns. Beyond Shendi, *Talahawiyya* picked up one of Khashm al-Mus's agents. He reported that the Berber column had been deterred from advancing by survivors of Abu Tulayh. Armed with this good news, the flotilla was back at Gubba by sunset.

Percy Barrow, who had led a recce along the river bank to the south with his Hussars, reported that there were no movements from that direction. There seemed to be no immediate threat to the Expedition, and Wilson declared that he hoped to leave for Khartoum at midday on the 23rd. He had selected two of the steamers to make the journey – *Talahawiyya*, commanded by Khashm al-Mus, and *Bordain*, under his cousin, 'Abd al-Hamid Bey. These were the largest of the four steamers, but they still reminded Wilson of 'penny steamers' on the Thames. Having got in, though, the two steamers would be too big to get out through the cataracts with the rapidly falling Nile. Wilson would have to use Gordon's smaller steamers for the return.

The two officers originally selected to go with him were reduced to one – Eddie Stuart-Wortley. In place of Dickson, whose leg had been shattered at Abu Tulayh, Wilson chose Captain Fred Gascoigne of the Blues, on the basis of his experience in the eastern

Sudan. Both of these officers would remain in Khartoum with Gordon. Beresford was now in such pain that he had been removed to the hospital, awaiting surgery. There was no prospect of his accompanying the steamers. Wilson would have with him Captain Lionel Trafford and twenty-one men of the Royal Sussex Regiment as the sole British fighting contingent. In addition, there would be 110 Jihadiyya, a few Bashi-Bazuks, and the Turco-Egyptian crews.

The twenty-two men of the Sussex Regiment were supposed to arrive in Khartoum wearing red coats, to demonstrate the fact that they were really British soldiers. When Wilson ordered the coats to be brought, it was discovered that the whole bale had been lost during the night-march. The Camel Corps carried red jumpers in addition to their grey ones, and the Heavies managed to produce enough to fit out the Sussex, who found the whole process absurd. 'Haven't we thrashed these niggers in grey?' one private was heard to mutter. 'What fucking use is there in dressing us up in red now? They'll not think us the same fellows whose acquaintance they made at Abu Klea.'[59]

From sunrise the next morning, the men struggled to get the steamers ready. There was no supply of wood in the area, so Wilson ordered the Camel Corps to smash up all the *sagiyyas* along the river bank. This in itself was a painstaking task, as every work party had to be protected by a covering party. The wood was not ideal fuel – it was hard and bulky, and burned too fast. Meanwhile, the Royal Navy artificers did their best to prepare the boats to resist heavy fire, and to overhaul the engines. The Egyptian soldiers and their families had to be removed, and ammunition put on board. Noon came and went, and still the steamers were not ready. By the time they were shipshape it was sunset, and Wilson postponed the start until first light the following day.

Wilson knew that the odds of reaching Khartoum and getting back alive were slim. They would probably face dervish artillery all the way up to the town, and a few sharpshooters at the Sixth Cataract – the Sabaluka gorge – would be fatal. They could not carry enough fuel for more than a day or so. This meant that

Wilson would have to land parties continually to demolish *sagiyyas*, with covering troops. Finally, they would have to run the gauntlet of the dervish batteries at Halfaya and Omdurman. One well-directed shell could send either of the steamers to the bottom. Wilson, who knew that Gordon was in the habit of observing everything from his terrace with a telescope, hoped that he would spot their advance fifteen or twenty miles away, and create a diversion. His plan was to steam into the town at full speed, blasting the shore batteries with broadsides from the nine-pounders and small-arms volleys.

At 0800 hours the following morning, *Bordain* and *Talahawiyya* cast off, carrying their twenty-two British redcoats, on the last desperate attempt to save Gordon and Khartoum.

13

On 20 January a knot of camel-riders couched their beasts in the Mahdi's camp on the west bank of the White Nile, south of Omdurman fort. The tribesmen, travel-stained and weary, were ushered quickly into the Mahdi's presence. They had ridden non-stop from Metemma with bad news: the British had defeated the dervish army at Abu Tulayh, and again at Gubbat al-Krumat. They had met up with Gordon's steamers and were about to embark for Khartoum.

All day the camp was filled with wailing and shrieking as the widows and children of dead dervish warriors received the news of their loss. Rudolf Carl von Slatin, who had fallen from grace with 'Abdallahi and was now in chains, had not heard anything like it since he had left Darfur. The Mahdi's strictures forbade the expression of grief for those who had been killed in battle, and Slatin concluded that something very serious must have happened to make people openly flout the rules. When he found out the truth from his guards, he was flushed with excitement. 'What news!' he wrote later. 'My heart was literally thumping . . .'[60]

The Mahdi was alarmed. He and 'Abdallahi at once tried to stop the mourning. According to Slatin, though, it continued for hours. To cover the noise, the Mahdi ordered his artillery-men to fire a hundred-and-one-gun salute, as if in celebration of a great victory.

Gordon, who had taken to sleeping during the day, was awoken in the palace about three and a half miles to the west by the crash of ordnance from the direction of Omdurman. It sounded like a salute, and he counted the shots carefully as he dressed in his white uniform. He donned his tarboosh, crossed the corridor outside, and passed through a door which led up to the terrace. For two weeks he and his soldiers had been on starvation rations, and like a condemned man Gordon had taken solace in smoking his cigarettes, the only commodity of which he had an abundant supply.

From the terrace he turned his telescope across the White Nile. What he saw did not suggest a celebration. Bevies of dervish women were wailing and tearing out their hair. Gordon's favourite spy, a Shaygiyya girl, returned across the river that night and informed him that the dervishes had suffered defeats at the hands of the British. The salute had been a ruse.

Gordon lost no time in spreading word among his troops. Their morale was sorely in need of a boost. Two weeks earlier the garrison at Omdurman, under a Sudanese officer named Farajallah Pasha, had surrendered to the dervishes. Farajallah had made a heroic stand, but had been starved into submission. Gordon, who had been unable to get supplies to him, had permitted him to surrender. Farajallah had marched his Jihadiyya out of the fort and taken the oath of fealty to the Mahdi. He was now an officer in the dervish army.

The day after Omdurman had fallen, thousands of civilians from Khartoum had hurried to the Mahdi's camp. Gordon had apparently approved of this defection, and had sent a letter with them asking the Mahdi to feed them. The plight of his nine thousand soldiers, and the twenty thousand civilians left in the city, though, was pitiful. The dervishes were now surrounding Khartoum on three sides, and had cut off all supplies. Food reserves had run out at the end of December. Gordon had ordered the crop on Tuti island to be harvested under the covering fire of a fort he had had built there. The crop amounted to two hundred ardebs. This and the last of the biscuit were distributed among the soldiers.

It had lasted less than a week. When it was finished, Gordon instructed the Greek consul, Nikolaos Leontides, with a merchant named Bordeini Bey and half a company of troops, to scour the city for hidden supplies. They discovered some sacks of grain buried under the ground and a little left in the stores of various merchants, but once again it was enough for only a few days. Both civilians and troops then took to slaughtering donkeys, mules and horses, and to hunting dogs and rats in the streets. Gordon ordered his committee to collect all the cattle left in the town. There were only twenty-eight, and they were in poor condition. They were slaughtered by turns and a meat ration issued to the troops every three days.

The civilians had eaten everything – gum arabic, palmetto fibre, animal-skins, and even the pith of palm-trees that had been cut down. People began to fall dead in the street. Gordon detailed a section of guards for each quarter of the town to bury them, but they lacked the energy. Even Gordon's offer of two dollars to anyone who interred a corpse proved futile. The soldiers were in such poor condition that they stood to on the ramparts like living corpses themselves. Many had grotesquely bloated limbs from consuming only gum arabic and water.

Gordon must have smiled when he realized that the hundred-and-one-gun salute from the Mahdi's camp was a trick. It was a carbon copy of a scam he had himself used back in September, to celebrate the supposed advance of the Relief Column on Met-emma. At that point, the Relief Expedition had not even left Cairo. Gordon had continued to make superhuman efforts to fight the propaganda war. He had held constant musters, parades and reviews to impress the citizens. Every two weeks or so he had had posters put up, announcing that British, Indian or Turkish soldiers were on their way, via Kassala, Berber or Dongola. He had even drawn pictures of the various nationalities on his posters, their faces suitably flushed with victory. He claimed that the British were sailing upriver in no less than eight hundred armed steamers, each of which held ten men.

To make his stories more convincing, he had hired all the empty houses along the Blue Nile waterfront as quarters for the expected British officers. He had had them fitted out with furniture, and commissioned potters to make water-jars. He had engaged cooks and servants, drawn up contracts with butchers and bakers to supply them with victuals, and even detailed steamers to bring in firewood and vegetables for them. To add even more conviction to the pretence, he had inspected the quarters personally, declared that more furnishing was required, and authorized the spending of a further 20,000 piastres. He told the manager of the Treasury that they must be ready for occupation at any moment.

Since the Mahdi had arrived outside Omdurman on 24 October, Khartoum had been almost constantly under fire. Gordon would sit placidly by night at a window in the west wing of the palace, with a light behind him, cocking a snook at snipers and gunners. He would record the near misses meticulously in his journal. On 12 December he mentioned that an artillery shell had fallen into the Nile in direct line with the window he was sitting at. He estimated that the enemy had fired no less than two thousand artillery shells at Khartoum in all, but had caused only three deaths. He sent his boy buglers to the terrace to snipe back at the enemy, or give out confusing bugle-calls. Some of them were so small they had to stand on stools to see over the parapet.

During his sojourn across the White Nile, the Mahdi had written no less than nine letters to Gordon, all of them urging him to surrender. With the first of these he had sent him a full set of dervish costume – patched *jibba*, baggy *sirwal*, sandals, skullcap, and palmetto-fibre belt. It was tit-for-tat for the Turkish dress Gordon had offered him, but Gordon did not see the humour in it. He saw only that he had underestimated the Mahdi and, instead of laughing, kicked the garments across the room in a fit of pique.

On 22 October a letter from the Mahdi had informed Gordon that Stewart, Power and Herbin had been killed. As confirmation, he had enclosed some documents from *Abbas*. Gordon refused to believe it, declaring that the documents had never been on *Abbas*, and had been taken from one of his messengers. It was not until 3 November, when a letter arrived from Kitchener corroborating the claim, that he finally accepted it. For days afterwards he wrestled with his conscience, pouring out the pros and cons of his guilt in his diary. 'I cannot get out of my head the *Abbas* catastrophe,' he wrote two days later, '. . . as far as human foresight goes I did all my possible. Why did you [I] let them go? . . . I will own that, without reason . . . I have never been comfortable since they left . . . It is very sad, but, being ordained, we must not murmur.'[61] Gordon added that he thought it a nemesis on the execution of the two pashas – Hassan and Sa'id – suggesting that he was not entirely convinced they had been guilty.

The Mahdi's last letter had offered him a safe conduct to British lines, revealing that Mohammad Ahmad no more grasped Gordon's character than Gordon had his. Gordon could easily have left Khartoum had he wished to do so, but evacuating himself would have meant betraying those he had sworn to protect. What troubled him most, indeed, was the knowledge that, had he not been there, the population could long ago have surrendered to the Mahdi's mercy. They had endured endless hardship for his sake: thousands of troops had died defending them. The way Gordon saw it, it was his duty to share their fate, whether the British government abandoned them or not. 'I declare *positively*,' he had written in his journal on 9 November, 'and *once and for all that I will not leave the Sudan until every one who wants to go down is given the chance to do so, unless* a government is established which relieves me of the charge.' Even if an emissary arrived and ordered him to leave, he added, 'I WILL NOT OBEY IT BUT WILL STAY HERE AND FALL WITH THE TOWN.'[62]

On the night following the artillery salute, Gordon convened a meeting of his committee in the house of Faraj Pasha, commander of the Jihadiyya, in which he was represented by his Chief Clerk, Giriagis Bey. Through Giriagis, Gordon told the council that the British would soon arrive, but assured them that when they did so he would remain in Khartoum 'and die with the soldiers'. According to the merchant Bordeini Bey, who was present at the meeting, the news that the British were on the doorstep raised morale to unprecedented heights.

Across the White Nile, the Mahdi was also holding council. Mohammad Ahmad had been disturbed by the British victories in the north, and almost all of his counsellors were advising him to withdraw back to Kordofan. The only dissenting voice was that of his uncle, Mohammad 'Abd al-Karim, who pointed out that if a single Englishman, Gordon, had caused them so much trouble, an army of Englishmen in Khartoum would be truly formidable. Instead of waiting for Gordon to surrender, they must attack Khartoum now, *before* the British arrived. It was an opportune moment. Deserters from Gordon's forces confirmed that provisions in the town were now virtually finished, and that the soldiers were too weak to resist an attack.

Sometime later, another deserter told the Mahdi of a serious gap in Khartoum's southern defences. On the White Nile side, opposite Omdurman, and just north of the village of Kalakla, the Nile waters had receded to expose about a thousand yards of poorly defended land. There had been a ditch and a bank here before the flood, but it had been partly eroded by the inundation. Gordon was aware of the gap, and had sent his battalions to improve the ditch, but they had been discouraged by dervish fire from across the river. The ditch was still no more than two yards deep, and would not prevent a determined attack. To the west, the flood plain was covered in a shallow film of water. The ditch itself was full of mud, but was not defended by troops. Gordon had positioned two barges on the river near the gap, each one manned by a platoon.

14

Days passed without any sign of British steamers, and the morale of the government troops began to droop once more. 'Gordon Pasha used to say every day, "They must come tomorrow,"' recalled Bordeini, 'but they never came and we began to think that they must have been defeated by the rebels after all.' Gordon had all the ammunition moved along the waterfront, to the Catholic church, where it would be safer behind thick stone walls. He had a mine primed in the church, with a fuse linked to the palace, so that it could be blown if necessary. He had long ago had two massive mines set up in the basement of the palace itself, ready to blow himself to smithereens before the dervishes could capture him. The small steamer *Mohammad 'Ali* was kept moored and provisioned at the palace jetty, to provide an escape-route for the consuls and other prominent citizens.

On Sunday 25 January the sun came up weak and pallid. The morning was cold, and the Nile was at its lowest, a dirty brown trickle between mud-banks and shoulders of dried mud like cracked and broken leather. Gordon was on the terrace with his telescope at first light, scanning the dervish positions. In wad an-Nejumi's camp at Kalakla, near the White Nile, to the south-west, thousands of dervish warriors had left their positions and were couching and loading camels. Gordon sent his ADC, Khalil Agha Orfali, a Syrian ex-Bashi-Bazuk, to the telegraph office on the ground floor to order the men stood to. He expected an attack. He instructed the officers on the defences to hold their positions until 0800 hours the following morning, when, he assured them, British troops would arrive.

He called his Chief Clerk, Giriagis Bey, and had him convene a committee meeting in his office at the palace. Once again, Gordon did not attend in person. Instead, Giriagis relayed his instructions that every male in Khartoum above the age of eight years must be collected and told to line the defences alongside the troops.

After the meeting Bordeini Bey asked to see Gordon and was shown into his room next door. Gordon was sitting on a divan near a table on which Bordeini saw two full boxes of cigarettes. When the Bey entered, Gordon pulled off his tarboosh and flung it moodily at the wall. 'I have nothing more to say,' he told him. 'People will no longer believe me, and I have told them over and over that help would be here, but it has never come, and now they must see I tell them lies. If this, my last promise, fails, I can do no more. Go and collect all the people you can on the lines and make a good stand.'[63]

Bordeini realized that Gordon was more agitated than he had ever seen him, and in fact had been too upset to attend the meeting. This was why he had sent Giriagis instead. His hair seemed to have turned white overnight. Gordon told Bordeini that if the attack came, he should stay in his house until he sent for him. 'Now leave me and let me smoke these cigarettes,' he said. They were Gordon's last recorded words.

After sunset there were three other visitors: consuls Martin Hansall and Nikolaos Leontides, and a Greek doctor. They remained with him until midnight. After they had gone, Gordon stayed up for another hour, writing, chain-smoking and occasionally pacing the room. At one in the morning he called his ADC, Orfali, and told him to check with the telegraph room to see if there was any news from the defences. Orfali returned minutes later to report that all was quiet.

Half an hour afterwards Gordon heard the sound of gunfire from the southern ramparts. Orfali told him that there had been a minor attack on Burri fort, but that it had been repulsed. Gordon then prepared for bed. After closing all the doors along the corridor, Orfali went down and instructed the duty telegraph clerk to notify him immediately if there were any developments. He then retired to his room.

At about 0300 hours, Orfali roused Gordon and told him the Mahdi had launched an attack from the direction of the White Nile. Gordon threw on his dressing-gown and prepared for action, but the first reports suggested that the attack had been broken off.

Soon after, though, both Gordon and Orfali heard shooting, and several orderlies ran down from the terrace and told them that waves of dervishes were flooding into the town.

The Mahdi and 'Abdallahi had crossed the White Nile by boat shortly after last light, and joined their hordes under 'Abd ar-Rahman wad an-Nejumi near Kalakla. At midnight, just as Gordon was bidding farewell to Hansall and Leontides, the Mahdi had given wad an-Nejumi the order to attack. The dervishes had advanced so silently on the gap in the defences that the troops manning the ramparts further to the east never heard a sound. They were not aware that an attack was in progress until minutes before the enemy crossed the line. The troops had been expecting an assault from the west, near Burri, believing that the gap was too muddy for an offensive.

The dervishes burst suddenly out of the night, carrying old *angarebs* to help them breast the deep mud. Some waded waist deep into the slough and allowed themselves to be used as stepping-stones by their advancing companions. Others found the ground in places less muddy than they had expected. Within minutes they were inside the town. Sentries opened fire blindly in the darkness. The starving soldiers awoke to find the enemy scrambling over the parapet in thousands, screaming death to the unbelievers.

The 5th Egyptian Regiment, under Colonel Hasan Bey al-Bahnassi, saw the enemy racing towards them. 'They came in shouting,' said Sid 'Ahmad 'Abd ar-Razak, a subaltern of the 4th battalion. 'They broke in near the White Nile. We fired in that direction, and when we saw the enemy were behind us, Nos. 3 and 4 companies formed square, and we remained firing until the square was broken, then we formed groups and fell back on the 1st Regiment. The [dervishes] broke in amongst us and there was a mêlée, then some [of us] were taken prisoner, and others were killed.'[64]

The government Jihadiyya, manning the wall further along, were attacked simultaneously by massed assault parties. They smashed against the Burri gate, west of the palace, and the Masalamiyya gate, to the south. In places the Sudanese troops put up a stiff resistance. 'Though we went on firing our rifles until they were too hot to hold,' said a survivor, Yuzbashi (Captain) 'Abdallah Adlan, '[the dervishes] finally poured over the ramparts by sheer force of numbers, and anyone who remained standing was killed. Life was dear, and many of us threw ourselves down among the dead and wounded while the dervishes passed over us into the town.'[65]

Faraj Pasha, the Commander-in-Chief, had been at Buri when the assault began. He rode down the defences on a horse, bawling at his men to hold steady. When he reached the Masallamiyya gate, though, he realized that the dervishes were inside, and that the game was up. According to some witnesses, he threw a civilian coat over his uniform and ordered the sentry to open the gate. He told his men to stop firing, and surrendered to the enemy.

The dervishes surged through the native town and dashed across the open space to the Blue Nile waterfront. Aroused by the noise, the population ran outside to see warriors teeming through the streets. Many civilians were butchered where they stood. The dervishes, wild with victory, broke into the houses, massacring, raping, pillaging and looting. 'The whole town was now filled with the screams of the people and the shouts of the [dervishes],' wrote Nushi Pasha, in his official report based on eye-witness accounts. 'They killed everyone they met, attacked the inhabitants in their houses and slaughtered them and ransacked everywhere.'[66] Other eye-witnesses reported that the Mahdi's men systematically raped the fairer-skinned women, especially Egyptians, and women of the Ja'aliyyin and Shaygiyya tribes. Some officers shot their wives and children, then put bullets through their own heads, rather than allow them to fall into dervish hands. Mohammad Pasha Hussain, the Head of Finance, saw his daughter and her husband murdered in front of him, and refused to flee with his friends. Instead he hurled curses on the Mahdi at the onrushing warriors until they silenced him permanently.

They caught the Greek consul, Nikolaos Leontides, in his house, and severed both his hands at the wrists before cutting off his head.

They smashed their way into the house of another Greek family nearby, shooting the father through the forehead and cleaving his twelve-year-old son's head with an axe, splattering brain matter and blood over his pregnant wife, who was claimed as a concubine by wad an-Nejumi. Almost all the Egyptian Copts in the town were murdered. Among the dead was the American consul, a Copt called Aser, who died of a heart attack when his brother's head was struck off before his eyes.

Many people were betrayed by their former slaves and servants. Austrian consul Martin Hansall's servant led a party to his house. In the courtyard, they found Hansall's carpenter, Mulatte Skander, whose head they cut off. Hansall himself came downstairs, un-armed, to find Skander's headless corpse lying in a pool of blood. A second later the warriors hacked off Hansall's head, and in a killing frenzy stabbed both his dog and his parrot. They took man, dog and parrot outside, doused them in alcohol, set them on fire, and tossed them into the Blue Nile.

Franz Klein, a Hungarian Jew who had converted to Catholicism, and who had been the official tailor to many governors-general of the Sudan, was seized in his house and had his throat cut from ear to ear in front of his Italian wife and five children. His eighteen-year-old son was speared to death, and his daughter raped.

On the waterfront, the brother left in charge of the Catholic Mission, Domenico Polinari, opened the gate a crack. He found the guards chopped to pieces, and thousands of chanting dervishes standing over their bodies, brandishing bloody spears and swords. He slammed the gate shut and fled with some black workers to a hay shed in the corner of the ornate garden. Seconds later, dark figures burst through the gate and swarmed over the high walls. The blacks lost their nerve and quit their hiding-place, only to be caught and dismembered by the dervishes. Every man employed in the Mission grounds was killed. Polinari remained concealed, but could hear clearly their shrieks of terror, and the dry thwack of the dervish swords. A group of warriors came into the hut and poked their spears into the hay. Astonishingly, they missed him.

Dawn was already gathering over Omdurman, blood-red streaks gashing the night sky. Further along the Nile bank, hundreds of Mahdist banners were bobbing around the palace, and scores of dervish warriors were massing. According to one account, they were reluctant to enter, since several former palace servants had told them it was mined. But Gordon had abandoned the idea of blowing himself up, which would have been suicide, and therefore an act of cowardice and a betrayal of faith.

How Gordon actually died is a mystery. The figure of the hero standing on the palace steps in full uniform, sheathed sword at his belt, revolver unfired, with a host of spear-toting dervishes below him, is a familiar icon of the British Empire. The concept of martyrdom, with its Messianic overtones, was dear to the Victorian mind, and that this is how it happened seems somehow obvious to us, mainly because of George William Joy's famous painting *The Death of Gordon*. Lytton Strachey's embellishment in his biographical essay *The End of General Gordon*, suggesting that there was a dramatic pause while Gordon and the dervishes contemplated each other, has also added to the myth. The 1960s film *Khartoum*, starring Charlton Heston as Gordon, has the dervishes actually backing away when Gordon appears.

This image, though, is based on an account by Bordeini Bey, who had last seen Gordon hours before, and seems highly unlikely. Bordeini stated that Gordon was on the roof terrace in his dressing-gown until first light, when he descended to his room and dressed in his uniform. He then stood outside the door of his office, which was situated at the head of the stone steps leading down to the palace entrance.

A moment later, four dervishes came up the stairs. At least one of them had worked as a servant here previously, and knew the layout of the place. According to some accounts, Gordon demanded, 'Where is your master, the Mahdi?' The first man, a tribesman of the Danagla named Taha Shahin, ignored the question and bawled, 'O cursed one, your day has come!' He ran his spear into Gordon's body. Gordon staggered, made a gesture of contempt, and turned his back. Taha stabbed him again, between the shoulder-blades. Gordon collapsed in a gush of blood. Taha's three companions then came forward and hacked at the body with their swords until he was dead.

It might be better for posterity, perhaps, to leave Gordon standing there at the top of the steps, passively waiting for a martyr's death. His ADC, Orfali, though, describes a very different passing – one that has Gordon fighting to the bitter end. This story cannot be dismissed, because, unlike Bordeini, Orfali was certainly present in the palace when the dervishes entered it, and his account is rich in the sort of convincing detail the other stories lack.

Orfali relates that within five minutes of Gordon learning that the dervishes had broken into the town, he had organized a defence of the palace. He stationed more than fifty soldiers and servants at windows, at the door on the ground floor, and on the roof terraces. Each man was armed with a Remington and had 120 rounds of ammunition. As the dervish mass streamed into the garden, cascades of fire roared out of the windows and rained down from the roof. About seventy warriors were killed or wounded. They were quickly replaced by their comrades, who ran round the walls and climbed over the vine trellis at the back. 'They were met with the fire from the windows and terraces,' recalled Orfali. 'They came in great numbers, very quickly. Some ran to the entrance, killed the guards, and opened the door. Then they all ran to the [ground floor] door and killed the telegraph clerks.'[67]

Some hared up the stairs on the right and began to slaughter the soldiers on the terrace. Others broke down the door into the upper corridor with axes, only to find Charles Gordon waiting for them with a loaded Webley revolver in one hand, a drawn sword in the other, and a grim look on his face. As they staggered back in surprise, he fired five or six rounds, knocking down two of them. He ran his sword through another, then began to reload his pistol, but at that moment some warriors who had entered from the other end of the corridor smashed through the door behind him. Orfali, standing next to him, rushed to block their way. A spearman stabbed him in the face. Gordon ran to help, but was hit by a hurled spear that glanced off his left shoulder. Ignoring the wound, he opened rapid fire. Orfali, with blood streaming down his face, fired blindly at point-blank range. Three bodies hit the floor, and the rest retreated, several of them losing blood.

Gordon was bleeding slightly from the glancing spear wound. Orfali's face was covered in blood, but the wound was not as severe as it looked. They retired to Gordon's room and reloaded their weapons. Gordon's left hand was already black with powder burns from his rapid firing. A moment later, they heard more dervishes clumping up the stairs, and ran out to meet them. Just as they reached the head of the stairs, a dervish leaned out of an office door and rammed a spear into Gordon's left shoulder from behind. Orfali chopped at the man's hand, almost cutting it off. The dervish toppled across the corridor and down the stairs, and was impaled on the spear of one of his comrades coming up. At almost the same moment, a warrior on the top step cut Orfali's leg with his blade.

More warriors were bounding down the corridor behind them. They were trapped on both sides. Another dervish slashed Orfali's left hand. Gordon hacked him down with his own blade, and kicked him in the head. A tall black man, skulking in the doorway of one of the rooms, stepped out suddenly and fired at Gordon with a revolver. Gordon staggered, hit in the breast. He brought his own pistol up, and snapped a shot at the big warrior, knocking him flat.

Before he had even fallen, dozens more warriors sprinted up the corridor behind him. Gordon and Orfali blasted off their last rounds, then turned and tried to fight their way downstairs with their swords. They forced their way step by step, fighting shoulder to shoulder, cutting and thrusting, until they reached the bottom. By this time, Gordon had lost so much blood that he could scarcely stand. A last thrust from a spearman took him in the right hip, and he sank down on the mat at the base of the staircase. Orfali tried to back into the Finance Office nearby, but was knocked senseless with a club. He lay there among the corpses until afternoon. When he came round, he saw Gordon's body lying where it had fallen, covered in blood and flies. His head had been cut off.

Orfali's account is the most detailed of all the versions of

Gordon's death, but may not be the final word. Another eye-witness, a servant of Giriagis Bey, claimed that Gordon was not killed in the palace at all, but shot in the street while leading a party of soldiers and servants towards Martin Hansall's house. Yet another eye-witness on the dervish side, a former clerk from el-Obeid named Ibrahim Sabir, claimed that Gordon was shot by a standard-bearer called Mursal Hammuda while standing at the top of the steps. Only when the body had rolled to the ground was it identified as that of Gordon. A chief called Babikr Koko came riding up on a horse, cut off Gordon's head with his sword, stuffed it in a leather bag, and rode away.

What happened to Gordon's body is uncertain. Most probably it was simply dropped into the Blue Nile. The river to which he had returned over and over again in his life became his final resting place.

The killing, raping, torture and looting in Khartoum continued until 1700 hours, when the Mahdi ordered it stopped. By that time, as many as ten thousand men, women and children may have been massacred.

Rudolf Carl von Slatin, still in chains at the dervish camp in Omdurman, had been up all night. He knew that something was afoot, but had not been told that the dervish army had advanced. He had just fallen asleep at dawn when he was awoken by the clatter of musketry and the roar of artillery-fire from across the river. He realized that the Mahdi must have launched an offensive. 'Excited and agitated,' he wrote, 'I awaited the result with intense impatience. Soon shouts of rejoicing and victory were heard in the distance, and my guards ran off to find out the news. In a few minutes they were back again, excitedly relating how Khartoum had been taken by storm and was now in the hands of the Mahdists.'[68]

At first he was not inclined to believe them. Crawling out of his tent, though, he saw that the camp was jam-packed with thousands of exultant warriors, most of them gathered before the pavilions of the Mahdi and the Khalifa 'Abdallahi. Suddenly, Slatin noticed a slave marching directly towards him followed by a crowd of crying people. The slave, one of 'Abdallahi's warriors, whom

Slatin recognized as a southerner called Shatta, was carrying something wrapped in a bloody cloth. Shatta halted before Slatin and made an insulting gesture. Then he unwrapped the cloth, and showed Slatin the severed head of Charles George Gordon. 'Is this not the head of your uncle, the unbeliever?' he leered.

Slatin was staggered. For a moment his heart seemed to stop. Then he recovered his self-control. He studied Gordon's familiar features, looked the slave in the eye, and said quietly, 'What of it? A brave soldier, who fell at his post. Happy is he to have fallen. His sufferings are over.'[69]

15

At noon on 28 January, the steamer *Bordain* rounded Tuti island, followed closely by *Talahawiyya*. Both steamers were cruising at full speed. From *Bordain*'s midship turret, Lieut. Colonel Sir Charles Wilson and his deputy, Captain Fred Gascoigne, got their first look at the palace at Khartoum. Even without field-glasses they could see that it was wrecked. Khashm al-Mus, who was also with them, was anxious to know if they could see the Egyptian flag that Gordon always flew from the roof. 'Neither Gascoigne nor I could see a trace of it anywhere,' Wilson recalled.[70]

The steamers had been under fire since they had been spotted by dervish lookouts near Halfaya, an hour earlier. Four guns, hidden in *sagiyya* pits on the east bank, had begun rumbling, sending shells screeching over them and smacking into the river. Scores of Remingtons had opened up from six or seven hundred yards, the rounds pattering audibly like hailstones against the boats' sides. Wilson had ordered his Sudanese gunners to reply with their trusty nine-pounder mountain-guns. The cannon were soon roaring from the decks, shrouding them in smoke, through which the black gunners, clad only in loincloths, could be glimpsed. The red-jacketed men of the Sussex Regiment fired volleys with their Martini-Henrys, but the dervishes were well dug in and neither the shellfire nor the musketry had much apparent effect.

Scanning the bank with his field-glasses, Wilson had noticed that Halfaya itself looked derelict, and that there were some large boats lying off the shore. This was curious, as he knew the Mahdi had no boats – and judging by the intense incoming fire, Gordon's men were not there. As the steamers came abreast of the lower end of Tuti island, the shooting stopped and the smoke cleared. Wilson and Gascoigne gained a clear view of the palace above the trees.

Khashm al-Mus's anxiety showed on his face. He told Wilson that he was certain something had happened. Khartoum must have been taken by the Mahdi, otherwise the flag would have been kept flying, and there would have been no boats at Halfaya. 'I could not believe this,' Wilson said. 'At any rate, we could not stop now until we were certain all was over.'[71]

Moments later, as *Bordain* and *Talahawiyya* approached the Moghran point, where the Blue and White Niles meet, two guns punched out smoke from the right bank, in Khor Shambat, just north of Omdurman. The rounds whacked into the water, hurling waves against the hulls. The clack and patter of rifle-fire started again, and to his consternation Wilson saw puffs of smoke bursting out among the vegetation on both banks. He could see no one, and could not tell if both sides were directing fire at the steamers, or at each other.

To solve the problem he directed *Bordain*'s skipper to steer near to Tuti, and scrambled out of the turret. Leaning over the gunwale on deck, he shouted for the news. The only answer was a fusillade of .43 calibre Remington rounds that zipped around him like flies. Wilson scuttled back into the turret, convinced that the dervishes now held Tuti but hoping desperately that Gordon was still holding Khartoum. There was the crunch of artillery from about twelve hundred yards away on the right, and Wilson realized that the battery at Omdurman fort had now got the steamers in range. He ordered the mountain-guns to fire back. Watching the strikes with his field-glasses, he noticed that a flotilla of *nuggars* and troop-carriers was moored near the fort. This was perplexing, because

Khashm al-Mus had told him that Gordon always kept these vessels under his own guns at Khartoum.

As they rounded the Moghran, the city hove into full view off the starboard bow. 'We came to the junction of the two Niles,' Wilson said, 'when it became plain to everyone that Khartoum had fallen into the Mahdi's hands – hundreds of dervishes with banners were on the sand-spit ready to oppose a landing, and no flag was flying.'[72]

Gunfire was sizzling out at the gunboats from Khartoum, and Wilson listened in vain for the sound of shooting inside the town that might indicate that Gordon was still under siege. This, the absence of the Egyptian ensign, and the fact that none of Gordon's steamers came out to help them, was conclusive proof that they had arrived too late. There was no time to contemplate this, though, for dervish rounds were slapping into them from all sides.

Wilson ordered *Bordain* to turn about and steam at full speed back through the deadly gauntlet of the dervish guns. For those on the steamers, the world had become a hell of choking smoke, the deafening crump of bursting shells, and bullets whining across their bows. 'Looking out over the stirring scene,' Wilson said, 'it seemed almost impossible that we should escape.'[73] Suddenly, a shell whomped into the deck, splitting open the cabin, and clanging into the magazine. The boat rocked perilously, but the shell failed to explode. When the smoke cleared, Wilson noted to his horror that *Talahawiyya*, ahead of them, had run aground.

To make it worse, the Jihadiyya had stopped firing. Khashm al-Mus rolled himself up in a rug and lay pathetically in a corner. Like the soldiers under his command, he was aware that his wife and children were now slaves or concubines of the Mahdi. Wilson realized that he might soon be facing a mutiny from Khashm al-Mus and the Sudanese troops, but for now the Sanjaq was too stunned to do anything. Wilson decided to eliminate the thought from his mind until they were clear of immediate danger.

The redcoats of the Sussex Regiment fought on stoically. They were picked marksmen, and they continued to load and fire, taking aimed shots at the enemy. Wilson saw dozens of dervishes fall under their tattoo of fire.

Bordain steamed past her consort, and moments later *Talahawiyya* freed herself and followed in her wake. Shortly after, she was holed by a shell, but steamed on, round the Moghran point, past the snipers on Tuti. It was like a voyage through the deepest reaches of a Gothic nightmare. For another two hours they withstood the onslaught of dervish shells and rifles. When they finally pulled clear of Halfaya, Wilson knew that they had witnessed a miracle: only one good shot had been needed to sink either of the steamers, and they had been under continuous enemy fire for four solid hours.

Wilson, having escaped almost certain death for the second time in two weeks, lowered his field-glasses and sat down, shell-shocked. It was only then that the enormity of the failure struck him. 'To me the blow was crushing,' he wrote. 'Khartoum had fallen and Gordon dead! – for I never for a moment believed he would allow himself to fall into the Mahdi's hands alive. Such was the ending of all our labours and of his perilous enterprise. For months I had been looking forward to the time when I should meet Gordon again . . . and now all was over, it seemed to me too cruel to be true.'[74]

16

When darkness fell, it came like the answer to a prayer. Wilson ordered the steamers tied up at an island south of the Sabaluka gorge, and dispatched scouts back towards Khartoum to find out the fate of Gordon. The scouts returned the same night to say that Khartoum had been taken on the 26th, and Gordon killed. At first light the next morning, the flotilla set off to take the bad news back to Gubba.

For the past days, the Nile had been falling almost visibly – up to three feet a day. Both the steamers were larger than those normally used to shoot the cataracts at low Nile: the original plan had been to return with two of Gordon's small vessels. The steamers entered the Sabaluka Cataract at about 1230 hours. All seemed to be going well. The sun drifted over the gorge, and was sinking into the desert beyond. Suddenly there was a deafening clang from *Talahawiyya*. She had hit a submerged rock, and a large hole had been ripped in her skin under the waterline. Artificers jumped into the river to examine her hull, but there was no hope. She was already taking on water and listing badly. In a matter of minutes she was sinking. The soldiers abandoned her, piling into the boat she had been towing. Captain Trafford of the Royal Sussex and Lieutenant Eddie Stuart-Wortley of the Intelligence Department managed to salvage her two mountain-guns, but lost almost all of the ammunition.

Now there was only *Bordain*. When night came Wilson ordered her tied up again. After dark, a tribesman approached her, sending word that he was an envoy from the Mahdi. Wilson allowed him on board, and the man handed him a letter from Mohammad Ahmad himself, calling on him to surrender. Wilson was all for ignoring it, but after the courier had gone, Khashm al-Mus argued that they should play for time. He wrote a letter back saying that if a safe-conduct pass were given to him, he would deliver the British to the dervishes at Wadi Habeshi further downstream. Wilson reluctantly accepted the trick, but insisted that no promises would be given on his part. Khashm al-Mus hoped that this ploy would cause the dervishes to hold off at least until *Bordain* got past Wad Habeshi, where they had a battery and a fort. Wilson planned to run the gauntlet at Wadi Habeshi at full steam with all guns blazing.

The next day *Bordain* negotiated the rest of the narrow gorge of Sabaluka without incident. All day, though, Wilson had to wrestle with suspicions and rumours that the Shaygiyya Bashi-Bazuks were about to mutiny. What disturbed him most was a feeling that Khashm al-Mus's letter to the Mahdi was a real offer to sell the British out, rather than the ruse he had pretended. The day passed peacefully enough, though, and the next morning Wilson began to feel that they were going to make it back to Gubba after all. That afternoon, *Bordain* was steaming ahead at full speed when there was an almighty crunch. Everyone on deck was sent flying. The paddles stopped abruptly. Wilson did not need an expert to tell him that her hull had been ruptured. Like *Talahawiyya*, she began taking on water very rapidly. Wilson suspected that the captain had wrecked her on purpose, but there was no time for recriminations: she had to be abandoned at once.

Wilson ordered the men to disembark on the large island of Mernat nearby. His force was now stranded forty miles upstream from their base, with no transport. He quickly devised a plan of action. He would send Eddie Stuart-Wortley down to Gubba on the boat, to inform Boscawen of the situation. Boscawen would dispatch another steamer at once. Fred Gascoigne would also be sent downstream in a *nuggar* carrying the wounded. Wilson, Trafford, and the Royal Sussex, the Jihadiyya, the Bashi-Bazuks and the crews, would march up the west bank to meet the rescue craft. The plan had one flaw – the Jihadiyya refused to march. This was mutiny, but Wilson knew there was nothing he could do. The next step would be defection to the enemy. He decided to send Stuart-Wortley down with the boat anyway, and hoped the Jihadiyya would not make a move before the steamer arrived.

Just after last light, Stuart-Wortley set off in a *nuggar* with four men of the Sussex Regiment and eight Sudanese. The only obstacle was the dervish post at Wadi Habeshi, and he hoped to sneak past hidden by the darkness. Bearing in mind Wilson's suspicion that the wreck of *Bordain* might have been deliberate sabotage, he told his pilot that, should the boat 'strike a rock' on the way down, he would kill him without hesitation. They made good time, and soon the dervish post loomed out of the darkness. As they approached, the pilot manned the tiller while the soldiers lay under blankets in the bottom of the boat. Stuart-Wortley pointed his pistol at the pilot's head.

Just as they were nearing the place, a huge moon shot up over the right bank. The pilot had to keep the *nuggar* as near to the bank as possible to make use of the deepest channel, and the boat was clearly silhouetted in moonlight. Stuart-Wortley peeped over the gunwale, and saw cooking fires twinkling along the opposite bank. He could make out the groups of dervishes sitting around them. By some marvel, none of the enemy saw them. The *nuggar* was passing the last flicker of fire, and it seemed for an incredible moment that they had got through. Then Stuart-Wortley saw a dervish look up and shade his eyes against the moon. 'He jumped to his feet with excitement,' he recalled, 'and shouted out *"Fuluka ingleezi!"* [British boat] Immediately hundreds of enemy sprang up, seized their rifles, and began to pour in a fairly heavy fire at us.'[75]

He screamed at the troops to man the oars and pull for their lives. Remington rounds pitched out of the night, thumping against the gunwales and ricocheting off the oars. Incredibly, no one was hit, and within minutes the current had pulled the boat out of range. The men worked the oars valiantly. Wadi Habeshi was left behind and the river became as silent as the grave. No one else challenged them. At 0400 hours they hauled the *nuggar* ashore at Gubba.

Quickly they located the command post, and found that Boscawen had gone down with malaria, and that command had been assumed by Lieut. Colonel M. Willson of the Scots Guards. A courier was dispatched at once for Korti, to inform Wolseley that Gordon was dead. By afternoon, *Safia* had been prepared and steamed off upriver to rescue Wilson. She was commanded by Captain Lord Beresford himself, now recovered from his boil, and delighted to have a chance to play a part in the final drama.

Meanwhile, Wilson had set up a defensive position on the island where he had landed. He was worried about the loyalty of the Sudanese soldiers, and next morning his worst suspicions were confirmed when the former commander of *Talahawiyya*, 'Abd al-Hamid Bey, and his company of Shaygiyya irregulars, went over to the enemy. To his credit – and to Wilson's surprise – Khashm al-Mus refused to join him.

On 3 February Wilson heard the thunder of guns from downstream. Trafford ran off up the bank with a party of scouts to find out what was happening. He returned to tell Wilson that *Safia* was abreast of Wadi Habeshi and engaged in a gun-battle with the dervish battery there. Wilson ordered his force to cross to the east bank on the boat, and move north to meet *Safia*. They traversed the river under heavy fire from dervish troops, who had arrived that morning, but Wilson managed to get all his men to the east bank without casualties.

They marched north until they were opposite the dervish position at Wadi Habeshi. Wilson saw *Safia*, apparently drifting in midstream, under fire from dervish guns only three hundred yards away. Shortly, a boat arrived from her with a message from Beresford. It was bad news: *Safia*'s boiler had been burst by a dervish shell, and was under repair. Beresford needed Wilson's help.

Beresford had tried to run the dervish battery, sailing through at full steam with guns blasting. One man had been killed and another injured in the leg. Just when he believed he had got through, the boiler had taken a hit. Two engine-room artificers had been carried up from the depths with their boiled flesh hanging in strips from the bones. A stoker had been burned to death. Henry Benbow, the chief engineer, had emptied the boiler, put out the fires, and started to hammer out a new boiler-plate. The plate had to be fitted and bolted from inside, but even hours after it had been emptied, the iron was still red hot. Finally, a Sudanese youth agreed to go inside. Benbow had the boiler filled with cold water twice, and emptied again, and had the men smear the youth's skin with tallow. The boy entered, but was back a moment later – the heat was still unendurable. After a brief interlude, he entered again and this time stayed inside long enough to fit the plate and pass the bolts through. He emerged unscathed.

Fortunately Wilson had salvaged his mountain-guns from *Bordain*, and ordered the crews to give covering fire. While the boiler was being repaired, his nine-pounder was slapping shells constantly across the river into the dervish entrenchments. Wilson also ordered the Jihadiyya and Sussex to fire controlled volleys. They kept up the fire resolutely for hours. No dervish could show his head at Wadi Habeshi without being shot at. From the decks of *Safia*, a Gardner machine-gun pumped out round after round, its sputtering punctuated by steady roars from one of the steamer's own four-pounder mountain-guns. So effective was this, and Wilson's supporting fire, that the dervish gunners failed to get off a single shot at *Safia* for the rest of the day. Their snipers, though, managed to kill two and wound twenty-five of Wilson's force. When darkness fell, hiding *Safia* in its folds, Wilson moved his exhausted men two miles downstream to a defensive position that an advance party had already set up.

The hole in *Safia*'s boiler had been repaired by 1900 hours. At first light the fires were stoked up again and Beresford managed to turn the steamer about under heavy fire and run back towards Gubba. On the way, he picked up Gascoigne with the wounded, stranded in their *nuggar* on a sandbank. Further on, he also lifted Wilson and his company. They arrived back at base just before sunset on 4 February. At first light the following day, Wilson left for Korti with an escort of the Guards Camel Regiment, to brief Wolseley on the fall of Khartoum.

17

That week had been one of terrible anxiety for Garnet Wolseley. 'Having led storming parties,' he wrote, 'I can assert them to be child's play compared with the strain which a General situated as I have been for some days past, has to undergo . . . When . . . I am left a week without news of what is going on . . . the tension on all vital parts of the bodily system becomes almost intolerable.'[76] On 4 February, just as he was going to dinner in the mess-tent, the bomb dropped. A messenger came in with a dispatch from Gubba: Khartoum was taken, and Gordon presumed dead. Wolseley had lost the game.

For days Wolseley continued to grasp at straws. When Wilson himself arrived at Korti on 9 February, the C.-in-C. quizzed him obsessively. On learning that no shots had been fired at the steamers from Khartoum itself, he wired Hartington in London that Wilson might have been mistaken. Gordon might still be holding out, in the Catholic Mission, or somewhere else. There were no rumours from native sources of the fall of Khartoum, he said: the Mudir of Dongola had claimed it was impossible that the Mahdi had taken the city on the 26th. Wolseley preferred to believe this rather than the stark truth from Wilson, who had seen the place with his own eyes.

Wilson was a 'nervous, weak unlucky creature',[77] Wolseley claimed. He had 'lost his nerve' at Abu Tulayh. He had delayed two days before embarking for Khartoum on the steamers. Had he left on the 20th, he could have been in Khartoum by the 25th – the day before Khartoum fell. He would in all probability have saved Gordon. Even the stress he had suffered was Wilson's fault, for failing to send dispatches.

Wolseley's invective against Wilson in his journal turned to vitriol as it slowly dawned on him that the report was true: Gordon really was dead, and Wolseley's chance of eternal glory had been cruelly snatched away. There would be no historic handshake on the waterfront at Khartoum under the flag, to be recorded in every illustrated newspaper, to be known by every schoolchild for generations to come, as familiar as 'Doctor Livingstone, I presume'. Wolseley rambled a great deal in his diary about it being all for the best, and about the Almighty moving in mysterious ways, but it was clear that he needed a scapegoat, and Wilson had been elected.

Had Wolseley been capable of seeing beyond his disappointment, he would have realized that his bitterness against Wilson was unfair, and his calumnies unfounded. No officer who had truly 'lost his nerve' could have shown the resoluteness Wilson had displayed at Abu Kru, when he had pushed the square forward under heavy fire in a manner that had been nothing short of heroic. Even seasoned veterans had thought that they would never get out of it alive. Wilson's readiness to embark on the steamers to Khartoum, on what must have appeared virtually a suicide mission, showed, as correspondent Alex MacDonald commented, 'the boldness of a lion'.

Wolseley insisted over and over that had his favourite, Stewart, not been wounded, Gordon would still be alive. He repeated interminably that if Wilson had embarked on *Bordain* and *Talah-*

awiyya on 20 January, the day after Abu Kru, he could have been at Khartoum on the 25th, and thus saved the city. Wolseley never seems to have paused for reflection. If he had done so, he would have realized that Wilson could not possibly have left on the steamers on the 20th, since they had not then arrived at Metemma. They had not appeared, in fact, until 0930 hours on 21 January. Even then, Wilson could not have left on them right away. The Egyptian soldiers and their families had first to be disembarked, and the steamers had to be overhauled and supplied with fuel. Wolseley had himself instructed Wilson not to leave until Beresford had declared the steamers ready.

Even if Wilson *had* set off immediately, he could not have travelled any faster than he did. 'If I could have started on the 22nd,' he wrote, 'which I do not admit, I could only have reached Khartoum by mid-day on the 26th, Gordon having been killed at daybreak that morning. The water was exceptionally low, and I had enormous trouble getting up the cataracts.'[78] The very earliest Wilson could have left was 22 January, and, as he pointed out, he had every reason to believe that dervish forces were advancing from both north and south. As commanding officer – whether he liked it or not – he could not leave his force where it was without finding out if it was likely to be attacked.

It is, of course, possible that the approach of British redcoats might have dissuaded the Mahdi from his assault on Khartoum, but it is by no means certain. Given the fact that the dervish army was at least sixty thousand strong, and armed with Krupps and Nordenfeldts, it would not have been surprising if the Mahdi had laughed at Wilson's twenty-two soldiers in red jumpers. And since it was the news of his defeat at Abu Tulayh that had prompted his decision to attack the city anyway, it is just as likely that he would have resolved to launch his offensive even if Wilson had left a day earlier. Wolseley behaved as if the 26 January attack on Khartoum were part of a rigid plan that had been decided months before. In fact, the Mahdi had decided on the spur of the moment that Khartoum had to be taken before the British arrived: 'Our Only General' had been out-generalled by a Sufi holy man.

At Korti, Wolseley asked Wilson to explain in writing why he had 'delayed for two days' at Gubba, and sent the explanation to Hartington. He did not refer at all to the much more serious delay in reaching Metemma that had come about as a result of his own instructions to Herbert Stewart. Had Stewart's spearhead force marched directly to Metemma instead of waiting for ten days at Jakdul, it would have taken the dervishes by surprise. The Camel Corps could have been at Metemma by 5 January, and the bloody battles of Abu Tulayh and Abu Kru need not have been fought. Wilson could have been in Khartoum by 10 January. 'Nothing is more certain,' wrote Wilson, 'than if Stewart had gone straight across in his march, he would have met with no opposition in the desert, and but slight resistance at Metemma . . . and Khartoum and Gordon would have been saved . . . for want of a thousand camels the game was lost.'[79]

Certainly Wolseley had been let down by Sir Redvers Buller, who had not provided enough camels. But the lack of camels need not have prevented Stewart from reaching Metemma in a single dash. Wolseley's insistence that every man should have his own camel was based on ignorance – the belief that British soldiers could not cross the desert on foot. This was entirely untrue. Metemma lay only 175 miles from Korti, and the route was well supplied with water. British infantrymen could easily cover this distance with camels to carry their equipment and supplies. This was proved conclusively later, when the Royal Irish Rifles marched from Korti to Gubba, and when the Guards Camel Regiment marched back from Gubba to Dongola without their camels. In both cases these marches took place in the hot season, and in neither case did the units concerned lose a single man.

Wolseley's idea of using men picked from all the units of the British army was a remarkable innovation, but in practice it was a waste of time, because the Gordon Relief Expedition needed trained foot-soldiers more than it needed 'special' troops. In particular, Wolseley bowed to the very conventions he claimed to be flouting, when he made up half the Camel Corps from supposedly 'crack' cavalry units. Three battalions of line infantry regiments, such as Graham had deployed at et-Teb and Tamaai, would have done the job just as well.

As for the irreplaceability of Herbert Stewart, this, too, was Wolseley's call. Why did he fail to appoint a second-in-command of requisite experience, in case Stewart became a casualty? He knew perfectly well that Wilson was bound by army regulations to take over if Stewart went down. The idea that he had 'really' appointed Burnaby as Stewart's 2i/c is simply a myth – one of those imponderable 'what-ifs' that punctuate history. Judging by Burnaby's performance at Abu Tulayh, *if* he had gone to Khartoum instead of Wilson, no one would have returned to tell the tale.

In fact Wilson behaved admirably as a commander, and Wolseley was psychologically incapable of taking responsibility for his own mistakes. The greatest of these by far was in adopting the Nile route in the first place. Wolseley's advance of a thousand miles from Cairo was handled superbly, yet from the beginning its adoption smacked of exhibitionism. It is as if Wolseley had set out deliberately to demonstrate his administrative excellence, rather than simply to do the job. His plan, with its four hundred boats, its boatmen imported from Canada and west Africa, its specially picked troops, its supply columns and its intricate lines of communication, was over-elaborate. Weeks had been lost simply waiting for the boats to be built from scratch.

A brigade of ordinary troops, supported by a baggage-train of camels, could have marched from Suakin to Berber on foot in ten days. The desert route was not only well supplied with water, it was also inhabited, and stocked with pasture for the camels. In the winter of 1882–3, Hicks's force of Egyptian conscripts had marched this way without difficulty. Did Wolseley really believe it was 'impossible' for professional British troops? Even the fall of Berber need not have prevented him from using this route – in practice the situation would have been no different from the march across the Bayuda, in which the original intention was to capture Metemma. Instead of hundreds of miles of unwieldy lines of communication between Cairo and Korti, the Expedition would have had a solid beach-head only a few days behind it, guarded and supplied by the Royal Navy.

Wilson quickly realized that his Commander-in-Chief intended to make him a scapegoat, but accepted it with characteristic dignity. He knew he had done his duty, whatever Wolseley might say. He also emerged with more honour than Lord Charles Beresford, who had gone to rescue Wilson's force but had ended up being rescued by him. Without Wilson's cool-headed deployment opposite Wadi Habeshi, when *Safia* was in dire straits, she would almost certainly have been sunk, and everyone on board captured or killed. Wolseley ignored Wilson's action at Wadi Habeshi, but wrote that Beresford had 'behaved splendidly'. He also ignored the fact that the broken square at Abu Tulayh was partly his friend's fault. Beresford could have helped exonerate Wilson, but played Judas by claiming that his naval artificers had reported the steamers ready for action by the morning of 22 January. This was an outright lie, and Beresford was forced later to retract it by an indignant Alex MacDonald, the *Daily News* man, who had been present at Gubba and knew that the artificers had not even touched the steamers until the following day.

18

Early on the morning of 5 February – the day Wilson left Gubba for Korti – Queen Victoria barged into the cottage of her private secretary, Sir Henry Ponsonby, adjoining her estate at Osborne on the Isle of Wight. Ponsonby, who had just finished breakfast with his wife and daughter, was astonished to see his monarch standing in his living-room, looking pale and shaken. 'It's too late!' she whispered. 'Khartoum has fallen. Gordon is dead.'

The Queen blamed neither Wolseley nor Wilson for the disaster, but set it firmly on the shoulders of her private *bête noire*, Prime Minister William Ewart Gladstone. Later that day she telegraphed to the cabinet without cipher and without apparent editing, 'These news from Khartoum are frightful, and to think that all this might have been prevented and many precious lives saved by earlier action is too frightful.'

The Queen wanted to say much more. Nothing that had happened in her reign filled her with more disgust than the death of Gordon. Gladstone, she told her private secretary, was a man without regard for the honour of the British Empire. It was a sorry day when he had been elected Prime Minister. 'Mr G,' she said, 'wraps himself up in his own *incomprehensible delusions and illusions* refusing to read what is in every paper and everyone's mouth.'

The Queen believed that she had her finger on the mood of the country, and in this case she was right. There had scarcely ever been such a sense of outrage. The public had followed news of the Relief Expedition anxiously in the popular press, with every expectation of success. Britain was the most powerful nation on earth: the map of the world was everywhere splashed with red, illuminating the far horizons of an empire on which the sun never set. That her government had prevaricated so long over the fate of a national hero, and that her army had failed to reach Khartoum in time to save him, was an utter disgrace. As Baring himself commented, '[Gordon] seemed to embody in his own person the peculiar form of heroism which is perhaps most of all calculated to move the Anglo-Saxon race.'[80]

To the nation, as to the Queen, it was patently clear who was at fault. As Baring himself said, 'a great and *inexcusable* mistake was made in delaying so long the dispatch of the Gordon Relief Expedition'.[81] Now the newspapers, pubs, streets and music-halls were full of invective against the Prime Minister. The GOM or 'Grand Old Man' of British politics was inverted overnight to the MOG, 'the Murderer Of Gordon'.

Gladstone tried to fight his corner, but his voice was drowned in the hubbub and clamour for revenge. The government was forced to give way to public opinion. On 6 February, only twenty-four hours after the Queen had heard the news, Wolseley was astonished to receive instructions from the War Office that he was not to withdraw, and that his advance on Berber would be supported. Sir Gerald Graham was to be sent back to Suakin to fight a second round with 'Osman Digna.

Wolseley rightly divined that this was mere politics. 'In fact,' he wrote in his diary, 'the Cabinet today have realized that nothing could save them except a spirited policy, and their telegram to me is the result.'[82] He also knew that the fall of Khartoum had changed everything. The Mahdi now held the capital. He was the *de facto* military power in the Sudan, and all the tribes that had remained on the sidelines would soon join him. Wolseley could not take Khartoum without reinforcements, and could not now advance until the cool season, which would mean his troops sweltering out the summer in apathy and boredom under a tropical sun.

Four days later the River Column fought a successful action at Kirkbekan, downstream from Abu Hamed, killing more than two thousand dervishes. The news, which reached Wolseley the following day, was marred by the death of the Column's commander, Major General William Earle. Command devolved on Wolseley's man, Major General Henry Brackenbury, who reached Abu Hamed on 24 February.

By then, though, the wind had changed. From Gubba, Redvers Buller, the general of whom so much had been expected, announced that the forward base could not be held. There were rumours of the advance of a dervish force fifty thousand strong. Buller dumped the stores in the Nile, scuttled the last two steamers, and abandoned the base. The Desert Column which had set out from Korti so confidently on 30 December marched back, a rag-tag army on foot, many of the men bootless, and with little to eat but the precious camels that had brought them there. There was no prospect of taking Berber. Sadly, Wolseley ordered Brackenbury to turn the River Column around and sail back whence it had come.

Three weeks later, Wolseley received a *most confidential* telegram from Hartington explaining that a crisis had blown up with Russia in Afghanistan. The Russians had attacked the remote village of Penjeh in British-protected territory, and some Afghans had been killed. The attack flouted the work of a British boundary commission that was already taking great pains to delineate the frontier, and was clearly 'unprovoked aggression'. Parliament supported Gladstone, and had voted £11 million to underwrite a war with Russia. Wolseley was informed that 'imperial interests' might dictate a complete withdrawal from the Sudan.

As usual, Wolseley saw through the rhetoric. He realized that Gladstone had no intention of fighting a war with Russia. It was a heaven-sent excuse for 'the old impostor' finally to wash his hands of the Sudan. As Wolseley predicted, nothing was to come of the 'Penjeh Crisis' – the Russians backed down – but Wolseley's force was out of the Sudan by the end of July. In May, Sir Gerald Graham's task force sailed from Suakin, having once again fought a series of bloody battles with the Beja, but achieved nothing. The first round of the ultimate imperial adventure was over, and the British had lost.

Wolseley's attempts to pin everything on Wilson came to naught. Back in London, he repeated in private the libel that Wilson had delayed at Gubba – now extending the delay magically from two to three days. In a statement in the House of Commons, though, Lord Hartington expressed the government's gratitude and admiration for the expedition led by Wilson to Khartoum. Hartington added that he was aware of the criticism that had been levelled at 'this gallant officer' for his 'alleged slight delay', but he felt that Sir Charles was completely exonerated. 'Many men in your position would have hesitated after the hard fighting and losses the force had sustained, and which I believe were not anticipated by Lord Wolseley,' a friend wrote to Wilson. 'You did all that a man could do, and so far as I can see, you and your companions on that most hazardous expedition deserve the greatest praise.'[83]

Wolseley's plan had backfired on him badly. The enchanted Ashanti Ring was broken, never to be reforged. Sir Herbert Stewart had died of his wound at Jakdul on the way back to Korti, and was buried there: his grave remains there to this day. Sir Evelyn Wood resigned as Sirdar of the Egyptian army. He and Sir Redvers Buller were put out to graze in office jobs, where they could indulge their alcoholism and taste for good living to the full. As for Wolseley, it was his name, rather than Wilson's, that was besmirched. The sentence he unofficially pronounced on Wilson – that he would never again see active service – also rebounded on him. Though he eventually rose to fill the shoes of his detested rival, the Duke of Cambridge, as Field Marshal and Commander-in-Chief of the British army, he was never to fight another campaign.

Neither did Gladstone escape fallout from the disaster. Before the last British troops had left the Sudan, he was out of office. On 9 June the Liberal government fell, to be replaced by Lord Salisbury's Conservatives. The Mahdi himself lasted only another eleven days. By 20 June he was dead. Some said he died of typhoid or smallpox, others of self-indulgence or poison, administered by a concubine whose children his army had killed. He was succeeded by the man who had first recognized him as the Expected One at al-Masallamiyya, only five heady years earlier – 'Abdallahi wad Torshayn, a simple nomad from the *goz* of Darfur, who was to become supreme ruler of the Sudan for fourteen years.

Part Six

1

In the early hours of 13 March 1896, Herbert Kitchener was woken up in his residence in Cairo by the sound of pebbles rattling against his window. Irritated, he lit his lamp. Outside, on the lawn below, stood his night watchman, and his ADC, Captain Jemmy Watson of the 6oth Rifles. Watson was waving a piece of paper. Kitchener descended in his pyjamas, and Watson handed him the paper, grinning silently. It was a decoded telegram from the War Office in London, ordering Kitchener to begin an immediate advance on Dongola: Gordon had been dead eleven years, but at last the reconquest of the Sudan was to begin. When Captain Lord Athlumney of the Coldstream Guards arrived moments later, Kitchener was holding the lamp in one hand, the paper in the other, doing an ecstatic dance with Watson.

Kitchener's meteoric rise had taken him to the rank of Sirdar of the Egyptian army at the age of only forty-one. Garnet Wolseley was a viscount, a field marshal and Commander-in-Chief of the British army, and Major General Sir Evelyn Wood, VC, was his Adjutant General. William Ewart Gladstone had been back in office and out again since the fall of Khartoum, to be replaced both times by Lord Salisbury and his Conservative government. Salisbury acted as both Prime Minister and Foreign Secretary: his Secretary of State for War was Lord Lansdowne. Sir Evelyn Baring, now Lord Cromer, had made himself indispensable in Egypt as British agent, especially so since the Khedive Tewfiq had died prematurely in 1892 and had been succeeded by his eighteen-year-old son, Abbas Hilmi II.

Kitchener owed his appointment as Sirdar to Cromer. He was disliked by the new Khedive and detested by most of his comrades, but Cromer was a banker by birth and instinct, and Kitchener's parsimony appealed to him. Once a staunch exponent of abandonment, Cromer had grown proprietorial towards the Sudan when it had become obvious that both Italy and France had designs on her. Handed the port of Massawa in 1884, Italy had used it as the corner-stone for her new colony of Eritrea. Six years later she had annexed Kassala, a town considered to lie in the Sudan. Rumours of French activity in the southern Sudan had, in 1895, resulted in a warning from Britain that any attempt by France to establish her influence there would be considered 'an unfriendly act'.

Cromer had long since come to the view that a reconquest of the Sudan was inevitable. But having spent years nursing the Egyptian economy back to health, he had no intention of handing the operation over to a spendthrift. Not only did Kitchener have a reputation for meticulous planning, he was also obsessively mean. When the previous Sirdar, Wolseley nominee Major General Sir Francis Grenfell, was recalled to England on the death of Tewfiq, Cromer deftly inserted Kitchener into his place.

It was not a popular appointment. Kitchener suffered from some of the disadvantages of his former chief, Lieut. Colonel Sir Charles Wilson, whom he had loyally defended against Wolseley's canards. In the British army, conformity and 'fitting in' were everything. Cleverness, ruthlessness and originality were nothing. Courage was valued. So were good manners, modesty, chivalry and a devotion to duty. The ideal officer evinced a congenial extraversion: sportiness, 'chumminess', and an easy-going amateurism in everything.

Kitchener scorned amateurism. He was shy, aloof and withdrawn, often execrably rude, inconsiderate and insufferable, and had no time for the sacred cows of the military hierarchy: the rule book, 'pecking order' and the chain of command. He was an individualist and an original thinker of genius, with a drive and thoroughness probably unequalled in the Victorian army, if ever: Lord Curzon called him '[a] devouring mass of molten energy'.[1] As brilliant a general as Wolseley, he was free of the corroding vanity and pettiness that had Wolseley continually sniping even at friends such as Stewart and Buller. While Wolseley had hatched the Gordon conspiracy largely as a means of showering himself with glory, Kitchener needed no one's approval. He was impervious to the opinions of others. 'He did not pose for posterity,' wrote Lord Asquith, 'he never laid himself out either for contemporary or posthumous applause.'[2]

His subordinates found him distant, autocratic and formidable – more a ruthless precision machine than 'one of the boys' – he would later be known as 'the Sudan Machine'. But Kitchener was also capable of profound affection, generosity and warmth, and beneath the hard outer shell had a deep feeling for his comrades and his men – a trait easily observed in his concern for his friend John Hammill Stewart. In his private moments, he was a passionate gardener and an ardent collector of fine porcelain.

While Wolseley had found an opportunity to criticize Sir Charles Wilson for his lack of combat experience, however, no one could argue that Kitchener was an 'intellectual soldier'. As Cromer himself commented, he had his 'honourable scars' to prove it. These had been acquired in 1888 at Handub, fifteen miles from Suakin, when, as governor-general of the eastern Sudan, he had attempted to snatch Beja leader 'Osman Digna.

The Handub raid might have succeeded had Kitchener's Bashi-Bazuks and irregulars not fled when the Beja had attacked from the rear. Kitchener had rallied his handful of regulars on a hillock, and had ridden forward, heedless of the grating bullets, expecting his troops to charge. It was while looking round to see if they were following that a .43 calibre round had shaved off his right ear-lobe, splintered his jaw, and driven a bone-fragment into his throat.

Miraculously, he managed to stay in the saddle. He did not get off his horse until he was safely back at the palace in Suakin, where he was helped down by his guards. By then his uniform was slick with blood, and he was in excruciating pain. Surgeon General Galbraith examined the wound, and realized that Kitchener had cheated death by a fraction of an inch. The splinter of bone had penetrated his windpipe and tonsils, and his neck was badly swollen. Galbraith was unable to find the bullet, and Kitchener said later that he had swallowed it. The medical officer thought the wound too severe to be dealt with at Suakin, and recommended that Kitchener should be sent straight back to Cairo in HMS *Starling*.

Ironically, it was almost exactly four years since Valentine Baker had been deserted by his Bashi-Bazuks in exactly the same place. Baker, who might possibly have become Kitchener's father-in-law, had died in 1887 in the Nile Delta. His life had ended in tragedy. His eldest daughter, Hermione, who had been in love with Kitchener, had died of typhoid around the time of the fall of Khartoum. Her mother had died a week later. Kitchener had returned from the Gordon Relief Expedition to find the Baker family in mourning. Legend has it that he carried a locket with Hermione's portrait in it for the rest of his life.

Within twelve months of the Handub raid, Kitchener had been promoted lieutenant-colonel, appointed Adjutant General of the Egyptian army, awarded a CB, made a Pasha, and created ADC to Queen Victoria. In August 1889 he had played a major role in the battle of Tushki, near the Sudanese frontier, when Sirdar Sir Francis Grenfell had foiled an attempted invasion of Egypt by the dervish general 'Abd ar-Rahman wad an-Nejumi. The battle had been fought almost entirely by the Egyptian army. Kitchener had led the cavalry contingent in a risky game of hit-and-run, slowing down the dervish advance until Grenfell's infantry brigade and artillery had come into action.

The dervishes had rushed in with their customary ferocity, but this time the Egyptian battalions had been ready for them. They had driven them off with disciplined fire, and advanced with fixed bayonets. The Mahdist army had broken up in disorder, and at that point Kitchener had charged at the head of two squadrons of Egyptian cavalry, and a squadron of the 10th Hussars – the only British unit on the field.

Among the enemy masses his riders spotted a camel laden with what they thought was a screw-gun. It was surrounded by forty men. After a short, sharp encounter, the Egyptian cavalry shot or cut down all but one of the dervishes, and killed the camel. They advanced to take possession of the 'gun' and found that it was a man – wad an-Nejumi himself. He had been wounded several times, but their last spray of fire had dealt the fatal wound. Next to him lay the body of his five-year-old son.

The Egyptian victory at Tushki was the point at which the new Egyptian army came of age. It was no longer the mob of demoralized conscripts who had marched to their deaths with Hicks and Baker. Grenfell's units – the Nile Frontier Force – were part of a different army, well trained, well disciplined, and well equipped. In all, it consisted of sixteen battalions of infantry – ten Egyptian, six Sudanese. There were eight squadrons of cavalry, four companies of Egyptian Camel Corps, and four of Sudanese Camel Corps. There was a battery of horse artillery, two field batteries, a battery of Maxim machine-guns, a transport battalion and a railway battalion. The total strength was about fifteen thousand men.

It was officered by both British and Egyptians. The British officers were seconded to the Foreign Office, and were given two-year contracts. The old guard of Turco-Egyptian officers had been carefully weeded out. A military academy had been set up, and a fresh influx of young blood revitalized the junior level of command. Two of the Egyptian battalions were commanded exclusively by Egyptian officers.

After Shaykan and et-Teb, popular opinion had been that the Egyptian *fellahin* would never make good soldiers. But the British were past masters at forging fine fighting units out of what had appeared to be unpromising material. They knew that it was not physical prowess that made an army, but confidence. In any case, the Egyptians did not lack martial qualities – on occasions they had fought well. They were amenable to discipline, could be steady, actually liked drill, and they were capable of incredible endurance.

The problem was that conscription in the old Egyptian army had been regarded as virtually a death-sentence. Conscripts had been dragged screaming in chains from their villages, to a life of drudgery and brutality from which they were unlikely to return unscathed. There was no specified period of service, no leave, no pension, poor food, and poor pay that was either in arrears, deducted for non-existent stoppages or embezzled wholesale by the officers. It is hardly surprising that potential recruits were ready to amputate their own fingers, or blind themselves in one or both eyes, to avoid service.

The new system introduced fairer treatment: conscripts were paid, fed and clothed well, and efforts were made to make sure their dues were not stolen or acquired by their officers. Most of all, the British tried to foster the kind of mutual regard that existed between commissioned ranks and men in their own army. This was a practice at which they excelled. British officers were not noted for professional competence. Garnet Wolseley, indeed, had complained after the Relief Expedition that many senior regimental officers were 'unfit for their positions', 'ignorant of the first principles of tactics or of the military art', and 'manifestly incompetent'.[3] This was certainly the case, but generations of experience in handling their social inferiors had taught them how to make themselves liked and admired. They were loved by their men, because they treated them as they might a cherished horse or dog. The men accepted this because the vast social gulf that existed between them made their superiors seem almost 'magical'.

The British had turned on this charm with their Egyptian troops, with some success. Within three years of the debacles of et-Teb and Shaykan there had developed a new sense of trust and affection between the ranks. As Winston Churchill put it, 'To such simple souls the white officer – rich, strange, sharp-spoken, just, and always apparently fearless – seemed a splendid demi-god – a being of superior knowledge and resource. Whatever the dangers he would help them out. Certainly he would never desert them. The only chance of safety was to stay by him.'[4]

Part of the new confidence stemmed from improved equipment. Gone were the Remingtons, to be replaced by quick-firing Martini-Henrys. The Gardners, Gatlings and Nordenfeldts that always jammed at the wrong moment had been replaced or supplemented by the Maxim. Introduced in 1885, too late for the Gordon Relief Expedition, the Maxim was the first 'true' machine-gun ever deployed. Unlike its predecessors it was fully automatic, operating on a trigger rather than cranking-handles. As long as there was pressure on the trigger, rounds were continually pumped into the chamber, fired and ejected. With only a single barrel, it was much lighter than the Gardner or Gatling, weighing only 40 lb, and unlike them also its barrel could be fully traversed from side to side. The most devastating small-bore weapon invented up to that point, it was the ancestor of all modern machine-guns, capable of rattling out ten rounds a second, and accurate up to two and a half thousand yards.

The new camel-corps – the *hajana* – bore little resemblance to Wolseley's camel regiments. By now every aspect of camel-handling had been carefully studied, and the *hajana* used only the best camels – the off-white Bishari breed reared by the Beja in the Red Sea hills. The Egyptian cavalry, too, were no longer the craven troops who had bolted at et-Teb. They took the best recruits out of every annual intake. Although their British officers thought them poor horsemen, and despaired of getting a glorious cavalry charge out of them, they were regarded as 'steady' – which in British eyes was compliment enough.

The Sudanese battalions were the cream of the new army. The Jihadiyya were more difficult to train than the *fellahin*, but were aggressive and dashing in battle. While the Egyptians served with the colours for only six years, the Sudanese were lifetime pro-fessionals, most of them Nubas from the Nuba mountains, or Nilotic tribesmen from Equatoria – tall, spindly Shilluk, Dinka or Nuer, who had grown up naked in the swamps and savannahs, herding cattle. They were treated as well as any soldiers in the world, with good pay, good rations, and an allowance for their wives and children. 'I can quite understand now the affection every British officer in a Sudanese regiment entertains for these cheery, kindly, very human creatures,' wrote *Times* correspondent E. F. Knight. 'They are ferocious in battle, but they do not appear to be cruel . . . they are not cold blooded murderers of women and children and never inflict on wounded or dead foemen . . . abominable mutilations.'[5]

2

In March 1895, six years after the battle of Tushki, two ragged figures stumbled down the escarpment above the First Cataract at Aswan, leading a lame and limping camel. Both men were dressed head to foot in soiled Arab robes, but only one was an Arab – a withered old tribesman of the Kababish named Hamed Ghargosh. The other was an Austrian – Rudolf Carl von Slatin, former governor of Darfur, former prisoner of the dervishes, and lately unofficial consultant to the Khalifa 'Abdallahi. He had finally escaped after almost twelve years in the Mahdist camp.

Though Slatin had several times been thrown into prison by the Khalifa, who had never fully trusted him, he had always managed to reinstate himself. He had a magnetic personality, a charm and mystique that 'Abdallahi had not been able to resist. Free to wander in the streets of Omdurman, he had been contacted by Kababish agents dispatched by Egyptian army intelligence chief, Major Reginald Wingate of the Royal Artillery, who had snatched him on 18 January 1885.

Some hours after sunset on that day, he had sneaked out of his *tukul* to meet a guide called Zaki Belal, who had whisked him out of the city by donkey and camel. At a secret rendezvous in the desert, Zaki had introduced him to another Kabbashi, Hamid wad Hussain, who had been waiting with three camels. Slatin reckoned that 'Abdallahi would not miss him until morning prayer, and this gave them twelve or fourteen hours' start.

He had been hoping that he would be able to make a single dash for the frontier, but the camels turned out to be of poor quality and had to be exchanged on the way. Eventually Slatin and his guides had swum the beasts across to the west bank of the Nile, using inflated water-skins. They had worked their way through the warren of hills on the east bank, at one stage missing a patrol of sixty dervishes by a hair's breadth. Finally, Slatin had been handed over to Hamed Ghargosh, who fell ill in the course of their six-day march together. The one camel they were left with developed a sore on its foot, and Slatin was obliged to stitch on a leather 'shoe' as he had seen camel-herders do in Darfur.

Slatin's appearance caused a sensation in the mess of the Egyptian Frontier Field Force. At first the officers wondered who this shabby, subdued character was. When he whispered in Arabic that he was 'Salateen', Captain Jemmy Watson of the 60th Rifles – later to be Kitchener's ADC – immediately ordered him a bottle of beer and made him drink it: a real Arab would have turned it down, he said.

The Force commander, thirty-nine-year-old Lieut. Colonel Archibald Hunter, of the Royal Lancashire Regiment, arrived shortly afterwards, and was so delighted on hearing of Slatin's escape that he had the band summoned to play the Austrian national anthem. Slatin was sent to bathe and rest, and by evening a full set of officer's kit had been found for him. When he entered the mess again for dinner washed, shaved and in uniform for the first time since the day of his surrender, every officer stood to attention, while the band played 'God Save the Kaiser'. Slatin took his place at the mess-table with tears streaming down his face. His determination to survive at any cost had been vindicated. It was, he said, 'as though I had just woke up from an evil dream'.[6]

In Cairo, Slatin was debriefed by Reginald Wingate, the arche-typal military intelligence officer – a small, terrier-like man with boundless energy and equally boundless inquisitiveness. A Scots-man from a large family, he had a courteous manner, an incisive mind, a photographic memory and a gift for languages. He had begun his career as ADC to Sir Evelyn Wood, and would end it as both Sirdar of the Egyptian army and governor-general of the Sudan.

Wingate had two characteristics that were vital to the spy-master: an obsessive, childlike curiosity and infinite patience. While the death of Gordon had killed the interest in the Sudan for many of his brother officers, it had only whetted his appetite. Day by day, year by year, Wingate had built up a database of information about the enemy. Slowly, he created a staff of intelligence officers. Steadily they began to construct networks of agents penetrating every corner of the Sudan.

In 1892, Wingate, together with agents from the Vatican, secured the escape of Father Joseph Ohrwalder and two Roman Catholic nuns. Ohrwalder's book *Ten Years' Captivity in the Mahdist Camp*, edited by Wingate, had been a major contribution to the British propaganda effort, as well as a mine of information about the dervishes. Wingate's own book, *Mahdism and the Egyptian Sudan*, a massive compendium of virtually everything known about the Mahdist movement, was also published in 1892.

Many officers despised Slatin for changing his religion, and becoming an 'adviser' to the enemy. Major Lord Edward Cecil, one of Kitchener's ADCs, son of Prime Minister Lord Salisbury, detested his 'perky manner' and his continuous references to 'mysterious sources of information'. Wingate, though, found in him a soulmate. They became close friends, and Slatin was eventually appointed Deputy Director of the Intelligence Department. Slatin's book, *Fire and Sword in the Sudan*, also edited by Wingate, was to become a best-seller. More important, though, was the light Slatin was able to shed on 'Abdallahi's character, his modus vivendi, and the inner workings of the Mahdist state, to which he had been privy.

The key aspect of Slatin's new information concerned the rifts that had appeared in dervish solidarity since the Mahdi's death. 'Abdallahi had been named Mohammad Ahmad's successor both during his life and on his deathbed, but the Mahdi's family – the *Ashraf* ('nobility') – had not taken kindly to the idea of being led by a rough and uneducated nomad from the *goz*.

Although 'Abdallahi's power was based on his Baggara horsemen, they were a double-edged sword. Like all nomads, they resented authority, even that of their own kinsman, 'Abdallahi, whom they never considered a superior. In Baggara society, a sheikh ruled only by the consent of his tribesmen. Nomad custom was governed by *'urf*, a set of unwritten traditions handed down over generations. A sheikh had no means of enforcing *'urf* or of punishing offenders. Murder or injury was regulated by the law of *tha'r* – the blood feud. Adultery was the responsibility of the husband: the seduction of an unmarried woman that of the father and brothers. Other breaches of the code were punished by a simple refusal by tribesmen to cooperate with the offender. This meant, essentially, that he was disowned by his tribe. In the *goz*, a man without a tribe was a man under a death-sentence, because he could be robbed and murdered by enemies without invoking *tha'r*. It was the threat of a relentless pursuit of revenge continuing for generations that kept reckless murder and rapine in check.

'Abdallahi's Baggara troops felt little personal loyalty to the Khalifa as a leader, but followed him because of the possibilities of plunder. Sorely in need of their support, 'Abdallahi allowed them to assume the role the Bashi-Bazuks had played under Turco-Egyptian rule. The nomads behaved with equal cruelty and rapaciousness. 'Twenty or thirty Baggara arrive at a place accompanied by their slaves,' wrote *Times* man E. F. Knight. 'They read out to the people the Khalifa's proclamation with regard to taxation, and then seize all the land and all the cattle. They apportion to the original inhabitants only just so much land as will enable them to procure the barest subsistence, then enter into possession of all the remainder. The bygone Egyptian *regime* at its very worst was never so bad as this.'[7]

Of the northern, riverain tribes, the Ja'aliyyin were the most powerful. Proud of their pure Qurayshite ancestry, they looked down on the Baggara and resented their ascendancy. They had joined the Mahdi largely for economic reasons – to get rid of crippling taxes and reinstate the slave trade – but now found themselves dominated by crass and primitive nomads from the west. In 1894, the Ja'aliyyin sheikh of Metemma, 'Abdallah wad Sa'ad, attempted to get backing from the British for a rising against the Khalifa. His plea was turned down, as the time was not yet judged ripe – but Wingate filed away the knowledge carefully for future use.

The Khalifa was aware of wad Sa'ad's treachery, but decided to bide his time. Meanwhile, though, he put no further trust in the Ja'aliyyin. All top military posts were given to Baggara tribesmen, and all Ja'aliyyin units strengthened by Baggara troops.

The threat from the Ashraf was always present. 'Abdallahi exiled the Mahdi's cousin, Mohammad Khalid, the former governor of Darfur – the man who had made Slatin kiss his feet, and had tortured Major Hamada to death – to the swamps of Equatoria. He removed Mohammad al-Khayr, the Mahdi's former teacher, who had sent the steamer *el-Fasher* to pursue Stewart, and whose men had fought at Abu Tulayh, from his position as governor of Berber. He had many of the Mahdi's wives and children carefully watched. Even the brilliant wad an-Nejumi, the victor of Shaykan and Khartoum, was exiled to Dongola to remove him from court.

Of the Mahdi's old guard, the only man 'Abdallahi did not pursue was 'Osman Digna, whose Beja tribesmen inhabited their own world, aloof from the politics of the Nile Valley and the western Sudan. 'Osman always behaved self-effacingly when in the Khalifa's presence.

The tension between 'Abdallahi and the Ashraf reached its climax in 1891, when the Khalifa unearthed a conspiracy to oust him, led by Mohammad ash-Sharif, the second Khalifa. He went about dealing with the plot in a tortuous way. He pardoned Mohammad ash-Sharif, undermined his support by arresting and confiscating the property of his partisans, then performed a treacherous turn-about by having him thrown into prison, claiming that he had been told to do so in a vision. Seven of the chief conspirators were sent to Fashoda and beaten to death by Zaki Tamal, a Mandala from Darfur, who had assumed the role of 'Abdallahi's chief executioner. Among the executed conspirators were the Mahdi's uncle, Mohammad 'Abd al-Karim, whose staunch advice had encouraged the Mahdi to move on Khartoum, and Ahmad Sulayman, former chief of the *bayt al-mal*. Zaki Tamal was himself later accused of treachery and walled up alive.

'Abdallahi's ambition had been to continue the jihad or holy war against unbelievers and apostates – the first nominee being the Egyptian state, under the Khedive Tewfiq. In 1885, a dervish advance towards Egypt from Dongola had been defeated by the British and Egyptian armies at Ginnis. 'Abdallahi had been distracted from the jihad by rebellions in Darfur and northern Kordofan, and by a full-scale invasion of the eastern Sudan by the Abyssinians, under King John II of Tigre. He had dealt with these problems piecemeal. Darfur had been pacified. The leader of the Kordofan rebellion, Kababish chief Salih wad Fadlallah, had been captured and killed. The Abyssinians had been routed at Gallabat, and King John's head had been brought to Omdurman and, like Gordon's before it, displayed on a spike.

Though 'Abdallahi had managed to survive all these challenges, his ruthlessness had gained him few sympathizers. The Ja'aliyyin were already making overtures to the enemy, and were ripe for revolt. The dervish Jihadiyya were also fertile ground for subversion. Many had been captured in the Mahdi's campaigns, and though they had fought well for the dervishes at Abu Tulayh and in other battles, it was rumoured that they disliked 'Abdallahi and would be ready to rejoin their old units if given the chance.

When Abu Anja died in 1889, 'Abdallahi himself had become less trustful of his Jihadiyya. They were gradually superseded as his household troops by the *Mulazimin*, half of them slave-riflemen from the south, and half free tribesmen from Kordofan and Darfur. The *Mulazimin* numbered about nine thousand, and were commanded by 'Abdallahi's son, Shaykh ad-Din.

After the defeat of wad an-Nejumi at Tushki, 'Abdallahi had begun to show signs of paranoia. He had started to withdraw behind walls and bodyguards. He had built a new perimeter around his quarters in Omdurman, containing his own house, that of his brother Ya'gub — now commanding the Black Standard division — and the *Mulazimin* quarters. He no longer appeared at the Friday parade — a custom established by the Mahdi — but attended only four times a year, on the great festivals. Even then, he arrived surrounded by his guards.

Like most despots, 'Abdallahi ruled by fear, and had manoeuvred himself into a position where he could trust no one. Wingate thought he was hanging on only by the skin of his teeth.

On 1 March 1896 an Italian army, eighteen thousand strong, was wiped out at Adowa, in Abyssinia, by King Menelik of Shoa – later to become the Emperor Menelik II. This calamity, one of the worst ever suffered by a European army in Africa, spelt the end of Italian ambitions in Abyssinia for more than a generation. Italy's immediate concern, though, was the safety of her garrison at Kassala, now threatened by the Khalifa's man 'Osman Digna.

On 12 March the Italian Ambassador in London respectfully requested the Prime Minister, Lord Salisbury, to initiate an action in the Sudan to distract the dervishes from Kassala. The request provided a convenient peg on which to hang an invasion. The British public had never forgotten the national humiliation over the death of Gordon and the fall of Khartoum, and the desire for revenge was still smouldering. Salisbury's government had already been voted out of office once for failing to do anything about it. Now, Salisbury saw a chance of killing two birds with one stone – assisting the Italians, and occupying the northern Sudan. There was no question at this stage, though, of a full-scale reconquest. While Dongola Province was under dervish control, there would always be a threat to Egypt. The immediate objective was to secure a buffer zone between the central Sudan and the Egyptian frontier.

Soon after breakfast on 13 March, the Egyptian cabinet met and approved the decision to invade the Sudan. Within twenty-four hours, Lieut. Colonel Archibald Hunter, commanding the Nile Frontier Force at Wadi Halfa, received the order to advance. Hunter was delighted. For months the dervishes had been raiding his frontier outpost at Sarras, a fort perched on a crag of black basalt overlooking the Nile, thirty-five miles south of Wadi Halfa. Hunter, a cool but truculent officer, had been restrained from swatting these flea-bite attacks by Kitchener. Now, all that had changed. 'Am as pleased as Punch,' he wrote to his brother. 'It can make a man or a mouse out of me – Never was so pleased in my life.'[8]

The forty-year-old son of a wealthy Glasgow merchant, Hunter was a brave, blunt, brutal warrior – a drinker and womanizer who was consequently idolized by his men. He was also an old campaigner in the Sudan. His first encounter with the dervishes had come more than a decade earlier, when, after the failure of the Gordon Relief Mission, the Khalifa had pushed his forces north towards the Egyptian frontier. In December 1885 Hunter had been badly wounded at Kosha, near the Third Cataract, just before Anglo-Egyptian forces had turned back the Khalifa's army at Ginnis. In a skirmish he had shot dead six of the enemy with a Winchester rifle at close-contact range, before being himself shot in the right arm. For this action he had been awarded the DSO. He had also fought with distinction at Tushki in 1889.

Hunter's orders were to move immediately with a small spearhead force and secure the Nile-side village of Akasha as a forward operating base. It lay fifty miles south of Sarras. Kitchener knew from Wingate's intelligence briefs that there was no enemy presence at Akasha. The dervish frontier garrison was at Firka, sixteen miles further south, tacked on to a Nubian village beneath a sawtooth mountain on the west bank of the Nile.

Firka lay on the remote Kerma–Sarras reach of the Nile, at the southern end of a labyrinth of plunging khors and spurs known as the *Batn al-Hajar*, the 'Belly of Stones' – some of the worst country in the northern Sudan. From the Second Cataract, twelve miles upstream from Wadi Halfa, the Nile snaked through a moonscape of bluffs and fractured knolls, cut by the shoals of the Dal Cataract, following fault-lines in the basement complex. In places the sheer wind-carved hulks of the hills pressed right up to the water's edge; in others the river bank was no more than a rough terrace, a few yards wide, criss-crossed by plunging defiles. The Nile was sparsely inhabited here by Nubians of the Mahas and Sukkot tribes, who scratched out a living from tiny patches of alluvial soil. Hamlets of a few mud-brick houses were crammed awkwardly between rock and river. In places the cultivable patches were so high that two *sagiyyas* had to be employed in tandem to relay the water.

On the east bank, the only viable route passed through a maze of gorges that towered in places more than fifteen hundred feet above the plain. Their ragged spines were dotted with the ruins of ancient watchtowers, forts and temples, dating back to Pharaonic times. Away east, as far as the eye could see, lay a wild confusion of hogsback ridges, and peaks as sharp as icicles. Pools of orange sand lay in hollows against the base of the hills, and in the beds of khors that sliced through the stone labyrinth like giant sabre-cuts.

The Firka garrison was commanded by Hamuda Idris, an *emir* of the Habbaniyya, a Baggara tribe from Darfur. His warriors, four thousand strong, were mainly Baggara nomads, with contingents of Ja'aliyyin and Danagla. The footmen, armed with swords and spears and a few rifles, were divided into four battalions or *rub's*, made up of all three tribes in varying proportions. The fourth element in the dervish force was the Jihadiyya riflemen, commanded by Baggara chiefs Yusuf Anjar and Dudu wad Badr, both from the Khalifa 'Abdallahi's own tribe, the Ta'isha.

Kitchener's objective was to capture Dongola. His first action would be to wipe out or capture Hamuda's garrison, using Akasha as a jumping-off point. Unlike Wolseley eleven years earlier, though, he was in no hurry. Akasha had once been the terminus of a railway, constructed by Isma'il Pasha and refurbished by Wolseley too late to help the Gordon Relief Mission. The line was still in working order as far as Sarras, but beyond that it had been demolished by dervish patrols. Kitchener intended to reconstruct the line, first from Sarras to Akasha, then further south. Until the railway was completed, Akasha would be supplied by relays of 4,500 camels, which were to be shipped from Cairo on barges. Fortified posts would be set up along the caravan route to protect the convoys at night.

Kitchener had worked out a complex line of communication and supply. It began in Cairo, extended almost eight hundred miles south by railway to Balliana on the Nile, in Upper Egypt, and continued by Messrs Cook Nile steamers to Aswan. Here, stores and men would once more be loaded on railway carriages and trans-shipped seven miles past the First Cataract. From Shellal, just south of Aswan, a second flotilla of gunboats, steamers, barges and *felukas* – Egyptian Nile boats – would transport men and materiel to Wadi Halfa, where they would be loaded on railway trains for the third time. The railway would carry them to within marching distance of the forward base.

Hunter's advance guard consisted of the 13th Sudanese battalion, under Major J. Collinson of the Northamptonshire Regiment, two squadrons of Egyptian cavalry under Captain R. G. Broadwood of the 12th Lancers, a camel corps company and a mule-mounted battery. On 15 March the mounted contingent left Wadi Halfa, heading south. Hunter entrained the infantry to Sarras, from where they marched south to rendezvous with the mounted troops. By 18 March the entire column was on its way to Akasha through the Belly of Stones.

Hunter hugged the river bank where he could, but this was not possible in most places. On the way his force passed several deserted villages of the local Sukkot tribe, whose population had been so persecuted by the Baggara that they had migrated to Egypt lock, stock and barrel. Hunter's cavalry and camel corps fanned out into the rocky warrens ahead, scouring the area for dervishes. Not a living soul was seen. Four days after setting out, Hunter's column marched into Akasha.

The village had been founded by a holy man whose tomb was still to be seen there, and was noted for its medicinal hot springs. Its gravel banks were thick with forests of tamarisk trees, and looking south, the Nile scintillated like mercury between the arms of serrated dark ridges that closed in from either side. Hunter's units began to convert the village into a fortress, digging trenches and throwing up gun-banks. By the end of the month a second column had come in escorting six hundred baggage-camels. The 11th and 12th Sudanese battalions followed, commanded by forty-four-year-old Major Hector MacDonald of the Royal Fusiliers, a tough veteran who had seen action in the Afghan war in 1879, had marched with Roberts to Kabul, and had fought at Kandahar, and at Majuba Hill in South Africa in 1881. The son of a humble Scottish crofter, MacDonald had spent nine years as an enlisted man and NCO, attaining the rank of sergeant in the Gordon

301

Highlanders before being commissoned. He took command of the entire forward base.

Further north, a complex game of military musical chairs was being conducted as reserves were called up, battalions were swapped and regiments were shunted around. A British battalion, the 1st North Staffords, was deployed in Wadi Halfa, so that six Egyptian battalions could be freed to move to the front. A four-gun battery of Maxim machine-guns was formed from units of the British army of occupation – the North Staffords and the Connaught Rangers – and sent to the forward base. The Egyptian army Railway Battalion was mustered at Aswan, and parts for the reconstruction of the line – sleepers, rails, bolts and fishplates – began to pile up on the platforms there ready for the shift to Sarras.

On 29 March Kitchener arrived at Wadi Halfa with his Chief of Staff, Lieut. Colonel Leslie Rundle of the Royal Artillery. Within two days, the whole intricate clockwork of communications, over almost a thousand miles between Cairo and Akasha, was in motion. It was a tribute to the organizing genius of Herbert Kitchener. 'The first and not the least remarkable instance,' wrote Winston Churchill, 'of [the Sirdar's] strange powers of rapid and comprehensive arrangement.'[9]

By mid-April, the Railway Battalion, under Lieutenant Stevenson of the Royal Engineers, was working flat out in rough country south of Sarras. The navvies, who carried Remington rifles, were also protected by pickets of the 7th Egyptian battalion. The men were mostly new to the job, and had to be trained as they worked by half a dozen professional platelayers from the Egyptian Railway Department, who acted as foremen. Soon the battalion was laying half a mile a day, and every mile nearer to Akasha shortened the distance over which the camel caravans had to work. Locomotives rattled backwards and forwards to the Railhead camps each day, carrying rails, sleepers and other components, and food and water for the crews.

Parallel with the railway work, another Sapper officer, Lieutenant M. G. E. Bowman-Manifold, was supervising the stringing of a telegraph line as far as Akasha, with sixteen civilian engineers. The mistakes of Wolseley's Bayuda crossing were not to be repeated. Manifold had begged his telegraph wire from the Egyptian Telegraph Department, but as no signalling equipment was available, he ingeniously constructed his own out of two electric bells and two telephone receivers he discovered at Wadi Halfa.

Meanwhile, Kitchener had not forgotten the desert approaches. His old comrades from the 'Ababda, commanded by Bashir Bey, rode out to the wells in the Nubian desert at Murrat and Bir al-Haymur, to prevent dervish patrols from outflanking the British advance.

At first light on 1 May Kitchener arrived at Akasha on a tour of inspection, with an escort under his cavalry commander, Major John Burn-Murdoch of the Royal Dragoons – a former subaltern in the Heavy Camel Regiment. An hour later, a party of 'Ababda came loping in on their camels, reporting that they had been attacked by twenty dervish cameleers in a wadi four miles to the east. One of their number had been killed and one captured. Soon after, another scout arrived to say that eighty dervish camel-men had been spotted moving past his post.

Kitchener dispatched Burn-Murdoch at once with four British officers, and three squadrons of cavalry to cut off the dervish party. They would be followed up by half a battalion of the 11th Sudanese under Major G. W. Jackson of the Gordon Highlanders. Burn-Murdoch's horsemen scouted to the south. Six and a half miles towards Firka, in a long sandy valley hemmed in by sharp peaks, they came across fresh camel-tracks. Burn-Murdoch rode to the head of the valley, expecting to see a handful of cameleers, and ran smack into a large dervish force of cavalry and infantry, fifteen hundred strong.

He had happened across a major raiding party that the Firka garrison commander, Hamuda Idris, had sent to cut the railway from Sarras. Burn-Murdoch took one look and galloped back to his squadrons, bawling at them to withdraw. It was too late. At that moment, the Baggara cavalry broke over the ridge at the end of the valley and hurtled towards them, their spearheads sparkling in the sunlight. On their flank was a knot of camel-men, and behind them the dark mass of the spearmen.

The Baggara horsemen were moving towards the Egyptians at breakneck speed, filling the narrow tunnel between the rocks with shrouds of fine yellow-ochre dust, as dense as a fog. Burn-Murdoch bellowed out the order to wheel into line, and face the enemy charge. Only part of the rear squadron heard it. About sixteen men, including the four British officers, turned into the eye of the dervish attack. The enemy hit them, half blinded by the dust. Some of the Baggara passed clean through their ranks. For a few seconds the Egyptian troopers thrust with their lances, slashed with their sabres and blasted off their pistols. In that brief moment no less than a dozen Baggara fell dead in the sand. Stunned, they retreated. Burn-Murdoch pulled the rest of the squadron together, and they began chasing the Baggara helter-skelter back down the defile. The dust was so dense that at one point a British officer found himself riding cheek-by-jowl with a Baggara horseman who did not realize there was an enemy beside him. The pursuit was stopped short when the squadron ran into a wall of fire from the dervish infantry.

The two squadrons that had not heard the order to wheel came cantering up the defile, and all three units dismounted. They ran into the cover of some rocky knolls near the end of the tunnel, and started ripping out volleys from their Martini-Henry carbines. The dervishes skirmished towards them, shooting. Rounds whipped and whined off the rocks. It was near noon and the sky was a merciless blue, without a single cloud. The heat pulsed out, magnified by the stones all around them. Both men and horses were racked with thirst – one soldier died of dehydration.

Concentrated firing from the troopers drove the dervishes off, and soon Burn-Murdoch's force was joined by his second-in-command, Captain Brentwood, and a party of scouts, and then by the 11th Sudanese under Major Jackson. They arrived just in time to see the enemy withdrawing. The Egyptian force had lost one man killed and eight wounded, one mortally. Six of the injured had been hit by bullets, and three had been cut by swords and spears. A British officer, Captain H. G. Fitton, of the Royal Berkshire Regiment, was among them. The first blood of the reconquest had been drawn.

4

Kitchener had a choice of two ways of approaching Firka – the River Route or the Desert Route. The Desert Route lay to the east of the central massif of Dal mountain, through the rocky valleys and defiles, where the 1 May fight had taken place. The River Route lay to the west of the mountain, and passed nearer to the Nile bank, touching it in three places. The River Route was the more difficult: it was crossed by a series of plunging cliffs, and in one place, just north of the village of Sarkamatto, the bank was so narrow that the troops would have to pass in single file. A few dervish sharpshooters there would be able to hold back the entire column. Kitchener was confident, though, that the enemy would not be expecting an approach from this direction, and decided to send his main infantry and artillery force that way. The mounted troops would cut across the desert. The approach from both sides would take place at night, and the assault force would swoop suddenly out of the desert at first light.

By 6 June the build-up was complete. The railway had reached the wells of Ambigol, where several narrow khors opened out into an amphitheatre of rock, surmounted by stone sangars. The distance the camel supply caravans had to cover was now reduced by half. The telegraph line had long since reached Akasha. Masses of supplies, and an assault force of nine thousand men of the Egyptian army were gathered at the forward base.

The infantry division, commanded by Lieut. Colonel Archibald Hunter, was divided into three brigades: No. 1, under forty-two-year-old Major David F. 'Taffy' Lewis of the Cheshire Regiment, No. 2, under Hector MacDonald, and No. 3, under forty-seven-year-old Major John G. Maxwell of the Black Watch. Each brigade was made up of three battalions – all MacDonald's were Sudanese, all John Maxwell's were Egyptians, and Taffy Lewis's were a mixed bag of both. Another Sudanese battalion, the 12th, under Major Charles Townshend of the Indian Staff Corps – the hero of Chitral, and later the villain of Kut – was to go with the mounted troops, riding baggage-camels.

The mounted column, under Burn-Murdoch, would consist of six squadrons of Egyptian cavalry, the entire strength of the Camel Corps, under Major R. J. Tudway, Essex Regiment, a battery of Horse Artillery under Captain R. E. Young of the Royal Artillery, and the North Staffords' half of the Maxim machine-gun battery.

The other half, the two guns crewed by thirty Connaught Rangers, were to accompany the infantry, together with two batteries of half a dozen Krupp mountain-guns. Medical detachments were to follow each force, with about a hundred camels for medical supplies and a further hundred for spare ammunition.

The timing of the operation had been kept under wraps by Intelligence Director Reginald Wingate and his Deputy, Rudolf von Slatin, who were both to ride with Kitchener's staff. Constant cavalry patrols around Akasha had prevented curious Arabs from prying, and for the past three days all irregular scouts and spies had been grounded in case they might be double-agents. In Firka, though, the dervishes had a feeling that something was in the wind. On the afternoon of 6 June, just as the Egyptian troops were getting ready to march off, a patrol of Ja'aliyyin and Danagla camel-men approached silently under cover of the hills. They were led by 'Osman Azraq, a fanatically devoted adherent of the Khalifa, who had spent years brutalizing the peaceful inhabitants of Nubia, devastating entire villages and impressing men into military service and women and children into slavery. 'Osman had fought at Tushki under wad an-Nejumi, and had escaped. Four years later he had led a raid on the 'Ababda at Murrat wells in the Nubian desert and killed Salah Hussain, chief of the 'Ababda Field Force, who years earlier had guided Gordon and Stewart across the desert and who had avenged Stewart's death by killing his murderer, Sulayman Na'iman wad Gamar.

'Osman Azraq had been sent to Firka by the dervish governor

36. Major General Sir Herbert Kitchener. Kitchener became Sirdar of the Egyptian army at the age of forty-one, and meticulously planned the British reconquest of the Sudan. On 13 March 1896 he received the long-awaited order to advance.

37. The first action of the reconquest. On 1 May 1896, Major John Burn-Murdoch's Egyptian cavalry goes in pursuit of dervish raiders near Akasha, and runs into a much larger force.

38. The battle of Firka, 7 June 1896, from the foot of Firka mountain. Kitchener's forces attack at dawn, taking the dervishes by surprise after a brilliantly executed night-march through the Belly of Stones.

39. The battle of Firka. At 0700 hours on 7 June, Major David Lewis's 1st Egyptian Brigade advances into the dervish camp, clearing it house by house.

40. The battle of 'Atbara, 8 April 1898. The Cameron Highlanders, the point battalion of the British brigade, are the first to breach the dervish zariba on the left of the line. Inside, they find themselves in a living hell of bayonets, swords and spears.

41. The *emir* Mahmud. Captured at the battle of 'Atbara, Mahmud – a cousin of the Khalifa – had sealed his own fate by ignoring the advice of 'Osman Digna and choosing a position within a short march of Kitchener's forces.

42. The battle of Omdurman, 2 September 1898. View from a British gunboat over Kitchener's main position at al-'Ijayja, and the battlefield on Kerrari plain.

43. The battle of Omdurman: Gunners of the Anglo-Egyptian flotilla give defensive fire against the dervish advance. Each of Kitchener's ten-strong flotilla carried five or six heavy guns and four Maxim machine-guns.

44. The main dervish attack at Omdurman, 0645 hours, 2 September 1898. Perhaps the best and bravest force the British ever faced in North Africa, this was an army of warriors who had thrown to the wind every military complication but qualities of courage and determination.

45. Lieut. Colonel Hector MacDonald. One of Kitchener's toughest fighters, MacDonald was the son of a Scottish crofter and had risen through the ranks. Trapped between two huge dervish divisions at Omdurman, MacDonald deployed his 1st Egyptian Brigade brilliantly, wheeling his ranks to face the force behind him with only minutes to spare.

46. The charge of the 21st Lancers at Omdurman. The last regimental charge ever made by the British cavalry, the Lancers believed they were attacking a few hundred dervishes but failed to see two thousand more concealed in the khor. The action lasted only two minutes, but in that time three VCs were won, and seventy-one lancers and a hundred and nineteen horses were wounded or killed.

47. The dervish dead around the Black Standard at Omdurman. Of the vast dervish army that had massed at first light on 2 September 1898, nearly eleven thousand were dead and sixteen thousand wounded.

48. Kitchener enters Omdurman on the evening of 2 September 1898. For the Sirdar, this was the culmination of years of meticulous planning. By the time he reached the Khalifa's house, though, he found that 'Abdallahi had flown.

49. Scenes in Omdurman and Khartoum after the battle.

50. Raising the flag in Khartoum, 3 September 1898. After the Union Jack and the Egyptian flag were run up on the roof of the ruined palace, there was a service in memory of Gordon. By the time the service had finished, many of those who had fought the dervishes so stoically, including Kitchener himself, were in tears.

51. British soldiers visiting the ruins of Khartoum after the battle of Omdurman. Vengeance for Gordon had been the rallying cry of Kitchener's reconquest, and many soldiers were anxious to see the place where their hero had fallen.

of Dongola, Mohammad wad Bishara, a Ta'ishi of 'Abdallahi's tribe, who had become nervous about Anglo-Egyptian activity on the border. He had given 'Osman orders to assume command of the Firka garrison from Hamuda Idris, whose performance had been lacklustre.

In Firka, Hamuda had been demoted to the command of a *rub'* of infantry mostly consisting of his own Habbaniya tribe. Too late, 'Osman had embarked on a more active strategy. Today in particular, his luck was out. Kitchener's troops were actually preparing to march, but 'Osman's view of Akasha was obscured by a swirling dust-storm and he saw nothing. He rode back to Firka and reported that all was quiet.

A little later, both columns set off. The cavalry, camelry and horse artillery vanished into the hills. Kitchener himself rode with the infantry division. The men, Sudanese and Egyptian, in their tall tarbooshes with neck flaps, their khaki drill jackets, breeches and puttees, coiled in among the rocks like a giant serpent. The hooves of the dozens of artillery mules clicked on the stones. The wind dropped, the sunlight spilt in brilliant cascades through a horizontal slash in the sky. Soon the light faded and dissolved into darkness. The men had made good time in the daylight, but now had to scramble across rocky drywashes, and up the sides of steep slopes in pitch darkness. There was no moon. Discipline was rigid: no talking, no smoking, no lights, no bugles. If the enemy were encountered they were to be bayoneted silently. Any soldier abusing these orders would be shot at dawn.

The soldiers staggered on, stifling their curses. All the khors ran down into the river, so the column's direction was always across them. It took four hours to trek four miles, but by 2200 hours Lewis's 1 Brigade, on point, had descended on to the narrow plain a mile north of the ruined village of Sarkamatto. Firka mountain towered above them, invisible in the darkness. The dervish camp lay only three miles to the south.

The troops had a bite to eat and lay down for an hour. Then they moved off again to negotiate the worst part of the route – a narrow landbridge above the Nile waters, in places no more than six feet wide. There was room for only one man at a time, and a bottleneck quickly formed. To make things worse, the movement had become urgent. The redness of dawn was glimmering over the eastern sky, and the assault force had to be in position by first light. Kitchener sent repeated messages to his brigade commanders to hurry, and the NCOs hustled their soldiers, sending them monkey-running across the rocky shelf.

On the map this stretch was marked 'impassable', and yet Kitchener got the entire column over without mishap – three brigades of infantry, horses, twelve mountain-guns on mules and two hundred camels, in absolute silence and with no light other than the stars. It was an impressive feat. Below them the river rushed, roaring through the Dal Cataract, drowning the noise of stumbling hooves.

From Firka village, now a mile to the south, but hidden by a rise, there came the sudden throb of tom-toms. Kitchener listened, afraid that this was the alarm-call he had been dreading. If the enemy advanced now, his infantry would be caught like sheep in the narrow defile between Firka mountain and the river. He waited tensely, but there was no movement, and he realized that the drums signified only the call to prayers. This meant that the dervishes had no inkling of the menace lurking in the shadows.

The flame-coloured band across the sky began to broaden, revealing the stark outline of Firka mountain. The angular pink granite had been shaved by erosion into successive terraces, and as Lewis's brigade passed its foot, silent orders went out to deploy in line. To their left lay only a rough scrub of acacia and tamarisk that gave way to taller groves of palm-trees along the river. As Lewis's men formed up ready to assault the village, MacDonald's brigade fanned out on their left, prepared to make a flanking movement, then wheel into the attack. Maxwell's brigade lay behind in reserve. The mules carrying the mountain-guns emerged from the ranks, and picked their way up to the higher ground, where the gunners began to unload them methodically and screw the guns together. There was a halt while the infantry formed columns of companies.

The red glow of first light was already melting into the ochres of dawn. The dervish camp, though, was still hidden by the low ridge. The men waited. The silence was unearthly, foreboding. It seemed impossible that the enemy had not seen or heard them coming – six thousand men and hundreds of mules and camels.

It was 0500 hours. Dawn had blossomed into blue day. Kitchener gave the order to advance, and at precisely that moment a single rifle shot cracked out from the slope of the mountain above them. Five dervishes in white robes could be seen bounding wildly uphill towards a stone sangar overlooking the valley. The alarm had been given. A second later a Maxim gun clanked out, bringing the sentries down one by one. Just as the last two topped a spur, and turned back to fire, there was an echoing burst of shell-fire from the unseen side of the hill: Burn-Murdoch's desert column had arrived with perfect timing – his horse artillery was already in place.

In Firka, the dervishes were taken completely by surprise. They had just finished morning prayers, and were assembled in their units on the river bank listening to their daily orders. When the first shot rang out, they looked up to see the lower slopes of Mount Firka swarming with enemy troops. Whiffs of smoke and the boom and crash of shells told them that the 'Turks' were firing at them. In seconds, white-clad figures, grasping Remingtons, were running in all directions, making for their earthworks. The Jihadiyya and the Habbaniya rub' ran for the hills to the east.

The 10th Sudanese battalion under Lewis, on the left of his brigade, topped the rise and saw their objective for the first time. The native Nubian village of mud houses lay nestled in the date groves along the river bank, running south for at least a mile. The dervish camp of straw shelters and tents lay on the rocky shoulder to the east of the village. Across the front of the village, though, facing them, lay a natural ridge of weathered boulders, which had been improved by breastworks and festooned with flags.

The 10th Sudanese opened fire. Many dervishes were still running pell-mell for cover, but the fizz of smoke and the whine of lead from every direction told the attackers that some of the enemy were shooting back. Thinking that the action would be over before he got there, *Times* correspondent E. F. Knight galloped to the front and saw the Sudanese running forward in line, with their rifles still on their shoulders. Already the scene was a confusion of noise and smoke. From the right came the roaring volleys of Taffy Lewis's brigade, from the left the staccato patter of fire as the troops skirmished forward. From the terraces of the mountain John Burn-Murdoch's horse artillery battery crumped, and nearer at hand, the mountain-guns rolled and thundered. In answer, growing steadily more powerful, came the rattle of defensive fire.

The 3rd and 4th Egyptian battalions began to jog out of the tunnel between the mountain and the Nile, moving quickly left and right. Mountain-gun shells and a stream of rounds from the Maxims wheezed over their heads. Hector MacDonald's brigade came up at the double, in a line of battalion columns, and deployed facing the rocky ridge. Before they could get within two hundred yards of it, fifty Baggara horsemen broke from cover, men in flying robes on small dark horses, uttering guttural roars and brandishing spears, swords and rifles. They were led by the garrison commander, Hamuda Idris, and Jihadiyya chief Yusuf Anjar.

The hoofbeats pounded fast on the soft, stony ground. The Baggara hung together for a moment, small, lithe men with pointed goatee beads and shaven skulls, their predator's eyes fixed on the encroaching troops. The Sudanese soldiers took careful aim and fired independently. The fusillade sounded like a single blast. For a second there was a mad confusion of horses crashing into each other, dust, smoke and yells, the crack of limbs breaking, and the heavy thud of bodies. Not a single rider survived the deadly cordon of fire.

Now wild with excitement, the Sudanese battalion rushed forward to the breastworks with bayonets flashing. Some of the dervishes, shocked at the sudden destruction of their horsemen, ran. They took cover behind a second ridge, but the Sudanese chased them, thrusting, stabbing, and firing at point-blank range. Soon, dozens of dead littered the rocks. The dervishes fled over another ridge, and ran towards the river.

MacDonald's brigade turned towards the village. Lewis's was already advancing on it from the north, and Maxwell's brigade had now moved up to fill the gap between the two. The three infantry brigades now formed a continuous line, effectively surrounding the dervish camp. Several hundred dervish warriors, including 'Osman Azraq, escaped along a secret path to the south, or plunged into the Nile and swam across. Kitchener could have ordered his cavalry and the 12th Sudanese to cut them off, but was wary of completing the circle in case his troops came under fire from their own side.

The initial defence had collapsed. MacDonald's men were chasing the enemy across a swampy isthmus on to an island in the Nile. Lewis's men advanced on the village, fighting house to house. Some of the Baggara ran out of their huts and defended them-selves with swords and spears. The Egyptians surrounded them and gouged them to death with their bayonets. Some dervishes remained inside, firing through windows and loopholes. The Egyptian and Sudanese troops blitzed them with return fire. In one corner of the village, 126 bodies were piled up on each other. In a single courtyard, eighty corpses were found. By 0720 hours, before the heat of the day had come on, the village had been cleared. Up on the spur of the hill, Kitchener ordered the Maxim gunners to stop firing and conserve ammunition. Eight hundred dervishes lay dead on the field. Six hundred were wounded, and there were five hundred prisoners. Kitchener's force had lost only twenty dead and eighty-three wounded.

Kitchener rode into the village solemnly with Wingate, Slatin and his staff. The victory was, he knew, not one of courage alone, but of careful planning. The element of surprise had been perfect. The difficult night-march had gone off splendidly. But most of all, Kitchener felt, it was a vindication of British leadership and train-ing. The much-disparaged Egyptian troops — the men who had panicked and run at et-Teb — had fought brilliantly. While many of the Sudanese troops were veterans, not one of the Egyptians had been in action before. This day Baggara warriors had run in panic from Egyptian peasants, and had heard yells of derision from soldiers they had previously rated as cowards. The British were proud of them. 'Such is the result of twelve years' careful training of the once despised fellahin by British officers,' wrote *Times* correspondent E. F. Knight. 'I am very pleased to be able to say . . . [that] the Egyptian troops, concerning whom so many disparaging things have . . . been written, greatly distinguished themselves.'[10]

The strangest scenes came after the fighting was done. Many of the soldiers in the Sudanese battalions recognized old comrades among the captured enemy Jihadiyya. For a moment it was almost as if they had just completed a friendly football match – there was embracing, inquiries about friends and relatives, and the victorious Sudanese doled out cigarettes and handed round water-bottles. One soldier from a Sudanese battalion actually recognized his own father among the dead Mahdist riflemen, and asked permission to prepare him for burial. Almost before the smoke had cleared, Jihadiyya who had just been fighting for their lives against the Egyptians were clamouring to join them. There were over a hundred new volunteers for the Sudanese battalions from the Mahdist ranks.

The Jihadiyya were not the only ones who encountered old acquaintances. Rudolf von Slatin was scouring the battlefield for familiar faces among the slain, and identified the body of Hamuda Idris, whom he had met at Omdurman. At about 0900 hours, while Kitchener was establishing his headquarters in a cluster of mud houses, Slatin rode up and dismounted. He was standing outside the new HQ when a wounded dervish *emir* was brought up on a donkey – a brawny, stout man with a white beard and a sympathetic expression. When he saw Slatin, he slipped out of the saddle and hurried to embrace him. The two exchanged warm greetings. The *emir* was Sheikh el-Obeid of the Ja'aliyyin – the holy man whose warriors had cut Gordon's telegraph line in 1884 and had captured Halfaya. The sheikh had been kind to Slatin while he was under suspicion in Omdurman, and his kindness now reaped its reward. Slatin was delighted to see him.

The local tribesmen, Nubians of the Mahas tribe, welcomed

Kitchener and his force as liberators. To them, the dervishes had been an army of occupation who had been persecuting them for too long: stealing their produce, their sheep and goats, and forcing their men into service. Only two Mahas families in Firka had willingly collaborated with the dervishes, and after the battle they were ostracized for ever. The depth of local feeling against these collaborators can be gauged by the fact that the names of their families are remembered to this day, more than a hundred years later.

5

After the battle of Firka, Kitchener did not engage the enemy again for five months, and in that time almost everything went wrong. His troops in Akasha were plagued first with dysentery, then cholera. Three hundred and sixty-four men died – British, Egyptian and Sudanese. The Nile was far lower than usual, preventing the use of steamers, and the seasonal north wind that Kitchener was relying on to power his *nuggars* failed to arrive.

The Sudanese summer, often unbearable, was attended by a freak scorching wind from the south. Hector MacDonald's 2 Brigade, marching across a desert short-cut to take up a new forward position, was decimated by dehydration. Eight Sudanese riflemen expired from water loss before they even made the first water-depot. The war correspondents christened it the 'Death March'. Archibald Hunter privately accused Kitchener of 'murdering' his own men.

The furnace wind was replaced by the worst rainstorm in living memory. Between Sarras and Akasha, where the railway followed the bed of the Khor Ahrusa, the rain drowned the track for twelve miles and washed away the ballast, leaving sleepers and rails hanging in the air. The army was stranded at Kosha with rations for only five days.

Kitchener rode to Akasha in a single night, and immediately began to organize repair work. He detailed units to rebuild the embankment, and others to scour the desert for the missing sleepers. While they were working, another storm destroyed a further eight miles of track. He had five thousand men labouring round the clock, and he joined in with them in his shirt-sleeves, helping to lay out the rails. When they flagged in the blinding heat, he rode along the lines chatting to them in Arabic. Kitchener's personal leadership was inspirational – the line was replaced in only a week.

In early September, when the Nile was in flood, there was another setback. The steamer *Zafir*, specially designed by Kitchener and his cavalry chief, John Burn-Murdoch, for the campaign, had been brought up to Kosha in sections and assembled there. She was a state-of-the-art gunboat, a 135-foot ironclad, stern-wheeled, with extra armaments, protection for troops on deck, and a shallow draught. Kitchener claimed that she was worth more to him than a battalion of infantry. On her maiden voyage, though, her cylinder burst, putting her *hors de combat* for weeks. After the months of anticipation, this was too much for the Sirdar. He vanished into the cabin of another steamer and wept.

In Dongola, dervish governor Mohammad wad Bishara was aware of Kitchener's misfortunes, and was itching to hit the Egyptian force while it was down. From Omdurman, though, 'Abdallahi instructed him to wait for reinforcements. Wad Bishara did not believe that these reinforcements would arrive, and instead began to prepare defensive positions at Kerma, the ancient capital of Nubia, where the tortuous, rocky defiles of Mahas country ended and the broad, fertile flood plains of the Danagla region began.

On 10 September Wingate reported to the Sirdar that his agents had spotted an enemy build-up at Kerma. Kitchener moved with incredible speed. Using a combination of railways and steamers, he had concentrated thirteen thousand men at Delgo, capital of the Mahas region, within only two days. Within eight, his force had arrived at Abu Fatma, only three miles north of Kerma.

Kerma, like Firka, lay on the east bank of the Nile. The river guarded Kitchener's right flank, and was secured by a flotilla of gunboats, *Tamai*, *Abu Klea* and *Metemma*, under thirty-five-year-old Commander Stanley Colville, RN. The four steamers bristled with mountain-guns and Maxims manned by the men of the Royal Marine Artillery. A fourth steamer, *et-Teb*, had got stuck on a rock in the Hannek Cataract and had been left behind. Two unarmoured steamers, *Dal* and *Akasha*, each carried a company of the North Staffordshire Regiment.

At first light on Saturday 19 September, Kitchener trotted into Kerma at the head of a troop of Egyptian cavalry. The town and the fort were completely deserted. As the sun rose above the desert behind him, though, the Sirdar understood what had occurred. Wad Bishara's men had slipped across the Nile in the night and were now manning entrenchments among the palm-groves at Hafir, on the west bank, about half a mile upstream. Kitchener scanned the dervish position with his field-glasses. Moored against the far bank were about thirty *nuggars* and a small steamer, *at-Tahira* – the boats the enemy had evidently used to cross the Nile. Their trenches and gun-pits extended for almost a thousand yards along the river, and above the palm-trees, among the mud-brick houses, the Sirdar could see the brilliant white *jibbas* of scores of tribesmen on foot. Beyond them, where the palms gave way to the desert, he could make out the flash of leaf-bladed spears as a host of Baggara cavalry banked and wheeled. Just visible to his left lay the palm-shrouded island of Artagasha, and nearer, to his right, the bow-shaped rump of Badin island.

Kitchener ordered his horse artillery battery to shift their Krupps along the river bank to the south, opposite the dervish fortification. Their instructions were to give covering fire for the gunboats. It occurred to him that if he sent his steamers directly upriver to Dongola, the enemy would fear they were going to be cut off from their base, and would almost certainly pull out. It was an inspired plan, but first the flotilla had to run the gauntlet of wad Bishara's defences, which included five Krupp breech-loaders. This was to prove no easy task.

At 0630 hours, half a dozen guns of the horse artillery belched flame from the east bank. Shells droned across the river and crashed into the enemy positions: for a moment the entire thousand yards of defences were laced in smoke. The dervish riflemen opened fire: some of their rounds spattered ineffectually off the bank. The range was too great for their Remingtons, and they caused not a single casualty.

The three gunboats beat up against the current to the enemy position, followed by *Dal* and *Akasha*, carrying the Staffords. On his flagship, *Tamai*, Stanley Colville now understood why wad Bishara had sited his defences half a mile upstream from Kerma. The dervish position lay where the Nile became a narrow bottle-neck between the west bank and Artagasha island. To get into this channel the steamers would have to place themselves in harm's way – well within range of enemy batteries and snipers. There was no other way through: the eastern channel of the island was blocked by shallows.

Colville's vessels came up fighting like old-time galleons. The Marine gunners blasted off their ordnance at the dervish emplace-ments: the Maxims traversed the parapets, rattling rimfire. The Staffords fired controlled volleys from the decks of their boats. In moments the steamers were wreathed in smoke. The dervish bat-teries barked back at them, their shells whaling across the water, ripping up the surface into waves. Remington bullets clanged against steel hulls. A Krupp shell punched through *Abu Klea*'s skin just above the waterline, but did not explode. Three shells hit *Metemma* – one through her smoke-stack, one through her main cabin, and a third through the shield of the gun in her bows. On *Tamai*, Colville's wrist was shattered by a bullet, and Armourer-Sergeant Richardson of the Royal Marine Artillery was shot dead manning a Maxim gun. Twelve other men were wounded. The duel became so hot that Colville pulled *Tamai* out of the fray and beat downstream to request more covering fire from the artillery.

Minutes later she was back for a second run. The horse batteries blatted out shell after shell, but still could not silence the enemy guns long enough for the steamers to get through. The heads of the palm-trees were full of dervish sharpshooters, raking the steamers' decks with rifle-shot – from their elevated positions they could shoot behind the guns' protective shields. *Metemma* turned and steamed back towards Kerma, followed by dervish jeers.

The battle had been raging for two and a half hours. Kitchener realized that the gunboats simply could not knock out the dervish defences, and decided on another tactic. He ordered two field batteries, one horse battery, and the Maxim battery, under Major C. S. B. Parsons of the Royal Artillery, to ford the shallows to Artagasha island. From here, at four thousand yards, they could get a better crack at wad Bishara's trenches. At the same time he placed three battalions of infantry directly opposite the dervish position, with a rocket detachment. He then instructed Lieutenant de Rougemont, RN – now in command of the flotilla – to make a flying run past the enemy at full steam.

It was a bold gamble. At 0900 hours eighteen guns opened up with a shocking barrage of fire from Artagasha. They knocked out three of the five dervish guns within minutes. Simultaneously, infantry and rocket fire burst out from the west bank. The heads of the palm-trees erupted in flames, and dervish snipers fell out of them yelling, their *jibbas* on fire. One of the guns on the island smacked a hole through the dervish steamer *at-Tahira*. She listed over on one side, and sank a moment later. At 1000 hours the gunboat flotilla steamed past the enemy, let off a single broadside, and sailed on jubilantly towards Dongola.

Wad Bishara had lost the game. He had been severely wounded by a fragment of shrapnel. His lieutenant 'Osman Azraq had also been badly injured. His dervishes kept up unfocused fire for the rest of the day while the Egyptians dropped shell after shell into their trenches. After dark, when the shooting stopped, wad Bishara pulled his men out and headed south for Dongola. They left behind them more than two hundred dead.

The retrieval of Dongola was now in Kitchener's grasp. It lay only thirty-six miles to the south, on the opposite bank. His forces outnumbered wad Bishara's by about three to one. At first light next day, his men fetched the dervish *nuggars* over to the west bank, and Kitchener began moving his thirteen thousand troops and 3,200 horses and camels across. By the afternoon of 21 September the entire Egyptian force was ready to march. The gunboat flotilla had by that time returned from Dongola. They had reached the town on the afternoon of the 19th, shelled the garrison, and captured a fleet of *nuggars*. The dervish force from Hafir under wad Bishara had not reached Dongola until the following night. The wounded dervish chief had begun to prepare a defence. To hamper his preparations, Kitchener sent *Abu Klea*, commanded by Lieutenant David Beatty, RN – the future naval hero and First Lord of the Admiralty – back to Dongola.

While Beatty was fighting a duel with wad Bishara's guns, Kitchener's force was marching south. By noon the next day they were at Sowarat, a large village on a wide fertile plain six miles north of Dongola. The army rested for the remainder of the 22nd, and at 0300 hours the next morning the final march began.

When the first streaks of crimson fire lit up the horizon to the east, Kitchener was delighted to see *Zafir* steam into view. The steamer he had claimed worth 'a battalion of infantry' had been repaired in time for the last act. As the day opened like a box, the army fanned out into extended order. It was the largest force commanded by a British officer since the Crimean War. The three original brigades – Lewis's, MacDonald's and Maxwell's – formed into line. In the centre were the artillery batteries, with the men of the North Staffordshire Regiment, and the Maxim gunners of the Staffords and Connaught Rangers. The Rangers stood out in their red tunics – the only flash of scarlet among the serried ranks of khaki and yellow ochre. On the right the cavalry and camel corps wheeled and strutted. On the left, the gunboats, now augmented by *Zafir*, puffed smoke.

The sky was a flawless blue. On the flat plain nothing stirred but the Egyptian army advancing on the small town. Suddenly, though, a tight body of Baggara horse, in dazzling white *jibbas*, with banners streaming and spears gleaming, came pounding towards the invaders on a tide of dust. They were so few in number compared with their enemy that a sigh of admiration went up. For a moment it looked as if they were determined to make a suicidal charge. A second later, though, they broke off and wheeled back towards the town. Kitchener ordered Burn-Murdoch to go after them with his cavalry, horse artillery and camel corps. This was exactly what the Baggara had planned. The pursuit distracted the Anglo-Egyptians from the main dervish force, which was already hurrying south towards the Bayuda desert. Burn-Murdoch never caught the Baggara. They outrode his squadrons and managed to rendezvous later with wad Bishara and 'Osman Azraq at ed-Debba. All the cavalry made it across the Bayuda to Metemma.

The Anglo-Egyptians captured a number of detached parties and stragglers, and about eight hundred Jihadiyya surrendered. By noon, the Egyptian flag was flying once more over the Muderiyya that Kitchener had first seen as a subaltern twelve years earlier. He was satisfied with his relatively inexpensive victory, happy that he had liberated the whole of the Sudan's northern province from the tyranny of the Khalifa's rule.

Part Seven

1

In Omdurman, 'Abdallahi realized that the fall of Dongola would soon be followed up by a full-scale invasion that would reach into the very heart of his state. In September 1896 he sent instructions to his *emirs* in Kordofan and Darfur to bring their Baggara armies to the capital, to prepare for the onslaught he knew would soon come.

In fact, he knew more than the British Prime Minister, Lord Salisbury, whose government was under the impression that the reconquest of the Sudan was at an end. Even Cromer had envisaged a consolidation period of three or four years before any further move was made. Kitchener disagreed. His force was large, but nowhere near as large as the army 'Abdallahi could muster against him. It would be militarily disastrous to leave his forces static in the northern Sudan. Soon after capturing Dongola, he left for Cairo and London to ask for funds to continue the advance.

He arrived in England in November to find his star in the ascendant. He was lionized by the public, promoted to major-general, knighted, and invited to stay at Windsor Castle with the Queen. He found her most sympathetic. On the day he had taken Dongola, she had completed sixty years on the throne, becoming the longest reigning monarch in British history. The following year, 1897, she would celebrate her Diamond Jubilee. This occasion would be the crowning glory of an age. For Queen Victoria, the death of Gordon and the fall of Khartoum had been her nadir – to recapture Khartoum and avenge Gordon in her jubilee year, or closely following it, would redeem everything.

To Cromer, as always, it was a simple question of money. The Egyptian government had financed the Dongola campaign, but could not afford a further advance. He admitted that Kitchener had spent less than he had anticipated, and agreed that it would be cheaper to strike now while the iron was hot. If the British taxpayer was ready to shell out the half million pounds needed for the next phase, then Cromer would recommend an immediate advance.

Kitchener went to work with all his powers of persuasion on the Chancellor of the Exchequer, Sir Michael Hicks-Beach, whose reputation for tight-fistedness exceeded even his own. The Queen's cousin, Wolseley's old adversary the Duke of Cambridge, swung all the influence he could muster in Kitchener's favour. The tipping point, though, was the news that a French officer, Captain Marchand, had received authorization from his government to trek all the way across Africa to stake France's claim to the Upper Nile. He was already on African soil, and would set out from Brazzaville within a few months. On 16 November, the day Kitchener was knighted by the Queen, the Chancellor capitulated. Salisbury agreed not only to foot the bill, but also to provide British soldiers if they were needed. Kitchener left Britain for the Sudan five days later feeling ecstatic. Khartoum would be retaken, and Gordon avenged.

Kitchener had no intention of following Wolseley's line of advance through the Bayuda desert. The vast sweep in the Nile between Dongola and Abu Hamed – the Nile's 'question mark' – could be cut by a straight line. The 250-mile stretch of desert between Korosko and Abu Hamed had been a caravan route from time immemorial. Camels could do it in eight days, rather than the weeks it would take following the Nile, but Kitchener did not plan to use camels. He would attempt a feat of engineering the like of which had never been seen before: he would span the desert with a railway.

It was a truly courageous undertaking. The Nubian desert was virtually unexplored and unknown apart from the old caravan route, and that was waterless except for the wells at Murrat and Gabgaba. Moreover, the railway would be progressing directly into enemy territory, and the route could not even be reconnoitred as far as Abu Hamed. There were no maps of the desert, but it was believed to be too sandy, rocky and hilly for railway construction. In any case, no one had ever built such a railway before. Railway experts Kitchener had consulted in England had told him frankly that to build such a line was impossible.

Kitchener refused to be put off, and even exacerbated the difficulties by deciding to place the northern terminus of the line at Wadi Halfa instead of Korosko. There were good reasons for this: Halfa was the terminus of the Dongola line, and already had the necessary workshops and facilities. But while the Korosko route passed through the Murrat and Gabgaba wells, the Wadi Halfa route was entirely waterless.

The route was surveyed by Lieutenant Edward Cator of the Royal Engineers, who had the useful accomplishment of being a water-diviner. Cator set off by camel with an 'Ababda escort, carrying a sketch-map Kitchener had given him, marking two sites where he thought water might be found. By incredible luck, he divined water in both places. He also brought Kitchener cheering news about the route itself. The Sirdar had been right and the doubting Thomases wrong. The country between Wadi Halfa and Abu Hamed was not unduly hilly, rocky or steep. It was mostly flat sand. There was a gradual ascent up to sixteen hundred feet, but this would not present a major challenge. The only real problem would be the descent into Abu Hamed, which Cator had not been able to survey, as it lay within enemy territory.

Cator was one of Kitchener's 'Band of Boys' – a squad of young subalterns of the Royal Engineers to whom he had assigned the actual task of constructing 'the impossible railway'. Their kingpin was twenty-nine-year-old Percy Girouard, a French-Canadian from Montreal and a graduate of the Royal Military College, Kingston, who had cut his teeth on the Canadian Pacific. Girouard lived, breathed and slept railways, and had already been awarded the DSO for his work on the Dongola line. Smart, irrepressibly buoyant and direct, he was soon to prove himself Kitchener's most valuable assistant – so indispensable, in fact, that the Sirdar would put up with criticism from him that he would not tolerate from much more senior officers.

During his stay in London in November, Kitchener had ordered a number of locomotives. Girouard quizzed him about their specifications, then confidently announced that they would be quite useless. Kitchener shrugged and told him he had better go to England himself. 'But don't spend too much,' he added, 'because we are terribly poor.' One of the conditions Hicks-Beach had laid on Kitchener was that he must on no account exceed the budget of £240,000 being granted him for the railway. He was delighted when Girouard returned having obtained some locomotives for nothing. He had managed to borrow several seventy- and eighty-ton engines from the statesman Cecil Rhodes, who had earmarked them for use in the Cape Province and Natal. Girouard had also ordered fifteen new locomotives and two hundred wagons.

The railway was to be designated the SMR – the Sudan Military Railway. The first spadeful of sand had been lifted on 1 January 1897, and fifteen miles of track laid by the end of February, but it was not until May that work began in earnest. The Dongola line had by then reached its southern terminus at Kerma, and the platelayers, bankmakers, spikers and other crews who had worked on the Dongola line could be drafted to the SMR. These crews, who had begun in 1896 as apprentices laying half a mile a day, were now veterans who thought nothing of laying two miles a day. They joined the fifteen hundred new navvies on the desert line, bringing the total number of the labour force up to three thousand.

To keep these three thousand men alive, contented, fed and watered, and working at full capacity, was a Herculean task to which Kitchener's genius was particularly suited. The bulk of the force was maintained at Railhead, a nomadic encampment that vaulted forward every four or five days. The camp consisted of hundreds of tents, including mess-tents, a post and telegraph office, stores, station and water-tanks, and was protected by half an Egyptian battalion under a British captain, who commanded the entire working party.

The logistics of the water-supply alone were a nightmare. Each of the three thousand men at Railhead required twelve litres of water a day – a total of thirty-six thousand litres. Each day at noon a supply train arrived drawing half a dozen six-thousand-litre water-trucks, containing the water for the work-crews. In addition to this, it carried a reserve, and water for its own crew and escort. The train also had to pull its own water-supply – enough to keep its steam-engine working to Railhead and back. The amount of water required would, of course, increase as Railhead grew further away, until one third of its total capacity was taken up by its own water. The tanks at Railhead held a reserve for three days. If the train broke down or the line were cut or blocked for more than forty-eight hours, it was likely that everyone there would die.

It was in his work on the SMR that Kitchener really earned his nickname 'the Sudan Machine'. The railroad rattled forward with machine-like precision. The 'spearhead' of the line was the survey camp, which remained six miles in advance of Railhead. The survey party was commanded by two of the Sirdar's young Sapper officers, and consisted of a single British Sapper NCO, and eighteen Egyptian military surveyors, trained in the use of the theodolite and level.

The survey party was the 'brains' of the great iron serpent. Its job was to mark out the route with a numbered wooden peg, every hundred feet. Data on the height of the embankment or depth of the cutting required at each peg was sent back to the crew foremen at Railhead every day. In practice, the railway was made to conform as much as possible to the desert surface – the variation in height rarely exceeded two feet.

The survey party was supported by camel, and supplied with water and food from Railhead. It was thought strong enough to fight its way back to the main camp if attacked by dervish raiders. As a safety net, a force of 'Ababda camel-men patrolled the desert constantly, operating from their base at Murrat. They stayed forty miles ahead of the survey party, far enough to give a long warning should they spot a raiding party or come across fresh tracks.

Wingate believed that the lack of water on the route would

confine a raiding party to not more than three hundred men. This was the number that could be watered from the *gelta* or rainwater cistern at Jabal Kurur – at twelve hundred feet, the only place in the desert where rainwater collected. In May, Kitchener sent a camel corps detachment under Captain King to Jabal Kurur to empty the *gelta*, cutting off potential raiders' only water-supply.

Following the survey party came the bankmakers, fifteen hundred strong, who constructed the embankments and cuttings to the surveyors' stipulations. They worked one day in front of the other crews, building a mile and a quarter to a mile and a half of banks a day. Theirs was the most arduous task of all. While the platelayers rode to and fro on the locomotives, the bankmakers had to march to their place of work every morning carrying their tools, setting off two hours before dawn. They worked all day, shovelling sand in the baking sun, almost without a break, until sunset, when they had to march back to camp.

The platelayers followed the bankmakers. They numbered about a thousand men, and were divided into gangs. The platelayers' day would begin at dawn, when the 'materials train' arrived from Wadi Halfa, carrying two and a half thousand yards of rails, sleepers, bolts and fishplates. The platelayer gangs would shimmy aboard the lumbering train and ride out to the end of the line. There, the train would halt, and the gangs would clamber down. One gang unloaded the sleepers: another carried them to the embankment and laid them out. A third crew spaced them correctly and adjusted them so that they were at perfect right-angles. A fourth gang – 'the Rail Gang' – laid the rails on the sleepers. Other parties adjusted the rails, bolted the fishplates, or chalked the rails to show where they should be spiked.

The spiking gangs came next. They consisted of five men, two to lever up the sleeper, two to spike it, and one to superintend the work. They were followed by three or four men whose job was to straighten the rails using iron bars. This was possible because initially only alternate sleepers were spiked, leaving some play in the rails. Once a hundred yards of track had been laid, the locomotive would steam up to the end of the line once more and the whole process would begin again. After the engine came another spiking gang, who spiked the sleepers left by the first, and then a gang of straighteners, lifters and fillers-in, who lifted and packed earth under the sleepers to prevent subsidence, and straightened the rails once more. Finally an expert platelayer would inspect the line to make certain it was perfect. The labour would continue throughout the long roasting hours of the day, progressing at a steady rate of a mile and a half a day. The work ceased only at sunset, when the train would carry the exhausted men back over the track they had laid. At Railhead, they would eat their evening meal and fall into a deep sleep, under the watchful eyes of their guards. The fires flickered out and the great camp was lost in darkness, devoured by the vastness of the desert.

The iron road uncoiled yard by yard across the sands under the cloudless steel-blue sky. The Railway Battalion battled on through furnace heat, thirst, hunger, sickness and violent sandstorms. The number of men who gave their lives in its construction is not recorded. Since two of Kitchener's eight-strong band of boys – Lieutenant Edward Cator, who had completed the first survey, and Lieutenant R. Polwhele – died before it was completed, it is likely that the attrition rate among the labourers was also high. History has remained strangely silent about casualties on the SMR, but there were rumours of Kitchener's cruelty – of floggings and even hangings – and his apparent indifference to the use of severe punishments. 'There are many nameless mounds in the desert,' hinted Winston Churchill two years later, 'which mark the changing sites of Railhead Town, and show that nothing good is ever achieved in this world without someone having to pay the cost.'[1]

Kitchener was ubiquitously present, overseeing the unloading of steamers at Wadi Halfa, riding in the cab of the 'materials train' as it lumbered to Railhead, visiting Girouard or his comrades at the survey camp, chatting in Arabic with the platelayers, even driving the locomotives himself. Though Girouard and his crew had responsibility for the day-to-day running of the railway, none of them denied that it was Kitchener's plan, and Kitchener's glory. He may have been Sirdar, but he was first and foremost an engineer, and the executive decisions were his. Kitchener was spurred on by an obsession with detail and an inability to delegate that frequently led to utter exhaustion. His blunt bullying of his subordinates grew worse as the pressure mounted, and he suffered frequently from nervous indigestion and neuralgia caused by eye-strain. Deep down he knew that the railway was a huge gamble. It could be ruined any moment by a concerted effort on the part of the Khalifa 'Abdallahi.

3

If the Khalifa had adopted the role taken by T. E. Lawrence and his Bedouin on the Hejaz railway during 1916–18, his forces could have played havoc with Kitchener's advance. The supply train only needed to be held up for two days and the entire workforce would be doomed. Pinprick raids by warriors on fast camels, hitting locomotives, survey camp, water-installations, even embankments and rails, would have been a ceaseless thorn in the Anglo-Egyptian side.

Today, it seems obvious that the Khalifa's best strategy would have been to fight a guerrilla campaign. In 1897, though, T. E. Lawrence was only ten years old, and his brilliant epiphany on 'desert power' lay nineteen years in the future. To the Khalifa and his men, 'hit and run' was an alien idea. Brought up in the undulat-ing steppe of the *goz*, among horses and cattle, 'Abdallahi was unable even to conceive what a railway looked like, let alone its strategic potential. More importantly, his cultural perspective caused him to think of war almost entirely in terms of honour and courage. The enemy might possess all the technology in the world, but in the end, victory would be decided not by railways or steamers, but by a clash of fighters on the battlefield, just as it had been at Shaykan.

The Khalifa's 'master plan' was to allow Kitchener to penetrate deeper and deeper into his territory until his lines of communi-cation were over-extended. Then, his men tired, thirsty and fearful, he would be lured to a place of 'Abdallahi's own choosing, where his force, after being softened up by the *Mulazimin*, would be chopped to pieces in an irresistible charge by fearless warriors.

'Abdallahi was old in Sudanese terms – over fifty – and, like many who have come to power suddenly, was far gone in self-indulgence. Vanished were the sleek lines and corded muscles of the elephant- and giraffe-hunter he had been in his youth. The Khalifa had soared to incredible heights for a nomad born in the desert steppe of Darfur: clearly he was no ordinary man. He had always been the *éminence grise* behind the Mahdist movement. Without him, Mohammad Ahmad might never have been recognized as the Mahdi; without him the crucial Baggara tribes might never have joined the dervishes; without him, the Mahdi might never even have adopted firearms.

But his restricted background imposed limits on him. He was unable to grasp what a vast difference the railway made in terms of moving huge numbers of men and large amounts of arms and ammunition up to the front quickly. Neither did he appreciate that the Egyptian army of Kitchener was not the Egyptian army of Hicks. The dervishes had obliterated the Hicks column in 1883, and chased the British out of the country in 1885. He was convinced that, railway or no railway, they could do the same now.

He also believed that, like Wolseley, Kitchener would, in the end, use the Bayuda desert as his main line of advance. Consequently he decided to strengthen Metemma, the town lying at the end of the Bayuda route. It was the tribal capital of the Ja'aliyyin tribe, but the Khalifa knew they could not be trusted, and that their chief, 'Abdallah wad Sa'ad, had been in communication with the enemy.

In June 1897, 'Abdallahi called wad Sa'ad to Omdurman and told him that he must evacuate Metemma forthwith. His town had been designated as a garrison for the Baggara squadrons that his cousin, the *emir* Mahmud Ahmad, had recently brought in from the west. Wad Sa'ad was furious and decided to join the Anglo-Egyptians. Immediately on arriving back in Metemma, he sent two tribesmen across the desert on fast camels to contact the nearest Anglo-Egyptian force, at Merowe. The envoys were met by Kitchener's Chief of Staff, Leslie Rundle, now a major-general. The Ja'aliyyin asked for arms, ammunition and, if possible, soldiers. Rundle knew he had to act quickly, but was wary of a trap. He turned down the request for troops, but quickly assembled a caravan of rifles and ammunition, and sent it under escort to Metemma.

It was too late. On 1 July, the *emir* Mahmud, an arrogant young man of thirty-four, arrived at the head of between ten and twelve thousand Baggara warriors, with orders to wipe the Ja'aliyyin off the face of the earth. The Baggara attacked in strength. The Ja'aliyyin resisted bravely, but after a struggle the nomads captured the town and massacred two thousand men, women and children. Wad Sa'ad was killed in the fighting. Mahmud located his body, had his head cut off, and sent it triumphantly to Omdurman. He did not realize that, in his triumph, he had served his cousin's state the most serious blow it had ever sustained.

That June, Kitchener's morale was raised by a visit to Cairo for the parade commemorating the Queen's Diamond Jubilee. The Sirdar was aware that his campaign and his railway project, if successful, would be remembered as the very apogee of the British Empire in the Victorian age. After the ceremony, he and Hunter – now a major-general and military governor of Dongola – went into conclave with Cromer and planned the forthcoming invasion down to the last detail. Kitchener wanted to bring off a lightning offensive, but the speed of his advance would be hampered by the lack of water in the Nubian desert. To reach Abu Hamed and return to Halfa, a distance of 470 miles, his locomotives would need to pull no less than fourteen six-thousand-litre trucks, just for their own water-supply. This would severely limit the number of men and the amount of matériel the trains could carry at one time.

The Sirdar returned to Wadi Halfa to find a surprise waiting for him. In the officers' mess, Lieut. Colonel John Maxwell, CO of 3 Brigade and military governor of Halfa, offered him a whisky and soda. The Sirdar accepted gratefully, but when he tasted it almost spat it out. 'What's this?' he demanded. Maxwell grinned and told him that the 'soda' he was drinking had come from a well sunk in the Nubian desert. The site, excavated by one of his 'Band of Boys', Lieutenant George Gorringe, Royal Engineers, had been one of the two places where Edward Cator had divined water. Gorringe had found it after five weeks' work, at a depth of ninety feet. The second site had yielded water in even greater abundance. The two water-points, 77 and 126 miles from Wadi Halfa respectively, would become known to posterity as Station Four and Station Six.

Kitchener was ecstatic. This meant that the water-supply of his trains could be replenished en route to, and on the way back from, Abu Hamed. The turn-around time could be shortened, and the carrying capacity increased. Kitchener knew that these two discoveries were the key to victory: he must have said a silent prayer of thanks to his young comrade Edward Cator, who had died in February, before the fruits of his survey had come to light.

By 23 July, Railhead was at the highest point of its climb from Wadi Halfa, at sixteen hundred feet, 103 miles from the terminus. It had remained within its projected curve of six degrees, and within its gradient of not more than one in 120. Kitchener was aware that if the railway progressed much further it would be in reach of dervish raiding parties from Abu Hamed. The time had come for aggressive action.

The capture of Abu Hamed had been made more urgent by the fall of Metemma. If Mahmud's Baggara moved to reinforce it, the small town would become a far harder nut to crack. In the long run, though, the massacre of the Ja'aliyyin at Metemma had been a massive home goal for the Khalifa. It had cemented the enmity between the Ja'aliyyin and the Baggara once and for all. The victory also distracted the Baggara from their real objective. They were fresh from the *goz* of the west, and had come in the hope of plunder: Metemma provided everything they had dreamt of. The nomads ran amok in the town, among the slowly rotting bodies, raping and pillaging, and Mahmud found himself helpless to control them. They refused to send their loot to the *bayt al-mal*, and remained for months there, losing their edge to good living, and daily on the verge of mutiny.

Kitchener decided to go for Abu Hamed while the going was good. His first act was to dispatch his 'Ababda irregulars under their chief, 'Abd al-Azim Bey Hussain, on a reconnaissance mission to find out the enemy's strength. 'Abd al-Azim, the younger brother of Salah Bey Hussain, who had escorted Gordon across the desert in 1884, brought this off brilliantly. He spread his 150 camel-men out in the desert in ones and twos, so as not to raise suspicion, and converged on the village of Abtayn, seven miles south of Abu Hamed. They captured everyone they found in the desert, then surrounded the village so that no one could leave. 'Abd al-Azim called for the sheikh and questioned him carefully about the dervish garrison in Abu Hamed. When he had got all the information he needed, the 'Ababda watered their camels, and forced every man, woman and child to walk six miles into the desert with them – ensuring it would be hours before anyone could report their coming to the enemy. Then they rode fast back to their base at Murrat wells.

'Abd al-Azim's report revealed that the dervishes had only a small force in Abu Hamed – 450 Jihadiyya, fifty Baggara horsemen, and about six hundred warriors armed with swords and spears. They were commanded by an *emir* called Mohammad az-Zayn. The Khalifa could not maintain a larger garrison there because of the difficulties of logistics, but when the dervishes heard of the 'Ababda reconnaissance, they would certainly send reinforcements from Berber.

'Abd al-Azim had even ascertained that the Mahdist troops expected an attack by enemy gunboats when the Nile was in flood, about mid-August. To this end they had dug a series of shelter-trenches along the river. This was vital information because it suggested that an attack from the landward, in early August, would catch them napping.

On the basis of this report, Kitchener planned his move on Abu Hamed. It would be taken by a 'flying column' from Merowe, led by his best fighters, Archibald Hunter and Hector MacDonald. They would muster their forces at Kassinger, near Merowe, and march quickly along the Nile, hitting the town before reinforcements got there. The march-in would be modelled on that of Firka, and the element of surprise would once again be paramount, although the distance, at 131 miles, was much longer, and the weather much hotter.

Hunter left Kassinger on the last day of July, with his 'flying column' – the 9th, 10th and 11th Sudanese battalions, the 3rd Egyptians, a mule-mounted artillery battery with six Krupps, two Maxims, a Gardner and a Nordenfeldt. An Egyptian cavalry detachment, twenty-five strong, acted as his eyes and ears. The column moved on foot but was supported by a baggage-column of thirteen hundred camels. Hector MacDonald commanded the infantry brigade.

Determined not to commit Wolseley's folly on the Gordon Relief Expedition, Kitchener remained in touch with the force by telegraph. Hunter was accompanied by the ubiquitous telegraph-man, Lieutenant M. Bowman-Manifold, who had hired a host of donkeys to carry the telegraph wires. In the absence of saddles – and at the Sirdar's suggestion – he had simply looped the spools of wire around the donkeys' bellies, so that it unwound as they walked.

Hunter's plan was to march only at night to avoid being spotted. The country was less rocky than the Belly of Stones, but desolate, with vast sweeps of Nubian sand approaching close to the river. For long stretches there were no cultivated strips, no palm-groves, and no villages. It was hard going in pitch darkness, and during the day it was impossible for the troops to sleep. Daytime temperatures soared to 42° Centigrade, and there was no shade. Men began falling asleep during the night-marches. By 5 July three of the Egyptian battalion had died, and fifty-eight men had been left behind suffering from exhaustion.

On the way, Hunter passed the site of the battle of Kirkbekan, where Wolseley's River Column had won a redundant victory eleven years earlier. He also tramped through the village where

Stewart, Power and Herbin had been murdered, and even came across bits of the broken-up steamer *Abbas*. But Hunter was not a reflective man, and had no time to dwell on the past. The objective was everything. It became even more urgent when, on 4 August, a shot was fired at them, revealing that they had been compromised.

The pressure went up two more notches when, the next night, at al-Khula, they were joined by 'Abd al-Azim Bey's skirmishing force of 150 'Ababda camel-men. 'Abd al-Azim told Hunter that the dervishes in Abu Hamed were preparing to dig in for a fight, pending the arrival of a large force that had already been sent from Berber. Hunter decided to move on without delay.

At 0200 hours on the morning of 7 August the 'Flying Column' had reached the thick palm-groves of Ginnifab, only two miles from Abu Hamed. Hunter's force had covered the distance from Kassinger in seven and a half days, which, as one officer commented, 'considering the heat and the country traversed, shows the excellent marching power of the "black" and the Egyptian'.[2] Indeed, it was a tribute to the toughness of the Egyptian army that they had marched thirty-six miles in the last thirty-five and a half hours, and were still ready for the fight.

Hunter corralled the transport camels in a zariba by the Nile, and posted half the 3rd Egyptian battalion to guard them. Hunter and MacDonald squatted down together, while 'Abd al-Azim drew a sketch of Abu Hamed in the sand. The town was a maze of mud-brick houses, no more than six hundred yards long and a hundred wide, lying in a shallow crater inside a plateau that sloped up from the river. The crater was defended by shelter-trenches and by three stone watchtowers. The dervishes were stationed in the shelter-trenches, in loopholed houses on the east side of the town, and in the watchtowers. Hunter decided on a carbon copy of Kitchener's attack at Firka. The column would divide and attack from along the river bank and from the desert flank. They would go into action at first light.

At 0500 hours dawn was drawing up in magenta seams along the sugar-loaf terraces and ridges out in the Nubian desert. The Nile rippled on placidly along the green banks of Moghrat island,

and a slight breeze ruffled the heads of the massed date-palms. Hunter's force lay no more than a quarter of a mile on the desert side of Abu Hamed, concealed in the folds and crevices of the ground. They had formed into a crescent with the 9th Sudanese on the right, the 11th in the centre, and the 10th on the left. The artillery battery lay between the 9th and 11th, defended by the 3rd Egyptians. The village itself was uncannily silent. There was no sign of the enemy, and Hunter began to wonder if the dervishes had pulled out after all.

He sent Major Kincaid to reconnoitre and followed on with some of his staff. Kincaid trotted up to within eighty yards of the trenches, and scanned them with his field-glasses. He could see the earthworks clearly, but they appeared to be empty. He put away the glasses and took out his pocket-book to make notes. 'There is no . . .' he had written, when the *wht! wht! wht!* of enemy bullets shivered past him. He felt the shock-waves as they zipped past his ear. A second later a score of dark heads emerged from the trench he had thought was empty. A volley clattered out. Kincaid did not wait to observe the smoke-puffs, but tore back towards Hunter, thanking God that the dervish shots were going high. To his horror, he saw that Hunter and his staff had almost reached the crater's edge. In a moment there was another salvo from the trenches. Bursts of smoke erupted from behind the banks. Rounds lacerated the air. Again they went high. Hunter galloped back to his own lines, three hundred yards away, and yelled for the artillery to open fire.

The Krupps roared in unison. Shells hissed and slapped into the dervish trenches, detonating with deafening thuds in showers of gravel and umbrellas of dust. The Egyptian and Sudanese infantry had been lying prone on the ground. Under cover of shellfire, the battalion formed up. The troops executed their drill movements with elegant precision, in full view of the enemy, silhouetted against the rising sun on the crests of the hills.

Hunter realized that his gun batteries were achieving nothing but keeping the enemy's heads down. The dervishes were well protected, and the houses were invisible inside the dip. He had the battery shifted to within a hundred yards of the ramparts to enfilade the trenches. The gambit failed. The barrels could not be depressed low enough to fire into them. Instead, Hunter told MacDonald to advance to contact.

MacDonald, mounted on a horse behind his lines, ordered, 'Attach bayonets!' There was the crisp clack of steel on steel as the men fixed their pike-bayonets in a single drill movement. MacDonald bawled, 'Advance!' and the long lines of khaki-clad men, black and brown, in their ochre breeches, tall tarbooshes and puttees, their bodies criss-crossed with belts and bandoliers, moved off in step, and in perfect order, with colours flying.

The dervishes' Remingtons were more than ten years old, and had not been well maintained. Much of their ammunition was home-manufactured in Omdurman, and was either defective or under-strength. This restricted their range, and as the infantry advanced, the Mahdist force held their fire.

The Anglo-Egyptian force had to advance three hundred yards, most of it downhill. MacDonald's plan had been to approach to within a hundred yards and launch a terrifying bayonet charge. Instead, the 11th Sudanese, on the right of the line, suddenly broke into independent fire. The other two battalions quickly followed suit. Rounds pulverized the dervish trenches from three directions. Major H. M. Sidney of the Duke of Cornwall's Light Infantry, commanding the 10th Sudanese, could see a blue-on-blue incident developing. The three battalions were converging, and his battalion would soon come into the killing-ground of the 9th Sudanese. He gave the order to halt. Hector MacDonald himself rode out among the 9th furiously, swearing and knocking up rifle-muzzles. The other officers did the same.

At that moment the dervishes stood to and fired two terrific volleys, one after the other. The 10th battalion was caught marking time, and dozens of men crashed into the sand, dead or wounded. Major Sidney himself was shot dead, and another officer, Lieutenant Fitzclarence, was also killed. There were sixty-two other casualties, including a dozen dead.

The other battalions let out a roar of rage, and bounded towards the dervish trenches. The men's faces were distorted with fury, their eyes bulging, their bayonets flashing perilously. The dervishes never got off another shot. They took one look at the attackers, and a moment later were haring away for their lives out of their defences and into the village.

Minutes later the Sudanese battalions were in the streets, their bayonets clicking double-time. They proved expert street-fighters. 'The black is a splendid chap at house-fighting,' commented one officer. 'They rapidly worked through the place, though it must be admitted that some of their methods are almost as dangerous to friend as to foe.'[3] They would fire blind around corners before entering a street, even if their own troops were already in it. Before assaulting a house they would fire a volley into it – the rounds would pass through the soft mud walls and whip out the other side. If the dervishes came out, the Sudanese troops would bayonet them and pull the trigger at the same time. 'Nevertheless,' the officer went on, 'they are A1 at clearing the enemy out of a village. In a twinkling they were all over the place, on the roofs, through the windows, and in no time had worked through the place and formed up beyond, firing volleys at the few dervish cavalry, who were the only ones to escape.'[4]

Many of the dervish warriors fought to the death. Soon the garrison was devastated, with bloody piles of dead littering the streets. The dervishes suffered 450 dead, but only twenty wounded. The commander, Mohammad az-Zayn, was captured. Abu Hamed was in the hands of the Anglo-Egyptians by 0730 hours: the fighting had lasted scarcely an hour.

One Baggara sniper, though, refused to give up. He had barricaded himself into a small house by the river and held out for seven hours, shooting down six men sent to finish him off. Finally, Hunter ordered a pair of Krupps brought up. Shrapnel shells blew the house to pieces. An Egyptian soldier went forward to 'pick up the bits', and was shot down when the sniper appeared like a ghost in the ruins. The Krupps crashed out again, reducing the house to a pile of rubble, but the body of the lone sniper was never found.

Mohammad az-Zayn had surrendered to an Egyptian officer,

and Hunter quickly had him brought up. He proved to be an intelligent young man of the Ta'isha Baggara, no more than twenty-three years old, an ardent Mahdist, firmly committed to the Khalifa's cause. When Hunter asked him why he had fought in the face of such overwhelming odds, the youth answered that since the Anglo-Egyptians only outnumbered his force three to one, and his fighters were worth four of the enemy, he had thought he stood an even chance.

He also informed Hunter that the *emir* Mahmud Ahmad would be there in five days with his Baggara force from Metemma: Hunter would be a dead man, and all his troops with him. It was brave talk, but for Mohammad az-Zayn the war was over. He was sent to Egypt and remained a prisoner at Rosetta until 1901. Still, the prospect of dervish reinforcements, whether from Berber or Metemma, did perturb Hunter. Abu Hamed was isolated, and he was short of supplies. The Nile was rising, but no gunboats had arrived, and the railway still lay 130 miles away. He was not yet aware that the Sirdar had ordered his flotilla of steamers, *et-Teb*, *Tamai*, *Fateh*, *Nasr*, *Metemma* and *Zafir*, through the Fourth Cataract three days earlier, in anticipation of his victory. *El-Teb*, commanded by David Beatty, had been wrecked, but the five others had been hauled through on ropes by local Shaygiyya tribesmen and Egyptian soldiers. They were all at Abu Hamed by 29 August.

Neither was there any immediate threat from the enemy. The dervish relief force from Berber turned back on receiving news of the fall of Abu Hamed from the retreating cavalry. Far from arriving at Abu Hamed in five days, the *emir* Mahmud was still in Metemma, trying to get his recalcitrant Baggara to cross the Nile.

By 22 August, Metemma was threatened by the Egyptian Camel Corps under Major R. Tudway of the Essex Regiment, a veteran of the Mounted Infantry Camel Regiment, who had fought at Abu Tulayh eleven years earlier. Tudway was now occupying Jakdul wells in the Bayuda desert, together with an irregular force of Ja'aliyyin camel-men, known as 'Friendlies'.

In late August, Hunter sent his other irregulars – the 'Ababda, under 'Abd al-Azim Bey – south to Berber to reconnoitre the town. 'Abd al-Azim returned with the astounding news that it had been abandoned. Its commander, the *emir* Zaki 'Osman, had given up waiting for Mahmud's half-mutinous Baggara, and had pulled out.

On 5 September, Hunter arrived at Berber with four gunboats, carrying half the 11th Sudanese battalion. He simply walked into the town whose capture, back in May 1884, had proved a major strategic problem. Kitchener soon joined him, having ridden by camel across the Bayuda desert from Merowe. The Sirdar was aware of the dangers this easy victory promised. His lines of communication were badly stretched. The railway was still over a hundred miles away, and 'Abdallahi could, if he chose, be here long before it arrived. Mahmud Ahmad was at Metemma with twelve thousand Baggara. Kitchener's old adversary from Handub, 'Osman Digna, was at Adarama on the 'Atbara river, only eighty miles away, with two thousand Beja.

As he rode into the town, though, he could not suppress a sense of satisfaction. The second phase of the reconquest was over. The railway that everyone had said was impossible to build would soon reach the Nile. His forces had occupied Berber. Wolseley had failed to take it in 1885, yet the town he had always believed was the key to the Sudan had simply fallen into his hand.

5

It had taken the *emir* Mahmud ten days just to get his Baggara across the river to Shendi, on the west bank, ready to march to Berber. On 21 August he heard that Zaki 'Osman had withdrawn. The next day he received reports of Tudway and his seventeen hundred camel-corps and Ja'aliyyin 'Friendlies' at Jakdul. He was aware that if he moved north, the Ja'aliyyin would promptly reoccupy Metemma. In any case, his Baggara troops did not want to leave.

For the next four months, Mahmud squandered his time exchanging futile messages with his cousin, the Khalifa 'Abdallahi, while his Baggara locusts ate up all the food supplies left in Metemma. The corpses still lay stinking in the streets. The Baggara persecuted the remaining Ja'aliyyin womenfolk so badly that Mahmud was obliged to pack all females off to Omdurman by steamer. As soon as the food ran out, many of the nomads began to saddle their horses and head for home. They had had what they had come for – a few months of ease and luxury at the expense of the haughty Ja'aliyyin. Disease began to spread through the force, causing more desertions.

'Abdallahi advised Mahmud to pull back as far as the Sabaluka Cataract. This was sound advice. Protected by the gorge of Sabaluka, the Baggara would be safe from British gunboats. They could turn the narrow channels into an impregnable fortress, with sniper-points, gun-banks, and artillery batteries. It would hold back the Anglo-Egyptian advance for months. More important, they would be near enough to Omdurman for supplies to reach them. Mahmud brushed this advice aside. He may have been afraid that any withdrawal would be interpreted as a defeat, and cause more desertions among his nomads. He also believed that he could beat the Anglo-Egyptians, and was spoiling for a fight.

The odds were already mounting against him. At 0700 hours on the morning of 16 October the gunboat *Zafir* appeared suddenly opposite Metemma, together with *Fateh* and *Nasr*. The flotilla's chief, Commander Colin Keppel, RN, ordered his Royal Marine gunners to open fire at a range of four thousand yards. As Metemma itself lay more than half a mile from the bank, the gunboats concentrated on the six forts Mahmud had built by the river. In an hour two of them had been reduced to debris, and the gunboats manoeuvred opposite the remaining four. They pounded them with shrapnel and high-explosive shells until the walls crashed down and the dervishes fled. As soon as the survivors emerged, the boats' Maxims mowed them down.

The guns roared and rattled without pause until 1430 hours, when resistance ceased. The following day the boats returned for another four-hour pummelling, then sailed back downstream whence they had come. Their payloads were lighter by 650 shells, and several thousand machine-gun rounds, and they left behind an estimated five hundred enemy dead. Keppel had lost only one man killed.

On 31 October the railway reached Abu Hamed. It had taken nine months to span the Nubian desert, and it arrived with only seventeen miles of track and sleepers to spare. There was now a hiatus while more materials were imported, but Kitchener's plan was to extend it as far as Berber, then further south in reach of the confluence of the Nile and the 'Atbara, where he intended to establish his next – and final – forward operating base.

By January, Mahmud had realized that if he did not make an attempt to halt the enemy's advance, his army would simply disintegrate. On the 16th, he wrote to 'Abdallahi that he intended to cross to the east bank and march north against Anglo-Egyptian forces at 'Atbara. For weeks, he had been requesting 'Osman Digna to join his army in Metemma. The old fox had left his headquarters at Adarama in September, but resisted Mahmud's requests until ordered to reinforce him by the Khalifa himself. He arrived at Metemma on 16 February with five thousand Beja troops.

It was not a happy combination. Both the Baggara and the Beja had a reputation as fearless warriors, but they were quite different in character. The Beja, proud of their ancient roots, looked down on the Baggara as Arab parvenus. The milieu in which the Baggara were raised – the *goz* – was lush in comparison with the Red Sea hills. The Beja were not good mixers. They spoke Tu-Bedawi, a language not closely related to Arabic, and were dour, moody and intolerant of strangers. The Baggara, like most Arab nomads, followed a code that exalted hospitality and generosity as well as courage, toughness and loyalty. The Beja were among the hardiest and most courageous fighters in the Sudan, but they did not welcome outsiders. To expect them to fight well with the Baggara was expecting oil and water to mix.

'Abdallahi had written to his nephew to exercise tact in his dealings with 'Osman Digna. 'Osman was the senior *emir* and had answered the Mahdi's call when Mahmud had still been a youth. More important, 'Osman was the only dervish general who had fought the British. He knew that direct confrontation would be suicidal, and that guerrilla tactics were the only reliable approach. This advice cut no ice with Mahmud. He had never seen British troops in action, but had no intention of taking advice from a Bejawi, even a veteran like 'Osman, who was old enough to be his father.

Mahmud cannot be blamed entirely for his refusal to listen to 'Osman. To a Baggara nomad reared on the cult of bravery, and the heroic exploits of elephant- and giraffe-hunters, 'Osman's strategy must have seemed pusillanimous and feeble. Mahmud's remark that, while the Beja might have learned how to survive, they had not learned how to defeat the enemy, hinted at cowardice. This was hardly justified – the Beja had been fighting British-led and British troops for fourteen years, with some notable successes. The British considered them among the most dangerous foes they had ever encountered.

Mahmud was a young man riding the crest of his people's supremacy, caught up in his own sense of self-importance. He would have done well to listen to the advice of both 'Abdallahi and 'Osman, but he did not. His plan was simply to tramp up the banks of the Nile with his twelve thousand Baggara and smash Kitchener at the 'Atbara. 'Osman shook his head in despair. Marching along the river would expose their men to the fire of British gunboats. In a face-off with a well-disciplined and well-armed Anglo-Egyptian army, Baggara courage alone would not prevail. 'Osman suggested that they should strike away from the Nile at 'Aliyab, and march across the desert to the 'Atbara river. This would be a tall order, but the dervishes were hardy enough to withstand a desert march, and the enemy's steamers could not touch them there. Once they hit the 'Atbara river, they could decide on the next step.

As for provisions, their warriors could live on the nuts of the *dom* palm-trees that grew on the river banks in abundance. These nuts did not form part of their normal diet, but they could be ground up and baked into a kind of bread in an emergency.

'Osman appealed to the Khalifa for his opinion, but before an answer came back from Omdurman, Mahmud was already leading his army north along the river. Harassed by steamers all the way, precisely as 'Osman had predicted, he halted at 'Aliyab, where he received a letter from the Khalifa: he should follow 'Osman's suggestion, and turn away from the Nile.

Mahmud capitulated, and ordered his force to cross the forty miles of desert between 'Aliyab and the 'Atbara. It was a crippling march. The force carried no food and little water. Hundreds of tribesmen deserted on the way. By the time the remainder reached the 'Atbara, thirty hours out of 'Aliyab, they were exhausted, starving, and dying of thirst.

Here a new dispute broke out between Mahmud and 'Osman. The old warrior suggested moving east, upriver, to his old head-quarters at Adarama. Kitchener would not be able to ignore the concentration of such a large enemy force there, and would be obliged to attack before moving on Omdurman. His battalions would have to move up the 'Atbara without gunboats in support, and could be lured into a trap.

Once again, Mahmud simply ignored 'Osman and led his troops downriver towards the Anglo-Egyptian camp. On the way, though, he lost his nerve: perhaps, having seen Kitchener's gun-boats in action, he was, after all, chary of coming too close to them. Instead of pressing through his attack, he halted at the village of Nukhayla, about thirty-five miles east of the 'Atbara–Nile confluence, and ordered his men to build a defensive position on the river's floodplain.

For the final time, 'Osman ventured to advise him. The position he had chosen was not sound. It was on low ground by the river bank, and vulnerable to fire from the rocky bluffs above. The *dom* palm-groves along the river could easily be set on fire by enemy artillery. In any case, the place itself was too near Kitchener's base. The Anglo-Egyptian force could reach them in a single night's march. Mahmud disregarded him again, and did not bother to consult the Khalifa. 'Osman must have watched Mahmud's men building their thorn-zariba and trenches, with a feeling that they were digging their own graves. It was perhaps then that he decided to take no part in the coming battle.

6

'Osman was aware, too, that Kitchener's army no longer consisted only of Egyptian and Sudanese troops. Salisbury had given the Sirdar permission to call for a British force if he felt it was needed. On New Year's Day 1898, Kitchener wired Cromer, reporting a massive dervish advance from Omdurman. 'I think British troops should be sent to Abu Hamed,' he wrote, 'and that reinforcements should be sent to Egypt . . . The fight for the Sudan would appear to be likely to take place at Berber.'[5]

Kitchener probably knew that reports of an advance by the main dervish army, sixty thousand strong, were false. In early December, 'Abdallahi had attempted to revive flagging morale in Omdurman by holding a great parade. Afterwards the army had trekked out of the town as if starting for the north, but got only a few miles before halting. This, the Khalifa explained, was a result of disputes over command. In fact, the whole parade had been a bluff. 'Abdallahi's huge force was totally immobile: Kitchener's great strength – his logistics and supply system – was the Khalifa's Achilles' heel. He was unable to support so vast an army: his supply system was non-existent. He had, in any case, long ago decided on his strategy. He had advised his cousin to withdraw to Sabaluka, but Mahmud had rejected that advice. Now, Mahmud was on his own. If he halted Kitchener's advance, well and good. If not, the Khalifa would wait for the enemy and destroy them.

Kitchener's 'spin' worked. By the end of February a British infantry brigade, moved quickly by the railway, arrived at Berber. Kitchener had learned his lesson from Wolseley, and had asked for no special troops, only solid line infantrymen – the 1st Battalion the Lincolnshire Regiment, the 1st Battalion the Royal Warwickshire Regiment, and the 1st Battalion the Cameron Highlanders. The 1st Battalion the Seaforth Highlanders were to follow.

These units had been part of the British army of occupation in Cairo, and were under the command of fifty-five-year-old Major General William Gatacre, Middlesex Regiment, a lean, thin-faced authoritarian who was universally hated. The brigade also included a Field Company of the Royal Engineers, and a Royal Artillery battery equipped with some heavy ordnance not seen previously in the Sudan – two forty-pound howitzers, designed to drop shells inside trenches and to demolish buildings. The artillery company had also brought with them six five-inch howitzers and six Maxim machine-guns.

There had been great strides forward in personal weaponry since the Gordon Relief Expedition. While the Egyptians and Sudanese troops had Martini-Henrys, the British were now equipped with the .303 calibre Lee-Metford, produced in 1888. The Lee-Metford was the first magazine-rifle ever used by the British army – instead of having to ram the shells into the chamber by hand, they were now fed in automatically by a spring-loaded magazine. The cartridges were thrust into the chamber by a breech-block operated by a hand-worked bolt, and ejected by the same method. The rate of fire was so fast that independent fire sounded like a volley of machine-guns. The smaller calibre increased both range and accuracy. The weapon had a muzzle velocity of two thousand feet per second and a maximum range of three and a half thousand yards. In practical terms this meant that at effective range its copper-nickel plated lead round would punch through a brick wall nine inches thick and would penetrate a chunk of solid oak to a depth of twenty-seven inches.

The Martini's smoke problem had also been solved. The invention by Alfred Nobel in 1892 of cordite – a combination of nitroglycerine and nitrocellulose – meant that Lee-Metford cartridges were virtually smoke-free. This had created a revolution in infantry tactics. It meant that troops could now sustain rapid, accurate fire without their vision being obscured by smoke. The rifleman could fire from cover without exposing his position to the enemy, and attackers had to advance without a smokescreen across longer fields of fire.

Kitchener had now mustered an army of fourteen thousand men – British, Egyptian and Sudanese. On hearing that Mahmud had encamped at Nukhayla on 20 March, he immediately moved the bulk of his force up the 'Atbara to Ras al-Hudi, a site shaded by *dom* palm-groves, thirteen miles short of the dervish position. He arrived there on the 21st and at 1030 hours sent his cavalry contingent – seven squadrons and a Horse Artillery battery, under Lieut. Colonel Broadwood – out to hunt dervishes.

Broadwood's squadrons limped back into camp at midnight, carrying seven wounded troopers. They had left eight dead in the field, and had lost thirteen horses. Having cleared the country twenty-two miles up the river bank, one of the squadrons had been shadowed by Baggara horse, who had followed them back to the rendezvous. They had attacked suddenly out of the thick bush on the floodplain, but the Anglo-Egyptians had fought them off. Most casualties had been sustained during the follow-up, when Broadwood's men had gone on foot into the bush to search for the Baggara, and had run into a force much larger than they had anticipated.

For more than a week, Kitchener remained at Ras al-Hudi, hoping that Mahmud would initiate the attack. He was aware that the Baggara and Beja warriors were short of food. Every day deserters arrived at his camp, many of them suffering from diarrhoea as a result of eating *dom* nuts. The Sirdar was loath to advance, knowing that starvation would gradually wear Mahmud's troops down. On the other hand, though, he did not want the enemy to escape. If Mahmud pulled out suddenly, Kitchener would look foolish. He would also have a large army behind his left flank when he moved towards Omdurman.

Every day Broadwood's cavalry patrols scoured the river bank for dervish scouts. There were some inconclusive skirmishes. In the Anglo-Egyptian camp, the infantry grew restless, waiting for the order to march. On 27 March, *Zafir*, *Nasr* and *Fateh* steamed upriver from 'Atbara camp, carrying the 15th Egyptian battalion and 150 Ja'aliyyin Friendlies. They landed at Shendi, where Mahmud had dumped all his food supplies and left a host of wives and children. The Egyptians stormed the town, and the small Baggara garrison fled. The Friendlies pursued them, killed 160, and captured 650 women and children. For the Ja'aliyyin it was sweet revenge for the massacre at Metemma.

Still, Kitchener fretted at Ras al-Hudi. Three days after the capture of Shendi, he sent Hunter up the 'Atbara with six squadrons of horse, two companies of camelry, the Horse Artillery, and the Maxims and howitzers, to make a close reconnaissance of Mahmud's zariba. Hunter returned having ridden right up to the zariba itself, without casualties. He reported that it was impregnable.

On 31 March the Sirdar assembled his staff – Hunter, Gatacre, Wingate and the brigade commanders – for a council. Gatacre was for attacking Mahmud at once. Hunter, the only one who had actually seen the zariba, advised against it. Kitchener was inclined to agree with Gatacre, but Hunter's opinion dissuaded him – Hunter had long experience in the Sudan, and was known for his aggressive style. According to the textbook, Kitchener's army was not large enough to assault a defended position – he would have required at least ten thousand more troops for that.

The next day he wired Cromer that he was 'perplexed' at Mahmud's immobility. While he had no doubt that an attack on his zariba would succeed, he was worried that it might result in a large number of casualties. Cromer wired to London for advice. At the War Office, Garnet Wolseley was astonished by Kitchener's hesitancy – it was axiomatic that the decision could only be taken by the commander on the ground. He wired back to Cromer that the best action was for the Sirdar to decide.

Impressed by the fact that Hunter had demurred, Cromer advised postponement. By the time his wire arrived, though, Kitchener had changed his mind, feeling that he could hold off no longer. His supplies were being brought up from 'Atbara camp by camel caravan, protected by a small escort of camel-corps. As a logistics expert, he was acutely aware that Mahmud's Baggara cavalry could cut his supply lines at any time. Hunter had finally come round, and agreed that action must be taken. Kitchener resolved to hit the zariba on Good Friday, 8 April.

On 5 April Hunter led another reconnaissance mission to Nukhayla, and was almost caught when Mahmud's cavalry attacked unexpectedly. Meanwhile, Kitchener's main force had left Ras al-Hudi and advanced to Umm Dabiyya, from where it could advance to Nukhayla in a few hours. On the evening of Thursday 7 April the Anglo-Egyptian army paraded ready for the attack. 'Manifestly,' wrote Cromer, the only one of the players who had been involved since the beginning, 'the curtain had gone up on the last scene of the drama, which commenced with the destruction of General Hicks's army fifteen years previously.'[6]

7

Today, the land where Mahmud's zariba stood is cultivated by local farmers, but a century ago it was a wild belt of thick acacia scrub, with the many-branched trunks of *dom* palms tilting at strange angles above the forest. Neatly ploughed furrows now stand where tangled thorn-bush once grew, and the *dom* palms are gone. Due to erosion, the level of the land has dropped by several yards, so it is no longer possible to see precisely what the Anglo-Egyptian troops saw when they appeared suddenly on the bluffs above Mahmud's zariba, just before dawn on Good Friday, 8 April 1898.

The rocky terraces were bathed in the silky light of a moon that had come up around midnight. The zariba lay in shadow, about nine hundred yards away. There was no sound from the dervish camp, and some of the British began to believe that the enemy had pulled out. 'Soon we saw large fires appear in the valley beneath us,' recalled Lieutenant R. Meiklejohn of the Warwickshire Regiment, 'and we realized the enemy were still there!'

The zariba was a rough oval, its rear edge touching the river bank and its forward edge tucked beneath the hard black cliffs of the desert. The enclosure was partly set in the acacia forest, so that only the front face was clearly exposed. It was constructed of cut thorn-bush, and was about a thousand yards in diameter, the interior being crammed with tents and huts. Inside the thorn-fence the dervishes had dug a complex system of trenches, three feet deep. Their seven artillery pieces were distributed around the perimeter, in gun-pits protected by embrasures. In the centre was a redoubt protected by a second zariba five feet high. The cliffs on the northern side ascended about two hundred feet to a treeless stony plateau, giving way to the undulating dark sarir of the Nubian desert.

The Anglo-Egyptian army had been marching much of the night in square formation. Now, orders were given and passed along in whispers. The squares began to unhitch themselves joint by joint, reforming with splendid precision into columns of assault. Soon the army was arranged in buffalo horns around the front of the dervish camp – Maxwell's Sudanese on the right, MacDonald's in the centre, and Gatacre's British brigade on the left. The Egyptian brigade under Lewis was held in reserve at the rear, protecting the transport and water. The Egyptian cavalry was drawn up far to the left, and the artillery batteries positioned on the right and in the front centre. A Maxim battery lay on the left, next to a rocket detachment commanded by Lieutenant David Beatty, RN. In front of Beatty stood Kitchener's command post under the red flag.

The Sirdar waited patiently on his horse for full daylight to come, knowing that he had reached the current climax of his career. Today, the eyes of the world would be on him. Before his men had started their night-march the previous afternoon, he had sent a message round to all units. '*The Sirdar feels absolutely certain that every man will do his duty. He has only these words to say: Remember Gordon: the men before you are his murderers.*'[7]

To the waiting men, now lying or sitting on the hard ground, it seemed for ever before the last of the darkness shredded into tears and tatters. The pre-dawn had been chillingly cold, but when the first gleam of light edged along the skyline, spirits soared. The day came awake in a surge of latent heat – plumes of fire from beyond the eastern horizon. The dark pool of night was whipped into an angry turmoil of cloud, charcoal, grey, brown, flame-red and ochre-yellow. The whirlpool of cloud itself gave way to shades of blue, as the sun spread long flame-coloured fingers across the desert and along the river bank from the east. The insubstantial forms of the ridges, the *dom* palms, and the enemy enclosure tightened gradually into focus. The day seemed to bristle with low sound – the rustle of the spiked palm-heads, the flitting of birds in the acacia scrub, the rasp of insects. Lieutenant Meiklejohn saw a huge flock of vultures rise suddenly on the left in a snap of wings. They began to circle the camp ominously. 'They had doubtless gathered for the offal from the dervish camp,' he wrote, 'but it looked as if they realized they would soon have a feast.'[8]

At first, there seemed no life or movement in the enemy camp. Then a troop of Baggara horsemen cantered out to observe the enemy, and returned. Dark heads appeared from behind the thorn-fence, then vanished again. The fires began to flicker out. The light became clearer and clearer, casting long shadows across the rocky bluffs. Still there was silence but for the snorting of horses and the shuffling of booted feet.

Kitchener's plan was simple: he would hit the zariba with every gun he had, then send his infantry in for the kill. He glanced at his watch. 0615 hours. He issued a terse instruction to the gun battery on his right. An Egyptian crew slammed a twenty-five-pound double-weight shrapnel shell into the chamber of a twelve-pounder Krupp, and snapped the breech closed. 'Fire!' came an NCO's growl. A single flat *bang* shattered the silence. The round sawed across the nine-hundred-yard gap, searing the air, smacking to land with a blinding flash and a balloon of white smoke, followed by a miasma of fine dust. The circling vultures scattered. The resounding thump of the strike came back a second later. The soldiers sitting and lying on the ridge sprang up to observe the action. Two more quick crumps followed from the right, a fleeting pall of smoke, two brilliant shellbursts in the air among the *dom* palm-fronds on the river bank. Suddenly, a salvo of rockets shrieked out hysterically. The roofs of several huts burst into flame. Then the twelve Maxims to the left began to clatter out rimfire in unison, like a percussion band.

One by one the Krupp guns came into action, until all twenty-four were whomping out in ear-splitting crescendo, wrapping the ridge with smoke and dust. Quickly the air itself was alive with whirring shells and bullets, and soon the observers could see dirt, stones, bits of trees and fragments of animal and human bodies being flung up by the strikes. 'Now and then we saw one or two dervishes walking unconcernedly about in the zariba,' Meiklejohn said, 'despite the hail of shells, and sometimes shrapnel caught them and they sank down. A camel broke loose and hobbled about. Then a shell caught it and it vanished. Once I saw a body thrown a short distance into the air by a percussion shell.'[9]

For a while there was no reply from the enemy. 'Then suddenly I saw a flash in the zariba nearly opposite me,' recalled Meiklejohn. 'A shell whined and screeched over our heads and burst nearly half a mile in the rear. The men all laughed.'[10] Suddenly a host of dervish banners appeared in the zariba, dancing and fluttering in defiance. 'Instantly a storm of shrapnel was poured into them and they collapsed.'[11] There was an audible yell from the hidden dervish gunners and riflemen. More dervish shells whistled over the massed ranks on the ridge. Almost all went high, exploding harmlessly in the desert.

A great mantle of dust lay over the zariba, and under its cover the Baggara cavalry mustered, dodging out of the zariba by a gap in the rear face, working round to the right. According to some observers, the horsemen were wearing steel helmets and chainmail, looking like 'crusader knights'. Kitchener spotted the movement, and ordered eight squadrons of cavalry to escort two Maxims to check their advance. The cavalry rode to meet them at the trot, their progress veiled from the rest of the army by the thick dust. Twice the Baggara formed up as if ready to charge, but both times they dispersed as soon as the Maxims were brought into action. The rat-tat-tat-tat of the machine-guns was all the rest of the force could hear of the engagement, but each time the guns opened fire twenty Baggara horsemen fell out of the saddle.

Kitchener's three infantry brigades – thirteen thousand men – were in formation ready for the attack. The two Sudanese brigades were deployed in line, maximizing their fire-power. The British brigade, under Gatacre, on the right, was organized into a deeper configuration. The Sirdar's plan was that the front rank would advance, firing as they came, keeping the defenders' fire down.

The front rank would tear gaps in the zariba, and more densely packed companies behind would pour through these holes, supported by the fire of their comrades, and clear the zariba methodically.

The British brigade's formation was more dense than the Sudanese, because Gatacre had over-estimated the difficulties of crossing the zariba. The Cameron Highlanders were in the front rank, followed by the Lincolnshire Regiment, the Seaforth Highlanders, and the Royal Warwicks. The Camerons were to breach the zariba, and had been issued with leather gloves, billhooks to rip apart the branches, blankets to cover the thorns, and scaling ladders, two per company. At 0740 hours, Kitchener gave the order to lift the barrage. The guns went quiet abruptly. Horses galloped up, their harness jingling, pulling rumbling carriages ready to limber up the guns.

At 0810 hours, the Sirdar ordered the advance. His bugler sounded a thin, eerie note, which was quickly taken up and repeated from bugler to bugler all along the line. The Anglo-Egyptian force tensed for action. Here was the moment they had awaited for so long.

The Sudanese bands started thrashing out a hypnotic tattoo. Among the Camerons and Seaforths, the pipers struck up a stirring haw. The drums and fifes of the Warwicks and Lincolns rattled and wheezed. Queen's colours and battle colours fluttered among the British battalions. Major General Gatacre drew his sword, and advanced on foot to the head of the Camerons' point company – perhaps the last British brigade commander ever to lead his men into battle from the front. Beside him were his staff party, his ADC, Captain Ronald Brooke of the 7th Hussars, his chief clerk, Lance Sergeant Wyeth of the Army Service Corps, carrying a huge Union Jack, and his batman, Private Cross of the Camerons. Among the Sudanese brigades, Maxwell, MacDonald and Hunter also took the lead, but remained on horseback lest they be over-taken by their lanky Dinka, Shilluk, Nuer, and Nuba troops.

The British brigade moved forward, marching in slow time and drill-square exactness, in absolute silence. The officers remained poker-faced. NCOs snapped out commands, dressing the men in line. 'The discipline and coolness,' wrote one officer, 'was such that their advance was absolutely like a drill. They began by volley firing and changed by order to independent. Their shooting was excellent – not a dervish could live above ground.'[12]

The Highlanders' kilts swung, the sun glistened on their white helmets. Behind them, in their field khaki jackets and Wolseley helmets, the Lincolns, whom Kitchener reckoned 'first rate in every way', came on with perfect discipline, carrying their weapons at the slope with fixed bayonets. 'Silently and slowly we moved forward,' said Lieutenant Meiklejohn, 'wondering when the enemy would open fire, but still ominous silence reigned.'[13]

As the Camerons edged to the right, two companies of the Warwicks doubled into line. The troops strode on across no man's land. To their left, the massed Sudanese companies were shuffling forward fast as if desperate to see the whites of their enemy's eyes. The Camerons halted and fired in section volleys, the staccato report of their Lee-Metfords clearly distinguished from the thud of the Sudanese battalions' Martini-Henrys. The whole magnificent force, drums bashing, bands crashing out, colours flying, crested the ridge above the floodplain with the sun gleaming on twelve thousand bayonets. 'On the top of the rise,' Meiklejohn said, 'the "Halt" sounded, and we opened fire, the front rank kneeling, the rear standing. There was a terrific roar of musketry as twelve thousand rifles and twelve Maxims swept the enemy position.'[14]

The invaders had approached within three hundred yards of the zariba when all hell let loose. Fire spurted all the way along the dervish defences, flashes and blobs of smoke growing in frequency as the troops closed in. 'The bullets,' wrote *Daily News* correspondent G. W. Steevens, 'swishing and lashing like rain on a pond.'[15]

Among the leading company of the Cameron Highlanders, men dropped like stones. The lines quickly closed up, and the front ranks broke into crisp independent fire. Behind them, the Seaforths could only watch and follow helplessly. '[It] was a severe trial for young soldiers,' commented one officer. 'The Camerons had the excitement of firing; we following fifty or sixty yards in rear had nothing to do except watch their men dropping, and all the bleeding and doctoring and stretcher work . . . but the men never turned a hair.'[16]

Meiklejohn thought the shrill notes of enemy musketry were birds calling. 'An angry buzz passed me rather like some huge infuriated bee,' he said. 'Yet I was so taken up directing the fire of my company that I did not grasp its significance. But a few seconds later there was a clatter, and I saw one of my company roll over on the ground . . . shouts for stretcher-bearers came from different parts of the line . . . one or two men collapsed suddenly . . .'[17]

On the British left, the 11th Sudanese battalion under Major G. W. Jackson was closing in on the Lincolns, who in turn edged nearer to the Seaforths, cramming all the British troops into a single mass. The Lincolns and Seaforths poured down a steep watercourse in two streams. 'Then we went up the sloping, gravelly ground,' wrote Sergeant Tom Christian, 'with bullets glancing in all directions, but mostly overhead, for they never thought we'd have cheek enough to come close in ten minutes – which we thought years!'[18]

The gravel spattered in all direction from ricochets, and the air was full of the same chirping whistle Meiklejohn had mistaken for birdsong – the effect of the dervishes' home-made gunpowder – and the cracks and thumps of explosive bullets. The roar of musketry was so intense at close quarters that it drowned out even the boom of the guns.

Men were still falling thickly, especially among the Highlanders. They came on, without flinching, without speeding up, without ceasing their steady loading and firing. 'Nearly every one of us thought every moment was his last,' said Bandsman Learmonth of the Seaforths, 'for there was no shelter in the least. Had they been better marksmen it would have told far more for us.'[19]

On the left, Captain Hunter-Blair of the Maxim battery was ordered to run three guns up a small rise. Blair's mules shied from the noise, and the Egyptian gunners had to drag them forward by the heads and ears. Just as they reached the rise, one mule was hit and rolled off, his legs kicking convulsively. As the gunners wheeled the weapons into place, Lieutenant Meiklejohn's company moved up to cover them. The Warwicks reached the top of the ridge under heavy fire, and Meiklejohn heard a clump and turned to find Private Power lying on his face. 'A red patch was slowly spreading on the front of his tunic and his face was dead white,' he recalled. 'He only said, "They've done for me, sir." '[20]

Meiklejohn halted his men and gave the order to fire section volleys. A troop of Baggara horse advanced to within fifteen hundred yards, but the Warwicks and the Maxim gunners hit them with a combined broadside, killing twelve men and five horses. In the exchange, Private Southall was hit in the right shoulder by a massive home-made slug that smashed his collarbone and knocked him flying. After a moment he got up, approached his officer with blood soaking his tunic, saluted with his left hand, and asked permission to retire.

Almost at the same moment, another private had his stomach blasted open and the company Quartermaster, Dixon, dragged him away on a stretcher. Bullets were pinging off the shields of the Maxims, and ricocheting around the feet of the Warwicks. A private near Meiklejohn had his rifle smashed by a bullet, but escaped without a scratch. Below them, thirty dervishes had assembled outside the zariba and looked as if they were massing for a charge. The Warwicks let loose a torrent of fire, and the Maxim stitched a pattern across the ranks, mowing them down. There were two survivors, who simply turned and strolled away. When a Maxim opened up on the first, though, he lost his disdainful attitude and began to run. A second later he was riddled with bullets and fell in a shower of blood. Quartermaster Dixon fired at the other with his pistol and missed. Meiklejohn laughed at him. Cursing angrily, Dixon fired again, this time hitting the dervish between the shoulder-blades and sending him staggering.

The Sudanese battalions broke into a charge, screaming insults at the enemy. On the left, the British units kept up their drill-like, slow advance, still firing. Major General Gatacre's standard-bearer, Sergeant Wyeth, was hit in the thigh by a bullet that burst an artery. He collapsed behind the general, his leg pumping blood.

Gatacre had no time to attend to him. He was the first to reach the zariba. As he wrenched at the branches with his own hands, a huge dervish lunged at him with a spear. 'Give him the bayonet, lad!' Gatacre growled at his batman, Private Cross of the Camerons, who slammed his sword-bayonet into the tribesman's belly.

Gatacre found that the zariba was nowhere near as difficult as he had anticipated. 'A miserable affair,' commented Meiklejohn, 'a few branches of tangled camel thorn four feet high and a few feet thick.'[21] The Highlanders were able to cross it simply by laying blankets on the thorns. The Sudanese troops were vaulting over it with their long legs. Gatacre himself hurdled the thorn-bush and entered a nightmare. Everywhere there lay the dismembered limbs and body-parts of men, women, children, camels, donkeys and horses blown to pieces by shellfire. 'There were pits full of hobbled donkeys, alive, dead and wounded,' recalled telegraph-man Lieutenant Manifold, 'camels knocked inside out; dead and wounded men with burning garments; dead and wounded women, often naked, and shattered by shot and shell.'[22] There were men inside the pits, alive and dead, who had been chained to heavy logs. *Tukuls* and tents were a blazing inferno of flame from Beatty's incendiary rockets. The *dom* palms themselves were on fire – the entire enclosure was a hell of noise and smoke. Black smoke drifted across the ranks, and the air was permeated with the stench of cordite and of charred and burning flesh.

The place was honeycombed with shelter-trenches, and beyond them was the high thorn-fence of the redoubt in which the *emir* Mahmud had holed up. Many of the Camerons had halted at the thorn-fence and were pulling it to pieces so that the following companies could get through. Others, Camerons, Seaforths, Lincolns and Warwicks, pushed on by the pressure behind them, simply smashed their way in and hurled themselves, scratched, torn and bleeding, on the dervish defenders.

Once again, it was bayonet against sword and spear. But the quality of the British bayonets had improved in the thirteen years since et-Teb and Tamaai. For long minutes there was a bloody hand-to-hand tussle inside the zariba. The attackers were streaming into it, thousands upon thousands of men, crammed shoulder to shoulder, stabbing, thrusting, firing and gouging. 'We began bayoneting right and left,' said Private Fletcher of the Camerons, 'killed everyone we came across. I shall never forget the sickening sight it made for as long as I live.'[23]

Meiklejohn leapt over the thorns to find himself crashing face-down in the dust. 'Blimey! He's copped it,' he heard a voice say. A round smacked the earth an inch from his head, and he scrambled up to see two Highlanders crouching over another officer – it was Captain Findlay, commanding C Company of the Camerons, who had been mortally wounded. Findlay had led his company to the zariba, and as he crossed had been assaulted by two dervishes. He had dropped one with his revolver, but the other had put a Remington round through his body at short range. 'Go on, my company. Never mind me,' were his last words. Findlay's fellow officer, Major Urquart, had been shot in the groin through the sporran and was also dying in agony. Another officer of the Cameron Highlanders, Captain Baillie, had his kneecap sliced off by an explosive bullet as he breasted the thorn-fence.

Meiklejohn saw a dervish Krupp with the shrapnel-riddled bodies of its crew scattered around it. There was a group of dervishes about six yards in front, standing shoulder to shoulder, the light flashing on broad-swords and spears. Hazily, he heard his men cheer. Someone shouted, 'Now you're into them, Warwick-shire lads. Stick every mother's son!' Afterwards he retained only blurred images of bayonets and swords. 'Everyone went mad,' he said.

He dimly registered a dervish in a trench drawing a bead on him with a rifle. He spun instinctively and shot at him at ten yards' range. The shot missed, kicking up a spray of dirt by the dervish's shoulder. He saw a muzzle-flash from the warrior's Remington, and a round zapped past his ear. He had taken the second pressure for another shot, when two of his men hurled themselves on the dervish like demons. They rammed him repeatedly with their sword-bayonets, until he collapsed into the trench in a bloody pulp.

The ground was so criss-crossed with trenches that many of the assault troops fell headlong into them. 'It was as good as a circus,' said Tom Christian of the Camerons. '. . . There were two small trenches that made some of us fall, and that did us a good turn, for the bullets were flying thick just there, and I'm sure many owed their lives to falling down.'[24]

Meiklejohn ran to help one man whose bayonet had been grabbed by a Baggara warrior. The dervish was trying to get out his dagger, and the two men were circling in a mad waltz. Before the lieutenant reached him, the Tommy squeezed the trigger of his Lee-Metford. The Arab was blown backwards with a black-edged hole in the front of his *jibba*. Nearby, another Arab had a Warwick on the ground by the throat. The dervish was about to plunge a knife into him, when another soldier drove his bayonet into the man's kidneys. Not far away, Pioneer Corporal Jones, the Warwicks' carpenter, a six-foot giant, was hefting the axe he had brought with him. A Baggara poked at him with a spear. Jones dodged and brought his blade down with a tree-felling blow that cleft the warrior's head in two.

Meiklejohn advanced towards a *tukul* and came across a Baggara armed with a ten-foot spear. 'He saw me and the spear flashed upwards,' he recalled, 'but I was just in time. The point of my sword caught him full in the chest, and I felt nothing till the hilt came against his ribs. Letting my revolver loose I caught his hand, for he made one supreme effort, which nearly brought us both to the ground, then crumpled up.'[25] Meiklejohn picked up the spear, and was looking at the blood on it, when a half-naked woman suddenly jumped on him wielding a dagger. He held her off with his sword until two of his men dragged her away, swearing, biting and spitting. They found her small baby not far behind her.

The dervish defenders, overwhelmed by the artillery barrage and the assault, began to give ground. 'Our fellows had revenge for Gordon right enough,' said Corporal Farquharson of the Camerons. 'Everyone . . . had to be either bayoneted or shot, and some of them got both.'[26] In the centre, the 11th Sudanese battalion came up against Mahmud's redoubt and ran smack into the *emir*'s bodyguard. A well-aimed volley crackled out at them, and ninety out of the hundred soldiers went down. The other companies quickly closed up and advanced, firing as they came. The enemy riflemen got no second chance. All were shot or bayoneted. The 11th Sudanese, closely followed by the 10th, rushed into the redoubt and found Mahmud hiding under a bed. They dragged him out and stabbed him in the leg with a bayonet. They would have killed him, had not a British officer, Major Franks of the Royal Artillery, intervened.

The Anglo-Egyptian force began to chase the dervishes towards the river. The madness inside the zariba had lasted only five minutes, but in that time the Anglo-Egyptian force had suffered four hundred casualties. The Cameron Highlanders had come off worst. They had lost fifteen men killed, and forty-five wounded, five of them mortally. Fifteen Warwicks had been injured, mostly by sword-cuts or explosive bullets. Lieutenant Meiklejohn's comrade, Lieutenant Greer, had been stabbed in the thigh and was losing blood rapidly. Three of his men were already dead. Three officers of the Lincolns were dead or dying. The Seaforths had lost Lieutenant Gore, and six other officers were badly wounded. The Sudanese brigade had lost fifty-seven men killed and 386 wounded since the order to advance.

As they passed the rifle-pits, enemy warriors sprang up and fired at their backs. The Tommies and Jocks fell on them in a frenzy of bayoneting. Bullets whined in all directions. The force had been told not to shoot inside the zariba, but most of Kitchener's men had forgotten the order. 'Their bullets, as well as the enemy's, were whistling past pretty thickly,' Meiklejohn said, 'smashing through huts, or thudding into the ground, which in places was quite slippery with blood.'[27]

The attacking force had now pressed the dervishes clear to the river bank. The troops emerged from the smoke smeared with blood and gore, bayonets dripping, faces and uniforms black with dirt and smoke. Thousands of dervishes were skedaddling across the dry river bed, which was no more than a series of muddy pools. Some were shot down as deserters by their own side. The

British began to pot the fugitives with coolly aimed shots. 'Not twenty out of a hundred reached [the opposite bank],' said Tom Christian. 'For six thousand rifles were firing at them as quick as possible.'[28] It reminded Corporal Farquharson of 'a rabbit shoot at home'.[29]

Suddenly the Egyptian cavalry thundered by at the gallop, followed by the Camel Corps, pursuing the Baggara horse, who had played no part in the battle and had withdrawn under the leadership of 'Osman Digna. He had correctly predicted the outcome of the battle. Many dervish fugitives fled up the 'Atbara towards Adarama, leaving a trail of dead and wounded. They were cut off by a force of 'Friendlies' under Major G. E. Benson of the Royal Artillery, who killed another 350 and took almost six hundred prisoners. Only about a third of the force Mahmud had led out of Metemma lived to fight again.

On the river bank the firing slowly dwindled. The 'Atbara's bed was choked with dead and dying Baggara tribesmen. Corpses lay everywhere, even in the stagnant pools, where the water was red with blood. The bugles bleated out 'Ceasefire!' Those that had watches glanced at them, and could not believe that only fifteen minutes had passed since the first shell had been fired. The men had lived a whole lifetime in that quarter-hour. Five hundred and fifty-eight of their comrades were dead or wounded. They had taken out eight thousand of the enemy. They had destroyed an army composed of Baggara tribesmen – among the most fearsome warriors in Africa. Slowly they began to sort themselves out into their original companies. The NCOs took the roll. Men thought lost reappeared out of foxholes where they had fallen, grinning from blood-spattered faces.

There was a sudden hush as Kitchener rode down the reforming lines. The soldiers, black, white and brown, waved their bloody helmets and tarbooshes, and cheered for a solid five minutes. The Sirdar, prince of the stiff upper lip, the man they called the 'Sudan Machine', had tears streaming down his granite-like cheeks. 'He was,' commented one officer, 'quite human for a quarter of an hour.'[30] Kitchener's great gambit had come off. All the effort, the planning, the endless labour, the endless discussions, the countless telegrams, the unending obstacles, had been worth it. All had been pushed through by the will and determination of one man, and by the true grit, loyalty, dedication, courage and professionalism of the ordinary fighting soldier – British, Egyptian and Sudanese. As Kitchener himself told Wolseley a few months later, with characteristic modesty, 'I had such good men under me it would have been difficult to go wrong.'[31]

As he rode back across the field with Hunter, an officer cantered up with the news of Mahmud's capture. They turned and saw a group of Sudanese troops of the 10th Battalion marching up a tall, shaven-headed, sullen young man in an ornately patched *jibba*. He was limping and his garment was soaked with blood from his bayonet-wound. His hands were tied behind his back. As the two generals approached, he scowled at them. 'This is the Sirdar!' Hunter told him in Arabic. Mahmud scowled again. Kitchener told him to sit, and Mahmud sat down cross-legged. At the time this was interpreted as defiance – the vanquished customarily knelt – but it may have been simply because he was in agony from his untreated wound. 'Why have you come into my country to burn and pillage?' Kitchener demanded in Arabic.

'I must obey the Khalifa's orders, as you must obey the Khedive's,' he answered. It was a good answer, as Kitchener commented, but hardly the complete truth. If Mahmud had followed the Khalifa's advice, he would have now been at Sabaluka, still resisting Kitchener's advance.

Mahmud had been a victim of his own arrogance, as well as the indiscipline of his nomad troops. As the Sudanese riflemen dragged him away, though, he had a parting shot to fire at Kitchener. 'You will pay for all this at Omdurman,' he shouted. 'Compared with the Khalifa, I am but a leaf!'[32]

8

After taking Khartoum back in 1885, many of the *Ashraf* – the Mahdi's relatives – had occupied houses there. On the Mahdi's death, though, the Khalifa, fearing that it would become a focus of opposition, had visited Khartoum at the head of a detachment of Baggara horse, and ordered the town evacuated. A year later, after the Khalifa Mohammad ash-Sharif's coup attempt, 'Abdallahi had enforced this order, moving everyone across the river to Omdurman. Khartoum had been a ghost town ever since.

By 1898 Omdurman was a walled city, much larger than the small village it had been in Gordon's time, but still only a tiny fraction of the size it is today. Little remains of that town but the evocative names of its various quarters – *Mulazimin, bayt al-mal* – a stone archway, some earthworks, the Mahdi's tomb and the Khalifa's house. The earthworks are the relics of six forts 'Abdallahi had built on the banks of the Nile, facing Tuti island, as emplacements for his artillery. There were also forts on Tuti itself and on the east bank of the Nile, so that any gunboats cruising up to shell the town could be bombarded from both sides.

To the north of the town walls, two roads forked through a vast sprawl of mud huts and *tukuls* where the bulk of the dervish army was housed. Further north, the Omdurman road crossed two large khors – both of them now almost lost in the urban jungle. The first, Khor Shambat, drained water from the west in the rainy season: the second, Khor Abu Sunt, took its water from Jabal Surkab (known to the British as Jabal Surgham), a lone knoll – more of a rock pimple than a mountain – standing in the middle of Kerrari plain. A long sand-ridge ran west from the slopes of Surkab, high enough to conceal an army from view. North of the sand-ridge, Kerrari was a vast expanse of flat red ochre soil, sparsely scattered with acacia trees, bounded to the east by the river, and to the north by a labyrinth of low granite peaks and ridges 250 feet high, known as the Kerrari hills. The village of al-'Ijayja stood on the river bank, just to the south of the hills.

Inside the walled town of Omdurman stood the Khalifa's house, a stone's throw from the silver-capped *gubba* of the Mahdi's tomb, backing on to a large parade ground where 'Abdallahi regularly reviewed his troops. The house – later rebuilt as a museum – is a rambling structure of kiln-baked mud brick, opening from a small courtyard: a warren of connected rooms and staircases, containing the Khalifa's private retreat, his harem, and bathrooms with running water. The house had, by 1898, become 'Abdallahi's sanctum. Apart from his wives and concubines, only his half-brother Ya'gub was allowed past the inner court.

After his capture, Mahmud spread the rumour that the Khalifa's army at Omdurman was a hundred and seventy-five thousand strong. Though in reality it may not have been much larger than forty thousand, it was still a considerable force, and 'Abdallahi's options were limited by practical considerations. The near starvation of Mahmud's men had shown the difficulty of supplying a dervish army on the move. Beyond the Sabaluka gorge, the Khalifa no longer enjoyed the overwhelming support of the local population – indeed, the powerful Ja'aliyyin had joined the enemy. Any move along the river would expose his men to demoralizing fire from Kitchener's gunboat flotilla.

A month after the defeat of Mahmud, 'Abdallahi held a council at his house. Among the notables present were 'Osman Digna, who had come in with a force of Beja about seven hundred strong, and the Khalifa Mohammad Sharif, whom 'Abdallahi had paroled from prison. Also in attendance were 'Osman Azraq, who had escaped Kitchener at Firka by diving into the Nile, and Mohammad wad Bishara, the former dervish governor of Dongola.

The Khalifa seemed distracted and preoccupied, and gazed blankly into the middle distance. When Mohammad Sharif claimed that the Mahdi had told him in a vision that he should advance north and occupy the Sabaluka gorge, 'Abdallahi snapped back, 'When we want your opinion, we'll ask for it.'[33] 'Osman Digna agreed that Sabaluka would be a strategically sound site for a stand. He was supported by Ibrahim al-Khalil, 'Abdallahi's cousin and a brother of Mahmud, who was currently the commander of the Kara garrison, a division of the Green Standard, based in Omdurman.

'Abdallahi endorsed the council's decision to build forts at Sabaluka, but remained secretly unconvinced. He had long ago chosen the site for his showdown with the 'Turks'. The Mahdi had once prophesied that a large force of infidels would be defeated on the plain of Kerrari, north of Omdurman. This would be a doubly fitting battlefield, because it lay near the village where Mohammad Ahmad had grown up. 'Abdallahi's strategy had always been to draw the invaders in until their lines of communication were over-stretched. Then, when they were cut off, hungry, thirsty, afraid and far from home, the massed dervish army would come in for the *coup de grâce*. In his heart, he never lost his conviction that it was at Kerrari that the last great battle would be fought.

Apart from marching out to meet the invaders, 'Abdallahi had two options. He could withdraw back to the safety of Kordofan, or he could remain inside the walled city and fight the enemy street by street. Retreat had some supporters, but to the Khalifa it was a non-starter. It would imply defeat, not least because it meant abandoning the Mahdi's tomb. A nomad from the *goz*, 'Abdallahi personally found the idea of burying holy men under ornate domes distasteful, but he was aware of the tomb's powerful political and religious symbolism: it was no coincidence that he had built his house almost in its shadow. As for fighting in the streets, this was not the Baggara way. Born on the open *goz*, the cattle-nomads were used to vast free panoramas, and felt hemmed in and claustrophobic in city streets.

'When intractable desires are thwarted by reality,' the psychologist Norman Dixon has written, 'there is a tendency to hark back to the memory of earlier gratifications.'[34] The defeat of Hicks at Shaykan, which had delivered the Sudan into Mahdist hands, was just such a gratification for 'Abdallahi. The pattern of its success was engraved indelibly on his mind. He would repeat this success by luring the enemy into his selected killing-ground at Kerrari.

Here, his riflemen, the *Mulazimin*, commanded by his son, Shaykh ad-Din, would act the part Abu Anja's Jihadiyya had played against Hicks. They would break down the enemy's resistance by constant fire, preparing them for a heart-stopping rush by the Black Standard division under his half-brother, Ya'gub.

In his determination to recreate the conditions of Shaykan, 'Abdallahi overlooked the shortcomings of his chosen battlefield. Denied water, Hicks's column had been dying of thirst. Kitchener's army would be fighting with their backs to the Nile, their access to water guaranteed by a squadron of gunboats bristling with ordnance. The dense forest that had hidden the Jihadiyya from Hicks's column did not exist at Kerrari, and it was going to be difficult for the Khalifa's riflemen to get into position in the face of Kitchener's long-range guns.

'Abdallahi ignored all these considerations and placed his faith in God and the undoubted courage of his warriors. He sought no less than the utter destruction of Kitchener's force – a massacre as complete as that of Shaykan. This was to be no street skirmish, but Armageddon: the final showdown between the 'red-faced infidels' and the forces of the righteous. Despite the superior fire-power of the Anglo-Egyptian army, his confidence was not entirely un-founded. If the dervishes managed to engage the enemy in hand-to-hand combat, as they had at Abu Tulayh, the battle could go either way.

In his base at 'Atbara, Herbert Kitchener was perfectly aware of this. His goal was in sight and he did not intend to squander the years of preparation. His advance on Omdurman would be supported by a flotilla of ten gunboats and five steamers, armed to the teeth. As the steamers would not be able to pass through the Sabaluka gorge before August, when the Nile began to rise, this ruled out any move before the following September. Four months in their summer quarters at Darmali, near the mouth of the 'Atbara, proved more deadly to the British than dervish bullets. By August there were fifty new graves in the cemetery there.

The railway reached 'Atbara on 3 July 1898. It soon began to ferry up reinforcements and new matériel for Kitchener's army. Among the first consignments were sections for three new gun-boats, *Melik*, *Sheikh* and *Sultan*. These pocket steamers would be assembled at the Nile-side workshops at 'Abadiyya. They were not paddle-steamers, but modern twin-screw armour-plated boats, each carrying five or six heavy guns and four Maxims.

The railway brought a fourth Egyptian brigade under Lieut. Colonel John Collinson of the Northamptonshire Regiment, a former battalion commander who had fought at Firka and the 'Atbara. A second British brigade also arrived, with four infantry battalions, the Grenadier Guards, the Lancashire Fusiliers, the Northumberland Fusiliers, and the 2nd Battalion the Rifle Brigade. The British contingent, commanded by Brigadier Neville Lyttel-ton of the Rifle Brigade, brought with it more tons of fearsome weaponry. This included nine-pounder field-guns, five-inch how-itzers, two giant forty-pounder guns manned by the Royal Garri-son Artillery, and two Maxim batteries, manned by gunners from both the Royal Artillery and the Royal Irish Fusiliers. There was also a British cavalry unit, the 21st Lancers − actually the 21st Hussars renamed and armed with lances.

William Gatacre was given command of both British brigades, and handed his first brigade over to Brigadier Andrew Wauchope of the Black Watch, who had fought previously with Graham in the eastern Sudan.

Apart from Collinson's 4th Egyptian Brigade, Kitchener had also increased his Egyptian contingent by two camel-corps com-panies, a squadron of cavalry, and the Ja'aliyyin Friendlies, now 2,500 strong, commanded by Major Eddie Stuart-Wortley, the officer who had run the gauntlet of dervish guns at Wadi Habeshi in 1885.

Like the Gordon Relief Expedition thirteen years earlier, the final phase of Kitchener's long advance attracted the attention of the great and noble, and many socially connected officers clam-oured for inclusion in the campaign. Among them were Frederick Roberts, the son of Wolseley's great rival, Lord Roberts; Prince Francis of Teck, brother of the Duchess of York; and Prince

Christian Victor, the Queen's grandson. Another would-be recruit was the son of the late Lord Randolph Churchill, a former Leader of the House of Commons and Chancellor of the Exchequer, who, as opposition spokesman back in 1884, had accused Gladstone of abandoning Gordon. His name was Winston Spencer Churchill.

The man who would become the leading statesman of the twentieth century, and the single most famous Englishman who ever lived, was then twenty-three years old and a second lieutenant in the 4th Hussars. He had had a somewhat traumatic childhood. His father, who had died of syphilis two years earlier, had suggested that he join the army simply because he thought his son too stupid to sit for the Bar examination.

It had taken Churchill three attempts to pass the same Sandhurst entry examination Garnet Wolseley had polished off first time at sixteen, while working in a surveyor's office. Yet despite his supposed 'stupidity', Churchill – a future recipient of the Nobel Prize for Literature – had an unusually adept mastery of the spoken and written word. He had sponsored his military adventures by obtaining commissions for books and articles. He had already managed to wangle himself on active service in India and South Africa, largely by manipulating social connections, and saw no reason why he should not do the same in the Sudan. Kitchener disagreed, and rejected his application. The Sirdar disliked 'medal hunters' who tried to get in through the back door, as much as he detested journalists. In spite of personal appeals by Lady Churchill, a close acquaintance of Kitchener's, and even by the Prime Minister, Lord Salisbury himself, the Sirdar was adamant that he would not have Lieutenant Winston Churchill in his army. Privately, Churchill commented that Kitchener was 'no gentleman'. It was only when Major General Sir Evelyn Wood, currently Adjutant General, grew tired of Kitchener's 'picking and choosing' of officers recommended by the War Office, that the situation changed. Kitchener, Wood said, was Sirdar of the Egyptian army, but not the ultimate authority with regard to the British contingent. Without the Sirdar's approval, therefore, Churchill was attached as a supernumerary subaltern to the 21st Lancers and ordered to report to Abbassiyya barracks in Cairo. He embarked on a train for Marseilles a few days later, armed with a Mauser semi-automatic pistol he had bought in London, and a commission for a series of letters from the *Morning Post*.

On 23 August, Churchill arrived with his squadron at Kitchener's forward base at Wadi Hamed, a little to the south of Wadi Habeshi, where in 1885 the gunboat *Safia* had fought a duel with dervish guns. The long journey from Cairo had not been a happy one for the 21st Lancers. Confined to railway trucks for almost two continuous weeks, the regiment's horses – mostly small Syrian chargers – had lost condition, and more than fifty had had to be destroyed. One man had already died from heat exhaustion, and three others had been evacuated. On a personal level, Churchill found himself treated as an outsider by the other officers, who disdained his status as a freelance journalist, and regarded him as little more than a 'spy'.

Now he and his troopers were lost amid the bustle of almost twenty thousand British and Egyptian troops, scurrying to get ready for the two-hundred-mile push to the south. The entire force was concentrated along a strip of river bank two miles in length, protected on the desert side by a strong zariba. The advance began three days later from a forward base established opposite Jabal Royan, south of the Sabaluka gorge. Kitchener's army moved down the western bank of the Nile on a broad front, ready to assume fighting formation as soon as the enemy were spotted. It was a magnificent sight. 'In the clear air the amazing detail of the picture was displayed,' Churchill wrote. 'There were six brigades composed of twenty-four battalions; yet every battalion showed that it was made up of tiny figures, all perfectly defined on the plain. The cavalry, starting later, rode through the army . . . and the impression of straight lines and clean-cut blocks of men of varied race and different uniform, yet all clothed in the brown colours of field service, and all looking over the plain with interested and confident eyes, was one not to be forgotten . . .'[35]

The last clash of dervish and 'red-faced infidel' was about to begin.

9

At 1140 hours on 1 September, Kitchener was on the Kerrari plain, about seven miles north of Omdurman. The purple crusts of the Kerrari hills lay to his right and the cluster of mud houses at al-'Ijayja stood on the river behind him. Riding ahead of a party of staff officers, his intention was to ascend Jabal Surkab (Surgham) to have his first look at the enemy.

Less than an hour earlier, he had occupied al-'Ijayja. Now, five of his six infantry brigades were forming a vast protective semi-circle around the village, and were throwing up a zariba to defend the masses of artillery mules and 2,300 transport camels drawn up inside. The sixth brigade – Collinson's 4th Egyptians – were bivouacked in the centre as a reserve.

Behind the village the Nile ran high, steel grey in the noon sun, and resonant with the chugging of paddle-steamers, towing dozens of *nuggars*. From seven miles upstream came the boom and thump of guns. For fifty minutes Kitchener's armoured steamers had been destroying forts, dismembering batteries, and whacking gaps out of the walls of Omdurman. The whump of fifteen-pound shells was followed by the crackle of machine-gun fire. Further upriver, men of the 37th Field Battery, Royal Artillery, were winching their howitzers ashore through the mud of the east bank, having tried unsuccessfully to land on Tuti. They were about to christen their high-tech fifty-pound Lyddite shells – never before used in battle – by lobbing them into the belly of Omdurman.

Kitchener's big question had been whether the dervishes would march out, or would remain in Omdurman and fight in the streets – a thorny option from his point of view. His gunboats and howitzers were capable of razing the town to the ground, but that would mean a massacre of civilians, and would not necessarily wipe out the Khalifa's force. Rudolf von Slatin, Wingate's DAAG of Intelligence, riding with the Sirdar's staff, had impressed on Kitchener the psychological benefit of wrecking the Mahdi's tomb – a powerful rallying signal to the enemy. The Sirdar had tasked the howitzer battery first with punching out the tomb, and second, with making the streets of Omdurman an unsafe refuge for dervish fighters.

The dervishes, though, were not the kind to wait for the enemy to attack. They had begun to pour forth from the town the previous morning, twenty-four hours before the bombardment had started. The first to spot them had been the Egyptian cavalry under Robert Broadwood. At about 1100 hours on 1 September, Broadwood, commanding seventeen squadrons of cavalry and Camel Corps, had crested the sandy ridge west of Jabal Surkab and seen what appeared to be a dark discoloration hanging in the desert on the far side of the Khor Shambat, three miles to the south. Beyond this dark stain he could clearly see the maze of mud-brick houses standing north of Omdurman, and beyond them the city, with the dome of the Mahdi's tomb peeking over the walls.

Nearer to the river, Lieut. Colonel Rowland Martin, commanding the 21st Lancers, had seen the same dense black line about four miles to the south. He and his men had taken it for a zariba or a thorn forest, defended by a few white spots he thought were the enemy. At about 1105 hours, though, the 'zariba' suddenly began to move. Martin realized with a shock that it was the front line of the dervish army, the rest of which had been concealed in dead ground by the same sand-ridge Broadwood had just crossed.

As the dervishes approached, wave upon wave appeared suddenly from behind the khor, until the whole plain seemed black with them. Estimates of their numbers, which had begun with no more than three thousand, increased rapidly from fifteen thousand to twenty thousand, then to thirty and forty thousand. They were advancing quickly at a trot, a thousand banners flying amid their ranks, and mail-clad, helmeted horsemen frolicking to and fro. As they came nearer, the Lancer squadrons heard the crescendo of drums and horns, and – even more ominously – the mesmerizing chant of '*La ilaha illa-llah*' delivered from so many throats that it sounded to the British scouts like the roar of surf on the sea-shore.

Broadwood's squadrons began to beat a hasty retreat as Baggara outriders came near. The Camel Corps in particular was hampered by the slippery ground, damp after the rain. Captain Douglas Haig – a future field marshal, commanding an Egyptian cavalry squadron – ordered his men to dismount and cover the camel-men's retreat. Presently, the Camel Corps reached firmer ground, and the riders whipped their mounts into a gangly-legged trot, leaving their pursuers behind.

Rowland Martin of the 21st Lancers had climbed to the peak of Jabal Surkab, and from the heliograph station set up there by his signals section had had a message flashed to the Sirdar in al-'Ijayja. 'Dervish army coming out of Omdurman in battle array, estimated 35,000 advancing NORTH.' Kitchener, who had received the message sitting on a mud-brick wall in the village, eating a plate of bully beef and pickles, had been unperturbed. Only after he had finished his lunch had he set out to view the advance.

At a quarter to twelve, as Kitchener neared Surkab, a rider approached – a subaltern in the uniform of the Lancers, khaki drill peppered with ochre dust. He drew his horse alongside the Sirdar, a respectable distance to the rear. The officer was young. He had a pudgy face and a rather impertinent expression accentuated by his service helmet, which was pulled down to shadow his eyes. He saluted smartly. 'Sir,' he said. 'I have come from the 21st Lancers with a report.' The Sirdar nodded. 'The enemy are in sight,' the subaltern continued, 'apparently in large numbers. Their main body lies about seven miles away almost directly between our present position and the city of Omdurman. Up to 1100 hours they remained stationary, but at 1105 hours they were seen in motion. When I left forty minutes ago they were still advancing rapidly.'

Kitchener listened carefully as the two horses crunched forward through the sand, still wet after the rain. He reflected for what seemed like a long time, while the subaltern, somewhat overawed, studied the heavy moustaches, the cheeks burned raw by the sun, and the strange cast of his eyes. Finally, the Sirdar asked. 'How long do you think I've got?'

'You have at least an hour,' the officer replied smoothly. 'Probably an hour and a half, even if they come on at their present rate.'

Kitchener gave no sign that he accepted the estimate, but merely bowed slightly to dismiss the scout. Neither did he give any intimation that he had recognized him: his informant was none other than Second Lieutenant Winston Spencer Churchill, with the 21st Lancers, the man whose application to join the force Kitchener had rejected out of hand. Churchill had been half expecting him to demand, 'What the devil are you doing here?' Whether or not the Sirdar did recognize him will never be known.

Minutes later, Kitchener stood on a ridge of Surkab among the Lancers' signal section, where a rare photograph captured his image for posterity, spruce in his tight-fitting tunic, drill breeches, high boots and service helmet, pointing out enemy dispositions to his ADC. When he returned to the village Archie Hunter, who had been left to organize its defence, rode out to meet him. Hunter thought he looked worried, 'as if he had seen a ghost'. In fact, Kitchener was simply engaged: he was hoping that the enemy would attack that day, and that it would all be over by nightfall.

At 1400 hours he ordered the Anglo-Egyptian brigades to advance five hundred yards outside the zariba they had constructed, ready to take on the enemy. Colour Sergeant Edward Fraley of the Rifle Brigade recalled that his unit had been in camp only an hour when the order came. 'Of course we guessed something was up,' he wrote. 'I suppose we went about a mile or so perhaps less and then we formed up in line . . . well we heard they were coming on and stuck there for some time but they did not come . . .'[36]

In fact, only minutes after the Anglo-Egyptian battalions had marched out, pickets of the 21st Lancers out on the sand-ridge six miles away had been astonished to see the entire dervish army halt as if on a single command. The warriors let out a deafening roar of '*Allahu akbar*' ('God is great') and the *Mulazimin* fired their rifles into the air. The dervishes then lay down on the wet sand, and soon a galaxy of fires leapt up amongst them. There would be no battle that day.

The only fighting, indeed, was taking place on the east bank of the Nile, where Eddie Stuart-Wortley had been landed with his three thousand Friendlies, to take out dervish forts. While some of the tribes in Stuart-Wortley's company baulked at hand-to-hand fighting and simply fired their rifles into the air, the Ja'aliyyin, still driven on by the sacred urge for revenge, fought magnificently. They captured the main dervish headquarters on the east bank, killing 350 of the Khalifa's troops, losing sixty-five of their own men. The dervish survivors were dragged to the water's edge. There they were butchered mercilessly by the Ja'aliyyin in payback for the thousands of their fellow tribesmen Mahmud had left dead on the streets of Metemma.

On the west side of the Nile, news of the enemy's halt suggested strongly that they were preparing for a night attack – the one thing Kitchener feared. In the darkness the superiority of his weapons would be lost. Even with the powerful spotlights deployed by the gunboats behind him, and flares fired by the Royal Engineers, visibility would be no more than four hundred yards. This would be far too near for comfort with warriors as fast and courageous as the dervishes, who would close with them in under a minute. Bullet wounds would not stop them. If they managed to engage the Anglo-Egyptians at close quarters, then the issue would be decided by cold steel. 'The consequences of the line being penetrated in the darkness were appalling to think of,' wrote Churchill, '. . . a multitude of fierce swordsmen would surge through the gap, cutting and slashing at every living thing . . . regiments and brigades would shift for themselves and fire savagely on all sides, slaying alike friend and foe . . . only a few thousand . . . demoralized men would escape . . .'[37] Churchill's rather alarmist view was not shared by everyone: many British officers present believed that, though casualties might have been much higher if it came to a hand-to-hand clash, their dogged British, Sudanese and Egyptian troops would have held as steady as the men at Abu Tulayh, and given a good account of themselves.

If Kitchener feared a night attack, though, he did not show it. He could have ordered his troops to dig shelter-trenches, deployed them in a solid mass four deep, occupied the buildings of al-'Ijayja and set his guns in strong emplacements, but he did none of these things. In fact, while the Egyptian and Sudanese battalions under Hunter dug shallow trenches, the British brigades under Gatacre merely lay behind their thorn zariba. Kitchener kept them in open order, two deep, relying on the fire-power of the Lee-Metford, and the support of his Maxims and quick-firing artillery.

The afternoon was scorchingly hot. The sky was lucid, but the air was muggy at ground level as the sun vaporized the moisture from the night's rain. From their lying-up place the dervishes could see the lines of British and Egyptian cavalrymen watching them from the ridges of Surkab, and among the sandhills. More patrols of Baggara horse bounded forwards to scare off the silent watchers, but found them resolute – three Baggara skirmishers were killed and nine wounded. Corporal Harris of the 21st Lancers was wounded and his horse shot from under him.

The sound of the howitzers could be heard from the scouts' position. Some minutes after three, seven fifty-pound shells fired in succession with incredible accuracy smacked gaping holes in the three-foot-thick cupola of the Mahdi's tomb. The *gubba* was covered in dust and smoke for what seemed like hours. When the dust cleared, it became apparent that the top of the dome had been sliced flat like a decapitated egg. The British and Egyptian cavalry cheered. An awkward hush fell among the dervish ranks. The Khalifa 'Abdallahi, looking on from his command post in the Khor Shambat, cried, '*La hawa wa la guwa illa billah!* [There is no power and no might except in God!] They do not fear God, but have destroyed the *gubba*!'

He had soon recovered from the shock sufficiently to inform his warriors, 'We built the tomb with mud, and with mud we will rebuild it.' When a riderless horse passed through the dervish ranks, though, it caused more disquiet. The previous day the Khalifa had declared that the Prophet Mohammad would ride before them on horseback, leading the same host of avenging angels that had aided them at Shaykan. The riderless horse seemed a cruel parody of that vision.

The dervishes did not attack that night. After sunset, 'Abdallahi set up his tent in the Khor Shambat, arranged a number of *angarebs*, ordered tea, and called his counsellors to a meeting. 'Osman Digna, Ibrahim al-Khalil and 'Osman Azraq all argued that they should fall on the enemy by night. The idea was opposed by 'Abdallahi's son, Shaykh ad-Din, who voiced the Khalifa's own fears that at night the commanders would lose control of their *rub 's* (battalions). Some would desert. Others would wander off in the wrong direction.

The only major night attack the dervishes had pulled off successfully was the assault on Khartoum, thirteen years earlier. That had been an attack on starving, demoralized and poorly equipped Egyptian soldiers – a very different kind of operation from one against a well-armed enemy in the field. Shaykh ad-Din was also aware that the rifles of his fifteen-thousand-strong *Mulazimin* would be ineffective in the dark. 'Let us attack in the morning after dawn prayers,' he concluded. 'Let us not be like mice or foxes slinking into their holes by day and peeping out at night.'[38]

Many have commented on the Khalifa's lack of strategic ability, but few have understood that all military activity is decided more by cultural standards than by logic. In any case, in the absence of radio communications, controlling even the most disciplined of troops at night was almost impossible. Even the British, though they had conducted night-marches successfully, hardly ever attacked before first light. The idea was to approach by stealth, then launch an all-out frontal attack as soon as it was light enough to see, firing so rapidly that the defenders were obliged to remain in cover until the last ferocious rush with bayonets fixed.

It has become customary to mock the rigid formations British and British-led troops then adopted: their lack of facility for blending in with the landscape, crawling, jumping, rolling and hiding, in the modern manner. This is to overlook the fact that, in this vanished era, the sight of a rigidly disciplined army in immaculate uniform, carrying out drill movements with machine-like precision, and advancing slowly and inexorably under withering fire, was its own defence. It was a great deal more impressive and awe-inspiring to the enemy than that of soldiers who 'hid' in the bushes, or fired 'cowering' behind trees. In those days – except in special circumstances – strong men fought in the open and in the light: an axiom that Shaykh ad-Din's reference to 'mice and foxes' makes clear.

Kitchener and his intelligence officer, Wingate, did not, however, intend to leave the matter entirely to chance. After dark, Wingate's deputy, Slatin, approached a group of villagers in al-'Ijayja and told them in strict confidence that the Sirdar intended to attack the dervish army that night. In case the news did not filter through to the Khalifa, he dispatched two of his own spies to the enemy lines to spread the same story. Finally, when the gunboats returned from pounding Omdurman, Kitchener gave orders that their spotlights should be trained on the approaches to his zariba. The gunboats had to remain in midstream because of the threat from snipers, and the range of the lights was limited, but their unfamiliarity had a demoralizing effect on the enemy. The Khalifa himself was told that the British were 'watching' him, and promptly had his conspicuous tent pulled down.

'Stand to' bugles sounded at 0430 hours, and were joined by the clash of snare-drums, the whistle of fifes and the blare of trumpets. The Anglo–Egyptian infantry, most of whom had not slept, formed up, shivering, and loaded their rifles. Once again it had rained heavily in the night, and they were soaked through. Kitchener was expecting an attack at about 0530 hours. The Lancers saddled their horses and cleaned their carbines in lamplight. If the enemy did not appear by dawn, they were to deploy as reconnaissance patrols on Kerrari plain. The cavalrymen ate a breakfast of porridge, hard tack biscuits and bully beef, then stood silently by their mounts. 'Each man [had] his private thoughts,' wrote Corporal Wade Rix of the 21st, 'knowing that out there in the desert thousands of Dervishes fired with religious fervour were about to descend on us, their determined aim being literally to cut us to pieces.'[39]

By the time the Lancer regiment and the Egyptian cavalry left the zariba at 0520 hours the dervish army, hidden behind Jabal Surkab, was already on the move. It was one of the last medieval armies ever mustered on the field – at least forty thousand warriors, but perhaps more than fifty thousand – armed mostly with double-edged 'crusader' swords, straight daggers in arm-sheaths, elephant and rhino-hide shields, javelins and broad-bladed fighting spears, clad in the patched *jibba*, baggy *sirwal* and headcloths of the dervish devotee. Many were barefoot, moving at a jog-trot behind their *emirs*, some of whom were mounted on Arab ponies and wearing chainmail and steel helmets. Green, black, yellow and white banners fluttered and streamed from amid the ranks. As they moved, loose-limbed and lithe across the flat red sand, they chanted the full-throated hypnotic mantra that had bound Muslim armies together for centuries, '*La ilaha illa-llah*' . . . 'There is no god but Allah' – 'a tremendous roar,' one eye-witness observed, '. . . in waves of intense sound, like the tumult of the rising wind and sea before a storm'.[40]

The dervish front extended no less than five miles across the plain. On the far left was the Green Standard division, in three sections, commanded respectively by the Khalifa 'Ali wad Helu of the Dighaym – who had been with the Mahdi from the very beginning – by 'Abdallahi's son, Shaykh ad-Din, and by the truculent Baggara warrior 'Osman Azraq. These three sections, numbering about twenty-two thousand men, and including ten thousand *Mulazimin* armed with Remingtons, advanced past Jabal Surkab directly towards the Kerrari hills.

To the right of their line two groups peeled off. The smaller – about seven hundred Beja under 'Osman Digna – occupied the eastern end of the Khor Abu Sunt, to prevent enemy detachments from moving along the road into Omdurman. The larger, the White Standard division (actually the Kara garrison from Omdurman – there was no official 'White' standard) – four thousand men, under 'Abdallahi's cousin Ibrahim al-Khalil – made for the eastern side of Jabal Surkab before turning directly towards Kitchener's zariba at al-'Ijayja.

The Khalifa, who had declared on waking that he had seen both the Mahdi and the Prophet Mohammad in a vision, foretold a great victory. Anyone who died on the field of Kerrari, he declared, would go directly to paradise. Mounted on a large white Nubian donkey, he now rode forward at the head of his thousand-man bodyguard, followed by the Black Standard division under his brother Ya'gub. The Black Standard, twelve thousand strong, were to be held in reserve, to deliver the *coup de grâce* to the stricken enemy.

Many have claimed that 'Abdallahi was certain of victory, but it is impossible to know how confident he really was. On one hand, the Khalifa undoubtedly believed that God was on his side. His warriors were brave beyond question, and they were the cream of a nation – tall, powerful, strong and fast. They outnumbered the enemy, and they believed they could win in an honourable fight. Their morale was high. They were not cowed by the enemy's superior weapons, because they were blissfully ignorant of their power, and they sincerely believed that the 'Turks' they were up against were timid and cowardly folk.

On the other hand, the defeat of his cousin Mahmud back in April had clearly unnerved him, as had the power of the Lyddite shells fired at Omdurman the previous day, and the destruction of the Mahdi's tomb. Once he had made the decision to attack, though, he ignored what he did not wish to see and held on to the Mahdi's prophecy of victory, and the memory of that glorious day in 1883, when an army of tribesmen had wiped out Hicks.

As the light slowly thickened, Winston Churchill, commanding one of two Lancer vedettes sent to observe the enemy from the ridges of Surkab, gasped in astonishment. 'There in the plain lay the enemy,' he wrote, 'their numbers unaltered, their confidence and intentions apparently unshaken . . . great masses of men joined together by thinner lines. Behind and to the flanks were large reserves. From where I stood they looked dark blurs and streaks, relieved and diversified by an odd-looking shimmer of light from their spear-points.' Churchill penned a dispatch to the Sirdar, marked XXX for extreme urgency. 'The Dervish army is still in position a mile and a half southwest of Jabal Surgham (*sic*).'[41]

The sun rose at 0550 hours, a play of golden light probing in tentacles through a dense sheen of cloud. It was only then that the Lancer observation posts on Surkab realized that the enemy were actually moving – and moving fast. It was like a tide coming in. As the dervish masses advanced, patrols of Baggara cavalry romped forward to reconnoitre Surkab. Though Churchill's patrol and that of his comrade Lieutenant Robert Smythe were concealed among the rocks, a war correspondent – probably the ill-fated Hubert Howard of *The Times* – riding towards them was spotted by the Baggara, who opened fire with their Remingtons. 'Bullets whistling and splashing on rocks very close,' wrote Smythe. '[Colonel Martin] hearing this sends for me to retire at once . . . much excited and annoyed, and very fussy and saying I was unnecessarily exposing myself . . . It was the correspondent's fault . . . and after all it was only one private and myself, no great loss if we had been hit . . .'[42]

As the dervish masses rolled past the Lancers' position on the hill, the right flank under 'Osman Azraq began to wheel towards al-'Ijayja, and to fan out in a vast semi-circle ready to attack the zariba. The Kara men – the White Standard – to the south of Surkab swarmed over its lower slopes to threaten the Anglo-Egyptian left. The rest of the Green Standard, though, continued directly towards the Kerrari hills, where Broadwood's Egyptian cavalry and Camel Corps had taken up their positions. The Khalifa's last scouts had withdrawn the previous day, and the fact that he divided his forces suggests that he believed the main enemy position lay to the north.

Churchill's patrol charged down to the sand-ridge they had occupied the previous day, where they dismounted and lay in the path of the vast juggernaut. When the Khalifa's men were only four hundred yards away, Churchill had four troopers open up just for the hell of it – and to fire the first British shots of the battle. Rifle-fire crackled back, kicking up dust, and Churchill and his men scrambled to their horses. They were soon back on the slope of Surkab, where at one point White Standard troops passed only three hundred yards from them.

They were again spotted, but despite sporadic fire, Churchill decided to stay put. An order had come back from Kitchener instructing the Lancers to remain out as long as they could, and in any case, he knew something the dervishes did not. The moment they topped the ridge hiding them from the zariba, the gunboats and field batteries would open up. Churchill waited tensely, 'fascinated by the impending horror. I could see it coming. In a few seconds swift destruction would rush on these brave men.'[43]

He was distracted by two low crumps of cannon-fire from amid the dervish centre, now moving towards the zariba. To his surprise, the dervish guns had opened up first. Through his glasses he saw two puffs of smoke hanging in the air among the dark ranks of the enemy, and two canopies of dust leap up fifty yards short of the zariba. It looked as if the Khalifa's men had thrown down the gauntlet, Churchill thought, and moments later it was taken up by the Anglo-Egyptian artillery: white smoke spattered out all along the front of the zariba, the boom of the salvoes sounding to Churchill like distant thunder. He saw shell-bursts erupt over the heads of the advancing dervishes, and observed matchstick brown bodies dotting the red ground.

On his right, the Kara troops suddenly crested the ridge and let off their rifles, with a roaring invocation to God and the Prophet. At that moment, Churchill was alarmed to see a single Lancer officer, Lieutenant Connolly, galloping across their front only a hundred yards away. For a moment there was an ominous hiatus. Then the scene dissolved into chaos. Shells whistled and roared around them, smashing into the front ranks and bursting into shards of shrapnel over their heads. In seconds, the whole position was awash with flame, dust and smoke, and deadly cocktails of flying rocks, splinters and steel debris. Churchill, who was near enough to see the faces of the dervish warriors, estimated that twenty shells hit them in the first sixty seconds.

A mile and a half away, at al-'Ijayja, Lieutenant R. Meiklejohn of the Royal Warwicks, who had fought at Mahmud's zariba, had watched the Lancers scrambling up the hill and had heard the rapid fire as the dervishes shot at them. When two of their scouts had arrived with the news that the dervish army was on the move, he recalled, everyone was relieved that the waiting was over. The troops fell in quickly, eating a snatched breakfast as they trimmed the zariba. 'We had finished off our work,' Meiklejohn wrote, 'when suddenly a subdued, but general, exclamation of surprise made us look up. We saw a really wonderful sight. All along the crests of the high ground to our right front a regular forest seemed to be springing up, which resolved into a dense mass of banners. Then a solid black multitude of men began to appear for over two miles all along the crest line, in considerable depth, while we heard distant shouts and war cries. Soon after another mass appeared all over [Surkab] ridge, and along the British front, but these hung back a little as if waiting for the rest of the mighty army to come into line.'[44]

Gatacre's British brigades held the left of the zariba, and Hunter's Egyptian–Sudanese brigades the right. The British troops were stood to behind their thorn-fence, two ranks deep, with fixed bayonets, the front rank kneeling, the rear rank standing. Kitchener, seeing where the first thrust of the enemy would fall, paced up to the left of the zariba on his horse, and took up a position behind the men of the British 2nd Brigade, under Lyttelton. For the Rifle Battalion, the Lancashire and Northumberland Fusiliers, and the Grenadier Guards, it was their first sight of the dervishes in action.

To their right, facing 'Osman Azraq's men, were the veterans of Mahmud's zariba – the British 1st Brigade under Wauchope – the Seaforths and Camerons, the Lincolns and the Royal Warwicks. To their right stood Maxwell's 2nd Egyptian Brigade, with Mac-Donald's 1st Brigade to his right, and nearest to the Nile, Taffy Lewis's 3rd Brigade. Collinson's 4th Brigade was still in reserve.

As the dervishes wheeled into line, Meiklejohn saw his adjutant, Earle, galloping along the lines. 'Get into your places please, gentle-men,' he bawled. 'The show is starting!' The enemy were three thousand yards away when the artillery opened up on them. 'We were almost startled,' Meiklejohn recalled. 'The first shell burst a little short, but the second fell amongst them. Then the gunboats joined in, and white puffs of shrapnel showed up all over the enemy mass, while columns of dust indicated common shell. The enemy appeared to take no notice, except perhaps a slight quickening of pace ... one almost felt that nothing could stem the onslaught.'[45]

Out on Jabal Surkab, Winston Churchill had already snubbed one order from his CO to retire and was now dangerously near to the killing-ground of his own side's guns. His retreat would soon be cut off. When a second terse dispatch arrived ordering him back to the zariba, he told his men to mount. They trotted and cantered back towards al-'Ijayja, as shells from the gunboats' fifteen-pounders screeched over their heads, reducing the position they had just occupied to a cauldron of fire and dust.

The Lancers dismounted at the southern end of the zariba, and another of their officers, Captain E. F. Eadon, turned to watch the great masses of the enemy coming on. It was, he recalled, 'too magnificent for words – reckless in its bravery and devoid of all tactics. To hear the hum and cries and beating of drums of 30,000 men [sic], who could be seen slowly advancing, was as magnificent a spectacle as could be imagined ... I could see the shells dropping into their dense masses and killing heaps at a shot, but they still advanced.'[46]

Kitchener watched Ibrahim al-Khalil's division come on until it was within two thousand yards. It was Private Parragreen of the Grenadier Guards who fired the infantry's first bullet – a ranging shot for the rest of his battalion. The .303 round whistled unheard amid the cacophony of artillery fire, quickly followed by a louder roar as the Grenadiers let rip with company volleys. Great spurts of flame erupted from the massed ranks of 2 Brigade. Moments later 1 Brigade joined in, then Maxwell's 2nd Egyptian Brigade. 'A volume of fire burst out from the whole length of the zariba,' wrote Meiklejohn. 'Continual repetition on my part of the words of command "Ready" – "Present" – "Fire" – "Ready" in this rhythm, only varied by a shortening range ... The brunt of the attack seemed to be falling on the Lincolns and Sudanese on our right, but a huge mass were streaming down the slopes of our fire. I could see little trace of "sand spirits" from bullets in front of them, so concluded our elevation was correct, yet it seemed almost as if nothing could stop them.'[47]

Though the British riflemen were firing magazine-fed Lee-Metfords, in company volleys they used their weapons as breech-loaders, thrusting cartridges into the chamber one by one. Fingers shoved brass into breeches and worked bolts with the precision of automata. Officers snapped 'Fire!' twelve times a minute, until they were hoarse. The dervishes faced an impenetrable wall of fire, more daunting than any zariba – the thunder and shock of musketry, artillery and machine-gun fire alone was sickening. The British fired their Lee-Metfords so fast that they became too hot to hold and had to be swapped with those of the reserve behind them. The water in the Maxim barrels boiled and evaporated.

The flower of a generation was advancing on the invaders' position. The British, Egyptian and Sudanese soldiers played their part perfectly, but the dervishes, as Cromer later wrote, were 'beyond perfection'. It was truly the best and bravest army the British ever faced in north Africa, an army of warriors who had thrown to the wind every military complication but the core qualities of courage and determination. The future of a nation depended upon them, and they were ready to die in its defence.

Their losses were terrible. Whole families, whole clans, of tribesmen were swept away like chaff. Men fell, their bodies mangled, torn and shattered. The warriors closed the gaps and stormed forward shoulder to shoulder towards the fearsome dragon of fire. As one line vanished another leapt into its place, until it too was whipped to shreds by the merciless lash of shot and shell.

For a moment it seemed to the Anglo–Egyptian soldiers that the dervishes were invulnerable. But it was an illusion. They were flesh and blood, and nothing mortal could penetrate that concentration of fire. 'No European,' wrote Corporal Skinner of the 21st Lancers, 'would ever think of facing it the way these daring fanatics did.'[48] 'There is no doubt,' wrote Colour Sergeant Fraley of the Rifle Brigade,' . . . the Dervishes are very brave – to stick it like they did was wonderful . . . for a few paces [one group of dervishes] came on carrying a banner. First one dropped, then the fellow carrying the flag, another picked it up and still came on, when the two left almost dropped together, they marched straight to death right enough.'[49]

The Maxims, said Fraley, did 'awful execution'. The Maxim detachment of the Irish Fusiliers nearest to him held fire until the enemy were seven hundred yards away. 'Now!' the officer in charge yelled. 'Traversing fire begin.' The deadly weapons stitched left and right across the advancing ranks. The dervishes, wrote Fraley, 'simply fell down in a line, just the same as if they had been told to lie down, some of the bodies they saw afterwards had been hit with bullets five and six times in a line across their bodies before they fell.'[50]

But few dervishes got nearer than eight hundred yards. At some point it began to dawn on a critical mass of warriors that further advance was impossible. Step by step, their momentum ran out. Everywhere they were slowing down. Barked orders from their *emirs* were no longer heeded. The ground was strewn with dead in heaps, 'like snowdrifts', as Churchill commented. The commander of the main assault force, 'Osman Azraq, tried to shift the focus of the attack away from the deadly .303 Lee-Metfords to the Egyptian Brigades on the right, who were armed with the slower and shorter-range Martini-Henrys. It was too late. All around him, his assault force was breaking up into fragments, dissolving into the desert. The core of his army had simply ceased to exist.

Seeing all was lost, 'Osman Azraq mustered five hundred Baggara cavalry. He drew his sword, and took his position in front of them. Then, with his green standard flowing behind him, he led his horsemen directly towards a Maxim battery in the middle of the enemy zariba. It was, commented Meiklejohn, 'a most gallant attempt'. 'A murderous concentrated fire was turned on them,' he wrote, 'and they were literally mown down, yet they never faltered riding straight for us with wild cries and brandished weapons. A handful got within three hundred yards of us and I saw one solitary figure charging, so it seemed, our whole army single-handed for a few seconds, till horse and man collapsed in a heap.'[51] 'Osman himself got no nearer than four hundred yards, when he was hit in the thigh. He fell from his horse and was splattered by five or six more rounds as he crashed to the ground.

It was about 7.40 in the morning, only fifty minutes since the dervishes had come in sight of Kitchener's men. 'By now the dervishes were retiring everywhere,' wrote Meiklejohn, 'and the firing slackened . . . We got out the best company marksmen . . . and picked off most of them. One man refused to retire, but kept on firing at us till three of us gave him a kind of volley, when he fell.'[52]

The firing thinned out and stopped as the Anglo-Egyptian army surveyed the dreadful carnage they had delivered. The dervishes had sustained at least two thousand dead, and four thousand wounded, the Anglo-Egyptians less than a hundred casualties. Bodies littered the battlefield in piles – dead and wounded showing every horror gunshots could inflict. Dervishes were crawling away, blinded by the blood in their eyes, dragging shattered arms and the stumps of legs. Everywhere, injured warriors were throwing down their weapons, and trying to carry off those more dreadfully wounded than themselves. In the zariba a sense of both awe and pity enveloped the watching soldiers. Every man was aware consciously or unconsciously that he had witnessed something unique: the breathtaking courage of a people ready to die to maintain their own traditions against the encroachment of the technological world. No one there would ever see such a sight again. The battle was not yet over, but the heart of the dervish army had been ripped out – the last great hope of the Mahdiyya lay in the dust on Kerrari field, where, thirteen years earlier, the sage Mohammad Ahmad had predicted a great victory against the infidel.

10

In the Kerrari hills to the north, the rest of the Green Standard was fighting a running battle with Broadwood's Egyptian cavalry, Camel Corps and Horse Artillery. Broadwood withdrew and led the enemy on a 'wild goose chase' for three miles through the hills, before slipping back to the river bank, where his retreat was covered by the British gunboat *Melik*.

The Khalifa's Black Standard reserve was still in place behind Jabal Surkab. Kitchener could not see it, but calculated that it had not yet come into action. Any pursuit of the enemy, he reckoned, would come into contact with these fresh troops. The quickest way to Omdurman was to move east of Jabal Surkab, parallel to the Nile. At about 0730 hours, before the firing had ceased, the Sirdar had dispatched the 21st Lancers to the eastern side of Surkab to find out which way the enemy was retreating, and to spy out a clear route to Omdurman. If the way was open, the infantry would follow.

The Lancers' four squadrons surged towards the hill en masse, and from the ridge saw a long column of wounded dervishes trailing back towards the town. It was, thought Winston Churchill, commanding the second troop from the rear, clearly the occasion for a charge. 'That was the one idea that had been in all minds since we left Cairo,' he wrote. 'Of course there would be a charge. In those days, before the Boer War, British cavalry had been taught little else.'[53] The regiment dismounted in the hollow behind a hill five hundred yards east of Surkab, and awaited orders. The army was already advancing from al-'Ijayja – the British 1st and 2nd Brigades and the Egyptian 1st and 3rd Brigades were wheeling left directly towards Omdurman. Only Hector MacDonald's 2nd Egyptian Brigade would follow the retreating enemy to the west.

At 0830 hours precisely the Sirdar ordered Rowland Martin, commanding the Lancers, to harass the enemy on the left flank and try to cut them off from Omdurman. The dispatch reached Martin minutes later. He ordered his regiment to mount, and moved them forwards at a walk in 'column of troops' – sixteen troops of twenty to twenty-five men, one troop behind the other. Martin also sent out two patrols under Lieutenants A. M. Pirie and Robert Grenfell to scout ahead. Grenfell's patrol rode west of the ridge to look for the dervish reserve. Pirie's rode south, parallel with the Omdurman road, and after about a mile spotted a force of what he estimated to be about a thousand dervishes, blocking his path.

These were 'Osman Digna's Beja tribesmen, occupying the end of Khor Abu Sunt, where they had been sent early that morning to prevent just such a threat to Omdurman as the Lancers now presented. Almost all of them belonged to the ferocious Hadden-dowa tribe – the shock-haired spearmen and swordsmen who had massacred Baker's troops at the first et-Teb. Thirty-one of them had Remington rifles. Although Pirie could see the Haddendowa clearly enough to make a rough estimate of their number, he was not aware that a relatively deep watercourse lay concealed behind them. At exactly 0900 hours, Pirie's patrol returned to the main body of the Lancers to report.

Four of Kitchener's five brigades were now coming up behind them, and it was imperative for the cavalry to clear this last obstacle out of the way. The Lancers numbered about 440 men in all. The Beja outnumbered them more than two to one, but this was not a formidable ratio for mounted men against infantry. Pirie's report to Martin, however, stated that the enemy were standing on 'open ground'. Martin ordered his regiment to trot, and headed them south towards the Beja force.

Twenty minutes after Pirie had turned back, the Lancers came in sight of the Haddendowa, standing on a small ridge. Martin thought they numbered no more than three hundred, but probably believed that the remainder were hidden behind the ridge. What he did not know was that, in the short time that had elapsed since they had first been spotted, the cunning 'Osman Digna had prepared his last little surprise. He had reinforced his Beja with two thousand Baggara spearmen, who had moved into position from the slopes of Surkab, concealed inside the wadi. The Lancers now faced a force that outnumbered them by almost six to one, concealed in a deep watercourse that they would not see until it was too late. They were walking into a trap.

Martin turned the horsemen to the east, as if to outflank the enemy, riding across their face at about three hundred yards. Suddenly the riflemen among the Beja opened fire. 'We were in the lull of battle and there was complete silence,' Winston Churchill recalled. 'Forthwith from every blue-black blob [i.e. the enemy] came a white puff of smoke, and a loud volley of musketry broke the odd stillness.'[54] The range was short, and some of the dervish bullets went home. Along the line of jingling troopers, horses bolted and men fell. Martin was debating whether to continue his plan to outflank the enemy, when Lieutenant the Honourable Raymond de Montmorency, riding with B Squadron, blurted out, 'Why the blazes don't we charge those buggers before they shoot us down!'[55] Whether it was this that goaded Martin into changing his plan, or whether he had already decided, cannot be known. Whatever the case, seconds later, Martin ordered the bugler, Sergeant Knight, to sound, '*Right wheel into line.*' According to Winston Churchill, this was the first and last order given.

The whole regiment – all sixteen troops – turned neatly to face the knot of Beja on the ridge three hundred yards away. Martin spurred his horse on and led his men from the centre, thirty yards in front. Looking back, he saw his massed ranks of horsemen, helmets cocked across their eyes, lance-tips and sabres gleaming, leap forward at the gallop, into what would be the last regimental cavalry charge in British military history.

The little Syrian mounts thundered across the red ground. Most of the officers held their swords aloft. Martin himself drew neither sword nor pistol, and one of his squadron seconds-in-command, Captain Paul Kenna, of B Squadron, carried a lance. Churchill, riding a grey Arab polo-pony, spent the first few seconds sheathing his sword, drawing his Mauser from its wooden holster, and cocking it. He had long ago decided that because of an old shoulder injury, he would be better off using a pistol in hand-to-hand fighting. By the time he looked up, the enemy were only a hundred yards away – crouching figures, firing frantically, wreathed in smoke. To his left and right, he saw his fellow cavalrymen spread out in a fine line. Lances were angled low in the '*engage infantry*' position, and the horses going at a fast but steady gallop. Private A. Hewitt of B Squadron thought the pace perfect. 'It would have taken something rather solid to stop us,' he recalled.

Then, at only fifty yards, the scene was transformed. 'The blue-black men were still firing,' Churchill recalled, 'but behind them there now came into view a depression like a shallow, sunken road. This was crowded and crammed with men rising up from the ground where they had hidden. Bright flags appeared as if by magic . . . the Dervishes appeared to be ten or twelve deep at the thickest, a great grey mass gleaming with steel, filling the dry watercourse.'[56]

To Churchill's left, Raymond de Montmorency with B Squadron had a vivid impression of the enemy. 'Just before we hit them,' he said, 'I saw straight in front of me a khor with rocks on either side filled with a dense mass of Dervishes packed around three flags, yelling defiance at us, waving their spears and swords and firing their Remingtons, and amid the smoke and waving arms I could see their upturned faces grinning hate, defiance and satisfaction at us.'[57] Every man among the Lancers knew at that moment that they had ridden into a trap. The watercourse could not be jumped, but there was now no turning back. They were committed. The only effect of this revelation was that the men increased their pace to gain the momentum to carry them through. On the right flank, Churchill and his comrade Lieutenant Frederick Wormald curved their troops in slightly to take on the enemy left flank.

Seconds later, 440 British horsemen slammed into the dervish line at twenty miles an hour, with a mass of two hundred tons. The shock was tremendous. Most of the two hundred odd Beja standing on the lip of the khor were sent crashing into it or flying into the air, knocked senseless or impaled on the nine-foot lances. The Lancers let out a spontaneous roar. The dervishes screamed '*Allahu Akhbar!*' The wadi was four or five feet deep, and in a moment the Lancers' mounts were leaping into it. 'I checked my pony as the ground began to fall away beneath his feet,' Churchill wrote. 'The clever animal dropped like a cat . . . on to the sandy bed of the watercourse, and . . . I found myself surrounded by what seemed to be dozens of men.'[58]

Corporal Wade Rix of A Squadron remembered spearing a dervish in the left eye as his mount vaulted into the khor. 'The enormous impact and the weight of the man's body shattered the lance,' he wrote, 'and I cast the broken pieces from me. I quickly drew my sword just in time as another man pointed his flintlock, I struck him down and blood spattered his white robe. Then it was parry and thrust as I drove my horse through the mêlée.'[59]

For many seconds after the impact the whole battlefield became eerily silent. Time slowed to a snail's-pace crawl. For the Lancers, riding high on adrenalin, it was impossible to take it all in. Some later had no memory at all of what had happened. Actions immediately around them seemed ponderously slow, yet so inevitable that there was no time to feel real fear. The whole struggling, yelling, hacking, slashing mêlée seemed for a frozen moment like a silent circus act with a predetermined conclusion. 'The whole scene flickered exactly like a cinematograph picture,' Churchill recalled. '. . . I remember no sound: the whole event seemed to pass in absolute silence. The yells of the enemy, the shouts of the soldiers, the firing of many shots, the clashing of sword and spear, were unnoticed by the senses, unregistered by the brain.'[60] He had a fleeting impression of confusion: 'Terrified horses wedged in the crowd; bruised and shaken men, sprawling in heaps, struggled, dazed and stupid, to their feet, panted, and looked around them. Several troopers even had time to remount.'[61]

Churchill had hit the left flank, where the dervishes were scattered. Further to his left, where they were more densely packed, horses had been hamstrung by swords and knives as they jumped, or disembowelled by razor-sharp spears. Some chargers landed badly, stumbled and rolled, hurling their riders into the enemy. The troopers were at once set upon by swarms of dervishes, gaunt men in loincloths with mutton-greased mops of hair, who stabbed at their chests or hacked at their heads and necks. Others were dragged out of the saddle and shot or mutilated by the enemy. They fought back even when they were disarmed: Lancer and dervish locked together with their bare hands, rolling in the dust, gouging at each other's eyes and tearing at each other's throats.

Many troopers who remained seated skewered their opponents with their lances, only to find, as Rix had, that the shafts snapped in half, or the blades could not be withdrawn. They were obliged to abandon them and draw their sabres – a difficult cross-body action on a bucking horse with dervish warriors screaming death on all sides. Above the whinny of horses and the roar of the wounded and dying came the clash of steel on steel as the horsemen parried sword-blades and spearheads. Often the Haddendowa's heavy broad-swords shattered the lighter cavalry sabres and continued through to slice flesh. The dervishes sawed reins, girths and stirrup-leathers with their daggers. Pistol and rifle shots cracked out and buzzed among the heaving horde.

Colonel Martin, who had been first into the khor, had a lucky escape when his horse tottered and fell forward on its head. Dervish blades flashed towards him, but Martin managed to stay in the saddle and get his mount up and out of the converging crowd. His second-in-command, Major W. G. Crole-Wyndham, made a better landing, but just as he hit the wadi bed his charger was shot at point-blank range. It staggered a few yards then keeled over, giving Wyndham a chance to draw his Mauser pistol. With his sabre in one hand and his pistol in the other, he faced the dervish mass, ready to die. As the warriors surrounded him, Captain Paul Kenna, the lance-toting 2i/c of B Squadron, dashed past and pulled him bodily into the saddle. Kenna, who had left his lance stuck in a dervish body, was now armed with a revolver, which he emptied into the swaying mass. Suddenly his horse foundered under the weight. Both men slithered off, blasting off rounds at the enemy until they were separated in the throng.

Robert Grenfell's B Squadron troop, on Churchill's left, had been brought to a halt by the enemy, but Churchill did not see the carnage taking place there. His feeling was that the Lancers were still masters of the situation. Grenfell's own horse had been injured in the jump and threw him as it landed. He attempted to get it up, but was slashed across the back by a dervish sword, and stabbed in the wrist by a spear. As the lieutenant staggered, more black figures sprang on him for the kill, hewing his body to pieces. He died with eleven wounds to the head alone. All around him his men were being dragged down and butchered – ten of his troop were killed and eleven wounded, a casualty rate of almost a hundred per cent.

Private Thomas Byrne, riding with a B Squadron troop, was hit in the right arm by a dervish bullet before the leap into the khor, and reined in behind C Squadron, unable to use his lance. As he drew his sabre an agonizing bolt of pain shot through his arm. He landed well, and was desperately searching out a path through the enemy when he came upon Lieutenant the Honourable R. Molyneux of the Blues, attached to C Squadron, on foot. Molyneux's horse was dead, and he had a deep cut across the hand that was pumping blood. His pistol had been knocked out of his hand, and he was currently dodging the blows of the four dervish attackers who surrounded him. Molyneux called to Byrne for help. 'All right, sir, I won't leave you,' Byrne answered.

He veered round on his mount and barged straight into Molyneux's four assailants, sending them reeling. As he brought his sabre down, though, it fell from his grip. Almost at the same time, a dervish spiked him in the ribs with a spear. A stain of blood spread across the front of his jacket. As the rest of the warriors turned to deal with Byrne, Molyneux ran, scrambling out of the khor. Byrne wheeled his horse and followed, teetering in the saddle from blood-loss.

On the right of the line, Winston Churchill, with A Squadron, had bounded through the khor in seconds but found its opposite bank blocked by Haddendowa warriors. He had an impression of dervishes running to and fro. One fell down in front of him, poised with his sword for a hamstringing cut. Churchill leaned over and fired at him twice from three yards. As he straightened, he saw another dervish in front of him with a raised broad-sword. He fired his Mauser at such close range that its muzzle actually struck the man as he passed. To his left he saw a horseman in chainmail, and fired at him. The horseman turned away, but Churchill could not tell if his shot had struck home. He slowed his horse and looked about him, taking in a mass of dervishes to his left, but spotting not a single Lancer. He had a momentary but terrifying impression that he was the only survivor of the charge.

To his right, Frederick Wormald had come across a warrior whose chainmail turned his blade as he slashed at him. He reeled back, his sword badly buckled, but as the armoured fighter came in for the kill, a mounted private rode in at the gallop and speared him through the iron rings, his lance passing right through the warrior's body with the momentum of his charge. Another A Squadron officer, Lieutenant Robert Smythe, recalled fighting his way frantically through the crush. 'Am met by swordsman on foot,' he wrote. 'Cuts my right front. I guard it with sword. Next, man with fat face all in white having fired, missed me, throws up both hands. I cut him across the face. He drops. Large bearded man in blue, with two-edged sword and two hands cuts at me. Think this time I must be done for but my pace tells and my guard carries it off. Duck my head to spear thrown which just misses me . . .'[62]

On the far left, D Squadron under Captain Frederick Eadon were badly beleaguered. Sergeant Freeman was scythed across the face, the blow shearing off his nose, gouging his cheek, and almost severing his lips. Blood gushed in torrents over his khaki jacket. Nearby, Lieutenant C. S. Nesham, the youngest subaltern in the regiment, had climbed the far side of the khor when a dervish suddenly sprang up and seized his bridle. Nesham swung his sword, but another warrior cut his right hand at the wrist, almost through the bone. Two more blades slashed him simultaneously in the leg and the left shoulder. Nesham's right hand was hanging off, and his left arm paralysed. Death looked certain. A dervish grabbed his right leg and another his left and both tried to pull him back into the khor. In the process, Nesham's spurs dug accidentally into the horse's flanks, and his mount leapt forward shrieking, cantering across the flat ground to safety.

Further to his right, Thomas Byrne, losing blood from two wounds, had managed to stay on horseback, seeking out the rest of his troop. He found only Lieutenant Raymond de Montmorency and six troopers – all that was left of it. '[Byrne] was as pale as death and reeling in his saddle,' de Montmorency recalled, '. . . so I told him he might fall out, but he answered, "No, no, sir, I'm all right. Fall in No. 2 Troop – where are the devils?" '[63] De Montmorency was looking for his troop sergeant, Lance Sergeant Edward Carter, a superbly professional soldier, who he knew would have been there – something had happened to him. He turned and headed back into the khor to look for Carter and came on Crole-Wyndham, just separated from Kenna. The regimental 2i/c was running as fast as he could, with his pistol raised in his right hand. He had, incredibly, managed to fight his way out of the khor on foot, but was being chased by a Baggara horseman.

De Montmorency spurred his mount towards the dervish and, when the warrior turned tail, plugged him between the shoulders with a snap shot from his pistol. A moment later, de Montmorency had plunged back into the fray, finding a bloody jumble of mutilated bodies. The sight made him furious and he rode on swearing to himself, shooting down every dervish he came across with silent satisfaction. He could not find Carter, but instead he found the body of his friend Robert Grenfell, so badly hacked about that at first he thought it was Robert Smythe of A Squadron. Just then, he looked up and saw Paul Kenna, who had managed to remount his foundered horse, together with an NCO, Corporal Fred Swarbrick. De Montmorency called them over to help him retrieve Grenfell's body. While the two men stood guard, de Montmorency dismounted and lifted the shattered corpse on to his horse. The horse bolted, and the body fell. Swarbrick and Kenna chased it and brought it back, but by the time they arrived a hundred dervishes were closing in on them. De Montmorency made a last effort to lift the heavy body, then abandoned it and sprang on to his horse, only just in time. The three men rode off in a hail of bullets.

The dervishes pursued them out of the khor, but suddenly ran into a rattle of carbine fire. The regiment was already beginning to regroup on the far side of the wadi at about 150 yards. Survivors had dismounted and were ripping off salvoes to cover their comrades. The last men out were two troopers of B Squadron, Privates William Brown and Andrew Rowlett. Rowlett had been with Grenfell's troop, and had been unhorsed and stabbed in both arms. Brown, himself wounded, had already dragged another trooper, John Varney, to safety, and had gone back into the khor to pull Rowlett out. Brown and Rowlett emerged from the living hell at about 0930 hours, when time was beginning to flow again for the men of the 21st Lancers. Their walk through the valley of death had lasted less than two minutes. In that time, three VCs had been won – by de Montmorency, Kenna and Byrne – and seventy-one men and 119 horses wounded or killed.

11

A myth grew up that the Khalifa had actually been present to watch the fight in the Khor Abu Sunt, but this is unlikely. At 0930 hours he was still with his Black Standard division, concealed behind Jabal Surkab, debating whether or not to send them into action against Hector MacDonald's 1st Egyptian Brigade. MacDonald, holding Kitchener's right flank, had separated from the other five brigades and was marching around the western side of Surkab hill. For the past three hours 'Abdallahi had been seeing dead and dying carried back from the killing-ground in front of al-'Ijayja, and was aware that his first big gambit had failed. He had held the Black Standard in reserve to deliver the final blow to his enemies. Now, it represented the last ditch defence of the Mahdist state. MacDonald's Brigade numbered three thousand riflemen of the 2nd Egyptian battalion, and the 9th, 10th and 11th Sudanese. The Black Standard outnumbered them five to one, but consisted mostly of spearmen and swordsmen. The Khalifa's ten thousand trained riflemen – the *Mulazimin* – under his son, Shaykh ad-Din, and the Khalifa 'Ali wad Helu, had vanished hours ago into the Kerrari hills, in pursuit of Broadwood's cavalry and Camel Corps. Broadwood's brilliant strategy in leading them astray was now bearing fruit.

'Abdallahi was faced with a dilemma. Should he order his brother, Ya'gub, commanding the Black Standard, to attack at once, or should he wait for his son to return with the *Mulazimin*? He lost valuable minutes pondering this question. In the end, Ya'gub pre-empted him. Since 0900 hours, the Khalifa's half-brother and sole confidant had stood on a ridge with the sacred black flag flying behind him. Below, his division was drawn up in twenty-three ranks, amid scores of fluttering banners, across a four-thousand-yard front. He had been watching MacDonald's troops marching past north-east of him in echelons, with increasing impatience, waiting for the order from 'Abdallahi. At 0930 hours, he saw the flags of his nephew's Green Standard troops on the horizon to the north, but knew they were too far away to assist him.

Ya'gub was a scholarly man, a superb organizer and administrator, who was intensely loyal to his brother. It was the sight of the body of his cousin, Ibrahim al-Khalil – gunned down leading the White Standard in the attack on the zariba – that finally galvanized him into action. The body was being carried towards Omdurman on an *angareb*, covered in a white headcloth. On learning that it was his cousin, Ya'gub snapped. Without waiting for 'Abdallahi's orders, he leapt into the saddle and brandished his spear, bawling, '*Ansar*, look at us now! Young men like Ibrahim al-Khalil have gone to the eternal resting place. Here we are still on horseback . . . A *tebeldi* [baobab] tree has fallen. A *tebeldi* has fallen on the infidels! Raise your banners aloft and let your horses charge!'

He galloped along the front line of his army shouting crazily. 'A *tebeldi* has fallen!' and the dervishes answered by raising their spears and swords grimly. Ya'gub returned to his command post under the Black Standard, then faced directly towards MacDonald's advancing brigade and rode towards it on his charger. With a thunderous roar, and a furious fusillade of fire from their weapons, the last hope of the dervish army followed him.

MacDonald saw Ya'gub's standards before he saw the dervishes, and noticed the Khalifa's own black flag amongst them. The canny Scotsman was aware that another dervish division lay behind him, and shortly his lookouts spotted the warriors of the Green Standard in the Kerrari hills. They were two miles away, and flagging after chasing Broadwood, but MacDonald knew they would become a problem before long. He sent a dispatch rider to Taffy Lewis, commanding the 3rd Egyptian Brigade, asking him for reinforcements to watch his back. Lewis had been ordered by Kitchener to advance directly towards Omdurman, and refused. For the moment, MacDonald was on his own.

The former Highlander sergeant realized that he ran the risk of being ground between two divisions outnumbering him five to one, but resolved to deal with the situation in a calm and deliberate manner. He maintained his customary air of confidence, despite the fact that he had been kicked by a horse and was in agony with a broken foot. 'The force in front of me was a very large one,' he wrote, 'and I knew the force on my right was a very large one, so I decided to defeat if possible the nearer force before the other could join.'[64] When his leading Sudanese companies got the jitters and opened fire on the dervishes out of range, he personally rode along the front line knocking up their muzzles, exactly as he had done at Abu Hamed. This was a doubly brave act for MacDonald, who only the previous day had received a death-threat from one of his own soldiers.

MacDonald soon realized he was not entirely alone. Two companies from Maxwell's brigade, hidden on the other side of the knoll, had cleared dervishes off the heights of Surkab with the bayonet and were already sniping at Ya'gub's men. Making use of their covering fire, MacDonald ordered his artillery run out. The Egyptian crews set up their eighteen field-guns and eight Maxims methodically. The dervishes were coming on at a walk, with Ya'gub, mounted on his horse and brandishing his spear, leading from the front. MacDonald waited until they were within eleven hundred yards before ordering 'Fire!'

The earth moved under the Black Standard advance. Spouts of dust, smoke, rock splinters, and shrapnel spiralled among their ranks in deadly vortices. Maxim rounds splattered out, decimating the forward lines. Everywhere, men pitched over, mutilated by flying debris or raked with bullet wounds. The racket alone was nerve-shattering, but the dervishes kept on coming. 'Their advance was very rapid and determined,' MacDonald said later, 'and though they appeared to be mowed down by the artillery and Maxims they still pressed on in such numbers and so quickly that I brought up the infantry in line with the guns.'[65]

Kitchener, riding with Maxwell's brigade, could not see the Black Standard but heard the roar of gunfire from beyond the hill. Peering through his field-glasses, he observed that MacDonald had run out his artillery and was deploying his infantry in line. A moment later the Black Standard itself came into view, its fifteen thousand warriors moving with the same jaunty man-eating confidence the Green and White Standards had displayed earlier that morning. Kitchener had found the missing part of his jigsaw. At once he began frantically moving his brigades about like chess-pieces, sending Wauchope's 1st British Brigade – Highlanders, Warwicks and Lincolns – and Taffy Lewis's 3rd Egyptian Brigade into line to present a more continuous front. Broadwood's Camel Corps raced up on MacDonald's right, and Maxwell's and Lyttelton's brigades pressed west over the slopes of Surkab.

Shortly, Lyttelton's 32nd Battery, Royal Artillery, arrived at a breathless gallop with their mules and began to unpack their fifteen-pounders and Maxims on the western slope of Surkab. Within minutes the field-guns were pounding Ya'gub's right flank, and the Maxims spitting lead. An artillery subaltern even had two Maxims hauled up to the very summit of the knoll, from where they dropped scorching fire on the enemy from an elevation of 328 feet. The Black Standard's right flank withered under the onslaught and simply faded away. The whole vast arena west of the hill was littered with a mass of dead and dying men. Thousands of dervishes, realizing that the battle was lost, turned tail and headed back towards Omdurman.

The rest of Ya'gub's command, though, still threatened Mac-Donald's Egyptians and Sudanese. 'In spite of the hail of lead now poured at effective ranges into their dense masses,' MacDonald recalled, 'they still pressed forward in the most gallant manner.'[66] Then, as the dervish vanguard arrived within four hundred yards, the Martini-Henrys of the Sudanese and Egyptian infantrymen came into their own. Exposed in the middle of a coverless plain, these troops, many of whom had fought at Firka, Abu Hamed, and the 'Atbara, stood their ground against the vast throng bearing down on them. Their world went silent. There was nothing but the incessant, all-pervading ritual of loading, aiming and firing. They were shooting independently, without orders, but their fire became a continuous tempest roar. The Egyptian gun-crews began to load case-shot, slapping round after round into chambers. Within the last few minutes, MacDonald's eighteen guns hit the Black Standard with no less than 450 shells.

The dervishes were living a torment of searing flame and thunderous noise that no human being could have stood for long. Yet they refused to retreat. Six hundred yards from the maw of MacDonald's steadfast Sudanese rifles, Ya'gub himself was punched by a surge of Maxim fire. He fell from the saddle and was already dead when he hit the ground. Two Baggara horsemen dismounted to pick up his body but were quickly blasted off their feet. Every dervish who tried to shift their dead leader bit the dust. Furious, Baggara cavalry rushed the Sudanese line, screaming revenge. Most were brought down by coolly aimed shots before they got within a hundred yards, but a handful succeeded in getting right up to the line, and hurling their spears among the black troops.

Retreating dervishes rallied round the black flag, but were mown down in dozens. When Kitchener rode down from the slopes of Surkab with his staff, the Khalifa's dark banner was flying over a domain of devastation – a hundred dead and two hundred wounded lay around it in swaths of blood. No sooner had the Sirdar's men seized the black flag than a galloper reined in his horse and delivered alarming news. The Green Standard, fifteen thousand strong, was falling on MacDonald's brigade from the north.

Quickly, Kitchener dispatched the nearest British battalion, the Lincolns, to MacDonald's aid. The crack unit of the 1st British Brigade, renowned for their marksmanship, sprinted off at the double, growing tinier and tinier as they were devoured by the colossal scale of Kerrari plain.

MacDonald's 10th and 11th Sudanese and 2nd Egyptian battalions were still facing the warriors of the Black Standard in line, with the 9th Sudanese in column, in reserve. As the enemy began to melt away, MacDonald realized that his men were coming under enfilade fire from Shaykh ad-Din's *Mulazimin* riflemen, now moving up fast on his right. His front-line battalions were facing the wrong way, and for a moment it seemed that his men would be taken from the rear by the vast new horde of dervishes rushing on through the dust and smoke.

This was the critical moment of the entire battle. MacDonald knew it, but never lost his nerve. As soon he was sure the Black Standard had lost its momentum he transferred the 11th Sudanese and a gun battery to the new front. The 9th Sudanese, until now in reserve, wheeled from column into line on the right without orders. MacDonald now had two battalions facing each side. The Green Standard were coming on at a pace, firing their Remingtons rapidly. Among MacDonald's ranks, men dropped like flies. A hundred and twenty riflemen were killed and wounded in these first minutes alone, and the casualty rate among the artillerymen ramped up.

Aware that once the dervish mass closed with his men there would be a massacre, MacDonald never wavered. He was watching the last thrust of the Black Standard attack as closely as a hawk. A moment later, when he judged it had failed completely, he switched the 10th Sudanese and another battery to the new line, and ordered the 2nd Egyptians to wheel diagonally to their right, so that his brigade now formed an L shape, with the long side facing the warriors charging from the north. As smoke billowed around him, and bullets whipped overhead, MacDonald remained cool enough to call the officers of the 9th Sudanese and give them a rocket for moving without orders. 'I want your movements and behaviour just as they would be on the training ground,' he told the CO, Major C. F. Walter of the Lancashire Fusiliers.

The three Sudanese battalions in the long arm faced their enemy countrymen with resolution. Their firing, though, was wild. The troops blasted away without restraint, until their rifles were hot and their ammunition exhausted. In minutes they were calling for more rounds, which their officers doled out in twos and threes in an attempt to steady them. Shells and Maxim rounds erupted from the batteries, but the Green Standard horde came nearer and nearer. Soon, the Sudanese battalions were down to three bullets each, and the men – hardy Nuba, Dinka, Shilluk and Nuer – readied themselves to give the dervishes a greeting of cold steel. The Green Standard loomed over the tiny brigade like a tidal wave over a drifting boat. The leading dervishes were already within a hundred yards, and it seemed that nothing could prevent a clash.

It was at this precise moment that the men of the Lincolnshire Regiment sprinted up out of the desert, carrying their rifles at the trail. The Sudanese soldiers, seeing them, let out long hoots of welcome like Red Indian cries. The leading company of the Lincolns, under Captain R. P. Maxwell, formed up on the right. Winded from their run across the desert, they controlled their breathing for a moment, then started up with independent fire. They fired with such accuracy that the van of the Green Standard vanished. Bloody corpses and wounded hit the earth. After two minutes, when the whole battalion was in place, the order to cease independent fire was given. The Lee-Metfords went silent as the rest of the dark mass came on. 'Ready – Present – FIRE!' came the orders. Company volleys seared across the open ground, adding to the blast of the Maxims, field-guns and Martini-Henrys. The shooting was fast and fearful, and within minutes every man in the Lincolns had blatted out an average of sixty rounds. The whooping dervishes among the Green Standard faltered, then checked their advance. Then they turned and made off. The men facing them,

British and Sudanese, were few in number, but fierce and dogged, and their armaments were lethal.

Suddenly, when all looked finished, an array of four hundred Baggara horse broke from the faltering ranks in a chilling, suicidal rush. It was the Mahdiyya's last valiant gasp. The Baggara were far from the rolling grasslands of their beloved *goz*, far from their water-pools, their giraffe and elephant hunts, and their 'silver with hair'. They burst into a gallop at five hundred yards – some carried *shalagais*, others rode to certain death with no weapon at all. The Sudanese battalions fired. Death rolled over the horsemen like a tide. Not a single cavalryman reached the ranks of MacDonald's wedge of fighting men.

Kitchener's entire advance force of five brigades, with all his artillery, had now formed an extended line, about two miles long. The dervishes – Black and Green Standards – were withdrawing into the desert. The Egyptian cavalry under Broadwood formed up on the right ready to give chase. All along the line, firing dropped to a few half-hearted rounds, then stopped altogether. Of the vast dervish army that had massed at first light that morning, nearly eleven thousand were dead and sixteen thousand wounded. The corpses, scattered and in piles, some smoking from gunshot wounds, were almost as many as those of Hicks's column at Shaykan, a decade and a half earlier. The Mahdist state that had effectively come into being on that day had now ceased to exist. At 1130 hours, Major General Sir Herbert Kitchener, Royal Engineers, Sirdar of the Egyptian army, put down his field-glasses. The faintest flicker of a smile showed on the normally deadpan face. 'I think the enemy have had a good dusting,' he said.

12

'Abdallahi wad Torshayn had not remained on the field to witness the end of his army, and the end of his regime. He had known before the Black Standard moved that everything was lost. When the news of his brother Ya'gub's death was brought to him, though, he was staggered. From this point on he took no further interest in the battle. He wanted to remain on the field and await death, sitting on his *furwa*, or saddle-fleece, in the traditional Sudanese manner. He might have done so, had not 'Osman Digna, the eternal survivor, turned up at the command post and had him lifted on to his white Nubian donkey. 'This is not the end,' the veteran warrior told him. 'One day you and I will die on horseback, but it is no use waiting here on your *furwa*.'[67]

'Osman Digna walked with him until he joined the great column making their way back to Omdurman, lost amongst them, another faceless defeated man.

'Abdallahi was praying inside the remains of the Mahdi's tomb when he received word that Kitchener had entered the city. Hardly a single building remained untouched by the gunboats' shelling, which had not yet ceased. Everywhere there were dead and dismembered animals and people – everywhere lay the stench of death. 'Abdallahi emerged from the tomb with the same stupefied expression that he had worn since hearing of his brother's death, but was now lucid enough to order a general evacuation to the west.

The Sirdar did not arrive at 'Abdallahi's house until after dark, and by that time the Khalifa had flown. It was here that Kitchener came as close to death as he had ever been on the campaign, when a shell fired by a gunboat on the Nile burst overhead, raining down shrapnel. One fragment killed Hubert Howard, the *Times* correspondent who had ridden with the 21st Lancers and survived the charge into Khor Abu Sunt. When two more British shells walloped into the debris, Kitchener beat a hasty retreat.

It was Slatin who reported that the Khalifa had left two hours earlier, heading south. Kitchener dispatched Broadwood and his cavalry after him. Broadwood's men rode until 2200 hours that night, when they made camp. The following day they returned to report that 'Abdallahi had given them the slip. That morning, the Sirdar ordered the Mahdi's tomb destroyed. Mohammad Ahmad's bones were disinterred and thrown unceremoniously into the Nile, where the Mahdi's men had hurled Charles Gordon's headless body fourteen years earlier. He pondered what to do with Mohammad Ahmad's skull, and toyed with the idea of using it as an ashtray or desk ornament. Finally, he had it buried in a Muslim cemetery in an unmarked grave.

Later that day he sailed up the river on a gunboat to Khartoum, landing on the jetty outside Gordon's now wrecked and rubble-strewn palace. The ruined city around which his thoughts had revolved for so many years, but which he had never seen, seemed to echo with the voices of the dead. The Sirdar examined the palace and identified the stairs under which, or on which, Gordon had met his end.

The following day a memorial service for Gordon was held in the ruins of the palace, attended by detachments from each battalion of the Anglo-Egyptian army. The troops were drawn up in echelons on the bank of the Blue Nile, with the gunboat *Melik* and other steamers at anchor behind them. On this spot, fourteen years earlier, Gordon and Stewart had alighted from the steamer *Tewfiqiyya* to a tumultuous welcome from the crowds. Most of those who had been present on that day in 1884, Gordon, Stewart, Power, Hansall, Leontides, Turco-Egyptian officials, and soldiers of the 1st Sudan Brigade, were now dead. The troops who had belatedly avenged their comrades were called to attention. The Union Jack was run up on the palace roof, followed by the red Egyptian flag. *Melik* fired a salute. An order of 'Present arms!' thundered out, and three crisp drill moves were carried out in perfect unison. The soldiers stood silently, their officers at the salute, while the band of the Grenadier Guards played 'God Save the Queen', the Khedival anthem, and finally, in honour of Gordon, the 'Dead March' from *Saul*.

Kitchener called for three cheers each for the Queen and the Khedive, and was in turn cheered uproariously by his men. By the time the service had finished, many of those who had fought the dervishes so stoically, including Kitchener himself, were in tears. 'The Sirdar, who is, as a rule, absolutely unmoved,' wrote an eye-witness, 'had great round tears on his cheeks.'[68] In the palace garden afterwards, the Sirdar shook hands with all his senior officers and thanked them. 'He spoke in affecting words of Gordon,' one officer remembered, 'and of the long years he had spent recovering the lost Sudan, and all he owed to those who had assisted him. The lines of thought had gone out of his face. His manner had become easy and unconstrained. He was happy.'[69]

Within three days, Kitchener would be called to Fashoda to deal with Captain J. B. Marchand's party, who had marched across Africa and were now staking a French claim to the White Nile. Kitchener had carried sealed orders from Cromer, stitched inside his jacket, throughout the campaign, to be opened only after the capture of Khartoum. For now, though, he could sit back and enjoy what was without doubt the high point of his life. Though he was soon to become Lord Kitchener of Khartoum, and would end his career as Secretary of State for War, nothing would be quite so perfect ever again. First the attempted rescue, and later the avenging of Gordon, had taken the best years of his life, and in return had made him all he had become.

Within two years, though, the Victorian era would be over. The world stood poised on the brink of a new age, an age that would bring with it such tides of destruction that the casualties on the field of Omdurman would pale into insignificance. Very soon, the glory of the Sudan campaign would fade into the ignominious debacle of the Boer War, and into the horrors of the First World War, when, on the first day of the Somme in 1916, the British – among them men who had fought at Omdurman – would be ordered to make a frontal assault on artillery and machine-guns and would be mown down just as the dervishes had been at Kerrari. The only difference was that the British army would on that day suffer three times the casualties the Khalifa's army had sustained – the highest number, indeed, ever suffered in a single day by any army in history.

Looking back from 1916 to those Indian summers, the twilight of Victorian times, before aircraft, motor cars, telephones and dreadnoughts, the British experience in the Sudan would seem like a dream from another dimension – the last great romantic adventure of the imperial age.

13

At first light on 24 November 1899, fifteen months after the battle of Omdurman, an Egyptian–Sudanese force eight thousand strong waited for dawn in the long grass at Umm Dibaykarat in Kordofan. The force – consisting of two Sudanese battalions, an Egyptian infantry company, some former Mahdist Jihadiyya, Camel Corps, Egyptian cavalry and artillery batteries – was commanded by Reginald Wingate, who, since January, had been the new Sirdar of the Egyptian army.

Two days earlier, Wingate's men had smashed a dervish column under the Khalifa's relative Ahmad Fadil at Abu 'Adil, killing four hundred warriors and capturing a number of women and children and large amounts of supplies. The following day a deserter had reported that 'Abdallahi wad Torshayn himself was encamped seven miles south-east of the village of al-Jadid. 'Abdallahi's army was seven thousand strong, but was cut off from its water-supply by Wingate's advance. The tables had turned completely since 1883, when Hicks's column had been denied water by the dervish horde.

At about 0510 hours, the government force saw a legion of dark shapes hurtling towards them out of the *goz*. This was 'Abdallahi's last advance, and – incredibly – he had learned no lessons about modern fire-power from his previous experiences. The dervish *Mulazimin* attacked with customary élan, firing as they came. Maxim guns, twelve-pound field-guns and Martini-Henry volleys greeted them, hiccupping out across the grasslands. Once more, and for the final time, the dervish attack wilted under a wall of lead and shrapnel. The *Mulazimin* ran.

The Sudanese battalions leapt after them with fixed bayonets. Advancing no more than three hundred yards, the 9th Sudanese came across a huddle of bodies lying in the grass. Among them was the corpse of 'Abdallahi wad Torshayn.

'Abdallahi had died a brave man's death, leading his last army from the front. When defeat had seemed inevitable, he had finally sat down on his *furwa* with his most trusted *emirs* and waited for death in the time-honoured Sudanese way. So died one of the most remarkable, but least celebrated men in the history of north-east Africa – an illiterate Baggara nomad whose vision had provided the momentum for the Mahdist revolution. The man who had limped into al-Masallamiyya with a galled donkey in 1880, with nothing to his name but a water-skin and a spare shirt, had touched the skies. If Mohammad Ahmad had been the figurehead of the Mahdiyya, 'Abdallahi had provided much of its motive force. This man, born in a hut on the open grasslands, brought up in the saddle, had helped create the world's first Islamic state, and had ruled it for fourteen years. Now, his blood stained the red soil of the *goz*, where long ago he had hunted elephant and giraffe with spears, in a simpler, less complicated world. The forest of Shaykan, where fifteen years earlier his life had taken its momentous turning, lay no more than two days' march away.

The Mahdiyya died at Umm Dibaykarat, but Mahdism did not. It simply went underground, where it remained throughout the fifty-seven years of Anglo-Egyptian rule. After the Sudan's independence in 1956, Islamic politics again reared its head. From 1964 it was dominated by Hassan at-Turabi, a lawyer with a PhD from the Sorbonne, whose Islamic Charter Front party called for an Islamic orientation of the country, along the lines envisaged by the Mahdi and the Khalifa 'Abdallahi.

Turabi and his brother-in-law, Sadiq al-Mahdi, grandson of Mohammad Ahmad and leader of the Mahdist Umma party, were the power behind the coup that expelled the regime of Ja'afar Nimairi in 1989, and installed in his place the current president, 'Omar al-Bashir.

It was through the sponsorship of Hassan at-Turabi that, in 1994, the Saudi-Arabian terrorist chief Osama bin Laden made his home in the Sudan, where he remained for four years. During this time at-Turabi became bin Laden's mentor, profoundly influencing his ideology, and helping to construct al-Qaeda as the terrorist organization it would become. Bin Laden left the Sudan for Afghanistan in 1998, a very different man from the one who had arrived there: his pronouncements against the Americans, and the 'apostate' Muslim regimes of the Arab world, in some cases match those of the Mahdi almost word for word. The tragedy of 9/11 in New York, masterminded by bin Laden, was thus an expression of the same sentiments articulated by the Mahdi in his revolt, and, at least in part, a settling of scores for the ten thousand dervishes who fell under Kitchener's guns at Kerrari, just over a hundred years before.

Epilogue: The Survivors

Sir Herbert Kitchener, 1st Earl Kitchener of Khartoum: Kitchener's careful handling of Captain Marchand at Fashoda averted an international crisis, and he returned to Britain to be publicly lionized, thanked by Parliament, and awarded a baronetcy. When the Sudan was declared a Condominium to be ruled jointly by both Egypt and Britain, in January 1899, Kitchener fulfilled Gordon's recommendation by becoming governor-general, with full military and civil powers. From 1911 to 1914 he took over Cromer's old post of British agent and Consul General in Egypt. During this period he encouraged Arab resistance against the Ottoman Turks in the Hejaz – work that would come to flower as the Arab Revolt. He returned to Britain in 1914 as Secretary of State for War, raising an army a million strong to fight in the Dardanelles campaign, a plan that was in part the brainchild of the cavalry subaltern who, on 1 September 1898, had alerted him to the dervish advance, Winston Churchill – by then First Lord of the Admiralty. Kitchener was criticized for indecision during the Gallipoli operation, but probably found himself faced with an insoluble military dilemma. He was drowned in 1916 on a mission to Russia, when his ship hit a mine in the North Sea. On the same day, the Arab Revolt broke out in the Hejaz.

General Sir Reginald Wingate: Wingate succeeded Kitchener as Sirdar and governor-general of the Sudan, and presided over the construction of the new Anglo-Egyptian Condominium. In 1916 he was appointed British High Commissioner in Egypt, but was dismissed in 1919 after a disagreement with the British government over Egyptian Nationalism. He thereafter became a successful businessman, and died in 1953, aged ninety-two.

Major General Sir Hector MacDonald: The crofter's son and former Gordon Highlanders sergeant, the true British hero of

Omdurman, later saw service in the Boer War, and commanded the Highland Brigade. MacDonald was appointed commander of British troops in Ceylon, where, in 1903, he was involved in a homosexual scandal. In the wake of the trial of Oscar Wilde in 1895, this was not a sympathetic period for homosexuals, and faced with court-martial and public disgrace, MacDonald took a soldier's exit. He shot himself in a hotel room in Paris on the way back from an interview with Lord Roberts, the Commander-in-Chief.

The Khalifa 'Ali wad Helu: The veteran Mahdist *emir* who survived all the exigencies of the Mahdiyya, and co-commanded the Green Standard at Omdurman, remained with 'Abdallahi until the end. His body was found riddled with bullets, next to that of his chief, at Umm Dibaykarat.

('Osman) Shaykh ad-Din: 'Abdallahi's son, who commanded the *Mulazimin* at Omdurman, was wounded at Umm Dibaykarat and captured by Wingate. He died in prison at Rosetta in 1900, aged about twenty-five.

'Osman Digna: The great survivor of the Mahdiyya, and one of its few successful generals, escaped from Omdurman after seeing the Khalifa safely into the city. He later joined 'Abdallahi's forces in Kordofan, but once again escaped from British clutches at Umm Dibaykarat. He returned to the Red Sea hills and remained at large, moving from valley to valley and cave to cave, until 1900, when he was captured. He spent most of the rest of his life in prison at Rosetta and Tura, but was released in 1924 to make the hajj. He died at Wadi Halfa in 1926, aged about eighty-six.

The Gunboat *Melik*: The steamer that played a part in the bombardment of Omdurman and covered Broadwood's withdrawal at Kerrari was commanded by David Beatty and later by Charles Gordon's nephew, Captain W. 'Monkey' Gordon, RE. She was later docked on the Blue Nile at Khartoum, where she became an office and headquarters for the Blue Nile Sailing Club. The last of Kitchener's steamers, it still stands there in dry dock today. For some years, a *Melik* Restoration Society has been attempting to have the boat returned to Britain for refurbishing.

Major General Sir Archibald Hunter: Hunter had been

groomed by Kitchener to take over as Sirdar, but was wisely passed over by Cromer, who believed that his truculent character would turn him into a tyrant if he was given full military and civil power in the Sudan. Hunter had a successful military career, both in South Africa and as a staff officer with Kitchener in the First World War. He was Unionist MP for Lancaster from 1919 to 1922, and died in 1936.

Major General Sir William Gatacre: The martinet known as 'General Back-Acher', who had commanded the British division at Omdurman, met his nemesis later in South Africa, where he was dismissed from command in 1900. He became a rubber planter in Ethiopia, and died there of fever in 1906.

Sir Evelyn Baring, Lord Cromer: Remained British agent in Egypt until 1909, when he retired abruptly, having been de facto ruler of the country for more than a quarter of a century. Cromer retired uncelebrated, but was probably the most effective ruler in Egyptian history. Though he came to be regarded as almost a caricature of the British imperial bureaucrat, he was a man of conscience, who despised the corrupt ruling class, and struggled always to improve the lot of the Egyptian *fellahin*. The modern states of Egypt and the Sudan probably owe more to Cromer than to any other single individual. He died, aged seventy-six, in 1917.

Baron Sir Rudolf Carl von Slatin: Slatin remained a lifelong friend of Wingate, and was appointed Inspector General of the Sudan – a post created especially for him by his friend. He played a major part in the reconstruction of the country. Made a baron of the Austrian Empire, the outbreak of the First World War rendered his position as an Anglo-Egyptian official anomalous. He resigned in 1914, and became president of the Austrian Red Cross. He died in 1932.

The Khalifa Mohammad ash-Sharif: The Mahdi's cousin and son-in-law, long-term rival of 'Abdallahi, who was rumoured to have struck the blow that killed Hicks at Shaykan, did not join the Khalifa after Omdurman. He was arrested and executed by the British in August 1899, accused, perhaps unjustly, of trying to lead a Mahdist revival.

Field Marshal Viscount Garnet Wolseley: Wolseley, after Kitchener the most remarkable soldier of his era, never saw active service after the failure of the Gordon Relief Expedition. As Commander-in-Chief of the British army from 1895 to 1899, after his detested rival the Duke of Cambridge, Wolseley brought about major changes in the organization of the army, preparing it for the modern age. He died at Menton in France in 1913, aged eighty.

Field Marshal Sir Evelyn Wood, VC: Like Wolseley, Wood never saw active service after the Relief Expedition. He served in a variety of administrative posts, mainly under Wolseley, including Adjutant General. He retired as a field marshal in 1903, and died in 1919 aged eighty-one.

Major General Sir Charles Wilson, FRS: Wilson's career did not suffer, despite the calumnies poured on him by Wolseley, and he received a second knighthood for his part in the Relief Expedition. The founder of British geographical intelligence, he later became director-general of the Ordnance Survey of the United Kingdom, and ended his career as Director of Military Education. He died in 1905.

Major General Sir Redvers Buller, VC: Unlike Wood and Wolseley, Buller did see active service again. After many years at a desk, he was given command of British troops in the Boer War in 1899, but displayed a predictable lack of decisiveness and tactical imagination. Buller remained popular with the public, a factor which may have led to a conviction of his own indispensability. Given command at Aldershot, though, he was sacked after making an indiscreet speech at a public lunch, and was never offered another job.

Lieut. Colonel Henry de Coetlogon: De Coetlogon never returned to the Sudan. On arrival in Egypt in 1884, he became Commandant of Police at Asyut and later at Alexandria. He served in the British consular service, holding posts in the USA and Pacific. He retired in 1907 and died in Oxford in 1908.

The Sudan Military Railway: Later to become the Sudan Government Railway, the line Kitchener built still crosses the

Nubian desert – a lasting monument to British endeavour. Though many of the stations Kitchener built are now derelict, the railway is still in use from Khartoum to Wadi Halfa, conducting daily goods trains, and a passenger train once a week.

Lieut. General Sir Gerald Graham, VC: After his last campaign against 'Osman Digna in 1885, Graham became colonel-commandant of the Royal Engineers, a ceremonial post. He died in 1899, aged sixty-eight.

Sir Percy Girouard: Kitchener's chief engineer became president of state railways in Egypt, and later director of railways in South Africa during the war of 1899–1902. He was high commissioner of Nigeria, and governor and C.-in-C. of British East Africa, and later director-general of munitions during the First World War. After the war he became managing director of the engineering company Armstrong Whitworth. He was knighted in 1900, and died in 1932, aged sixty-five.

Admiral Lord Charles Beresford: One of the two main culprits of the near disaster at Abu Tulayh, Beresford's social status and connections insulated him from penalty. He became a full admiral in 1906 and was at various times a Member of Parliament. He died in Scotland in 1919.

Lieut. General Robert Broadwood: Kitchener's Egyptian army cavalry commander, who drew the Green Standard away from the main force during the battle of Omdurman, later returned to the British army and commanded a cavalry brigade in the Boer War. He was killed in action on the Western Front during the First World War in 1917, commanding the 57th Division.

Major General Lord Albert Gleichen, formerly Count Gleichen: The subaltern of the Guards Camel Regiment wrote a best-selling book about the Gordon Relief Expedition, *With the Camel Corps up the Nile*. He served with Kitchener on the Dongola Campaign in 1896, and transferred to the Egyptian army, serving as director of intelligence and Sudan agent in Cairo from 1901 to 1903. He commanded a division in the First World War. He died in 1937.

Gustav Klootz: The deserter survived the Mahdi, but did not live to see the end of his regime. He escaped from captivity in Omdurman but died on his way to the Ethiopian border in 1886.

Major General Charles Gordon: Gordon's reputation suffered in the Edwardian era, when, largely due to Lytton Strachey's acerbic portrait in *Eminent Victorians*, he came to be regarded as a British equivalent of the Mahdi – a religious fanatic, whose unbalanced behaviour in Khartoum brought about his own demise. A statue erected to his memory – where it rightly belonged, under the shadow of Nelson's column in Trafalgar Square – was later removed. Gordon's reputation deserves reinstatement. He did not save the country from invasion or disaster, but among the British heroes of all ages, there is perhaps no other who stands out so prominently as an individualist, a man ready to die for his principles. Here was one man among men who did not do what he was told, but what he believed to be right. In a world moving inexorably towards conformity, it would be well to remember Gordon of Khartoum.

Bibliography

'A Lieutenant Colonel', *The British Army*, London, 1899.

'An Officer', *Sudan Campaign 1896–1899*, London, 1899.

Alford, H. S. L., and Sword, W. D., *The Egyptian Sudan, Its Loss and Recovery*, London, 1898.

Arthur, Sir George (ed.), *Letters of Lord and Lady Wolseley 1870–1911*, London, 1922.

As-Sayid, Afaf Lutfi, *Egypt and Cromer – A Study in Anglo-Egyptian Relations*, London, 1968.

Atteridge, A. H., *The Dongola Expedition of 1896*, London, 1897.

Atteridge, A. H., *Towards Khartoum, The Story of the Sudan War of 1896*, London, 1897.

Babikr Badri, *The Memoirs of Babikr Badri*, 2 vols., London, 1969/80.

Barbour, K. M., *The Republic of the Sudan – A Regional Geography*, London, 1962.

Barthorp, M., *War on the Nile: Britain in Egypt and the Sudan 1882–1898*, Poole, 1984.

Bennet, E. N., *The Downfall of the Dervishes, Being a Sketch of the Sudan Campaign of 1896*, London, 1898.

Beresford, Charles, *Memoirs*, 2 vols., London, 1914.

Bermann, R. A., *The Mahdi Allah – The Story of the Dervish Mohammad Ahmad*, London, 1932.

Bey, Abbas, 'The Diary of Abbas Bey', *Sudan Notes and Records*, XXXII, Pt II, 1951, p.179.

Bloss, J. F. E., 'The Story of Suakin', *Sudan Notes and Records*, XIX, Pt II, 1936, p.271.

Blunt, W. S., *Gordon at Khartoum*, London, 1912.

Brackenbury, H., *The River Column: A Narrative of the Advance of the River Column of the Nile Expeditionary Force, and Its Return Down the Rapids*.

Bredin, G. R. F., 'The Life Story of Yuzbashi Abdallah Adlan', *Sudan Notes and Records*, XLII, 1961, p.37.

Brighton, T., and Anderson, D. N., *The Last Charge – The 21st Lancers and the Battle of Omdurman, 2 September 1898*, London, 1998.

Brook-Shepherd, G., *Between Two Flags – A Life of Baron Sir Rudolf von Slatin Pasha*, London, 1972.

Buchan, John, *Gordon at Khartoum*, London, 1934.

Burleigh, Bennet, *Desert Warfare*, London, 1884.

Burleigh, Bennet, *The Khartoum Campaign*, London, 1899.

Butler, W. F. Charles George G., *The Campaign of the Cataracts – Being a Personal Narrative of the Great Nile Expedition of 1884–5*, London, 1887.

Chenevix-Trench, C., *Charley Gordon – The Life of an Eminent Victorian Reassessed*, London, 1978.

Churchill, Winston S., *The River War*, 2 vols., London, 1899.

Churchill, Winston S., *My Early Life*, London, 1930.

Clark, 'The Manners, Customs and Beliefs of the Northern Beja', *Sudan Notes and Records*, XXI, 1938.

Colborne, J., *With Hicks Pasha in the Sudan: Being an Account of the Sennar Campaign in 1883*, London, 1884.

Corbin, Jane, *The Base: Al-Qaeda and the Changing Face of Global Terror*, London, 2002.

Cromer, Lord, *Modern Egypt*, 2 vols., London, 1909.

Cunnison, Ian, *Baggara Arabs – Power and Lineage in a Sudanese Nomad Tribe*, Oxford, 1966.

Cunnison, Ian, 'Blood Money – Vengeance and Joint Responsibility – The Baggara Case', in Cunnison, Ian, and Jones, Wendy, *Essays in Sudan Ethnography*, London, 1972.

Cunnison, Ian, 'Giraffe Hunting among the Humr Tribe', *Sudan Notes and Records*, XXXIX, 1958, pp.49–60.

Cunnison, Ian, 'Some Social Aspects of Nomadism among the Baggara', in *Nomadism and Economic Development in the Sudan*, Khartoum, 1962.

Davies, Reginald, *The Camel's Back – Service in the Rural Sudan*, London, 1957.

Dixon, Norman, *On the Psychology of Military Incompetence*, London, 1976.

Emery, Frank, *Marching over Africa: Letters from Victorian Soldiers*, London, 1986.

Encyclopedia of Islam, Leiden, 1985.

Etherington, Harry, 'Sent to Save Gordon', in Small, E. Milton (ed.), *Told from the Ranks*, London, 1898.

Fahmi, Khalid, *All the Pasha's Men*, London, 1997.

Farwell, B., *Prisoners of the Mahdi*, London, 1967.

Fitzmaurice, Lord Edmund, *Life of Granville — George Leveson Gower 1815–1891*, 2 vols., London, 1905.

Gleichen, Count Albert, *With the Camel Corps on the Nile*, London, 1889.

Gordon, C. G., *General Gordon's Last Journal*, London, 1885.

Gordon, M. A. (ed.), *Letters of Charles George Gordon to his Sister*, London, 1888.

Gray, R., *A History of the Southern Sudan 1839–1889*, London, 1961.

Gulla, Sheikh 'Ali, 'The Defeat of Hicks Pasha', *Sudan Notes and Records*, VIII, 1925, p.119.

Hake, A. E., *Gordon in China and the Soudan*, London, 1896.

Harrington, Peter, and Sharf, Frederic A. (eds.), *Omdurman 1898: Eyewitnesses Speak*, London, 1998.

Hicks, William, *The Road to Shaykan: Letters of General William Hicks Pasha Written during the Sennar and Kordofan Campaigns, 1883*, ed. M. W. Daly, Durham, 1983.

Hill, R., *A Biographical Dictionary of the Anglo-Egyptian Sudan*, Oxford, 1951.

Hill, R. (ed.), *The Sudan Memoirs of Carl Christian Giegler Pasha 1873–1883*, London, 1984.

Holt, P. M., *The Mahdist State in the Sudan — A Study of its Origins, Development and Overthrow*, Oxford, 1958.

Holt, P. M., 'The Place in History of the Sudanese Mahdiyya', *Sudan Notes and Records*, XL, 1959, pp.107–12.

Holt, P. M., and Daly, M. W., *A History of Sudan from the Coming of Islam to the Present Day*, London, 1989.

Hunter, A., *Kitchener's Sword Arm — The Life and Campaigns of General Sir Archie Hunter*, London, 1996.

Ibrahim, Ahmad Othman, 'Some Aspects of the Ideology of the Mahdiyya', *Sudan Notes and Records*, LIX, 1978, p.28.

Jackson, H. C. (trans.), *Black, Ivory and White — The Story of Zubayr Pasha*, London, 1913.

Jackson, H. C., *'Osman Digna*, London, 1926.

Jardine, Sir William, *The Naturalist's Library, Vol. V, Pachyderms*, London, 1836.

Keown-Boyd, H., *A Good Dusting: A Centenary Review of the Sudan Campaigns 1883–1899*, London, 1983.

Knight, E. F., *Letters from the Sudan*, London, 1896.

Knight, Ian (ed.), *Marching to the Drums – Eyewitness Accounts of War from the Kabul Massacre to the Siege of Mafeking*, London, 1999.

Kochanksi, Halik, *Sir Garnet Wolseley: Victorian Hero*, London, 1999.

Lehmann, Joseph H., *All Sir Garnet – A Life of Field Marshal Lord Wolseley*, London, 1964.

MacDonald, A., *Too Late for Gordon and Khartoum: The Testimony of an Independent Eye Witness of the Heroic Efforts for their Rescue and Relief*, London, 1887.

MacDonald, A., *Why Gordon Perished*, London, 1885.

MacMichael, H. A., *The Tribes of North and Central Kordofan*, London, 1912.

Magnus, Philip, *Kitchener – Portrait of an Imperialist*, London, 1958.

Mahdi, Mandour, *A Short History of the Sudan*, Oxford, 1965.

Marlowe, John, *Mission to Khartoum – The Apotheosis of General Gordon*, London, 1969.

Maxwell, Leigh, *The Ashanti Ring*, London, 1985.

Meredith, John (ed.), *Omdurman Diaries 1898 – Eyewitness Accounts of the Legendary Campaign*, London, 1998.

Middleton, Dorothy, *Baker of the Nile*, London, 1949.

Moore-Harrel, Alice, *Gordon and the Sudan 1877–1880 – Prolog to the Mahdiyya*, London, 2001.

Neillands, Robin, *The Dervish Wars: Gordon and Kitchener in the Sudan 1880–1898*, London, 1996.

Neufeld, K., *A Prisoner of the Khalifa – 12 Years Captivity at Omdurman*, London, 1899.

Nicoll, Fergus, *The Sword of the Prophet – The Mahdi of the Sudan and the Death of General Gordon*, London, 2004.

Nushi Pasha, 'General Report of the Siege and Fall of Khartoum', ed. R. Wingate, *Sudan Notes and Records*, XIII, Pt 1, 1930, pp.1–82.

Ohrwalder, Joseph, *Ten Years' Captivity in the Mahdi's Camp 1882–1892*, London, 1892.

O'Fahey, R. S., and Spaulding, J. L., *Kingdoms of the Sudan*, London, 1974.

Owen, T. R. H., 'The Haddendowa', *Sudan Notes and Records*, XX, Pt 2, 1937.

Paul, A., *A History of the Beja Tribes of the Sudan*, London, 1954.

Pollock, John, *Kitchener*, London, 1998.

Power, Frank, 'Massacre in the Desert', *The Times*, 18 December 1883.

Power, Frank, *Letters from Khartoum – Written during the Siege*, London, 1885.

Preston, Adrian (ed.), *In Relief of Gordon – Lord Wolseley's Campaign Journal of the Khartoum Relief Expedition – 1884–5*, London, 1967.

Prunier, Gerald, 'Military Slavery in the Sudan During the Turkiyya', in Elizabeth Savage (ed.), *The Human Commodity – Perspectives in the Trans-Saharan Slave Trade*, London, 1992.

Reid, R., 'The Khalifa Abdallahi', *Sudan Notes and Records*, XXXI, Pt 2, 1950, pp.254–73.

Risgnoli, C., 'Omdurman During the Siege', *Sudan Notes and Records*, XLII, 1967, pp.33–61.

Robson, B., *Fuzzy Wuzzy: The Campaigns in the Eastern Sudan 1884–85*, Tunbridge Wells, 1993.

Russell, Henry, *The Ruin of the Sudan*, London, 1892.

Sandars, G., 'The Besharin', *Sudan Notes and Records*, XVI, 1933.

Sandars, G., 'The Amarar', *Sudan Notes and Records*, XVIII, 1935.

Schweinfurth, G., *Heart of Africa*, London, 1872.

Shaked, Haim, *The Life of the Sudanese Mahdi*, New Jersey, 1978.

Shibeika, Makki, *The Independent Sudan: British Policy in the Sudan 1882–1902*, London, 1952.

Slatin, R. C., *Fire and Sword in the Sudan: A Personal Narrative of Fighting and Serving the Dervishes*, London, 1896.

Spiers, E. M., *The Late Victorian Army 1868–1902*, London, 1992.

Spiers, E. M. (ed.), *Sudan: The Reconquest Reappraised*, London, 1998.

Steevens, G. W., *With Kitchener to Khartoum*, Edinburgh, 1898.

Stevenson, R. C., 'Old Khartoum 1821–1883', *Sudan Notes and Records*, XLVII, 1966.

Stuart-Wortley, E. J. Montague, 'Reminiscences of the Sudan 1882–1899', *Sudan Notes and Records*, XXXIV, 1953, p.17.

Symonds, Julian, *England's Pride: The Story of the Gordon Relief Expedition*, London, 1965.

Theobald, A. B., *The Mahdiyya: A History of the Sudan 1881–1898*, London, 1967.

Thompson, Brian, *Imperial Vanities: The Adventures of the Baker Brothers and Gordon of Khartoum*, London, 2002.

Trimingham, J. S., *Islam in the Sudan*, London, 1965.

Udal, John, *The Nile in Darkness – Conquest and Exploration 1504–1862*, London, 1998.

Waller, John H., *Gordon of Khartoum – The Saga of a Victorian Hero*, New York, 1988.

Ware, J. R., and Mann, R. K., *The Life and Times of Colonel Fred Burnaby*, London, 1885.

Warner, Philip, *Dervish: The Rise and Fall of an African Empire*, London, 1973.

Watson, Charles, *The Life of Major General Sir Charles Wilson*, London, 1909.

Watson, Charles, 'The Campaign of Gordon's Steamers', *Sudan Notes and Records*, XII, Pt II, 1929.

Wilson, Charles, *From Korti to Khartoum*, London, 1885.

Wingate, R., *Mahdism and the Egyptian Sudan*, London, 1891.

Ziegler, Philip, *Omdurman*, London, 1973.

Zulfu, Isat, *Kerrari – the Sudanese Account of the Battle of Omdurman*, trans. P. Clark, London, 1973.

Notes

Prologue

1 Joseph Ohrwalder, *Ten Years Captivity in the Mahdi's Camp 1882–1892*, London, 1892, p.134.
2 *The Times*, 18 December 1883 (original reads 'Arabs' for 'dervishes').
3 ibid.
4 Sheikh 'Ali Gulla, 'The Defeat of Hicks Pasha', *Sudan Notes and Records*, VIII, 1925, p.119.
5 Frank Power, *Letters from Khartoum – Written during the Siege*, London, 1885, p.20.
6 ibid., p.14.
7 ibid., p.20.
8 Abbas Bey, 'The Diary of Abbas Bey', *Sudan Notes and Records*, XXXII, Pt II, 1951, p.179.
9 Ohrwalder, *Ten Years Captivity*, p.86.

Part One

1 Gerald Prunier, 'Military Slavery in the Sudan During the Turkiyya', in Elizabeth Savage (ed.), *The Human Commodity – Perspectives in the Trans-Saharan Slave Trade*, London, 1992.
2 William Hicks, *The Road to Shaykan: Letters of General William Hicks Pasha Written during the Sennar and Kordofan Campaigns, 1883*, ed. M. W. Daly, Durham, 1983, p.68.
3 ibid.
4 R. C. Stevenson, 'Old Khartoum 1821–1885', *Sudan Notes and Records*, XLVII, 1966, pp.1–37, 234.
5 Frank Power, *Letters from Khartoum – Written during the Siege*, London, 1885, p.25.

6 ibid., pp.35–6.

7 ibid., p.48.

8 ibid., p.53.

9 Lord Cromer, *Modern Egypt*, 2 vols., London, 1909, p.400.

10 Hicks, *The Road to Shaykan*, p.11.

11 Power, *Letters*, p.52.

12 Cromer, *Modern Egypt*, p.376.

13 Power, *Letters*, p.72.

14 John Pollock, *Kitchener*, London, 1998, p.12.

15 J. Colborne, *With Hicks Pasha in the Sudan: Being an Account of the Sennar Campaign in 1883*, London, 1884, p.10.

16 Cromer, *Modern Egypt*, p.219.

17 ibid., pp.403–4.

18 W. S. Blunt, *Gordon at Khartoum*, London, 1912, p.232.

19 Cromer, *Modern Egypt*, p.406.

20 'A Lieutenant Colonel', *The British Army*, London, 1899.

21 A. Paul, *A History of the Beja Tribes of the Sudan*, London, 1954, p.3.

22 *Sudan Notes and Records*, 1937.

23 ibid.

24 Bennet Burleigh, *Desert Warfare*, London, 1884, p.14.

25 Cromer, *Modern Egypt*, p.404.

26 Burleigh, *Desert Warfare*, p.15.

27 ibid., pp.15–16.

28 Brian Thompson, *Imperial Vanities: The Adventures of the Baker Brothers and Gordon of Khartoum*, London, 2002, p.223.

29 Burleigh, *Desert Warfare*, p.16.

30 ibid.

31 ibid., p.18.

32 Cromer, *Modern Egypt*, p.407.

33 ibid.

34 Makki Shibeika, *The Independent Sudan: British Policy in the Sudan 1882–1902*, London, 1952, p.224.

Part Two

1 E. Schweinfurth, *Heart of Africa*, London, 1872, p.66.
2 ibid.
3 H. C. Jackson (trans.), *Black, Ivory and White – The Story of Zubayr Pasha*, London, 1913, p.58.
4 P. M. Holt, *The Mahdist State in the Sudan – A Study of its Origins, Development and Overthrow*, Oxford, 1958, p.52.
5 R. Wingate, *Mahdism and the Egyptian Sudan*, London, 1891.
6 R. C. Slatin, *Fire and Sword in the Sudan: A Personal Narrative of Fighting and Serving the Dervishes*, London, 1896, p.143.
7 ibid., pp.143–4.
8 ibid., p.149.
9 ibid., p.151.

Part Three

1 C. Chenevix-Trench, *Charley Gordon: The Life of an Eminent Victorian Reassessed*, London, 1978, p.30.
2 ibid., p.190.
3 John Pollock, *Kitchener*, London, 1998, p.275.
4 Chenevix-Trench, *Charley Gordon*, p.196.
5 Joseph H. Lehmann, *All Sir Garnet – A Life of Field Marshal Lord Wolseley*, London, 1964, p.32.
6 ibid., p.134.
7 Chenevix-Trench, *Charley Gordon*, p.195.
8 ibid.
9 ibid., p.198.
10 Lord Cromer, *Modern Egypt*, 2 vols., London, 1909, p.426.
11 ibid., p.428.
12 Chenevix-Trench, *Charley Gordon*, p.231.
13 ibid., p.203.
14 ibid.
15 ibid., p.202.

16 Adrian Preston (ed.), *In Relief of Gordon – Lord Wolseley's Campaign Journal of the Khartoum Relief Expedition – 1884–5*, London, 1967, p.23.

17 ibid., p.6.

18 ibid., p.23.

19 Cromer, *Modern Egypt*, p.460.

20 Chenevix-Trench, *Charley Gordon*, p.276.

21 ibid., p.271.

22 Cromer, *Modern Egypt*, p.460.

23 ibid.

24 ibid., p.448.

25 W. S. Blunt, *Gordon at Khartoum*, London, 1912, p.517.

26 Cromer, *Modern Egypt*, p.437.

27 Pollock, *Kitchener*, p.278.

28 ibid.

29 E. J. Montague Stuart-Wortley, 'Reminiscences of the Sudan 1882–1899', *Sudan Notes and Records*, XXXIV, 1953, p.17.

30 Cromer, *Modern Egypt*, p.460.

31 ibid., p.410.

32 Makki Shibeika, *The Independent Sudan: British Policy in the Sudan*, London, 1952, p.225; 12/2/84, the Queen's italics.

33 ibid., p.227.

34 ibid.

35 Cromer, *Modern Egypt*, p.413.

36 Shibeika, *Independent Sudan*, p.225.

37 Preston (ed.), *Lord Wolseley's Campaign Journal*, p.166.

38 Sir George Arthur (ed.), *Letters of Lord and Lady Wolseley 1870–1911*, London, 1922.

39 Cromer, *Modern Egypt*, p.412.

40 Blunt, *Gordon at Khartoum*, p.262.

41 Bennet Burleigh, *Desert Warfare*, London, 1884, p.29.

42 ibid., p.204.

43 B. Robson, *Fuzzy Wuzzy: The Campaigns in the Eastern Sudan 1884–85*, Tunbridge Wells, 1993, p.50.

44 Burleigh, *Desert Warfare*, p.50.

45 ibid., p.61.

46 ibid., p.47.

47 ibid., p.106.

48 Frank Emery, *Marching over Africa: Letters from Victorian Soldiers*, London, 1986, p.134.

49 ibid.

50 Burleigh, *Desert Warfare*, p.49.

51 ibid.

52 Robson, *Fuzzy Wuzzy*, p.73.

53 Emery, *Marching over Africa*, p.134–5.

54 Burleigh, *Desert Warfare*, p.65.

55 ibid., p.102.

56 Emery, *Marching over Africa*, p.133.

57 Burleigh, *Desert Warfare*, p.72.

58 Cromer, *Modern Egypt*, p.414.

Part Four

1 M. A. Gordon (ed.), *Letters of Charles George Gordon to his Sister*, London, 1888, p.80.

2 Makki Shibeika, *The Independent Sudan: British Policy in the Sudan*, London, 1952, p.236.

3 A. E. Hake, *Gordon in China and the Soudan*, London, 1896, p.342.

4 Frank Power, *Letters from Khartoum – Written during the Siege*, London, 1885, p.97.

5 Lord Cromer, *Modern Egypt*, 2 vols., London, 1909, p.475.

6 C. G. Gordon, *General Gordon's Last Journal*, London, 1885, p.43.

7 Joseph Ohrwalder, *Ten Years Captivity in the Mahdi's Camp 1882–1892*, London, 1892, p.98.

8 ibid., p.45.

9 ibid., p.96.

10 ibid., p.98.

11 M. A. Gordon (ed.), *Letters of Charles George Gordon*, p.350.

12 Bennet Burleigh, *Desert Warfare*, London, 1884, p.305.

13 ibid., p.304.

14 Frank Emery, *Marching over Africa: Letters from Victorian Soldiers*, London, 1986, p.137.

15 Burleigh, *Desert Warfare*, p.194.

16 ibid., p.156.

17 Emery, *Marching over Africa*, p.138.

18 ibid.

19 Burleigh, *Desert Warfare*, p.157.

20 ibid., p.196.

21 ibid., p.197.

22 ibid., p.196.

23 ibid.

24 Emery, *Marching over Africa*, pp.138–9.

25 ibid., pp.137–8.

26 ibid.

27 Burleigh, *Desert Warfare*, p.165.

28 Cromer, *Modern Egypt*, p.416.

29 Power, *Letters*, p.99.

30 Winston S. Churchill, *The River War*, 2 vols., London, 1899.

31 C. Chenevix-Trench, *Charley Gordon – The Life of an Eminent Victorian Reassessed*, London, 1978, p.252.

32 Shibeika, *Independent Sudan*, p.297.

Part Five

1 W. F. Butler, *The Campaign of the Cataracts – Being a Personal Narrative of the Great Nile Expedition of 1884–5*, London, 1887, p.374.

2 Adrian Preston (ed.), *In Relief of Gordon – Lord Wolseley's Campaign Journal of the Khartoum Relief Expedition – 1884–5*, London, 1967, p.40.

3 John Pollock, *Kitchener*, London, 1998, pp.63–4.

4 Preston (ed.), *Lord Wolseley's Campaign Journal*, p.31.

5 Philip Magnus, *Kitchener – Portrait of an Imperialist*, London, 1958, p.54.

6 C. G. Gordon, *General Gordon's Last Journal*, London, 1885, p.201.

7 ibid., p.198.

8 ibid.

9 Joseph Ohrwalder, *Ten Years Captivity in the Mahdi's Camp 1882–1892*, London, 1892, p.130.

10 Magnus, *Kitchener*, p.57.

11 Preston (ed.), *Lord Wolseley's Campaign Journal*, p.31.

12 A. MacDonald, *Too Late for Gordon and Khartoum: The Testimony of an Independent Eye Witness of the Heroic Efforts for their Rescue and Relief*, London, 1887, p.72.

13 Ian Knight (ed.), *Marching to the Drums – Eyewitness Accounts of War from the Kabul Massacre to the Siege of Mafeking*, London, 1999, p.210.

14 Count Albert Gleichen, *With the Camel Corps on the Nile*, London, 1889, p.147.

15 ibid., p.157.

16 ibid.

17 ibid., p.71.

18 Knight (ed.), *Marching to the Drums*, p.213.

19 Preston, *Lord Wolseley's Campaign Journal*, p.101.

20 ibid., p.120.

21 Knight (ed.), *Marching to the Drums*, p.212.

22 ibid., p.213.

23 Gleichen, *Camel Corps*, p.88.

24 ibid., p.101.

25 ibid., p.103.

26 Knight (ed.), *Marching to the Drums*, p.212.

27 MacDonald, *Too Late for Gordon*, p.209.

28 Gleichen, *Camel Corps*, p.113.

29 ibid., p.118.

30 MacDonald, *Too Late for Gordon*.

31 ibid.

32 Charles Wilson, *From Korti to Khartoum*, London, 1885.

33 Gleichen, *Camel Corps*.

34 ibid.

35 Wilson, *Korti to Khartoum*, p.30.

36 Knight (ed.), *Marching to the Drums*, p.213.

37 Gleichen, *Camel Corps*, p.132.

38 Charles Beresford, *Memoirs*, 2 vols., London, 1914, p.266.

39 Knight (ed.), *Marching to the Drums*.

40 Wilson, *Korti to Khartoum*, p.30.

41 ibid., p.31.

42 Beresford, *Memoirs*, p.266.

43 Julian Symonds, *England's Pride: The Story of the Gordon Relief Expedition*, London, 1965, p.201.

44 J. R. Ware and R. K. Mann, *The Life and Times of Colonel Fred Burnaby*, London, 1885, p.304.

45 Gleichen, *Camel Corps*, p.135.

46 ibid.

47 Beresford, *Memoirs*, p.304.

48 Knight (ed.), *Marching to the Drums*, p.214.

49 Gleichen, *Camel Corps*, p.145.

50 MacDonald, *Too Late for Gordon*, p.206.

51 Beresford, *Memoirs*, p.276.

52 Gleichen, *Camel Corps*, p.156.

53 Beresford, *Memoirs*, p.276.

54 Wilson, *Korti to Khartoum*, p.71.

55 ibid.

56 Gleichen, *Camel Corps*, p.138.

57 MacDonald, *Too Late for Gordon*, p.255.

58 Gleichen, *Camel Corps*, p.172.

59 MacDonald, *Too Late for Gordon*, p.269.

60 R. C. Slatin, *Fire and Sword in the Sudan: A Personal Narrative of Fighting and Serving the Dervishes*, London, 1896, p.204.

61 C. G. Gordon, *Journal*, p.199.

62 ibid., pp.215–16; capitals and italics are Gordon's.

63 R. Wingate, *Mahdism and the Egyptian Sudan*, London, 1891, p.169.

64 ibid., p.518.

65 Nushi Pasha, 'General Report of the Siege and Fall of Khartoum', ed. R. Wingate, *Sudan Notes and Records*, XIII, Pt 1, 1930, pp.1–82.

66 ibid., p.80.

67 K. Neufeld, *A Prisoner of the Khalifa – 12 Years Captivity at Omdurman*, London, 1899, p.335.

68 Slatin, *Fire and Sword*, p.206.

69 ibid.

70 Wilson, *Korti to Khartoum*, p.172.

71 ibid.

72 ibid., p.174.

73 ibid., p.179.

74 ibid.

75 E. J. Montague Stuart-Wortley, 'Reminiscences of the Sudan 1882–
    1899', *Sudan Notes and Records*, XXXIV, 1953, pp.17, 44.

76 Preston (ed.), *Lord Wolseley's Campaign Journal*, p.129.

77 ibid., p.165.

78 Charles Watson, *The Life of Major General Sir Charles Wilson*, London,
    1909, pp.345–6.

79 ibid., p.347.

80 Lord Cromer, *Modern Egypt*, 2 vols., London, 1909, p.215.

81 ibid., p.33.

82 Preston (ed.), *Lord Wolseley's Campaign Journal*, p.138.

83 Halik Kochanksi, *Sir Garnet Wolseley: Victorian Hero*, London, 1999,
    p.351.

Part Six

1 Philip Magnus, *Kitchener – Portrait of an Imperialist*, London, 1958,
   p.369.

2 ibid., p.370.

3 Julian Symonds, *England's Pride: The Story of the Gordon Relief
   Expedition*, London, 1965, p.201. Symonds takes this to mean Charles
   Wilson. However, Wolseley clearly refers to *regimental* officers,
   whereas Wilson was a *staff* officer: his position was Adjutant General
   of Intelligence, i.e. a staff post.

4 Winston S. Churchill, *The River War*, London, 1899, Vol. 1, p.411.

5 E. F. Knight, *Letters from the Sudan*, London, 1896, p.135.

6 R. C. Slatin, *Fire and Sword in the Sudan: A Personal Narrative of
   Fighting and Serving the Dervishes*, London, 1896, p.401.

7 Knight, *Letters*, p.160.

8 A. Hunter, *Kitchener's Sword Arm – The Life and Campaigns of General
   Sir Archie Hunter*, London, 1996, p.43.

9 Churchill, *The River War*, p.118.

10 Knight, *Letters*, p.123.

Part Seven

1 Winston S. Churchill, *The River War*, London, 1899, pp.294–5.

2 'An Officer', *Sudan Campaign 1896–1899*, London, 1899, p.105.

3 ibid., p.109.

4 ibid., p.110.

5 Lord Cromer, *Modern Egypt*, 2 vols., London, 1909, p.296.

6 ibid.

7 John Meredith (ed.), *Omdurman Diaries 1898 – Eyewitness Accounts of the Legendary Campaign*, London, 1998, p.83.

8 ibid., p.89.

9 ibid., p.90.

10 ibid., p.30.

11 ibid.

12 'An Officer', *Sudan Campaign*, p.157.

13 ibid., p.90.

14 ibid.

15 M. Barthorp, *War on the Nile: Britain in Egypt and the Sudan 1882–1898*, Poole, 1984, p.148.

16 Meredith (ed.), *Omdurman Diaries*, p.60.

17 ibid., p.91.

18 Frank Emery, *Marching over Africa: Letters from Victorian Soldiers*, London, 1986, p.164.

19 E. N. Spiers (ed.), *Sudan: The Reconquest Reappraised*, London, 1998, p.60.

20 Meredith (ed.), *Omdurman Diaries*, p.91.

21 ibid., pp.92–3.

22 Spiers (ed.), *Sudan: The Reconquest Reappraised*, p.61.

23 ibid., p.60.

24 Emery, *Marching over Africa*, p.164.

25 Meredith (ed.), *Omdurman Diaries*, p.91.

26 Spiers (ed.), *Sudan: The Reconquest Reappraised*, p.60.

27 Meredith (ed.), *Omdurman Diaries*.

28 Emery, *Marching over Africa*, p.164.

29 Spiers (ed.), *Sudan: The Reconquest Reappraised*, p.60.

30 Churchill, *The River War*, p.437.

31 John Pollock, *Kitchener*, London, 1998, p.123.

32 ibid., p.120.

33 Isat Zulfu, *Kerrari – the Sudanese Account of the Battle of Omdurman*, trans. P. Clark, London, 1973, p.115.

34 Norman Dixon, *On the Psychology of Military Incompetence*, London, 1976, p.100.

35 Churchill, *The River War*, p.63.

36 Emery, *Marching over Africa*, p.168.

37 Churchill, *The River War*, p.102.

38 Zulfu, *Kerrari*, p.153.

39 T. Brighton and D. N. Anderson, *The Last Charge – The 21st Lancers and the Battle of Omdurman, 2 September 1898*, London, 1998, p.60.

40 Churchill, *The River War*, p.109.

41 Winston S. Churchill, *My Early Life*, London, 1930, p.181.

42 Brighton and Anderson, *The Last Charge*, p.61.

43 Churchill, *The River War*, p.115.

44 Meredith (ed.), *Omdurman Diaries*, p.183.

45 ibid., p.185.

46 Brighton and Anderson, *The Last Charge*, p.63.

47 Meredith (ed.), *Omdurman Diaries*, p.186.

48 Spiers (ed.), *Sudan: The Reconquest Reappraised*, p.70.

49 Meredith (ed.), *Omdurman Diaries*, p.170.

50 ibid.

51 ibid., p.187.

52 ibid.

53 Churchill, *My Early Life*, p.187.

54 ibid., p.188.

55 Brighton and Anderson, *The Last Charge*, p.79.

56 Churchill, *My Early Life*, p.189.

57 Brighton and Anderson, *The Last Charge*, p.91.

58 Churchill, *My Early Life*, pp.189–90.

59 Brighton and Anderson, *The Last Charge*, p.91.

60 ibid., p.87.

61 Churchill, *The River War*, p.136.

62 Peter Harrington and Frederic A. Sharf (eds.), *Omdurman 1898: Eye-witnesses Speak*, London, 1998, p.128.

63 Brighton and Anderson, *The Last Charge*, p.92.

64 Pollock, *Kitchener*, p.138.

65 ibid.

66 ibid.

67 Zulfu, *Kerrari*, p.222.

68 Pollock, *Kitchener*, p.141.

69 ibid.

INDEX

Ranks and titles given are generally the highest mentioned in the text.

432

Brentwood, Captain 304
Briggs, Surgeon 223
British army: Brigades; 1st Infantry in
Graham's force 109, 147, 155, 157;
Cavalry 109; 2nd Infantry in
Graham's force 146, 147, 154, 155;
1st Infantry in Kitchener's force
380, 381, 385, 397; 2nd Infantry in
Kitchener's force 380, 381, 385
10th Hussars 15, 108, 114, 115, 117,
123, 288; 13th Light Dragoons 18;
Royal Horse Guards 25; 17th
Lancers 77
19th Hussars; at et-Teb 105, 108,
114, 123; with Desert Column
184, 186, 191, 197–8, 206, 207,
214, 229, 232, 240
21st Lancers 365, 367, 370, 371, 375,
381, 385, 386–94
Mounted Infantry 105, 108, 115, 147,
155; Royal Sussex Regiment 147
Royal Artillery; camel battery 105,
108, 186; Scottish battery 113,
117–18, 147; M battery 145, 146,
154; 37th Field Battery 368; 32nd
Field Battery 397
Royal Engineers 18; 26th Field
Company 105
Grenadier Guards 365, 380, 381; 1st
Bn Black Watch 105, 108, 125; at
Tamaai 146, 148, 150, 153, 155,
158; East Yorkshire Regiment 9;
1st Bn Gordon Highlanders 105,
115, 116, 122, 147, 157; 3rd Bn
King's Royal Rifles 105, 116, 147;
Royal Irish Fusiliers 108, 116, 147,
278, 365, 383; Connaught Rangers
302, 306, 318; 1st Bn North
Staffordshire Regiment 302, 316,
318; 1st Bn Cameron Highlanders
343, 351, 352, 355, 357, 358, 380,
397; 1st Bn Lincolnshire
Regiment 343, 351–3 passim, 355,
358, 380, 381, 397, 399, 400;
Lancashire Fusiliers 365, 380;

Northumberland Fusiliers 365,
380; 2nd Bn Rifle Brigade 365,
380; Royal Sussex Regiment 186,
193, 198, 205, 210, 214, 216, 221,
240; on river steamers 251, 267,
269, 272, 274; 1st Bn Royal
Warwickshire Regiment 343, 351,
352, 354–8 passim, 380, 397; 1st
Bn Seaforth Highlanders 343, 351,
352, 353, 355, 358, 380, 397; 1st
Bn York & Lancaster Regiment; at
et-Teb 113–14, 116, 117–21; at
Tamaai 146, 149, 153, 155, 158
infantry training 11–12; background
110–11; artillery training 112–13;
cavalry training 112; weapons 112
Briton, HMS (screw corvette) 108
Broadwood, Captain R. G. 301
Broadwood, Lieut. Colonel Robert
345, 369, 385, 395, 401, 402, 412
Brocklehurst, Captain John 83, 87
Brooke, Captain Ronald 351
Brown, Private William 394
Buller: Brigadier Sir Redvers, VC;
commands 1st Infantry Brigade
108, 147; previous career 108–9;
character 109; and Relief
Expedition 170, 186; alcoholism
185, 284; fails to provide enough
camels 187, 278; laughs at
Beresford 204; Metemma
worthless 247; abandons Gubbat
base 282; given office job 283
Major General Sir Redvers, VC;
later life 411
Burdett-Coutts, Baroness 163
Burge, Private Bill: in Desert Column
190, 194, 199, 200, 206; at Abu
Tulayh 219, 225, 229
Burgevine, Henry, commander EVA
72
Burleigh, Bennet, *Daily Telegraph*
correspondent: at et-Teb 113, 115,
116, 118, 122, 125; at Tamaai
149–53 passim, 155, 156, 158

435